# THE RISE OF
# DAVID LEVINSKY

ABRAHAM CAHAN

# THE RISE OF
# DAVID LEVINSKY

BIBLIOBAZAAR

# THE RISE OF
# DAVID LEVINSKY

# CONTENTS

## BOOK V. I DISCOVER AMERICA

## BOOK VI. A GREENHORN NO LONGER

## BOOK VII. MY TEMPLE

## BOOK VIII. THE DESTRUCTION OF MY TEMPLE

# BOOK IX. DORA ✓

# BOOK X. ON THE ROAD ✓

# BOOK XI. MATRIMONY ✓

## BOOK XII. MISS TEVKIN

## BOOK XIII. AT HER FATHER'S HOUSE

## BOOK XIV. EPISODES OF A LONELY LIFE

# BOOK I

# HOME AND SCHOOL

# CHAPTER I

SOMETIMES, when I think of my past in a superficial, casual way, the metamorphosis I have gone through strikes me as nothing short of a miracle. I was born and reared in the lowest depths of poverty and I arrived in America—in 1885—with four cents in my pocket. I am now worth more than two million dollars  *wow.* and recognized as one of the two or three leading men in the cloak-and-suit trade in the United States. And yet when I take a look at my inner identity it impresses me as being precisely the same as it was thirty or forty years ago. My present station, power, the amount of worldly happiness at my command, and the rest of it, seem to be devoid of significance

When I was young I used to think that middle-aged people recalled their youth as something seen through a haze. I know better now. Life is much shorter than I imagined it to be. The last years that I spent in my native land and my first years in America come back to me with the distinctness of yesterday. Indeed, I have a better recollection of many a trifle of my childhood days than I have of some important things that occurred to me recently. I have a good memory for faces, but I am apt to recognize people I have not seen for a quarter of a century more readily than I do some I used to know only a few years ago

I love to brood over my youth. The dearest days in one's life are those that seem very far and very near at once. My wretched boyhood appeals to me as a sick child does to its mother.

I was born in Antomir, in the Northwestern Region, Russia, in 1865. All I remember of my father is his tawny beard, a huge yellow apple he once gave me at the gate of an orchard where he was employed as watchman, and the candle which burned at his head his body lay under a white shroud on the floor. I was less than three years old when he died, so my mother would carry me to the synagogue in her arms to have somebody say the Prayer for the Dead with me. I was unable fully to realize the meaning of the ceremony, of course, but its solemnity and pathos were not altogether lost upon me. There is a streak of sadness in the blood of my race. Very likely it is of Oriental origin. If it is, it has been amply nourished by many centuries of persecution

Left to her own resources, my mother strove to support herself and me by peddling pea mush or doing odds and ends of jobs. She had to struggle hard for our scanty livelihood and her trials and loneliness came home to me at an early period.

I was her all in all, though she never poured over me those torrents of senseless rhapsody which I heard other Jewish mothers shower over their children. The only words of endearment I often heard from her were, "My little bean," and, "My comfort." Sometimes, when she seemed to be crushed by the miseries of her life, she would call me, "My poor little orphan." Otherwise it was, "Come here, my comfort," "Are you hungry, my little bean?" or, "You are a silly little dear, my comfort." These words of hers and the sonorous contralto in which they were uttered are ever alive in my heart, like the Flame Everlasting in a synagogue

"Mamma, why do you never beat me like other mammas do?" I once asked her

She laughed, kissed me, and said, "Because God has punished you hard enough as it is, poor orphan mine."

I scarcely remembered my father, yet I missed him keenly. I was ever awake to the fact that other little boys had fathers and that I was a melancholy exception; that most married women had husbands, while my mother had to bear her burden unaided. In my dim childish way I knew that there was a great blank in our family nest, that it was a widow's nest; and the feeling of it seemed to color all my other feelings. When I was a little older and would no longer sleep with my mother, a rusty old coat of my deceased father's served me as a quilt. At night, before falling asleep, I would pull it over my head, shut my eyes tight, and evoke a flow of fantastic shapes, bright, beautifully tinted, and incessantly changing form and color. While the play of these figures and hues was going on before me I would see all sorts of bizarre visions, which at times seemed to have something to do with my father's spirit

"Is papa in heaven now? Is he through with hell?" I once inquired of my mother. Some things or ideas would assume queer forms in my mind. God, for example, appealed to me as a beardless man wearing a quilted silk cap; holiness was something burning, forbidding, something connected with fire while a day had the form of an oblong box

I was a great dreamer of day dreams. One of my pastimes was to imagine a host of tiny soldiers each the size of my little finger, "but alive and real." These I would drill as I saw officers do their men in front of the barracks some distance from our home. Or else I would take. to marching up and down the room with mother's rolling-pin for a rifle, grunting, ferociously, in Russian: "Left one! Left one! Left one!" in the double capacity of a Russian soldier and of David fighting Goliath.

Often, while bent upon her housework, my mother would hum some of the songs of the famous wedding bard, Eliakim Zunzer, who later emigrated to America.

I distinctly remember her singing his "There is a flower on the road, decaying in the dust, Passers-by treading upon it," his "Summer and Winter," and his "Rachael is bemoaning her children." I vividly recall these brooding airs as she used to sing them, for I have inherited her musical memory and her passionate love for melody, though not her voice. I cannot sing myself, but some tunes give me thrills of pleasure, keen and terrible as the edge of a sword. Some haunt me like ghosts. But then this is a common trait among our people.

She was a wiry little woman, my mother, with prominent cheek-bones, a small, firm mouth, and dark eyes. Her hair was likewise dark, though I saw it but very seldom, for like all orthodox daughters of Israel she always had it carefully covered by a kerchief, a nightcap, or—on Saturdays and holidays—by a wig. She was extremely rigorous about it. For instance, while she changed her kerchief for her nightcap she would cause me to look away

My great sport during my ninth and tenth years was to play buttons. These we would fillip around on some patch of unpaved ground with a little pit for a billiard pocket. My own pockets were usually full of these buttons. As the game was restricted to brass ones from the uniforms of soldiers, my mother had plenty to do to keep those pockets of mine in good repair. To develop skill for the sport I would spend hours in some secluded spot, secretly practising it by myself. Sometimes, as I was thus engaged, my mother would seek me out and bring me a hunk of rye bread.

"Here," she would say, gravely, handing me it. And I would accept it with preoccupied mien, take a deep bite, and go on filliping my buttons

I gambled passionately and was continually counting my treasure, or running around the big courtyard, jingling it self-consciously. But one day I suddenly wearied of it all and traded my entire hoard of buttons for a pocket-knife and some trinkets

"Don't you care for buttons any more?" mother inquired

"I can't bear the sight of them," I replied

She shrugged her shoulders smilingly, and called me "queer fellow."

Sometimes I would fall to kissing her passionately. Once, after an outburst of this kind, I said: "Are people sorry for us, mamma?"

"What do you mean?"

"Because I have no papa and we have no money."

Antomir, which then boasted eighty thousand inhabitants, was a town in which a few thousand rubles was considered wealth, and we were among the humblest and poorest in it. The bulk of the population lived on less than fifty copecks (twenty-five cents) a day, and that was difficult to earn. A hunk of rye bread and a bit of herring or cheese constituted a meal. A quarter of a copeck (an eighth of a cent) was a coin with which one purchased a few crumbs of pot-cheese or some boiled water for tea. Rubbers were worn by people "of means" only. I never saw any in the district in which my mother and I had our home. A white starched collar was an attribute of "aristocracy." Children had to nag their mothers for a piece of bread

"Mamma, I want a piece of bread," with a mild whimper

"Again bread! You'll eat my head off. May the worms eat you."

Dialogues such as this were heard at every turn

My boyhood recollections include the following episode: Mother once sent me to a tinker's shop to have our drinking-cup repaired. It was a plain tin affair and must have cost, when new, something like four or five cents. It had done service as long as I could remember. It was quite rusty, and finally sprang a leak. And so I took it to the tinker, or tinsmith, who soldered it up. On my way home I slipped and fell, whereupon the cup hit a cobblestone and sprang a new leak. When my mother discovered the damage she made me tell the story of the accident over and over again, wringing her hands and sighing as she listened. The average mother in our town would have given me a whipping in the circumstances. She did not

- recollection of his youth
- father had died before he was 3
- raised by his mother who didn't believe in "hitting" as discipline
- often called "my little bean" or "my comfort" by his mother
- were poor, could barely make ends meet
- Jewish

# CHAPTER II

WE lived in a deep basement, in a large, dusky room that we shared with three other families, each family occupying one of the corners and as much space as it was able to wrest. Violent quarrels were a commonplace occurrence, and the question of floor space a staple bone of contention. The huge brick oven in which the four housewives cooked dinner was another prolific source of strife. Fights over pots were as frequent and as truculent as those over the children

Of our room-mates I best recall a bookbinder and a retired old soldier who mended old sheepskin coats for a living. My memories of home are inseparable from the odors of sheepskin and paste and the image of two upright wooden screws (the bookbinder's "machine"). The soldier had finished his term of military service years before, yet he still wore his uniform—a dilapidated black coat with new brass buttons, and a similar overcoat of a coarse gray material. Also, he still shaved his chin, sporting a pair of formidable gray side-whiskers. Shaving is one of the worst sins known to our faith, but, somehow, people overlooked it in one who had once been compelled to practise it in the army. Otherwise the furrier or sheepskin tailor was an extremely pious man. He was very kind to me, so that his military whiskers never awed me. Not so his lame, tall wife, who often hit me with one of her crutches.

She was the bane of my life. The bookbinder's wife was much younger than her husband and one of the things I often heard was that he was "crazy for her because she is his second wife," from which I inferred that second wives were loved far more than first ones.

The bookbinder had a red-haired little girl whom I hated like poison. Red Esther we called her, to distinguish her from a Black Esther, whose home was on the same yard. She was full of fight.

Knowing how repulsive she was to me, she was often the first to open hostilities, mocking my way of speaking, or sticking out her tongue at me. Or else she would press her freckled cheek against my lips and then dodge back, shouting, gloatingly: "He has kissed a girl! He has kissed a girl! Sinner! Shame! Sinner! Sinner!"

There were some other things that she or some of the other little girls of our courtyard would do to make an involuntary "sinner" of me, but these had better be left out

I had many a fierce duel with her. I was considered a strong boy, but she was quick and nimble as a cat, and I usually got the worst of the bargain, often being left badly scratched and bleeding. At which point the combat would be taken up by our mothers

The room, part of which was our home, and two other single-room apartments, similarly tenanted, opened into a pitch-dark vestibule which my fancy peopled with "evil ones." A steep stairway led up to the yard, part of which was occupied by a huddle of ramshackle one-story houses. It was known as Abner's Court. During the summer months it swarmed with tattered, unkempt humanity. There was a peculiar odor to the place which I can still smell.

(Indeed, many of the things that I conjure up from the past appeal as much to my sense of smell as to my visual memory.) It was anything but a grateful odor

The far end of our street was part of a squalid little suburb known as the Sands. It was inhabited by Gentiles exclusively. Sometimes, when a Jew chanced to visit it some of its boys would descend upon him with shouts of "Damned Jew!" "Christ-killer!" and sick their dogs at him. As we had no dogs to defend us, orthodox Jews being prohibited from keeping these domestic animals by a custom amounting to a religious injunction, our boys never ventured into the place except, perhaps, in a spirit of dare-devil bravado

One day the bigger Jewish boys of our street had a pitched battle with the Sands boys, an event which is one of the landmarks in the history of my childhood

Still, some of the Sands boys were on terms of friendship with us and would even come to play with us in our yard. The only Gentile family that lived in Abner's Court was that of the porter. His children spoke fairly good Yiddish

One Saturday evening a pock-marked lad from the Sands, the son of a chimney-sweep, meeting me in the street, set his dog at me. As a result I came home with a fair-sized piece of my trousers (knee-breeches were unknown to us) missing

"I'm going to kill him," my mother said, with something like a sob. "I'm just going to kill him."

"Cool down," the retired soldier pleaded, without removing his short-stemmed pipe from his mouth

Mother was silent for a minute, and even seated herself, but presently she sprang to her feet again and made for the door

The soldier's wife seized her by an arm

"Where are you going? To the Sands? Are you crazy? If you start a quarrel over there you'll never come back alive."

"I don't care!"

She wrenched herself free and left the room.

Half an hour later she came back beaming

"His father is a lovely Gentile," she said. "He went out, brought his murderer of a boy home, took off his belt, and skinned him alive."

"A good Gentile," the soldier's wife commented, admiringly

There was always a pile of logs somewhere in our Court, the property of some family that was to have it cut up for firewood. This was our great gathering-place of a summer evening. Here we would bandy stories (often of our own inventing) or discuss things, the leading topic of conversation being the soldiers of the two regiments that were stationed in our town. We saw a good deal of these soldiers, and we could tell their officers, commissioned or non-commissioned, by the number of stars or bands on their shoulder-straps. Also, we knew the names of their generals, colonels, and some of their majors or captains. The more important manoeuvers took place a great distance from Abner's Court, but that did not matter. If they occurred on a Saturday, when we were free from school—and, as good luck would have it, they usually did—many of us, myself invariably included, would go to see them. The blare of trumpets, the beat of drums, the playing of the band, the rhythmic clatter of thousands of feet, the glint or rows and rows of bayonets, the red or the blue of the uniforms, the commanding officer on his mount, the spirited singing of the men marching back to barracks—all this would literally hold me spellbound

That we often played soldiers goes without saying, but we played "hares" more often, a game in which the counting was done by means of senseless words like the American "Eeny, meeny, miny, moe." Sometimes we would play war, with the names of the belligerents borrowed from the Old Testament, and once in a while we would have a real "war" with the boys of the next street

I was accounted one of the strong fellows among the boys of Abner's Court as well as one of the conspicuous figures among them. Compactly built, broad-shouldered, with a small, firm mouth like my mother's, a well-formed nose and large, dark eyes, I was not a homely boy by any means, nor one devoid of a certain kind of magnetism

One of my recollections is of my mother administering a tongue-lashing to a married young woman whom she had discovered flirting in the dark vestibule with a man not her husband

A few minutes later the young woman came in and begged my mother not to tell her husband

"If I was your husband I would skin you alive."

"Oh, don't tell him! Take pity! Don't."

"I won't. Get out of here, you lump of stench."

"Oh, swear that you won't tell him! Do swear, dearie. Long life to you.

Health to every little bone of yours."

"First you swear that you'll never do it again, you heap of dung."

"Strike me blind and dumb and deaf if I ever do it again. There."

"Your oaths are worth no more than the barking of a dog. Can't you be decent? You ought to be knouted in the market-place. You are a plague. Black luck upon you. Get away from me."

"But I will be decent. May I break both my legs and both my arms if I am not. Do swear that you won't tell him."

My mother yielded

She was passionately devout, my mother. Being absolutely illiterate, she would murmur meaningless words, in the singsong of a prayer, pretending to herself that she was performing her devotions. This, however, she would do with absolute earnestness and fervor, often with tears of ecstasy coming to her eyes. To be sure, she knew how to bless the Sabbath candles and to recite

*[handwritten margin note: I had fun w/ this dialogue,]*

the two or three other brief prayers that our religion exacts from married women. But she was not contented with it, and the sight of a woman going to synagogue with a huge prayer-book under her arm was ever a source of envy to her.

Most of the tenants of the Court were good people, honest and pure, but there were exceptions. Of these my memory has retained the face of a man who was known as "Carrot Pudding" Moe, a red-headed, broad-shouldered "finger worker," a specialist in "short change," yardstick frauds, and other varieties of marketplace legerdemain. One woman, a cross between a beggar and a dealer in second-hand dresses, had four sons, all of whom were pickpockets, but she herself was said to be of spotless honesty. She never allowed them to enter Abner's Court, though every time one of them was in prison she would visit him and bring him food

Nor were professional beggars barred from the Court as tenants. Indeed, one of our next-door neighbors was a regular recipient of alms at the hands of my mother. For, poor as she was, she seldom let a Friday pass without distributing a few half-groschen (an eighth of a cent) in charity. The amusing part of it was the fact that one of the beggars on her list was far better off than she

"He's old and lame, and no hypocrite like the rest of them," she would explain

She had a ferocious temper, but there were people (myself among them) with whom she was never irritated. The women of Abner's Court were either her devoted followers or her bitter enemies. She was a leader in most of the feuds that often divided the whole Court into two warring camps, and in those exceptional cases when she happened to be neutral she was an ardent peacemaker. She wore a dark-blue kerchief, which was older than I, and almost invariably, when there was a crowd of women in the yard, that kerchief would loom in its center

Growing as I did in that crowded basement room which was the home of four families, it was inevitable that the secrets of sex should be revealed to me before I was able fully to appreciate their meaning. Then, too, the neighborhood was not of the purest in town. Located a short distance from Abner's Court, midway between it and the barracks, was a lane of ill repute, usually full of soldiers. If it had an official name I never heard it. It was generally referred to as "that street," in a subdued voice that was suggestive either of shame and disgust or of waggish mirth. For a long time I was under the impression that "That" was simply the name of the street.

One summer day—I must have been eight years old—I told my mother that I had peeked in one of the little yards of the mysterious lane, that I had seen half-naked women and soldiers there, and that one of the women had beckoned me in and given me some cake

"Why, you mustn't do that, Davie!" she said, aghast. "Don't you ever go near that street again! Do you hear?"

"Why?"

"Because it is a bad street."

"Why is it bad?"

"Keep still and don't ask foolish questions."

I obeyed, with the result that the foolish questions kept rankling in my brain

On a subsequent occasion, when she was combing my dark hair fondly, I ventured once more: "Mamma, why mustn't I come near that street?"

"Because it is a sin to do so, my comfort. Fie upon it!"

This answer settled it. One did not ask why it was a sin to do this or not to do that. "You don't demand explanations of the Master of the World," as people were continually saying around me. My curiosity was silenced. That street became repellent to me, something hideously wicked and sinister

Sometimes some of the excommunicated women would drop in at our yard. As a rule, my mother was bitterly opposed to their visits and she often chased them out with maledictions and expressions of abhorrence; but there was one case in which she showed unusual tolerance and even assumed the part of father confessor to a woman of this kind. She would listen to her tale of woe, homesickness and repentance, including some of the most intimate details of her loathsome life. She would even deliver her donations to the synagogue, thus helping her cheat the Biblical injunction which bars the gifts of fallen women from a house of God

My mother would bid me keep away during these confabs of theirs, but this only whetted my curiosity and I often overheard far more than I should

Fridays were half-holidays with us Jewish boys. One Friday afternoon a wedding was celebrated in our courtyard. The procession emerged from one of the rickety one-story houses, accompanied by a band playing a solemn tune.

When it reached the center of the vacant part of the yard it came to a halt and a canopy was stretched over the principal figures of the ceremony.

Prayers and benedictions were chanted. The groom put the ring on the bride's finger, "dedicating her to himself according to the laws of Moses and Israel "; more prayers were recited; the bridegroom and the bride received sips of wine; a plate was smashed, the sound being greeted by shouts of "Good luck! Good luck!" The band struck up a lively tune with a sad tang to it

The yard was crowded with people. It was the greatest sensation we children had ever enjoyed there. We remained out chattering of the event till the windows were aglitter with Sabbath lights

I was in a trance. The ceremony was a poem to me, something inexpressibly beautiful and sacred.

Presently a boy, somewhat older than I, made a jest at the young couple's expense. What he said was a startling revelation to me. Certain things which I had known before suddenly appeared in a new light to me. I relished the discovery and I relished the deviltry of it. But the poem vanished. The beauty of the wedding I had just witnessed, and of weddings in general, seemed to be irretrievably desecrated

That boy's name was Naphtali. He was a trim-looking fellow with curly brown hair, somewhat near-sighted. He was as poor as the average boy in the yard and as poorly dressed, but he was the tidiest of us. He would draw, with a piece of chalk, figures of horses and men which we admired. He knew things, good and bad, and from that Friday I often sought his company. Unlike most of the other boys, he talked little, throwing out his remarks at long intervals, which sharpened my sense of his wisdom. His father never let him attend the manoeuvers, yet he knew more about soldiers than any of the other boys, more even than I, though I had that retired soldier, the sheepskin man, to explain things military to me.

One summer evening Naphtali and I sat on a pile of logs in the yard, watching a boy who was "playing" on a toy fiddle of his own making. I said: "I wish I knew how to play on a real fiddle, don't you?"

Naphtali made no answer. After a little he said: "You must think it is the bow that does the playing, don't you?"

"What else does it?" I asked, perplexed

"It's the fingers of the other hand, those that are jumping around."

"Is it?"

I did not understand, but I was deeply impressed all the same. The question bothered me all that evening. Finally I submitted it to my mother: "Mamma, Naphtali says when you play on a fiddle it is not the bow that makes the tune, but the fingers that are jumping around. Is it true?"

She told me not to bother her with foolish questions, but the retired soldier, who had overheard my query, volunteered to answer it.

"Of course it is not the bow," he said

"But if you did not work the bow the strings would not play, would they?" I urged.

"You could play a tune by pinching them," he answered. "But if you just kept passing the bow up and down there would be no tune at all."

I plied him with further questions and he answered them all, patiently and fondly, illustrating his explanations with a thread for a violin string, my mother looking from him to me beamingly

When we were through she questioned him: "Do you think he understands it all?" "He certainly does. He has a good head," he answered, with a wink. And she flushed with happiness

- Red Esther
- good Gentiles
  - lives in basement w/ 4 fams.
  - Naphtali

25

# CHAPTER III

THE tuition fee at a school for religious instruction or cheder was from eight to ten rubles (five dollars) for a term of six months. My mother could not afford it. On the other hand, she would not hear of sending me to the free cheder of our town, because of its reputation for poor instruction. So she importuned and harassed two distant relatives of ours until they agreed to raise part of the sum between them. The payments were made with anything but promptness, the result being that I was often turned out of school.

Mother, however, would lose no time in bringing me back. She would implore the schoolmaster to take pity on the poor, helpless woman that she was, assuring him, with some weird oaths, that she would pay him every penny. If that failed she would burst into a flood of threats and imprecations, daring him to let a fatherless boy grow up in ignorance of the Word of God. This was followed by similar scenes at the houses of my cousins, until finally I was allowed to resume my studies, sometimes at the same cheder, sometimes at some other one. There were scores of such private schools in our town, and before I got through my elementary religious education I had become acquainted with a considerable number of them

Sometimes when a teacher or his wife tried to oust me, I would clutch at the table and struggle sullenly until they yielded

I may explain that instruction in these cheders was confined to the Hebrew Old Testament and rudiments of the Talmud, the exercises lasting practically all day and part of the evening. The class-room was at the same time the bedroom, living-room, and kitchen of the teacher's family. His wife and children were always around. These cheder teachers were usually a haggard-looking lot with full beards and voices hoarse with incessant shouting.

A special man generally came for an hour to teach the boys to write. As he was to be paid separately, I was not included. The feeling of envy, abasement, and self-pity with which I used to watch the other boys ply their quills is among the most painful memories of my childhood

During the penmanship lesson I was generally kept busy in other directions.

The teacher's wife would make me help her with her housework, go her errands, or mind the baby (in one instance I became so attached to the baby that when I was expelled I missed it keenly)

I seized every opportunity to watch the boys write and would practise the art, with chalk, on my mother's table or bed, on the door of our basement room, on many a gate or fence. Sometimes a boy would let me write a line or two in his copy-book. Sometimes, too, I would come to school before the schoolmaster had returned from the morning service at the synagogue, and practise with pen and ink, following the copy of some of my classmates. One of my teachers once caught me in the act. He held me up as an ink-thief and forbade me come to school before the beginning of exercises

Otherwise my teachers scarcely ever complained of my behavior. As to the progress I was making in my studies, they admitted, some even with enthusiasm, that mine was a "good head." Nevertheless, to be beaten by them was an every-day experience with me

Overworked, underfed, and goaded by the tongue-lashings of their wives, these enervated drudges were usually out of sorts. Bursts of ill temper, in the form of invective, hair-pulling, ear-pulling, pinching, caning, "nape-cracking," or "chin-smashing," were part of the routine, and very often I was the scapegoat for the sins of other boys. When a pupil deserved punishment and the schoolmaster could not afford to inflict it because the culprit happened to be the pet of a well-to-do family, the teacher's anger was almost sure to be vented on me. If I happened to be somewhat absent-minded (the only offense I was ever guilty of), or was not quick enough to turn over a leaf, or there was the slightest halt in my singsong, I received a violent "nudge" or a pull by the ear.

"Lively, lively, carcass you!" I can almost hear one of my teachers shout these words as he digs his elbow into my side. "The millions one gets from your mother!"

This man would beat and abuse me even by way of expressing approval

"A bright fellow, curse him!" he would say, punching me with an air of admiration. Or, "Where did you get those brains of yours, you wild beast?" with a violent pull at my forelock

During the winter months, when the exercises went on until 9 in the evening, the candle or kerosene was paid for by the boys, in rotation. When it was my turn to furnish the light it often happened that my mother was unable to procure the required two copecks (one cent). Then the teacher or his wife, or both, would curse me for a sponge and a robber, and ask me why I did not go to the charity school

Almost every teacher in town was known among us boys by some nickname, which was usually borrowed from some trade. If he had a predilection for pulling a boy's hair we would call him "wig-maker" or "brush-maker"; if he preferred to slap or "calcimine" the culprit's face we would speak of him as a mason.

A "coachman" was a teacher who did not spare the rod or the whip; a "carpenter," one who used his finger as a gimlet, boring a pupil's side or cheek; a "locksmith," one who had a weakness for "turning the screw," or pinching

The greatest "locksmith" in town was a man named Shmerl. But then he was more often called simply Shmerl the Pincher. He was one of my schoolmasters.

He seemed to prefer the flesh of plump, well-fed boys, but as these were usually the sons of prosperous parents, he often had to forego the pleasure and to gratify his appetite on me. There was something morbid in his cruel passion for young flesh something perversely related to sex, perhaps. He was a young man with a wide, sneering mouth

He would pinch me black and blue till my heart contracted with pain. Yet I never uttered a murmur. I was too profoundly aware of the fact that I was kept on sufferance to risk the slightest demonstration. I had developed a singular faculty for bearing pain, which I would parade before the other boys. Also, I had developed a relish for flaunting my martyrdom, for being an object of pity

Oh, how I did hate this man, especially his sneering mouth! In my helplessness I would seek comfort in dreams of becoming a great man some day, rich and mighty, and avenging myself on him. Behold! Shmerl the Pincher is running after me, cringingly begging my pardon, and I, omnipotent and formidable, say to him: "Do you remember how you pinched the life out of me for nothing? Away with you, you cruel beast!"

Or I would vision myself dropping dead under one of his onslaughts. Behold him trembling with fright, the heartless wretch! Serves him right.

If my body happened to bear some mark of his cruelty I would conceal it carefully from my mother, lest she should quarrel with him. Moreover, to betray school secrets was considered a great "sin."

One night, as I was changing my shirt, anxiously manoeuvering to keep a certain spot on my left arm out of her sight, she became suspicious

"Hold on. What are you hiding there?" she said, stepping up and inspecting my bare arm. She found an ugly blotch. "Woe is me! A lamentation upon me!" she said, looking aghast. "Who has been pinching you?"

"Nobody."

"It is that beast of a teacher, isn't it?"

"No."

"Don't lie, Davie. It is that assassin, the cholera take him! Tell me the truth. Don't be afraid."

"A boy did it."

"What is his name?"

"I don't know. It was a boy in the street."

"You are a liar."

The next morning when I went to cheder she accompanied me

Arrived there, she stripped me half-naked and, pointing at the discoloration on my arm, she said, with ominous composure: "Look! Whose work is it?"

"Mine," Shmerl answered, without removing his long-stemmed pipe from his wide mouth. He was no coward

"And you are proud of it, are you?" "If you don't like it you can take your ornament of a son along with you.

Clear out, you witch!"

She flew at him and they clenched. When they had separated, some of his hair was in her hand, while her arms, as she subsequently owned to me, were marked with the work of his expert fingers.

Another schoolmaster had a special predilection for digging the huge nail of his thumb into the side of his victim, a peculiarity for which he had been named "the Cossack," his famous thumb being referred to by the boys as his spear. He had a passion for inventing new and complex modes of punishment, his spear figuring in most of them. One of his methods of inflicting pain was to slap the boy's face with one hand and to prod his side with the thumb of the other, the slaps and the thrusts alternating rhythmically. This heartless wretch was an abject coward. He was afraid of thunder, of rats, spiders, dogs, and, above all, of his wife, who would call him indecent names in our presence. I abhorred him, yet when he was thus humiliated I felt pity for him His wife kept a stand on a neighboring street corner, where she sold cheap cakes and candy, and those of her husband's pupils who were on her list of "good customers" were sure of immunity from his spear. As I scarcely ever had a penny, he could safely beat me whenever he was so disposed

—teachers had nicknames
— shmerl the Pincher —terrible brute

# CHAPTER IV

THE Cossack had a large family and one of his daughters, a little girl, named Sarah-Leah, was the heroine of my first romance.

Sarah-Leah had the misfortune to bear a striking resemblance to a sister of her father's, an offense which her mother never forgave her. She treated her as she might a stepdaughter. As for the Cossack, he may have cared for the child, but if he did he dared not show it. Poor little Sarah-Leah! She was the outcast of the family just as I was the outcast of her father's school.

She was about eleven years old and I was somewhat younger. The similarity of our fates and of our self-pity drew us to each other. When her father beat me I was conscious of her commiserating look, and when she was mistreated by her mother she would cast appealing glances in my direction. Once when the teacher punished me with special cruelty her face twitched and she broke into a whimper, whereupon he gave her a kick, saying: "Is it any business of yours? Thank God your own skin has not been peeled off."

Once during the lunch hour, when we were alone, Sarah-Leah and I, in a corner of the courtyard, she said: "You are so strong, Davie! Nothing hurts you."

"Nothing at all. I could stand everything," I bragged

"You could not, if I bit your finger."

"Go ahead!" I said, with bravado, holding out my hand. She dug her teeth into one of my fingers. It hurt so that I involuntarily ground my own teeth, but I smiled

"Does it not hurt you, Davie?" she asked, with a look of admiration

"Not a bit. Go on, bite as hard as you can."

She did, the cruel thing, and like many an older heroine, she would not desist until she saw her lover's blood

*vicious little thing*

31

"It still does not hurt, does it?" she asked, wiping away a red drop from her lips.

I shook my head contemptuously

"When you are a man you will be strong as Samson the Strong."

I was the strongest boy in her father's school. She knew that most of the other boys were afraid of me, but that did not seem to interest her. At least when I began to boast of it she returned to my ability "to stand punishment," as the pugilists would put it

One day one of my schoolmates aroused her admiration by the way he "played" taps with his fist for a trumpet. I tried to imitate him, but failed grievously. The other boy laughed and Sarah-Leah joined him. That was my first taste of the bitter cup called jealousy — it happens to us all

I went home a lovelorn boy

I took to practising "taps." I was continually trumpeting. I kept at it so strenuously that my mother had many a quarrel with our room-mates because of it

My efforts went for nothing, however. My rival, and with him my lady love, continued to sneer at my performances

O-kay.

I had only one teacher who never beat me, or any of the other boys. Whatever anger we provoked in him would spend itself in threats, and even these he often turned to a joke, in a peculiar vein of his own

"If you don't behave I'll cut you to pieces," he would say. "I'll just cut you to tiny bits and put you into my pipe and you'll go up in smoke." Or, "I'll give you such a thrashing that you won't be able to sit down, stand up, or lie down. The only thing you'll be able to do is to fly—to the devil."

This teacher used me as a living advertisement for his school. He would take me from house to house, flaunting my recitations and interpretations. Very often the passage which he thus made me read was a lesson I had studied under one of his predecessors, but I never gave him away

defending his mother's honor

Every cheder had its king. As a rule, it was the richest boy in the school, but I was usually the power behind the throne. Once one of these potentates (it was at the school of that kindly man) mimicked my mother hugging her pot of pea mush

"If you do it again I'll kill you," I said

"If you lay a finger on me," he retorted, "the teacher will kick you out.

Your mother doesn't pay him, anyhow."

I flew at him. His Majesty tearfully begged for mercy. Since then he was under my thumb and never omitted to share his ring-shaped rolls or apples with me

Often when a boy ate something that was beyond my mother's means—a cookie or a slice of buttered white bread—I would eye him enviously till he complained that I made him choke. Then I would go on eying him until he bribed me off with a piece of the tidbit. If staring alone proved futile I might try to bring him to terms by naming all sorts of loathsome objects. At this it frequently happened that the prosperous boy threw away his cookie from sheer disgust, whereupon I would be mean enough to pick it up and to eat it in triumph, calling him something equivalent to "Sissy."

The compliments that were paid my brains were ample compensation for my mother's struggles. Sending me to work was out of the question. She was resolved to put me in a Talmudic seminary. I was the "crown of her head" and she was going to make a "fine Jew" of me. Nor was she a rare exception in this respect, for there were hundreds of other poor families in our town who would starve themselves to keep their sons studying the Word of God

Whenever one of the neighbors suggested that I be apprenticed to some artisan she would flare up. On one occasion a suggestion of this kind led to a violent quarrel

One afternoon when we happened to pass by a bookstore she stopped me in front of the window and, pointing at some huge volumes of the Talmud, she said: "This is the trade I am going to have you learn, and let our enemies grow green with envy."

- Love lost → Sarah Leah
- Jealously gained
- excells academically
  └ mother wants D to have the best.
- after shunned, became bully

# BOOK II

ENTER SATAN

# CHAPTER I

THE Talmudic seminary, or yeshivah, in which my mother placed me was a celebrated old institution, attracting students from many provinces. Like most yeshivahs, it was sustained by donations, and instruction in it was free. Moreover, out-of-town students found shelter under its roof, sleeping on the benches or floors of the same rooms in which the lectures were delivered and studied during the day. Also, they were supplied with a pound of rye bread each for breakfast. As to the other meals, they were furnished by the various households of the orthodox community. I understand that some school-teachers in certain villages of New England get their board on the rotation plan, dining each day in the week with another family. This is exactly the way a poor Talmud student gets his sustenance in Russia, the system being called "eating days."

One hour a day was devoted to penmanship and a sorry smattering of Russian, the cost of tuition and writing-materials being paid by a "modern" philanthropist

I was admitted to that seminary at the age of thirteen. As my home was in the city, I neither slept in the classroom nor "ate days." The lectures lasted only two hours a day, but then there was plenty to do, studying them and reviewing previous work. This I did in an old house of prayer where many other boys and men of all ages pursued similar occupations. It was known as the Preacher's Synagogue, and was famed for the large number of noted scholars who had passed their young days reading Talmud in it.

The Talmud is a voluminous work of about twenty ponderous tomes. To read these books, to drink deep of their sacred wisdom, is accounted one of the greatest "good deeds" in the life of a Jew. It is, however, as much a source of intellectual interest as an act of piety. If it be true that our people represent a high percentage of mental vigor, the distinction is probably due, in some measure, to the extremely important part which Talmud studies have played in the spiritual life of the race

A Talmudic education was until recent years practically the only kind of education a Jewish boy of old-fashioned parents received. I spent seven years at it, not counting the several years of Talmud which I had had at the various cheders

What is the Talmud? The bulk of it is taken up with debates of ancient rabbis. It is primarily concerned with questions of conscience, religious duty, and human sympathy—in short, with the relations "between man and God" and those "between man and man." But it practically contains a consideration of almost every topic under the sun, mostly with some verse of the Pentateuch for a pretext. All of which is analyzed and explained in the minutest and keenest fashion, discussions on abstruse subjects being sometimes relieved by an anecdote or two, a bit of folklore, worldly wisdom, or small talk. Scattered through its numerous volumes are priceless gems of poetry, epigram, and story-telling

It is at once a fountain of religious inspiration and a "brain-sharpener." "Can you fathom the sea? Neither can you fathom the depths of the Talmud," as we would put it. We were sure that the highest mathematics taught in the Gentile universities were child's play as compared to the Talmud

In the Preacher's Synagogue, then, I spent seven years of my youthful life.

For hours and hours together I would sit at a gaunt reading-desk, swaying to and fro over some huge volume, reading its ancient text and interpreting it in Yiddish. All this I did aloud, in the peculiar Talmud singsong, a trace of which still persists in my intonation even when I talk cloaks and bank accounts and in English

The Talmud was being read there, in a hundred variations of the same singsong, literally every minute of the year, except the hours of prayer.

There were plenty of men to do it during the day and the evening, and at least ten men (a sacred number) to keep the holy word echoing throughout the night. The majority of them were simply scholarly business men who would drop in to read the sacred books for an hour or two, but there was a considerable number of such as made it the occupation of their life. These were supported either by the congregation or by their own wives, who kept shops, stalls, inns, or peddled, while their husbands spent sixteen hours a day studying Talmud

One of these was a man named Reb (Rabbi) Sender, an insignificant, ungainly little figure of a man, with a sad, child-like little face flanked by a pair of thick, heavy, dark-brown side-locks that seemed to weigh him down

His wife kept a trimming-store or something of the sort, and their only child, a girl older than I, helped her attend to business as well as to keep house in the single-room apartment which the family occupied in the rear of the little shop. As he invariably came to the synagogue for the morning prayer, and never left it until after the evening service, his breakfasts and dinners were brought to the house of worship. His wife usually came with the meal herself. Waiting on one's husband and "giving him strength to learn the law" was a "good deed."

She was a large woman with an interesting dark face, and poor Reb Sender cut a sorry figure by her side

Men of his class are described as having "no acquaintance with the face of a coin." All the money he usually handled was the penny or two which he needed to pay for his bath of a Friday afternoon. Occasionally he would earn three or four copecks by participating in some special prayer, for a sick person, for instance. These pennies he invariably gave away. Once he gave his muffler to a poor boy. His wife subsequently nagged him to death for it. The next morning he complained of her to one of the other scholars

"Still," he concluded, "if you want to serve God you must be ready to suffer for it. A good deed that comes easy to you is like a donation which does not cost you anything." I made his acquaintance by asking him to help me out with an obscure passage. This he did with such simple alacrity and kindly modesty as to make me feel a chum of his. I warmed to him and he reciprocated my feelings. He took me to his bosom. He often offered to go over my lesson with me, and I accepted his services with gratitude. He spoke in a warm, mellow basso that had won my heart from the first. His singsong lent peculiar charm to the pages that we read in duet. As he read and interpreted the text he would wave his snuff-box, by way of punctuating and emphasizing his words, much as the conductor of an orchestra does his baton, now gently, insinuatingly, now with a passionate jerk, now with a sweeping majestic movement. One cannot read Talmud without gesticulating, and Reb Sender would scarcely have been able to gesticulate without his snuff-box.

It was of tortoise shell, with a lozenge-shaped bit of silver in the center.

It gradually became dear to me as part of his charming personality.

Sometimes, when we were reading together, that glistening spot in the center of the lid would fascinate my eye so that I lost track of the subject in hand

He often hummed some liturgical melody of a well-known synagogue chanter.

One afternoon he sang something to me, with his snuff-box for a baton, and then asked me how I liked it

"I composed it myself," he explained, boastfully

I did not like the tune. In fact, I failed to make out any tune at all, but I was overflowing with a desire to please him, so I said, with feigned enthusiasm: "Did you really? Why, it's so beautiful, so sweet!"

Reb Sender's face shone

After that he often submitted his compositions to me, though he was too shy to sing them to older people. They were all supposed to be liturgical tunes, or at least some "hop" for the Day of the Rejoicing of the Law. When I hailed the newly composed air with warm approval he would show his satisfaction either with shamefaced reserve or with child-like exuberance.

If, on the other hand, I failed to conceal my indifference, he would grow morose, and it would be some time before I succeeded in coaxing him back to his usual good humor

Nor were his melodies the only things he confided to me. When I was still a mere boy, fourteen or fifteen years old, he would lay bare to me some of the most intimate secrets of his heart

"You see, my wife thinks me a fool," he once complained to me. "She thinks I don't see it. Do you understand, David? She looks up to me for my learning, but otherwise she thinks I have no sense. It hurts, you know." He was absolutely incapable of keeping a secret or of saying or acting anything that did not come from the depths of his heart. He often talked to me of God and His throne, of the world to come, and of the eternal bliss of the righteous, quoting from a certain book of exhortations and adding much

40

from his own exalted imagination. And I would listen, thrilling, and make a silent vow to be good and to dedicate my life to the service of God

"Study the Word of God, Davie dear," he would say, taking my hand into his.

"There is no happiness like it. What is wealth? A dream of fools. What is this world? A mere curl of smoke for the wind to scatter. Only the other world has substance and reality; only good deeds and holy learning have tangible worth. Beware of Satan, Davie. When he assails you, just say no; turn your heart to steel and say no. Do you hear, my son?"

The anecdotes and sayings of the Talmud, its absurdities no less than its gems of epigrammatic wisdom, were mines of poetry, philosophy, and science to him. He was a dreamer with a noble imagination, with a soul full of beauty

This unsophisticated, simple-hearted man, with the mind of an infant, was one of the most quick-witted, nimble-minded scholars in town.

His great delight was to tackle some intricate maze of Talmudic reasoning.

This he would do with ferocious zest, like a warrior attacking the enemy, flashing his tortoise snuff-box as if it were his sword. When away from his books or when reading some of the fantastic tales in them he was meek and gentle as a little bird. No sooner did he come across a fine bit of reasoning than he would impress me as a lion

On one occasion, after Reb Sender got through a celebrated tangle with me, arousing my admiration by the ingenuity with which he discovered discrepancies and by the adroitness with which he explained them away, he said: "I do enjoy reading with you. Sometimes, when I read by myself, I feel lonely. Anyhow, I love to have you around, David. If you went to study somewhere else I should miss you very much." On another occasion he said: "You are like a son to me, Davie. Be good, be genuinely pious; for my sake, if for nothing else. Above all, don't be double-faced; never say what you do not mean; do not utter words of flattery."

As I now analyze my reminiscences of him I feel that he was a yearning, lonely man. He was in love with his wife and, in spite of her devotion to him, he was love-lorn. Poor Reb Sender! He was anything but a handsome man, while she was well built and pretty. And so it may be that she showed more reverence for his learning and piety than love for his person. He was continually referring to her, apparently thirsting to discuss her demeanor toward him

"The Lord of the Universe has been exceptionally good to me," he once said to me. "May I not forfeit His kindness for my sins. He gives me health and my daily bread, and I have a worthy woman for a wife. Indeed, she is a woman of rare merits, so clever, so efficient, and so good. She nags me but seldom, very seldom." He paused to take snuff and then remained silent, apparently hesitating to come to the point. Finally he said: "In fact, she is so wise I sometimes wish I could read her thoughts. I should give anything to have a glimpse into her heart. She has so little to say to me.

She thinks I am a fool. There is a sore in here "—pointing at his heart.

"We have been married over twenty-two years, and yet— would you believe it?—I still feel shy in her presence, as if we were brought together for the first time, by a match-maker, don't you know. But then you are too young to understand these things. Nor, indeed, ought I to talk to you about them, for you are only a child. But I cannot help it. If I did not unburden my mind once in a while I might not be able to stand it."

That afternoon he composed what he called a "very sad tune," and hummed it to me. I failed to make out the tune, but I could feel its sadness

I loved him passionately. As for the other men of the synagogue, if they did not share my ardent affection for him, they all, with one exception, liked him. The exception was a middle-aged little Talmudist with a tough little beard who held everybody in terror by his violent temper and pugnacity. He was a pious man, but his piety never manifested itself with such genuine fervor as when he exposed the impiety of others. He was forever picking quarrels, forever challenging people to debate with him, forever offering to show that their interpretation of this passage or that was all wrong. The sound of his acrimonious voice or venomous laughter grated on Reb Sender's nerves, but he bore him absolutely no ill-will. Nor did he ever utter a word of condemnation concerning a certain other scholar, an inveterate tale-bearer and gossip-monger, though

*[handwritten margin note, left:]* He would be like a bottle ready to explode under the pressure

*[handwritten margin note, lower left:]* Who is this man?

a good-natured fellow, who not infrequently sought to embroil him with some of his warmest friends.

One Talmudist, a corpulent old man whose seat was next to Reb Sender's, was more inclined to chat than to study. Now and again he would break in upon my friend's reading with some piece of gossip; and the piteous air with which Reb Sender would listen to him, casting yearning glances at his book as he did so, was as touching as it was amusing

My mother usually brought my dinner to the synagogue. She would make her entrance softly, so as to take me by surprise while I was absorbed in my studies. It did her heart good to see me read the holy book. As a result, I was never so diligent as I was at the hour when I expected her arrival with the dinner-pot. Very often I discovered her tiptoeing in or standing at a distance and watching me admiringly. Then I would take to singing and swaying to and fro with great gusto. She often encountered Reb Sender's wife at the synagogue. They did not take to each other.

On one occasion my mother found Reb Sender's daughter at the house of prayer. Having her father's figure and features, the girl was anything but prepossessing. My mother surveyed her from head to foot

That evening when I was eating my supper at home my mother said: "Look here, Davie. I want you to understand that Reb Sender's wife is up to some scheme about you. She wants you to marry that monkey of hers. That's what she is after." I was not quite fifteen

"Leave me alone," I retorted, coloring

"Never mind blushing. It is she who tells Reb Sender to be so good to you.

The foxy thing! She thinks I don't see through her. That scarecrow of a girl is old enough to be your mother, and she has not a penny to her marriage portion, either. A fine match for a boy like you! Why, you can get the best girl in town."

She said it aloud, by way of flaunting my future before our room-mates. Two of the three families who shared the room with us, by the way, were the same as when I was a little boy. Moving was a rare event in the life of the average Antomir family

So basically once you were a class,
you stayed on that rung / didn't
go any higher

Red Esther was still there. She was one of those who heard my mother's boastful warning to me. She grinned. After a little, as I was crossing the room, she sang out with a giggle: "Bridegroom!"

"I'll break your bones," I returned, pausing

She stuck out her tongue at me

I still hated her, but, somehow, she did not seem to be the same as she had been before. The new lines that were developing in her growing little figure, and more particularly her own consciousness of them, were not lost upon me. A new element was stealing into my rancor for her—a feeling of forbidden curiosity. At night, when I lay in bed, before falling asleep, I would be alive to the fact that she was sleeping in the same room, only a few feet from me. Sometimes I would conjure up the days of our childhood when Red Esther caused me to "sin" against my will, whereupon I would try to imagine the same scenes, but with the present fifteen-year-old Esther in place of the five-year-old one of yore.

The word "girl" had acquired a novel sound for me, one full of disquieting charm. The same was true of such words as "sister," "niece," or "bride," but not of "woman." Somehow sisters and nieces were all young girls, whereas a woman belonged to the realm of middle-aged humanity, not to my world

Naphtali went to the same seminary. He was two grades ahead of me. He "ate days," for his father had died and his mother had married a man who refused to support him. He was my great chum at the seminary. The students called him Tidy Naphtali or simply the Tidy One. He was a slender, trim lad, his curly brown hair and his near-sighted eyes emphasizing his Talmudic appearance. He was the cleanliest and neatest boy at the yeshivah. This often aroused sardonic witticism from some of the other students. Scrupulous tidiness was so uncommon a virtue among the poorer classes of Antomir that the painstaking care he bestowed upon his person and everything with which he came in contact struck many of the boys as a manifestation of girl-like squeamishness. As for me, it only added to my admiration of him. His conscience seemed to be as clean as his finger-nails. He wrote a beautiful hand, he could draw and carve, and he was a good singer. His interpretations were as clear-cut as his handwriting. He seemed to be a Jack of all trades and master of all. I admired and envied him. His reticence piqued me and intensified his power over me. I strove to emulate

44

his cleanliness, his graceful Talmud gestures, and his handwriting. At one period I spent many hours a day practising caligraphy with some of his lines for a model

"Oh, I shall never be able to write like you," I once said to him, in despair

"Let us swap, then," he replied, gaily. "Give me your mind for learning and I shall let you have my handwriting."

"Pshaw! Yours is a better mind than mine, too."

"No, it is not," he returned, and resumed his reading. "Besides, you are ahead of me in piety and conduct." He shook his head deprecatingly and went on reading. He was one of the noted "men of diligence" at the seminary. With his near-sighted eyes close to the book he would read all day and far into the night in ringing, ardent singsongs that I thought fascinating. The other reticent Talmudists I knew usually read in an undertone, humming their recitatives quietly. He seldom did. Sparing as he was of his voice in conversation, he would use it extravagantly when intoning his Talmud

It is with a peculiar sense of duality one reads this ancient work. While your mind is absorbed in the meaning of the words you utter, the melody in which you utter them tells your heart a tale of its own. You live in two distinct worlds at once. Naphtali had little to say to other people, but he seemed to have much to say to himself. His singsongs were full of meaning, of passion, of beauty. Quite often he would sing himself hoarse

Regularly every Thursday night he and I had our vigil at the Preacher's Synagogue, where many other young men would gather for the same purpose. We would sit up reading, side by side, until the worshipers came to morning service. To spend a whole night by his side was one of the joys of my existence in those days

Reb Sender was somewhat jealous of him

Soon after graduation Naphtali left Antomir for a town in which lived some of his relatives. I missed him as I would a sweetheart

- finished elementary, went to yeshivah @ 13
- became friends w/ Reb Sender (father like figure) and Naphtali
- growing interest in the opposite sex, growing up.

45

# CHAPTER II

I WAS nearly sixteen. I had graduated from the seminary and was pursuing my studies at the Preacher's Synagogue exclusively, as an "independent scholar." I was overborne with a sense of my dignity and freedom. I seemed to have suddenly grown much taller. If I caught myself walking fast or indulging in some boyish prank I would check myself, saying in my heart: "You must not forget that you are an independent scholar. You are a boy no longer."

I was free to loaf, but I worked harder than ever. I was either in an exalted state of mind or pining away under a spell of yearning and melancholy—of causeless, meaningless melancholy.

My Talmudic singsong reflected my moods. Sometimes it was a spirited recitative, ringing with cheery self-consciousness and the joy of being a lad of sixteen; at other times it was a solemn song, aglow with devotional ecstasy. When I happened to be dejected in the commonplace sense of the word, it was a listless murmur, doleful or sullen. But then the very reading of the Talmud was apt to dispel my gloom. My voice would gradually rise and ring out, vibrating with intellectual passion

The intonations of the other scholars, too, echoed the voices of their hearts, some of them sonorous with religious bliss, others sad, still others happy-go-lucky. Although absorbed in my book, I would have a vague consciousness of the connection between the various singsongs and their respective performers. I would be aware that the bass voice with the flourishes in front of me belonged to the stuttering widower from Vitebsk, that the squeaky, jerky intonation to the right came from the red-headed fellow whom I loathed for his thick lips, or that the sweet, unassertive cadences that came floating from the east wall were being uttered by Reb Rachmiel, the "man of acumen" whose father-in-law had made a fortune as a war-contractor in the late conflict with Turkey.

All these voices blended in a symphonic source of inspiration for me. It was divine music in more senses than one

The ancient rabbis of the Talmud, the Tanaim of the earlier period and the Amorairn of later generations, were living men. I could almost see them, each of them individualized in my mind by some of his sayings, by his manner in debate, by some particular word he used, or by some particular incident in which he figured. I pictured their faces, their beards, their voices.

Some of them had won a warmer corner in my heart than others, but they were all superior human beings, godly, unearthly, denizens of a world that had been ages ago and would come back in the remote future when Messiah should make his appearance

Added to the mystery of that world was the mystery of my own singsong. Who is there?—I seemed to be wondering, my tune or recitative sounding like the voice of some other fellow. It was as if somebody were hidden within me. *trying to find himself*

What did he look like? If you study the Talmud you please God even more than you do by praying or fasting. As you sit reading the great folio He looks down from heaven upon you. Sometimes I seemed to feel His gaze shining down upon me, as though casting a halo over my bead

My relations with God were of a personal and of a rather familiar character.

He was interested in everything I did or said; He watched my every move or thought; He was always in heaven, yet, somehow, he was always near me, and I often spoke to Him as I might to Reb Sender

If I caught myself slurring over some of my prayers or speaking ill of another boy or telling a falsehood, I would say to Him, audibly: "Oh, forgive me once more. You know that I want to be good. I will be good.

I know I will."

Sometimes I would continue to plead in this manner till I broke into sobs.

At other times, as I read my Talmud, conscious of His approval of me, tears of bliss would come into my eyes

I loved Him as one does a woman.

*[left margin, handwritten, vertical:] Amen. understanding is all we want & from God we get it.*

Often while saying my prayers I would fall into a veritable delirium of religious infatuation. Sometimes this fit of happiness and yearning would seize me as I walked in the street

"O Master of the World! Master of the Universe! I love you so!" I would sigh. "Oh, how I love you!"

I also had talks with the Evil Spirit, or Satan. He, too, was always near me. But he was always trying to get me into trouble

"You won't catch me again, scoundrel you," I would assure him with sneers and leers. Or, "Get away from me, heartless mischief-maker you! You're wasting your time, I can tell you that."

My bursts of piety usually lasted a week or two. Then there was apt to set in a period of apathy, which was sure to be replaced by days of penance and a new access of spiritual fervor.

One day, as Reb Sender and I were reading a page together, a very pretty girl entered the synagogue. She came to have a letter written for her by one of the scholars. I continued to read aloud, but I did so absently now, trailing along after my companion. My mind was upon the girl, and I was casting furtive glances

Reb Sender paused, with evident annoyance. "What are you looking at, David?" he said, with a tug at my arm. "Shame! You are yielding to Satan."

I colored

He was too deeply interested in the Talmudic argument under consideration to say more on the matter at this minute, but he returned to it as soon as we had reached the end of the section. He spoke earnestly, with fatherly concern: "You are growing, David. You are a boy no longer. You are getting to be a man. This is just the time when one should be on his guard against Satan."

I sat, looking down, my brain in a daze of embarrassment

"Remember, David, 'He who looks even at the little finger of a woman is as guilty as though he looked at a woman that is wholly naked.'" He quoted the Talmudic maxim in a tone of passionate sternness, beating the desk with his snuff-box at each word

As to his own conduct, he was one of three or four men at the synagogue of whom it was said that they never looked at women, and, to a very considerable extent, his reputation was not unjustified

"You must never tire fighting Satan, David," he proceeded. "Fight him with might and main."

As I listened I was tingling with a mute vow to be good. Yet, at the same time, the vision of "a woman that is wholly naked" was vividly before me

He caused me to bring a certain ancient work, one not included in the Talmud, in which he made me read the following: "Rabbi Mathia, the son of Chovosh, had never set eyes on a woman.

Therefore when he was at the synagogue studying the Law, his visage would shine as the sun and its features would be the features of an angel. One day, as he thus sat reading, Satan chanced to pass by, and in a fit of jealousy Satan said: "'Can it really be that this man has never sinned?' "'He is a man of spotless purity,' answered God

"'Just grant me the liberty,' Satan urged, 'and I will lead him to sin.' "'You will never succeed.' "'Let me try.' "'Proceed.' "Satan then appeared in the guise of the most beautiful woman in the world, of one the like of whom had not been born since the days of Naomi, the sister of Tuval Cain, the woman who had led angels astray.

When Rabbi Mathia espied her he faced about. So Satan, still in the disguise of a beautiful woman, took up a position on the left side of him; and when he turned away once more he walked over to the right side again. Finally Rabbi Mathia had nails and fire brought him and gouged out his own eyes.

"At this God called for Angel Raphael and bade him cure the righteous man. Presently Raphael came back with the report that Rabbi Mathia would not be cured lest he should again be tempted to look at pretty women.

"'Go tell him in My name that he shall never be tempted again,' said God

"And so the holy man regained his eyesight and was never molested by Satan again."

The painful image of poor Rabbi Mathia gouging out his eyes supplanted the nude figure of the previous quotation in my mind

Reb Sender pursued his "exhortative talk." He dwelt on the duties of man to man.

"If a man is tongue-tied, don't laugh at him, but, rather, feel pity for him, as you would for a man with broken legs. Nor should you hate a man who has a weakness for telling falsehoods. This, too, is an affliction, like stuttering or being lame. Say to yourself, 'Poor fellow, he is given to lying.' Above all, you must fight conceit, envy, and every kind of ill-feeling in your heart. Remember, the sum and substance of all learning lies in the words, 'Love thy neighbor as thyself.' Another thing, remember that it is not enough to abstain from lying by word of mouth; for the worst lies are often conveyed by a false look, smile, or act. Be genuinely truthful, then. And if you feel that you are good, don't be too proud of it.

Be modest, humble, simple. Control your anger."

He worked me up to a veritable frenzy of penitence

"I will, I will," I said, tremulously. "And if I ever catch myself looking at a woman again I will gouge out my eyes like Rabbi Mathia."

"'S-sh! Don't say that, my son." About a quarter of an hour later, as I sat reading by myself, I suddenly sprang to my feet and walked over to Reb Sender

"You are so dear to me," I gasped out. "You are a man of perfect righteousness. I love you so. I should jump into fire or into water for your sake."

"'S-sh!" he said, taking me gently by the hand and pressing me down into a seat by his side. "You are a good boy. As to my being a man of perfect righteousness, alas! I am far from being one. We are all sinful. Come, let us read another page together."

Satan kept me rather busy these days. It was not an easy task to keep one's eyes off the girls who came to the Preacher's Synagogue, and when none was around I would be apt to think of one. I would even picture myself touching a feminine cheek with the tip of my finger. Then my heart would sink in despair and I would hurl curses at Satan

"Eighty black years on you, vile wretch you!" I would whisper, gnashing my teeth, and fall to reading with ferocious zeal

In the relations between men and women it is largely case of forbidden fruit and the mystery of distance. The great barrier that religion, law, and convention have laced between the sexes adds to the joys and poetry of love, but it is responsible also for much of the suffering, degradation, and crime that spring from it. In my case his barrier was of special magnitude.

Dancing with a girl, or even taking one out for a walk, was out of the question. Nor was the injunction confined to men who devoted themselves to the study of holy books. It was the rule of ordinary decency for any Jew except one who lived "like a Gentile," that is, like a person of modern culture. Indeed, there were scores of towns in the vicinity of Antomir where one could not take a walk even with one's own wife without incurring universal condemnation. There was a lancing-school or two in Antomir, but they were attended by young mechanics of the coarser type. To be sure, there were plenty of young Jews in our town who did live "like Gentiles," who called the girls of their acquaintance "young ladies," took off their hats to them, took them out for a walk in the public park, and danced with them, just like the nobles or the army officers of my birthplace. But then these fellows spoke Russian instead of Yiddish and altogether they belonged to a world far removed from mine. Many of these "modern" young Jews went to high school and wore pretty uniforms with silver-plated buttons and silver lace.

To me they were apostates, sinners in Israel. And yet I could not think of them without a lurking feeling of envy. The Gentile books they studied and their social relations with girls who were dressed "like young noblewomen" piqued my keenest curiosity and made me feel small and wretched

The orthodox Jewish faith practically excludes woman from religious life.

Attending divine service is not obligatory for her, and those of the sex who wish to do so are allowed to follow the devotions not in the synagogue proper, but through little windows or peepholes in the wall of an adjoining room. In the eye of the spiritual law that governed my life women were intended for two purposes only: for the continuation of the human species and to serve as an instrument in the hands of Satan for tempting the stronger sex to sin. Marriage was simply a duty imposed by the Bible. Love? So far as it meant attraction between two persons of the opposite sex who were not man and wife, there was no such word in my native tongue. One loved one's wife, mother, daughter, or sister. To be "in love" with a girl who was an utter stranger to you was something unseemly, something which only Gentiles or "modern" Jews might indulge in

But at present all this merely deepened the bewitching mystery of the forbidden sex in my young blood. And Satan, wide awake and sharp-eyed as ever, was not slow to perceive the change that had come over me and made the most of it

51

There was no such thing as athletics or outdoor sports in my world. The only physical exercise known to us was to be swinging like a pendulum in front of your reading-desk from nine in the morning to bedtime every day, and an all-night vigil every Thursday in addition. Even a most innocent frolic among the boys was suppressed as an offense to good Judaism

All of which tended to deepen the mystery of girlhood and to increase the chances of Satan.

I must explain that although women could not attend divine service except through a peephole, they were free to visit the house of worship on all sorts of other errands. So some of them would come with food for the scholars, others with candles for the chandeliers, while still others wanted letters read or written. One of the several rabbis of the town was in the habit of spending his evenings reading Talmud in the Preacher's Synagogue, so housewives of the neighborhood, or their daughters, would bring some spoon, pot, or chicken to have them passed upon according to the dietary laws of Moses and the Talmud

I would scrutinize the faces and figures of these girls, I would draw comparisons, make guesses as to whether they were engaged to be married (I did not have to speculate upon whether they were already married, because a young matron who would visit our synagogue was sure to have her hair covered with a wig). It became one of my pastimes to make forecasts as to the looks of the next young woman to call at the synagogue, whether she would be pretty or homely, tall or short, fair or dark, plump or spare. I was interested in their eyes, but, somehow, I was still more interested in their mouths. Some mouths would set my blood on fire. I would invent all sorts of romantic episodes with myself as the hero. I would portray my engagement to some of the pretty girls I had seen, our wedding, and, above all, our married life. The worst of it was that these images often visited my brain while I was reading the holy book. Satan would choose such moments of all others because in this manner he would involve me in two great sins at once; for in addition to the wickedness of indulging in salacious thoughts there was the offense of desecrating the holy book by them

Reb Sender's daughter was about to be married to a tradesman of Talmudic education. I did not care for her in the least, yet her approaching wedding aroused a lively interest in me

Red Esther had gone out to service. She came home but seldom, and when she did we scarcely ever talked to each other. The coarse brightness of her complexion and the harsh femininity of her laughter repelled me

"I do hate her," I once said to myself, as I heard that laugh of hers

"And yet you would not mind kissing her, would you, now?" a voice retorted

I had to own that I would not, and then I cudgeled my brains over the amazing discrepancy of the thing. Kissing meant being fond of one. I enjoyed kissing my mother, for instance. Now, I certainly was not fond of Esther. I was sure that I hated her. Why, then, was I impelled to kiss her? How could I hate and be fond of her at once? I went on reasoning it out, Talmud fashion, till I arrived at the conclusion that there were two kinds of kisses: the kiss of affection and the kiss of Satan. I submitted it, as a discovery, to some of the other young Talmudists, but they scouted it as a truism. A majority of us were modest of speech and conduct. But there were some who were not

- 16 — the pains of growing up, of trying to find yourself
- becoming more and more interested in girls
- what women really are = tools for temptation
- curiosity ... grows ...

# CHAPTER III

WHEN I was a little over eighteen the number of steady readers at the Old Synagogue was increased by the advent of a youth from the Polish provinces.

His appearance produced something of a sensation, for, in addition to being the son of a rich merchant and the prospective son-in-law of a celebrated rabbi, he was the possessor of a truly phenomenal memory. He was well versed in the entire Talmud, and could recite by heart about five hundred leaves, or one thousand pages, of it. He was generally called the Pole. He was tall and supple, fair-complexioned, and well-groomed, with a suggestion of self-satisfaction and aloofness in the very sinuosity of his figure. His velvet skull-cap, which was always pushed back on his head, exposed to view a forelock of golden hair. His long-skirted, well-fitting coat was of the richest broadcloth I had ever seen. He wore a watch and chain that were said to be worth a small fortune. I hated him. He was repugnant to me for his Polish accent, for his good clothes, for his well-fed face, for his haughty manner, for the servile attention that was showered on him, and, above all, for his extraordinary memory. I had always been under the impression that the boys of well-to-do parents were stupid. Brains did not seem to be in their line. That this young man, who was so well supplied with this world's goods, should possess a wonderful mind as well jarred on me as an injustice to us poor boys

I would seek comfort in the reflection that "the essence of scholarship lay in profundity and acumen rather than in the ability to rattle off pages like so many psalms." Yet those "five hundred leaves" of his gave me no peace.

Five hundred! The figure haunted me. Finally I set myself the task of memorizing five hundred leaves. It was a gigantic undertaking, although my memory was rather above the average.

I worked with unflagging assiduity for weeks and weeks. Nobody was to know of my purpose until it had been achieved. I worked so hard and was so absorbed in my task that my interest in girls lost much of its usual acuteness. At times I had a sense of my own holiness. When I walked through the streets, on my way to or from the synagogue, I kept reciting some of the pages I had mastered. While in bed for the night, I whispered myself to sleep reciting Talmud. When I ate, some bit of Talmud was apt to be running through my mind. If there was a hitch, and I could not go on, my heart would sink within me. I would stop eating and make an effort to recall the passage

It was inevitable that the new character of my studies should sooner or later attract Reb Sender's attention. My secret hung like a veil between us.

He was jealous of it. Ultimately he questioned me, beseechingly, and I was forced to make a clean breast of it

Reb Sender beamed. The veil was withdrawn. Presently his face fell again

"What I don't like about it is your envy of the Pole," he said, gravely.

"Don't take it ill, my son, but I am afraid you are envious and begrudging.

Fight it, Davie. Give up studying by heart. It is not with a pure motive you are doing it. Your studies are poisoned with hatred and malice. Do you want to gladden my heart, Davie?"

"I do. I will. What do you mean?" "Just step up to the Pole and beg his pardon for the evil thoughts you have harbored about him."

A minute later I stood in front of my hated rival, thrilling with the ecstasy of penitence.

"I have sinned against you. Forgive me," I said, with downcast eyes

The Pole was puzzled

"I envied you," I explained. "I could not bear to hear everybody speak of the five hundred leaves you know by heart. So I wanted to show you that I could learn by heart just as much, if not more."

A suggestion of a sneer flitted across his well-fed face. It stung me as if it were some loathsome insect. His golden forelock exasperated me

"And I could do it, too," I snapped. "I have learned more than fifty leaves already. It is not so much of a trick as I thought it was."

"Is it not?" the Pole said, with a full-grown sneer

"You need not be so stuck up, anyhow," I shot back, and turned away

Before I had reached Reb Sender, who had been watching us, I rushed back to the Pole

"I just want to say this," I began, in a towering rage. "With all your boasted memory you would be glad to change brains with me."

His shoulders shook with soundless mirth

"Laugh away. But let Reb Sender examine both of us. Let him select a passage and see who of us can delve deeper into it, you or I? Memory alone is nothing."

"Isn't it? Then why are you green with envy of me?" And once more he burst into a laugh, with a graceful jerk of his head which set my blood on fire

"You're a pampered idiot."

"You're green with envy."

"I'll break every bone in you."

We flew at each other, but Reb Sender and two other scholars tore us apart

"Shame!" the Talmudists cried, shrugging their shoulders in disgust

"Just like Gentiles," some one commented

"It is an outrage to have the holy place desecrated in this manner."

"What has got into you?" Reb Sender said to me as he led me back to my desk

I resumed studying by heart with more energy than ever. "That's all right!" I thought to myself. "I'll have that silk-stocking of a fellow lick the dust of my shoes." I now took special measures to guard my secret even from Reb Sender. One of these was to take a book home and to work there, staying away from synagogue as often as I could invent a plausible pretext. I was lying right and left. Satan chuckled in my face, but I did not care. I promised myself to settle my accounts with the Uppermost later on. The only thing that mattered now was to beat the Pole

The sight of me learning the Word of God so diligently was a source of indescribable joy to my mother. She struggled to suppress her feeling, but from time to time a sigh would escape her, as though the rush of happiness was too much for her heart

Alas! <u>this happiness of hers was not to last much longer</u>

*foreshadowing*

- rivalry between D | the Pole
- Pole has a good memory | D finds himself jealous of it
- D apologizes but P shoves it back in his face + they fight
  L for the sake of Reb Sender
- foreshadowing at end → something is going to happen either to his mother or himself.

# BOOK III

## I LOSE MY MOTHER

_↳ knew it... ≈_

# CHAPTER I

IT was Purim, the feast of Esther. Our school-boys were celebrating the downfall of Haman, and they were doing it in the same war-like fashion in which American boys celebrate their forefathers' defiance of George III. The synagogues roared with the booming of fire-crackers, the report of toy pistols, the whir-whir of Purim rattles. It was four weeks to the great eight-day festival of Passover and my mother went to work in a bakery of unleavened bread. She toiled from eighteen to twenty hours a day, so that she often dozed off over her rolling-pin from sheer exhaustion. But then she earned far more than usual. Including tips from customers (the baker merely acted as a contractor for the families whose flour he transformed into fiat, round, tasteless Passover cakes, or "matzoths") she saved up, during the period, a little over twenty rubles. With a part of this sum she ordered a new coat for me and bought me a new cap. I remember that coat very well. It was of a dark-brown cotton stuff, neat at the waist and with absurdly long skirts, of course. The Jewish Passover often concurs with the Christian Easter. This was the case in the year in question. One afternoon—it was the seventh day of our festival—I chanced to be crossing the Horse-market. As it was not market day, it was deserted save for groups of young Gentiles, civilians and soldiers, who were rolling brightly colored Easter eggs over the ground. My new long-skirted coat and side-locks provoked their mirth until one of them hit me a savage blow in the face, splitting my lower lip.

Another rowdy snatched off my new cap—just because our people considered it a sin to go bareheaded. And, as I made my way, bleeding, with one hand to my lip and the other over my bare head, the company sent a shower of broken eggs and a chorus of jeers after me

*[handwritten margin note: Always a mother...]*

*[handwritten margin note: The brute!]*

It was only a short distance from Abner's Court. When I entered our basement and faced my mother, she stared at me for a moment, as though dumfounded, and then, slapping her hands together, she sobbed: "Woe is me! Darkness is me! What has happened to you?"

When she had heard my story she stood silent awhile, looking aghast, and then left the house.

"I'm going to kill him. I am just going to kill him," she said, in measured accents which still ring in my ears

The bookbinder's wife, the retired soldier, and I ran after her, imploring her not to risk her life on such a foolhardy errand, but she took no heed of us

"Foolish woman! You don't even know who did it," urged the soldier

"I'll find out!" she answered

The bookbinder's wife seized her by an arm, but she shook her off. I pleaded with her with tears in my eyes

"Go back," she said to me, trying to be gentle while her eyes were lit with an ominous look

These were the last words I ever heard her utter

Fifteen minutes later she was carried into our basement unconscious. Her face was bruised and swollen and the back of her head was broken. She died the same evening

I have never been able to learn the ghastly details of her death. The police and an examining magistrate were said to be investigating the case, but nothing came of it

There was no lack of excitement among the Jews of Antomir. The funeral was expected to draw a vast crowd. But the epidemic of anti-Jewish atrocities of 1881 and 1882 were fresh in one's mind, so word was passed round "not to irritate the Gentiles." The younger and "modern" element in town took exception to this timidity. They insisted upon a demonstrative funeral. They were organizing for self-defense in case the procession was interfered with, but the counsel of older people prevailed. As a consequence, the number of mourners following the hearse was even smaller than it would have been if my mother had died a natural death. And the few who did take part in the sad procession were unusually silent. A Jewish funeral without a chorus of sobbing women was inconceivable in Antomir. Indeed, a pious matron who happens to come across such a scene will join in the weeping, whether she had ever heard of the deceased or not. On this occasion, however, sobs were conspicuous by their absence

"'S-sh! 's-sh! None of your wailing!" an old man kept admonishing the women

I spent the "Seven Days "(of mourning) in our basement, where I received visits from neighbors, from the families of my two distant relatives, from Reb Sender and other Talmudists of my synagogue. Among these was the Pole.

This time my rival begged my forgiveness. I granted it, of course, but I felt that we never could like each other    → sympathy

There was a great wave of sympathy for me. Offers of assistance came pouring in in all sorts of forms. Had there been a Yiddish newspaper in town and such things as public meetings, the outburst might have crystallized into what, to me, would have been a great fortune. As it was, public interest in me died before anything tangible was done. Still, there were several prosperous families of the old-fashioned class, each of which wanted to provide me with excellent board. But then Reb Sender's wife, in a fit of compassion and carried away by the prevailing spirit of the moment, claimed the sole right to feed me

"I'll take his mother's place," she said. "Whatever the Upper One gives us will be enough for him, too." Her husband was happy, while I lacked the courage to overrule them

As to lodgings, it was deemed most natural that I should sleep in some house of worship, as thousands of Talmud students did in Antomir and other towns.

To put up with a synagogue bench for a bed and to "eat days" was even regarded as a desirable part of a young man's Talmud education. And so I selected a pew in the Preacher's Synagogue for my bed. I was better off than some others who lived in houses of God, for I had some of my mother's bedding while they mostly had to sleep on hay pillows with a coat for a blanket

It was not until I found myself lying on this improvised bed that I realized the full extent of my calamity. During the first seven days of mourning I had been aware, of course, that something appalling had befallen me, but I had scarcely experienced anything like keen anguish. I had been in an excited, hazy state of mind, more conscious of being the central figure of a great sensation than

state of shock

of my loss. As I went to bed on the synagogue bench, however, instead of in my old bunk at what had been my home, the fact that my mother was dead and would never be alive again smote me with crushing violence. It was as though I had just discovered it. I shall never forget that terrible night

At the end of the first thirty days of mourning I visited mother's grave.

"Mamma! Mamma!" I shrieked, throwing myself upon the mound in a wild paroxysm of grief

The dinners which Reb Sender's wife brought to the synagogue for her husband and myself were never quite enough for two, and for supper, which he had at home, she would bring me some bread and cheese or herring. Poor Reb Sender could not look me in the face. The situation grew more awkward every day. It was not long before his wife began to drop hints that I was hard to please, that she did far more than she could afford for me and that I was an ingrate. The upshot was that she "allowed" me to accept "days" from other families. But the well-to-do people had by now forgotten my existence and the housewives who were still vying with one another in offering me meals were mostly of the poorer class. These strove to make me feel at home at their houses, and yet, in some cases at least, as I ate, I was aware of being watched lest I should consume too much bread. As a consequence, I often went away half hungry. All of which quickened my self-pity and the agony of my yearnings for mother. I grew extremely sensitive and more quarrelsome than I am naturally. I quarreled with one of my relatives, a woman, and rejected the "day" which I had had in her house, and shortly after abandoned one of my other "days."

Reb Sender kept tab of my missing "days" and tried to make up for them by sharing his dinner with me. His wife, however, who usually waited for the dishes and so was present while I ate, was anything but an encouraging witness of her husband's hospitality. The food would stick in my throat under her glances. I was repeatedly impelled abruptly to leave the meal, but refrained from doing so for Reb Sender's sake. I obtained two new "days." One of these I soon forfeited, having been caught stealing a hunk of bread; but I kept the matter from Reb Sender. To conceal the truth from him I would spend the dinner hour in the street or in a little synagogue in another section of the city. Tidy Naphtali had recently returned to Antomir, and this house of worship was his home now. His vocal cords had been ruined by incessantly reading Talmud at the top of his lungs. He now spoke or read in a low, hoarse voice. He still spent most of his time at a reading-desk, but he had to content himself with whispering

I found a new "day," but lost three of my old ones. Naphtali had as little to eat as I, yet he scarcely ever left his books. One late afternoon I sat by his side while he was reading in a spiritless whisper. Neither of us had lunched that day. His curly head was propped upon his arm, his near-sighted eyes close to the book. He never stirred. He was too faint to sway his body or to gesticulate. I was musing wearily, and it seemed as though my hunger was a living thing and was taking part in my thoughts

"Do you know, Naphtali," I said, "it is pleasant even to famish in company.

If I were alone it would be harder to stand it. 'The misery of the many is a consolation.'" He made no answer. Minutes passed. Presently he turned from his desk

"Do you really think there is a God?" he asked, irrelevantly

I stared

"Don't be shocked. It is all bosh." And he fell to swaying over his book

I was dumfounded. "Why do you keep reading Talmud, then?" I asked, looking aghast

"Because I am a fool," he returned, going on with his reading. A minute later he added, "But you are a bigger one."

I was hurt and horrified. I tried to argue, but he went on murmuring, his eyes on the folio before him

Finally I snapped: "You are a horrid atheist and a sinner in Israel. You are desecrating the holy place." And I rushed from the little synagogue

His shocking whisper, "Do you really think there is a God?" haunted me all that afternoon and evening. He appeared like another man to me. I was burning to see him again and to smash his atheism, to prove to him that there was a God. But as I made a mental rehearsal of my argument I realized that I had nothing clear or definite to put forth. So I cursed Naphtali for an apostate, registered a vow to shun him, and was looking forward to the following day when I should go to see him again

My interest in the matter was not keen, however, and soon it died down altogether. Nothing really interested me except the fact that I had not enough to eat, that mother was no more, that I was all alone in the world.

The shock of the catastrophe had produced a striking effect on me. My incessant broodings, and the corroding sense of my great irreparable loss and of my desolation had made a nerveless, listless wreck of me, a mere shadow of my former self. I was incapable of sustained thinking

My communions with God were quite rare now. Nor did He take as much interest in my studies as He used to. Instead of the Divine Presence shining down on me while I read, the face of my martyred mother would loom before me. Once or twice in my hungry rambles I visited Abner's Court and let my heart be racked by the sight of what had once been our home, mother's and mine. I said prayers for her three times a day with great devotion, with a deep yearning. But this piety was powerless to restore me to my former feeling for the Talmud

I distinctly recall how I would shut my eyes and vision my mother looking at me from her grave, her heart contracted with anguish and pity for her famished orphan. It was an excruciating vision, yet I found comfort in it. I would mutely complain of the world to her. It would give me satisfaction to denounce the whole town to her. "Ah, I have got you!" I seemed to say to the people of Antomir. "The ghost of my mother and the whole Other World see you in all your heartlessness. You can't wriggle out of it." This was my revenge. I reveled in it.

But, nothing daunted, the people of Antomir would go about their business as usual and my heart would sink with a sense of my helplessness.

I was restless. I coveted diversion, company, and I saw a good deal of Naphtali. As for his Free Thought, it soon, after we had two mild quarrels over it, began to bore me. It appeared that the huge tomes of the Talmud were not the only books he read these days. He spent much time, clandestinely, on little books written in the holy tongue on any but holy topics. They were taken up with such things as modern science, poetry, fiction, and, above all, criticism of our faith. He made some attempts to lure me into an interest in these books, but without avail. The only thing connected with them that appealed to me were the anecdotes that Naphtali would tell me, in his laconic way, concerning their authors. I scarcely ever listened to these stories without invoking imprecations upon the infidels, but I enjoyed them all the same. They were mostly concerned with their apostasy, but there were many that were not. Some of these, or rather the fact that I had first heard them from Naphtali, in my youth, were destined to have a peculiar bearing on an important event in my life, on something that occurred many years later, when I was already a prosperous merchant in New York. They were about Doctor Rachaeles, a famous Hebrew writer who practised medicine in Odessa, and his son-in-law, a poet named Abraham Tevkin. Doctor Rachacles's daughter was a celebrated beauty and the poet's courtship of her had been in the form of a long series of passionate letters addressed, not to his lady-love, but to her father. This love-story made a strong impression on me. The figures of the beautiful girl and of the enamoured young poet, as I pictured them, were vivid in my mind.

"Did he write of his love in those letters?" I demanded, shyly

"He did not write of onions, did he?" Naphtali retorted. After a little I asked: "But how could she read those letters? She certainly does not read holy tongue?"

"Go ask her."

"You're a funny fellow. Did Tevkin get the girl?"

"He did, and they have been married for many years. Why, did you wonder if you mightn't have a chance?"

"You're impossible, Naphtali."

He smiled

*[handwritten notes:]*

- was beaten by gentile soldiers, came home w/ split lip
- the maternal lion emerges to protect her son
  └ D's mother is beaten up + dies
- D in state of shock
- Reb takes him in
- D receives "days"
- Naphtali is back
- stories of love

# CHAPTER II

ONE afternoon Naphtali called on me at the Preacher's Synagogue

"Have you got all your 'days'?" he asked, in his whisper

"Why?"

He had discovered a "treasure"—a pious, rich, elderly woman whose latest hobby was to care for at least eighteen poor Talmudists—eighteen being the numerical value of the letters composing the Hebrew word for "life." Her name was Shiphrah Minsker. She belonged to one of the oldest families in Antomir, and her husband was equally well-born. Her religious zeal was of recent origin, in fact, and even now she wore her hair "Gentile fashion." It was a great sin, but she had never worn a wig in her life, and putting on one now seemed to be out of the question. This hair of hers was of a dark-brown hue, threaded with silver, and it grew in a tousled abundance of unruly wisps that seemed to be symbolic of her harum-scarum character. She was as pugnacious as she was charitable, and as quick to make up a quarrel as to pick one. Her husband, Michael Minsker, was a "worldly" man, with only a smattering of Talmud, and their younger children were being educated at the Russian schools. But they all humored her newly adopted old-fashioned ways, to a certain extent at least, while she tolerated their "Gentile" ones as she did her own uncovered hair. Relegating her household affairs to a devoted old servant, with whom she was forever wrangling, Shiphrah spent most of her time raising contributions to her various charity funds, looking after her Talmud students, quarreling with her numerous friends, and begging their forgiveness. If she was unable to provide meals for a student in the houses of some people of her acquaintance she paid for his board out of her own purse

Her husband was an exporter of grain and his business often took him to Koenigsberg, Prussia, for several weeks at a time. Occasions of this kind were hailed by Shiphrah as a godsend (in the literal sense of the term), for in his absence she could freely spend on her beneficiaries and even feed some of them at her own house

When I was introduced to her as "the son of the woman who had been killed on the Horse-market" and she heard that I frequently had nothing to eat, she burst into tears and berated me soundly for not having knocked at her door sooner

"It's terrible! It's terrible!" she moaned, breaking into tears again. "In fact I, too, deserve a spanking. To think that I did not look him up at once when that awful thing happened!"

As a matter of fact, she had not done so because at the time of my mother's death her house had been agog with a trouble of its own. But of this presently

She handed me a three-ruble bill and set about filling up the gaps in my eating calendar and substituting fat "days" for lean ones.

She often came to see me at the synagogue, never empty-handed. Now she had a silver coin for me, now a pair of socks, a shirt, or perhaps a pair of trousers which some member of her family had discarded. Often, too, she would bring me a quarter of a chicken, cookies, or some other article of food from her own table

My days of hunger were at an end. I lived in clover. "Now I can work," I thought to myself, with the satisfaction of a well-filled stomach. "And work I will. I'll show people what I can do."

I applied myself to my task with ardor, but it did not last long. My former interest in the Talmud was gone. The spell was broken irretrievably. Now that I did not want for food, my sense of loneliness became keener than ever. Indeed, it was a novel sense of loneliness, quite unlike the one I had experienced before

My surroundings had somehow lost their former meaning. Life was devoid of savor, and I was thirsting for an appetizer, as it were, for some violent change, for piquant sensations

Then it was that the word America first caught my fancy

The name was buzzing all around me. The great emigration of Jews to the United States, which had received its first impulse two or three years before, was already in full swing. It may not be out of order to relate, briefly. how it had all come about

An anti-Semitic riot broke out in a southern town named Elisabethgrad in the early spring of 1881. Occurrences of this kind were, in those days, quite rare in Russia, and when they did happen they did not extend beyond the town of their origin. But the circumstances that surrounded the Elisabethgrad outbreak were of a specific character. It took place one month after the assassination of the Czar, Alexander II. The actual size and influence of the "underground" revolutionary organization being an unknown quantity, St.

Petersburg was full of the rumblings of a general uprising. The Elisabethgrad riot, however, was not of a revolutionary nature. Yet the police, so far from suppressing it, encouraged it. The example of the Elisabethgrad rabble was followed by the riffraff of other places. The epidemic quickly spread from city to city. Whereupon the scenes of lawlessness in the various cities were marked by the same method in the mob's madness, by the same connivance on the part of the police, and by many other traits that clearly pointed to a common source of inspiration. It has long since become a well-established historical fact that the anti-Jewish disturbances were encouraged, even arranged, by the authorities as an outlet for the growing popular discontent with the Government.

Count von Plehve was then at the head of the Police Department in the Ministry of the Interior.

This bit of history repeated itself, on a larger scale, twenty-two years later, when Russia was in the paroxysm of a real revolution and when the ghastly massacres of Jews in Kishineff, Odessa, Kieff, and other cities were among the means employed in an effort to keep the masses "busy."

Count von Plehve then held the office of Prime Minister. To return to 1881 and 1882. Thousands of Jewish families were left homeless. Of still greater moment was the moral effect which the atrocities produced on the whole Jewish population of Russia. Over five million people were suddenly made to realize that their birthplace was not their home (a feeling which the great Russian revolution has suddenly changed). Then it was that the cry "To America!" was raised. It spread like wild-fire, even over those parts of the Pale of Jewish Settlement which lay outside the riot zone

This was the beginning of the great New Exodus that has been in progress for decades

My native town and the entire section to which it belongs had been immune from the riots, yet it caught the general contagion, and at the time I became one of Shiphrah's wards hundreds of its inhabitants were going to America or planning to do so. Letters full of wonders from emigrants already there went the rounds of eager readers and listeners until they were worn to shreds in the process

I succumbed to the spreading fever. It was one of these letters from America, in fact, which put the notion of emigrating to the New World definitely in my mind. An illiterate woman brought it to the synagogue to have it read to her, and I happened to be the one to whom she addressed her request. The concrete details of that letter gave New York tangible form in my imagination. It haunted me ever after

The United States lured me not merely as a land of milk and honey, but also, and perhaps chiefly, as one of mystery, of fantastic experiences, of marvelous transformations. To leave my native place and to seek my fortune in that distant, weird world seemed to be just the kind of sensational adventure my heart was hankering for.

*a new beginning*

When I unburdened myself of my project to Reb Sender he was thunderstruck

"To America!" he said. "Lord of the World! But one becomes a Gentile there."

"Not at all," I sought to reassure him. "There are lots of good Jews there, and they don't neglect their Talmud, either." The amount that was necessary to take me to America loomed staggeringly large. Where was it to come from? I thought of approaching Shiphrah, but the idea of her helping me abandon my Talmud and go to live in a godless country seemed preposterous. So I began by saving the small allowance which I received from her and by selling some of the clothes and food she brought me. For the evening meal I usually received some rye bread and a small coin for cheese or herring, so I invariably added the coin to my little hoard, relishing the bread with thoughts of America.

While I was thus pinching and saving pennies I was continually casting about for some more effective way of raising the sum that would take me to New York. I confided my plan to Naphtali.

71

"Not a bad idea," he said, "but you will never raise the money. You are a master of dreams, David."

"I'll get the money, and, what is more, when I am in America I shall bring you over there, too."

"May your words pass from your lips into the ear of God."

"I thought you did not believe in God."

"How long will you believe in Him after you get to America?"

· befriends a rich benefactor, Shiphrah Minsker
· no longer hungry
· longing for a fresh start in America
  └ starts saving to go to NY

# BOOK IV

# MATILDA

# CHAPTER I

I COULD scarcely think of anything but America. I read every letter from there that I could obtain. I was constantly seeking information about the country and the opportunities it held out to a man of my type, and cudgeling my brains for some way of scraping together the formidable sum. I was restless, sleepless, and finally, when I caught a slight cold, my health broke down so completely that I had to be taken to the hospital. Shiphrah visited me every day, calling me poor orphan boy and quarreling with the superintendent over me. One afternoon, after I had been discharged, when she saw me at the synagogue, feeble and emaciated, she gasped

"You're a cruel, heartless man," she flared up, addressing herself to the beadle. "The poor boy needs a good soft bed, fine chicken soup, and real care. Why didn't you let me know at once? Come on, David!"

"Where to?" I inquired, timidly.

"None of your business. Come on. I'm not going to take you to the woods, you may be sure of that. I want you to stay in my house until you are well rested and strong enough to study. Don't you like it?" she added, with a wink to the beadle

It appeared that her husband was away on one of his prolonged business excursions. Otherwise installing in her "modern" home an old-fashioned, ridiculous young creature like a Talmud student would have been out of the question

I followed her with fast-beating heart. I knew that her family was "modern," that her children spoke Russian and "behaved like Gentiles," that there was a grown young woman among them and that her name was Matilda

The case of this young woman had been the talk of the town the year before.

She had been persuaded to marry a man for whom she did not care, and shortly after the wedding and after a sensational passage at arms between his people and hers, she made her father pay him a small fortune for divorcing her

Matilda's family being one of the "upper ten" in our town, its members were frequently the subject of envious gossip, and so I had known a good deal about them even before Shiphrah befriended me. I had heard, for example, that Matilda had received her early education in a boarding-school in Germany (in accordance with a custom that had been in existence among people of her father's class until recently); that she had subsequently studied Russian and other subjects under Russian tutors at home; and that her two brothers, who were younger than she, were at the local Russian gymnasium, or high school. I had heard, also, that Matilda was very pretty. That she was well dressed went without saying

All this both fascinated and cowed me

Suddenly Shiphrah paused, as though bethinking herself of something. "Wait.

Don't stir," she said, rushing back. Ten or fifteen minutes later she returned, saying: "I was not long, was I? I just went to get the beadle's forgiveness. Had insulted him for nothing. But he's a dummy, all the same.

Come on, David."

Arrived at her house, she introduced me to her old servant, in the kitchen

"He'll stay a week with us, perhaps more," she explained. "I want you to build him up. Fatten him up like a Passover goose. Do you hear?"

The servant, a tall, spare woman, with an extremely dark face tinged with blue, began by darting hostile glances at me

"Look at the way she is staring at him!" Shiphrah growled. "He is the son of the woman who was murdered at the Horse-market."

The old servant started. "Is he?" she said, aghast

"Are you pleased now? Will you take good care of him?"

"May the Uppermost give him a good appetite."

As Shiphrah led me from the kitchen into another room she said: "She took a fancy to you. It will be all right."

She towed me into a vast sitting-room, so crowded with new furniture that it had the appearance of a furniture-store. There were many rooms in the apartment and they all produced a similar impression. I subsequently learned that the superabundance of sofas, chests of drawers, chairs, or bric-à-brac-stands was due to Shiphrah's passion for bargains, a weakness which made her the fair game of tradespeople and artisans. Several of her wardrobes and bureaus were packed full of all sorts of things for which she had no earthly use and many of which she had smuggled in when her husband and the children were out

Ensconced in a corner of an enormous green sofa in the big crowded sitting-room, with a book in her lap, we found a young woman with curly brown hair and sparkling brown eyes set in a small oval face. She looked no more than twenty, but when her mother addressed her as Matilda I knew that I was facing the heroine of the sensational divorce. She was singularly interesting, but pretty she certainly was not. Her Gentile name had a world of charm for my ear

One of the trifles that clung to my memory is the fact that upon seeing her I felt something like amazement at her girlish appearance. I had had a notion that a married woman, no matter how young, must have a married face, something quite distinct from the countenance of a maiden, while this married woman did not begin to look married.

Matilda got up, cast a frowning side-glance at her mother, and walked over to one of the four immense windows illuminating the room. Less than a minute later she turned around and crossed over to her mother's side

She was small, but well made, and her movements were brisk, firm, elastic

"Come on, mother, there's something I want to tell you," she said, a jerk of her curly head indicating the adjoining room

"I have no secrets," Shiphrah growled. "What do you want?"

A snappish whispered conference ensued, the trend of which was at once betrayed in an acrimonious retort by Shiphrah: "Just keep your foolish nose out of my affairs, will you? When I say he is going to stay here for some time I mean it. Don't you mind her, David."

"Mother! Mother! Mother!" Matilda trilled with a gesture of disgust, and flounced out of the room

I felt my face turning all colors, and at the same time her "Mother! Mother! Mother!" (instead of "Mamma! Mamma! Mamma!") was echoing in my brain enchantingly

Presently a fair-complexioned youth of eighteen or nineteen came in, apparently attracted by his mother's angry voice. He wore a blue coat with silver lace and silver buttons, the uniform of a Russian high school, which sent a flutter of mixed envy and awe through me. He threw a frowning glance at me, and withdrew. Two smaller children, a uniformed boy and a little girl, made their appearance, talking in Russian noisily. At sight of me they fell silent, looked me over, from my side-locks to the edge of my long-skirted coat, and then took to whispering and giggling

"Clear out, you devils!" Shiphrah shouted, stamping her foot. "Shoo!" A young chambermaid passed through the room, and Shiphrah stopped her long enough to introduce me and to command her to look after me as if I were one of the family—"even better."

- dreams of America stronger
- moves in w/ Shiphrah + fam
- S's daughter, Matilda
- "modern Gentiles" welcoming "old fashioned Jew"

# CHAPTER II

THE spacious sitting-room was used as a breakfast-room as well. It was in this room, on the enormous green sofa, that my bed was made for the night.

It was by far the most comfortable bed I had ever slept in

Early the next morning, after I finished my long prayer and had put away my phylacteries, the young chambermaid removed the bedding and the swarthy old servant served me my breakfast

"Go wash your hands and eat in good health. Eat hearty, and may it well agree with you," she said, with a compound of deep commiseration, reverence, and disdain. I went to the kitchen, where I washed my hands, and, while wiping them, muttered the brief prayer which one offers before eating. As I returned to the sitting-room I found Matilda there. She was seated at some distance from the table upon which my breakfast was spread. She wore a sort of white kimono. One did not have to stand on ceremony with a fellow who did not even wear a stiff collar and a necktie. Nor did I know enough to resent her costume. She did not order anything to eat for herself, not even a glass of tea. It seemed as though she had come in for the express purpose of eying me out of countenance. If she had, she succeeded but too well. Her silent glances fell on me like splashes of hot water. I was so disconcerted I could not swallow my food. There were centuries of difference between her and myself, not to speak of the economic chasm that separated us. To me she was an aristocrat, while I was a poor, wretched "day" eater, a cross between a beggar and a recluse. I dared not even look at her. Talmud students were expected to be the shyest creatures under the sun. On this occasion I certainly was

The other children entered the room. They were dressing themselves, eating and studying their Gentile lessons all at once. Matilda had a mild altercation with Yeffim, her eighteen-year-old brother, ordered breakfast for herself, and seemed to have forgotten my existence. Her mother came in and took to cloying me with food

At about 4 o'clock in the afternoon I was alone in the drawing-room. I stood at the piano—the first I had ever laid eyes on—timidly sounding some of the keys, when I heard approaching voices. With my heart in my mouth, I rushed over to the nearest window, where I paused, feigning interest in some passing peasant teams. Presently Matilda made her appearance. accompanied by two girl friends

The three young women were chattering in Russian, a language of which I understood scarcely three dozen words. I could conjecture, however, that the subject of their talk was no other than my own quailing personality

Suddenly Matilda addressed herself to me in Yiddish: "Look here, young man! Don't you know it is bad manners for a gentleman to stand with his back to ladies?"

I faced about, all flushed and scared

"That's better," she said, gaily. "Never mind staring at the floor. Give us a look, will you? Don't act as a shy bridegroom."

I made no answer. The room seemed to be in a whirl

"Why don't you speak?" Matilda insisted, concealing her quizzical purpose under a well-acted air of gravity

Her two friends roared, and, spurred on by their merriment, she continued to make game of me.

"Won't you give us one look, at least? Do, please! Come, my mother will never find out you have been guilty of a great sin like that."

I was dying to get up and fling out of the room, but I felt glued to the spot. Their cruel sport, which made me faint with embarrassment and misery, had something inexpressibly alluring in it

One of the two girls said something in Russian of which I caught the word "kiss" and which was greeted by a new outburst of laughter. I was terror-stricken

"Well, pious Jew!" Matilda resumed. "Suppose a girl were to give you a kiss.

What would you do? Commit suicide, would you? Well, never fear; we won't be as cruel as all that. I tell you what, though. I'll

Matilda is a tease but not in a good way ...

hide your side-locks behind your ears. I just want to see how you would look without them." At this she stepped up close to me and reached out her hands for my two appendages

I pushed her off. "Please, let me alone," I protested

"At last we have heard his voice. Bravo! We're making headway, aren't we?"

At this point her mother's angry voice made itself heard. Matilda desisted, with a merry remark to her friends

The next morning when she and I were alone she tantalized me again. She made another attempt to tuck my side-locks behind my ears. As we were alone I had more courage

"If you don't stop I'll go away from here," I said, in a rage. "What do you want of me?"

As I thus gave vent to my resentment I instinctively felt that, so far from causing her to avoid me, it would quicken her rompish interest in me. And I hoped it would

"'S-sh! don't yell," she said, startled. "Can't you take a joke?"

"A nice joke, that."

"Very well, I won't do it again. I didn't know you were a touch-me-not." After a pause she resumed, in grave, friendly accents: "Come, don't be angry. I want to talk to you. Look here. Is there any sense in your wasting your life the way you do? Look at the way you are dressed, the way you live generally. Besides, the idea of a young man like you not being able to speak a word of Russian! Aren't you ashamed of yourself? Why, mother says you are remarkably bright. Isn't it a pity that you should throw it all away? Why don't you try to study Russian, geography, history? Why don't you try to become an educated man?"

"The idea!" I said, with a laugh.

My confusion was gone, partly, at least. I looked her full in the face

She flared up. "The idea!" she mocked me. "Rather say, 'The idea of a bright young fellow being so ignorant!' Did you ever hear of a provoking thing like that?" There was a good deal of her mother's helter-skelter explosiveness in her

Now, that I had scanned her features in the light of the fact that she was a married woman, I read that fact into them. She did look married, I remarked to myself. Her exposed hair gave her an effect of "aristocratic" wickedness and wantonness which repelled and drew me at once. She was a girl, and yet she was a married woman. This duality of hers deepened the fascinating mystery of the distance between us

She proceeded to draw me out. She made me tell her the story of my young life, and I obeyed her but too willingly. I told her my whole tale of woe, reveling in my own rehearsal of my sufferings and more especially in the expressions of horror and heartfelt pity which it elicited from her.

"My God! My God!" she cried, gasping and wringing her hands. "Poor boy!" or, "Oh, I can't hear it! I can't hear it! It is enough to drive one crazy."

At one point, as I described the pangs of hunger which I had often borne, there were tears in her interesting eyes

When I had finished my story, flushed with a sense of my histrionic success, she ordered tea and preserves, as though to indemnify me for my past sufferings

"All the more reason for you to study Russian and to become an educated man," she said, as she put sugar into my glass. She cited the cases of former Talmudists, poor and friendless like myself, who had studied at the universities, fighting every inch of their way, till they had achieved success as physicians, lawyers, writers. She spoke passionately, often with the absurd acerbity of her mother. "It's a crime for a young man like you to throw himself away on that idiotic Talmud of yours," she said, pacing up and down the room fiercely

All this sounded shockingly wicked, and yet it did not shock me in the least

"I have a plan," I said

When she heard what I wanted to do she shook her head and frowned. She said, in substance, that America was a land of dollars, not of education, and that she wanted me to be an educated man. I assured her that I should study English in America and, after I had laid up some money, prepare for college there (she could have made me promise anything). But colleges in which the instruction was not in Russian failed to appeal to her imagination

Still, when she saw that my heart was set on the project, she yielded. She seemed to like the fervor with which I defended my cause, and the notion of my going to a far-away land was apparently beginning to have its effect. I was the hero of an adventure. Gradually she became quite enthusiastic about my plan.

"I tell you what. I can raise the money for you," she said, with a gesture of sudden resolution. "How much is it?"

When I said, forlornly, that it would come to about eighty rubles, she declared, gravely: "That's all right. I shall get it for you. Only, say nothing to mother about it." I thought myself in a flurry of joy over this windfall, but a little later, when I was left to myself, I became aware that the flurry I was in was of quite a different nature. When I tried to think of America I found that my ambition in that direction had lost its former vitality

I was deeply in love with Matilda — knew it

* forbidden romance *

• differences between Matilda | D.
• M teases D + chides him for not learning Russian
• M = married
→ • D "deeply in love w/ M"
    └ forbidden romance
• M agrees to help D pay for trip to America

# CHAPTER III

SHE continued to treat me in a patronizing, playful way; but we were supposed to be great friends and I asked myself no questions.

"The money is assured," she once announced. "You shall get it in a few days.

You may begin to pack your great baggage," she jested

My heart sank within me, but I feigned exultation

"Do you deserve it, pious soul that you are?" she laughed. And casting a glance at my side-locks, she added: "I do wish you would cut off those horrid things of yours. You won't take them to America, will you?"

I smiled. Small as was my stock of information of the New World, I knew enough of it to understand, in a general way, that side-locks were out of place there

She proceeded to put my side-locks behind my ears, and this time I did not object. She then smoothed them down, the touch of her fingers thrilling me through and through. Then she brought a hand-glass and made me look at myself.

"Do you see the difference?" she demanded. "If you were not rigged out like the savage that you are you wouldn't be a bad-looking fellow, after all.

Why, girls might even fall in love with you. But then what does a pious soul like you know about such things as love?"

"How do you know I don't?" I ventured to say, blushing like a poppy

"Do you, really?" she said, with mischievous surprise

I nodded

"Well, well. So you are not quite so saintly as I thought you were! Perhaps you have even been in love yourself? Have you? Tell me."

84

I kept silent. My heart was throbbing wildly.

"Do you love me?"

I nodded once more. My heart stood still.

"Kiss me, then."

She put my arms around her, made me clasp her to my breast, and we kissed, passionately

I suddenly felt ten years older

She broke away from me, jumping around, slapping her hands and bubbling over with triumphant mirth, as she shouted: "There is a pious soul for you! There is a pious soul for you!"

A thought of little Red Esther of my childhood days flashed through my brain, of the way she would force me to "sin" and then gloat over my "fall."

"A penny for your piety," Matilda added, gravely. "When you are in America you'll dress like a Gentile and even shave. Then you won't look so ridiculous. Good clothes would make another man of you." At this she looked me over in a business-like sort of way. "Pretty good figure, that," she concluded

In the evening of that day, when there was company in the house, she bore herself as though she did not know me. But the next morning, after the children had gone to school and her mother was away on her various missions, she made me put on the glittering coat and cap of her brother's Sunday uniform

"It's rather too small for you, but it's becoming all the same," she said, enthusiastically. "If mamma came in now she would not know you. But then there would be a nice how-do-you-do if she did." She gave a titter which rolled through my very heart. "Well, Mr. Gymnasist, [note] are you really in love with me?"

"Don't make fun of me, pray," I implored her. "It hurts, you know." "Very well, I sha'n't. But you haven't answered my question."

"What question?"

"What a poor memory you have! And yet mother says you have 'a good head.' Try to remember."

"I do remember your question."

"Then what is your answer?"

"Yes."

"Yes!" she mocked me. "That's not the way gentlemen declare their love." "What else shall I say?"

"What else! Well, say: 'I am ready to die for you. You are the sunshine of my life.'" "'You are the sunshine of my life,'" I echoed, with a smile that was a combination of mirth and resentment

"'You are my happiness, my soul. The world would be dark without you.'"

"I am no baby to parrot somebody else's words."

"Then you don't love me."

"Yes, I do. But I hate to be made fun of. Don't! Please don't!" I said it with a beseeching, passionate tremor in my voice, and all at once I clasped her violently to me and was about to kiss her. She put up her lips responsively, but suddenly she wrenched herself back

"Easy, easy, you saintly Talmudist," she said, good-naturedly. "You must not forget that you are not a gymnasist, that to kiss a woman is a sin, a great sin. You'll be beaten with rods of iron in the world to come. Well, good-by," she concluded, gravely. "I must go. Take off that coat and cap.

Mamma may come in at any moment." She showed me where to hang them [note: Gymnasist] A pupil of a gymnasium or high school

- M asks "Do you love me?" D says "Yes"
  They kiss
- a new chapter →

# CHAPTER IV

In my incessant reveries of her I developed the theory that if I abandoned my plan about going to America she would have her father send me to college with a view to my marrying her. Indeed, matches of this kind were not an unusual arrangement in our town (nor are they in the Jewish districts of New York, Philadelphia, Boston, or Chicago, for example)

My bed was usually made on the enormous green sofa in the spacious sitting-room. One night, when I was asleep on that great sofa, I was suddenly aroused by the touch of a hand

"'S-sh," I heard Matilda's whisper. "I want to talk to you. I can't sleep, anyhow. I don't know why. So I was thinking of all kinds of things till I came to your plan about America. It is foolish. Why go so far? Perhaps something can be done to get you into high school and then into the university."

"I have guessed it right, then," I exclaimed within myself. The room was pitch-dark. Her white kimono was all I could see of her

She explained certain details. She spoke in a very low undertone, with great earnestness. I took her by the hand and drew her down to a seat on the edge of the sofa beside me. She offered no resistance. She continued to talk, partly in the same undertone, partly in whispers, with her hand remaining in mine. I was aflame with happiness, yet I listened intently. I felt sure that she was my bride-to-be, that it was only a matter of days when our engagement would be celebrated. My heart went out to her with a passion that seemed to be sanctioned by God and men. I strained down her head and kissed her, but that was the stainless kiss of a man yearning upon the lips of his betrothed. I clasped her flimsily garmented form, kissed her again and again, let her kiss and bite me; and still it all seemed legitimate, or nearly so. I saw in it an emphatic confirmation of my feeling that she did not regard herself a stranger to me. That mattered more than anything else at this moment

"You're a devil," she whispered, slapping me on both cheeks, "a devil with side-locks." And she broke into a suppressed laugh

"I'll study as hard as I can," I assured her, with boyish exultation.

"You'll see what I can do. The Gentile books are child's play in comparison with the Talmud."

I went into details. She took no part in my talk, but she let me go on. I became so absorbed in what I was saying that my caresses ceased. I sat up and spoke quite audibly

"'S-sh!" she cautioned me in an irritated whisper

I dropped my voice. She listened for another minute or two and then, suddenly rising, she said: "Oh, you are a Talmud student, after all," and her indistinct kimono vanished in the darkness

I felt crushed, but I was sure that the words "Talmud student," which are Yiddish for "ninny," merely referred to my rendering our confab dangerous by speaking too loud

The next afternoon she kissed me once more, calling me Talmud student again.

But she was apparently getting somewhat fidgety about our relations. She was more guarded, more on the alert for eavesdroppers, as though somebody had become suspicious. My Gentile education she never broached again. Finally when a letter came from her father announcing his speedy return and Shiphrah hastened to terminate my stay at the house, Matilda was obviously glad to have me go.

"I shall bring you the money to the synagogue," she whispered as I was about to leave

I was stunned. I left in a turmoil of misery and perplexity, yet not in despair

When I returned to the synagogue everybody and everything in it looked strange to me. Reb Sender was dearer than ever, but that was chiefly because I was longing for a devoted friend. I was dying to relieve my fevered mind by telling him all and seeking advice, but I did not

"Are you still weak?" he asked, tenderly, looking close into niy eyes

"Oh, it is not that, Reb Sender." "Is it the death of your dear mother—peace upon her?"

"Yes, of course. That and lots of other things."

"It will all pass. She will have a bright paradise, and The Upper One will help you. Don't lose heart, my boy."

I ran over to Naphtali's place. We talked of Shiphrah and her children—at least I did. He asked about Matilda, and I answered reluctantly. Now and again I felt impelled to tell him all. It would have been such a relief to ease my mind of its cruel burden and to hear somebody's, anybody's opinion about it. But his laconical questions and answers were anything but encouraging *— reality sinks in*

I spent many an hour in his company, but he was always absorbed in the Talmud, or in some of his infidel books. The specific character of my restlessness was lost upon him

I was in the grip of a dull, enervating, overpowering agony that seemed to be weighing my heart down and filling my throat with pent-up sobs. I was writhing inwardly, praying for Matilda's mercy. It was the most excruciating pain I had ever experienced. I remember it distinctly in every detail. If I now wished to imagine a state of mind driving one to suicide I could not do it better than by recalling my mental condition in those days

In point of fact I took pride in my misery. "I am in love. I am no mere slouch of a Talmud student," I would say to myself

In the evening of the fourth day, as I was making a pretense at reading Talmud, a poor boy came in to call me out. In the alley outside the house of worship I found Matilda. She had the money with her

"I don't think I want it now," I said. "I don't care to go to America." "Why?" she asked, impatiently. "Oh, take it and let me be done with it," she said, forcing a small packet into my hand. "I have no time to bother with you. Go to America. I wish you good luck."

"But I'll miss you. I sha'n't be able to live without you."

"What? Are you crazy?" she said, sternly. "You forget your place, young man!"

She stalked hastily away, her form, at once an angel of light and a messenger of death, being swallowed up by the gloom

Ten minutes later, when I was at my book again, my heart bleeding and my head in a daze, I was called out once more

Again I found her standing in the lane

"I did not mean to hurt your feelings," she said. "I wish you good luck from the bottom of my heart."

She uttered it with a warm cordiality, and yet the note of impatience which rang in her voice ten minutes before was again there

"Try to become an educated man in America," she added. "That's the main thing. Good-by. You have my best wishes. Good-by."

And before I had time to say anything she shook my hand and was gone

- illusioning himself married to M
- ( knew M was a tease, doesn't care about him )
- M gives D the money, wishes him good luck

# CHAPTER V

A LITTLE over three weeks had elapsed. It was two days after Passover. I had just solemnized the first anniversary of my mother's death. The snow had melted. Each of my five senses seemed to be thrillingly aware of the presence of spring

I was at the railway station. Clustered about me were Reb Sender and his wife, two other Talmudists from the Preacher's Synagogue, the retired old soldier with the formidable side-whiskers, and Naphtali

As I write these words I seem to see the group before me. It is one of those scenes that never grow dim in one's memory

"Be a good Jew and a good man," Reb Sender murmured to me, confusedly. "Do not forget that there is a God in heaven in America as well as here. Do not forget to write us." Naphtali, speaking in his hoarse whisper, half in jest, half in earnest, made me repeat my promise to send him a "ship ticket" from America. I promised everything that was asked of me. My head was swimming

While the first bell was sounding for the passengers to board the train, Shiphrah rushed in, puffing for breath. I looked at the door to see if Matilda was not following her. She was not.

The group around me made way for the rich woman

"Here," she said, handing me a ten-ruble bill and a package. "There is a boiled chicken in it, and some other things, provided you won't neglect your Talmud in America."

A minute later she drew her purse from her skirt pocket, produced a five-ruble bill, and put it into my hand. That all the other money I had for my journey had come from her daughter she had not the remotest idea

I made my final farewells amid a hubbub of excited voices and eyes glistening with tears

~in a way, loses another family
*sets on his journey.

# BOOK V

# I DISCOVER AMERICA

# CHAPTER I

TWO weeks later I was one of a multitude of steerage passengers on a Bremen steamship on my way to New York. Who can depict the feeling of desolation, homesickness, uncertainty, and anxiety with which an emigrant makes his first voyage across the ocean? I proved to be a good sailor, but the sea frightened me. The thumping of the engines was drumming a ghastly accompaniment to the awesome whisper of the waves. I felt in the embrace of a vast, uncanny force. And echoing through it all were the heart-lashing words: "Are you crazy? You forget your place, young man!" When Columbus was crossing the Atlantic, on his first great voyage, his men doubted whether they would ever reach land. So does many an America-bound emigrant to this day. Such, at least, was the feeling that was lurking in my heart while the Bremen steamer was carrying me to New York. Day after day passes and all you see about you is an unbroken waste of water, an unrelieved, a hopeless monotony of water. You know that a change will come, but this knowledge is confined to your brain. Your senses are skeptical

In my devotions, which I performed three times a day, without counting a benediction before every meal and every drink of water, grace after every meal and a prayer before going to sleep, I would mentally plead for the safety of the ship and for a speedy sight of land. My scanty luggage included a pair of phylacteries and a plump little prayer-book, with the Book of Psalms at the end. The prayers I knew by heart, but I now often said psalms, in addition, particularly when the sea looked angry and the pitching or rolling was unusually violent. I would read all kinds of psalms, but my favorite among them was the 104th, generally referred to by our people as "Bless the Lord, O my soul," its opening words in the original Hebrew. It is a poem on the power and wisdom of God as manifested in the wonders of nature, some of its verses dealing with the sea. It is said by the faithful every Saturday afternoon during the fall and winter; so I could have recited it from memory; but I preferred to read it in my prayer-book. For it seemed as though the familiar words had changed their identity and meaning, especially those concerned with the sea. Their divine inspiration was now something visible and audible. It was not I who was reading them. It was as though the waves and the clouds, the whole far-flung scene of restlessness and mystery, were whispering to me: "Thou who coverest thyself with light as with a garment, who stretchest out the heavens like a curtain: who layeth the beams of his chambers in the waters: who maketh the clouds his chariot: who walketh upon the wings of the wind . . . So is this great and wide sea wherein are things creeping innumerable, both small and great beasts. There go the ships: there is that leviathan whom thou hast made to play therein . . . ."

The relentless presence of Matilda in my mind worried me immeasurably, for to think of a woman who is a stranger to you is a sin, and so there was the danger of the vessel coming to grief on my account. And, as though to spite me, the closing verse of Psalm 104 reads, "Let the sinners be consumed out of the earth and let the wicked be no more." I strained every nerve to keep Matilda out of my thoughts, but without avail

When the discoverers of America saw land at last they fell on their knees and a hymn of thanksgiving burst from their souls. The scene, which is one of the most thrilling in history, repeats itself in the heart of every immigrant as he comes in sight of the American shores. I am at a loss to convey the peculiar state of mind that the experience created in me

When the ship reached Sandy Hook I was literally overcome with the beauty of the landscape

The immigrant's arrival in his new home is like a second birth to him.

Imagine a new-born babe in possession of a fully developed intellect. Would it ever forget its entry into the world? Neither does the immigrant ever forget his entry into a country which is, to him, a new world in the profoundest sense of the term and in which he expects to pass the rest of his life. I conjure up the gorgeousness of the spectacle as it appeared to me on that clear June morning: the magnificent verdure of Staten Island, the tender blue of sea and sky, the dignified bustle of passing craft—above all, those floating, squatting, multitudinously windowed palaces which I subsequently learned to call ferries. It was all so utterly unlike anything I had ever seen or dreamed of before. It unfolded itself like a divine revelation. I was in a trance or in something closely resembling one

"This, then, is America!" I exclaimed, mutely. The notion of something enchanted which the name had always evoked in me now seemed fully borne out

In my ecstasy I could not help thinking of Psalm 104, and, opening my little prayer-book, I glanced over those of its verses that speak of hills and rocks, of grass and trees and birds.

My transport of admiration, however, only added to my sense of helplessness and awe. Here, on shipboard, I was sure of my shelter and food, at least.

How was I going to procure my sustenance on those magic shores? I wished the remaining hour could be prolonged indefinitely

Psalm 104 spoke reassuringly to me. It reminded me of the way God took care of man and beast: "Thou openest thine hand and they are filled with good." But then the very next verse warned me that "Thou hidest thy face, they are troubled: thou takest away their breath, they die." So I was praying God not to hide His face from me, but to open His hand to me; to remember that my mother had been murdered by Gentiles and that I was going to a strange land.

When I reached the words, "I will sing unto the Lord as long as I live: I will sing praise to my God while I have my being," I uttered them in a fervent whisper

My unhappy love never ceased to harrow me. The stern image of Matilda blended with the hostile glamour of America

One of my fellow-passengers was a young Yiddish-speaking tailor named Gitelson. He was about twenty-four years old, yet his forelock was gray, just his forelock, the rest of his hair being a fine, glossy brown. His own cap had been blown into the sea and the one he had obtained from the steerage steward was too small for him, so that gray tuft of his was always out like a plume. We had not been acquainted more than a few hours, in fact, for he had been seasick throughout the voyage and this was the first day he had been up and about. But then I had seen him on the day of our sailing and subsequently, many times, as he wretchedly lay in his berth. He was literally in tatters. He clung to me like a lover, but we spoke very little.

Our hearts were too full for words    In abs. and

As I thus stood at the railing, prayer-book in hand, he took a look at the page. The most ignorant "man of the earth" among our people can read holy tongue (Hebrew), though he may not understand the meaning of the words. This was the case with Gitelson

"Saying, 'Bless the Lord, O my soul'?" he asked, reverently. "Why this chapter of all others?"

"Because—Why, just listen." With which I took to translating the Hebrew text into Yiddish for him

He listened with devout mien. I was not sure that he understood it even in his native tongue, but, whether he did or not, his beaming, wistful look and the deep sigh he emitted indicated that he was in a state similar to mine

When I say that my first view of New York Bay struck me as something not of this earth it is not a mere figure of speech. I vividly recall the feeling, for example, with which I greeted the first cat I saw on American soil. It was on the Hoboken pier, while the steerage passengers were being marched to the ferry. A large, black, well-fed feline stood in a corner, eying the crowd of new-comers. The sight of it gave me a thrill of joy. "Look! there is a cat!" I said to Gitelson. And in my heart I added, "Just like those at home!" For the moment the little animal made America real to me. At the same time it seemed unreal itself. I was tempted to feel its fur to ascertain whether it was actually the kind of creature I took it for

We were ferried over to Castle Garden. One of the things that caught my eye as I entered the vast rotunda was an iron staircase rising diagonally against one of the inner walls. A uniformed man, with some papers in his hands, ascended it with brisk, resounding step till he disappeared through a door not many inches from the ceiling. It may seem odd, but I can never think of my arrival in this country without hearing the ringing footfalls of this official and beholding the yellow eyes of the black cat which stared at us at the Hoboken pier. The harsh manner of the immigration officers was a grievous surprise to me. As contrasted with the officials of my despotic country, those of a republic had been portrayed in my mind as paragons of refinement and cordiality. My anticipations were rudely belied. "They are not a bit better than Cossacks," I remarked to Gitelson. But they neither looked nor spoke like Cossacks, so their gruff voices were part of the uncanny scheme of things that surrounded me. These unfriendly voices flavored all America with a spirit of icy inhospitality that sent a chill through my very soul

The stringent immigration laws that were passed some years later had not yet come into existence. We had no difficulty in being admitted to the United States, and when I was I was loath to leave the Garden

Many of the other immigrants were met by relatives, friends. There were cries of joy, tears, embraces, kisses. All of which intensified my sense of loneliness and dread of the New World. The agencies which two Jewish charity organizations now maintain at the Immigrant Station had not yet been established. Gitelson, who like myself had no friends in New York, never left my side. He was even more timid than I. It seemed as though he were holding on to me for dear life. This had the effect of putting me on my mettle

"Cheer up, old man!" I said, with bravado. "America is not the place to be a ninny in. Come, pull yourself together." In truth, I addressed these exhortations as much to myself as to him; and so far, at least, as I was concerned, my words had the desired effect.

I led the way out of the big Immigrant Station. As we reached the park outside we were pounced down upon by two evil-looking men, representatives of boarding-houses for immigrants. They pulled us so roughly and their general appearance and manner were so uninviting that we struggled and protested until they let us go— not without some parting curses. Then I led the way across Battery Park and under the Elevated railway to State Street.

A train hurtling and panting along overhead produced a bewildering, a daunting effect on me. The active life of the great strange city made me feel like one abandoned in the midst of a jungle. Where were we to go? What were we to do? But the presence of Gitelson continued to act as a spur on me. I mustered courage to approach a policeman, something I should never have been bold enough to do at home. As a matter of fact, I scarcely had an idea what his function was. To me he looked like some uniformed nobleman—an impression that in itself was enough to intimidate me. With his coat of blue cloth, starched linen collar, and white gloves, he reminded me of anything but the policemen of my town. I addressed him in Yiddish, making it as near an approach to German as I knew how, but my efforts were lost on him. He shook his head. With a witheringly dignified grimace he then pointed his club in the direction of Broadway and strutted off majestically

"He's not better than a Cossack, either," was my verdict

At this moment a voice hailed us in Yiddish. Facing about, we beheld a middle-aged man with huge, round, perpendicular nostrils and a huge, round, deep dimple in his chin that looked like a third nostril. Prosperity was written all over his smooth-shaven face and broad-shouldered, stocky figure.

He was literally aglow with diamonds and self-satisfaction. But he was unmistakably one of our people. It was like coming across a human being in the jungle. Moreover, his very diamonds somehow told a tale of former want, of a time when he had landed, an impecunious immigrant like myself; and this made him a living source of encouragement to me

"God Himself has sent you to us," I began, acting as the spokesman; but he gave no heed to me. His eyes were eagerly fixed on Gitelson and his tatters

"You're a tailor, aren't you?" he questioned him

My steerage companion nodded. "I'm a ladies' tailor, but I have worked on men's clothing, too," he said

"A ladies' tailor?" the well-dressed stranger echoed, with ill-concealed delight. "Very well; come along. I have work for you."

That he should have been able to read Gitelson's trade in his face and figure scarcely surprised me. In my native place it seemed to be a matter of course that one could tell a tailor by his general appearance and walk.

Besides, had I not divined the occupation of my fellow-passenger the moment I saw him on deck? As I learned subsequently, the man who accosted us on State Street was a cloak contractor, and his presence in the neighborhood of Castle Garden was anything but a matter of chance. He came there quite often, in fact, his purpose being to angle for cheap labor among the newly arrived immigrants

We paused near Bowling Green. The contractor and my fellow-passenger were absorbed in a conversation full of sartorial technicalities which were Greek to me, but which brought a gleam of joy into Gitelson's eye. My former companion seemed to have become oblivious of my existence.

As we resumed our walk up Broadway the bejeweled man turned to me

"And what was your occupation? You have no trade, have you?"

"I read Talmud," I said, confusedly.

"I see, but that's no business in America," he declared. "Any relatives here?" "Well, don't worry. You will be all right. If a fellow isn't lazy nor a fool he has no reason to be sorry he came to America. It'll be all right."

"All right" he said in English, and I conjectured what it meant from the context. In the course of the minute or two which he bestowed upon me he uttered it so many times that the phrase engraved itself upon my memory. It was the first bit of English I ever acquired   *But no doubt, not the last*

The well-dressed, trim-looking crowds of lower Broadway impressed me as a multitude of counts, barons, princes. I was puzzled by their preoccupied faces and hurried step. It seemed to comport ill with their baronial dress and general high-born appearance

In a vague way all this helped to confirm my conception of America as a unique country, unlike the rest of the world

When we reached the General Post-Office, at the end of the Third Avenue surface line, our guide bade us stop

"Walk straight ahead," he said to me, waving his hand toward Park Row. "Just keep walking until you see a lot of Jewish people. It isn't far from here." With which he slipped a silver quarter into my hand and made Gitelson bid me good-by

The two then boarded a big red horse-car

I was left with a sickening sense of having been tricked, cast off, and abandoned. I stood watching the receding public vehicle, as though its scarlet hue were my last gleam of hope in the world. When it finally disappeared from view my heart sank within me. I may safely say that the half-hour that followed is one of the worst I experienced in all the thirty-odd years of my life in this country

The big, round nostrils of the contractor and the gray forelock of my young steerage-fellow haunted my brain as hideous symbols of treachery.

With twenty-nine cents in my pocket (four cents was all that was left of the sum which I had received from Matilda and her mother) I set forth in the direction of East Broadway

not a lot, even back then.

- arrive in America, fill of awe
- ~~meets~~ an fellow immigrant Gitelson.
- didn't get a job from the rich man but gained 25¢
- only 29¢ to name ... eck!

# CHAPTER II

TEN minutes' walk brought me to the heart of the Jewish East Side. The streets swarmed with Yiddish-speaking immigrants. The sign-boards were in English and Yiddish, some of them in Russian. The scurry and hustle of the people were not merely overwhelmingly greater, both in volume and intensity, than in my native town. It was of another sort. The swing and step of the pedestrians, the voices and manner of the street peddlers, and a hundred and one other things seemed to testify to far more self-confidence and energy, to larger ambitions and wider scopes, than did the appearance of the crowds in my birthplace

The great thing was that these people were better dressed than the inhabitants of my town. The poorest-looking man wore a hat (instead of a cap), a stiff collar and a necktie, and the poorest woman wore a hat or a bonnet

The appearance of a newly arrived immigrant was still a novel spectacle on the East Side. Many of the passers-by paused to look at me with wistful smiles of curiosity

"There goes a green one!" some of them exclaimed

The sight of me obviously evoked reminiscences in them of the days when they had been "green ones" like myself. It was a second birth that they were witnessing, an experience which they had once gone through themselves and which was one of the greatest events in their lives.

"Green one" or "greenhorn" is one of the many English words and phrases which my mother-tongue has appropriated in England and America. Thanks to the many millions of letters that pass annually between the Jews of Russia and their relatives in the United States, a number of these words have by now come to be generally known among our people at home as well as here. In the eighties, however, one who had not visited any English-speaking country was utterly unfamiliar with them. And so I had never heard of "green one" before. Still, "green," in the sense of color, is Yiddish as well as English, so I understood the phrase at once, and as a contemptuous quizzical appellation for a newly arrived, inexperienced immigrant it stung me cruelly. As I went along I heard it again and again. Some of the passers-by would call me "greenhorn" in a tone of blighting gaiety, but these were an exception. For the most part it was "green one" and in a spirit of sympathetic interest. It hurt me, all the same. Even those glances that offered me a cordial welcome and good wishes had something self-complacent and condescending in them. "Poor fellow! he is a green one," these people seemed to say. "We are not, of course. We are Americanized."

For my first meal in the New World I bought a three-cent wedge of coarse rye bread, off a huge round loaf, on a stand on Essex Street. I was too strict in my religious observances to eat it without first performing ablutions and offering a brief prayer. So I approached a bewigged old woman who stood in the doorway of a small grocery-store to let me wash my hands and eat my meal in her place. She looked old-fashioned enough, yet when she heard my request she said, with a laugh: "You're a green one, I see."

"Suppose I am," I resented. "Do the yellow ones or black ones all eat without washing? Can't a fellow be a good Jew in America?"

"Yes, of course he can, but—well, wait till you see for yourself."

However, she asked me to come in, gave me some water and an old apron to serve me for a towel, and when I was ready to eat my bread she placed a glass of milk before me, explaining that she was not going to charge me for it

"In America people are not foolish enough to be content with dry bread," she said, sententiously

While I ate she questioned me about my antecedents. I remember how she impressed me as a strong, clever woman of few words as long as she catechised me, and how disappointed I was when she began to talk of herself.

The astute, knowing mien gradually faded out of her face and I had before me a gushing, boastful old bore

My intention was to take a long stroll, as much in the hope of coming upon some windfall as for the purpose of taking a look

104

at the great American city. Many of the letters that came from the United States to my birthplace before I sailed had contained a warning not to imagine that America was a "land of gold" and that treasure might be had in the streets of New York for the picking. But these warnings only had the effect of lending vividness to my image of an American street as a thoroughfare strewn with nuggets of the precious metal. Symbolically speaking, this was the idea one had of the "land of Columbus." It was a continuation of the widespread effect produced by stories of Cortes and Pizarro in the sixteenth century, confirmed by the successes of some Russian emigrants of my time

I asked the grocery-woman to let me leave my bundle with her, and, after considerable hesitation, she allowed me to put it among some empty barrels in her cellar

I went wandering over the Ghetto. Instead of stumbling upon nuggets of gold, I found signs of poverty. In one place I came across a poor family who—as I learned upon inquiry—had been dispossessed for non-payment of rent. A mother and her two little boys were watching their pile of furniture and other household goods on the sidewalk while the passers-by were dropping coins into a saucer placed on one of the chairs to enable the family to move into new quarters

What puzzled me was the nature of the furniture. For in my birthplace chairs and a couch like those I now saw on the sidewalk would be a sign of prosperity. But then anything was to be expected of a country where the poorest devil wore a hat and a starched collar

I walked on

The exclamation "A green one" or "A greenhorn" continued. If I did not hear it, I saw it in the eyes of the people who passed me

When it grew dark and I was much in need of rest I had a street peddler direct me to a synagogue. I expected to spend the night there. What could have been more natural? At the house of God I found a handful of men in prayer. It was a large, spacious room and the smallness of their number gave it an air of desolation. I joined in the devotions with great fervor. My soul was sobbing to Heaven to take care of me in the strange country

The service over, several of the worshipers took up some Talmud folio or other holy book and proceeded to read them aloud in the familiar singsong.

The strange surroundings suddenly began to look like home to me

One of the readers, an elderly man with a pinched face and forked little beard, paused to look me over

"A green one?" he asked, genially.

He told me that the synagogue was crowded on Saturdays, while on week-days people in America had no time to say their prayers at home, much less to visit a house of worship

"It isn't Russia," he said, with a sigh. "Judaism has not much of a chance here."

When he heard that I intended to stay at the synagogue overnight he smiled ruefully

"One does not sleep in an American synagogue," he said. "It is not Russia." Then, scanning me once more, he added, with an air of compassionate perplexity: "Where will you sleep, poor child? I wish I could take you to my house, but—well, America is not Russia. There is no pity here, no hospitality. My wife would raise a rumpus if I brought you along. I should never hear the last of it."

With a deep sigh and nodding his head plaintively he returned to his book, swaying back and forth. But he was apparently more interested in the subject he had broached. "When we were at home," he resumed, "she, too, was a different woman. She did not make life a burden to me as she does here. Have you no money at all?"

I showed him the quarter I had received from the cloak contractor

"Poor fellow! Is that all you have? There are places where you can get a night's lodging for fifteen cents, but what are you going to do afterward? I am simply ashamed of myself."

"'Hospitality,'" he quoted from the Talmud, "'is one of the things which the giver enjoys in this world and the fruit of which he relishes in the world to come.' To think that I cannot offer a Talmudic scholar a night's rest! Alas! America has turned me into a mound of ashes."

"You were well off in Russia, weren't you?" I inquired, in astonishment.

For, indeed, I had never heard of any but poor people emigrating to America

"I used to spend my time reading Talmud at the synagogue," was his reply

Many of his answers seemed to fit, not the question asked, but one which was expected to follow it. You might have thought him anxious to forestall your next query in order to save time and words, had it not been so difficult for him to keep his mouth shut

"She," he said, referring to his wife, "had a nice little business. She sold feed for horses and she rejoiced in the thought that she was married to a man of learning. True, she has a tongue. That she always had, but over there it was not so bad. She has become a different woman here. Alas! America is a topsy-turvy country."

He went on to show how the New World turned things upside down, transforming an immigrant shoemaker into a man of substance, while a former man of leisure was forced to work in a factory here. In like manner, his wife had changed for the worse, for, lo and behold! instead of supporting him while he read Talmud, as she used to do at home, she persisted in sending him out to peddle. "America is not Russia," she said. "A man must make a living here." But, alas! it was too late to begin now! He had spent the better part of his life at his holy books and was fit for nothing else now. His wife, however, would take no excuse. He must peddle or be nagged to death. And if he ventured to slip into some synagogue of an afternoon and read a page or two he would be in danger of being caught red-handed, so to say, for, indeed, she often shadowed him to make sure that he did not play truant.

Alas! America was not Russia

A thought crossed my mind that if Reb Sender were here, he, too, might have to go peddling. Poor Reb Sender! The very image of him with a basket on his arm broke my heart. America did seem to be the most cruel place on earth

"I am telling you all this that you may see why I can't invite you to my house," explained the peddler

All I did see was that the poor man could not help unburdening his mind to the first listener that presented himself

He pursued his tale of woe. He went on complaining of his own fate, quite forgetful of mine. Instead of continuing to listen, I fell to gazing around the synagogue more or less furtively. One of the readers attracted my special attention. He was a venerable-looking man with a face which, as I now recall it, reminds me of Thackeray. Only he had a finer head than the English novelist

At last the henpecked man discovered my inattention and fell silent. A minute later his tongue was at work again

"You are looking at that man over there, aren't you?" he asked

"Who is he?"

"When the Lord of the World gives one good luck he gives one good looks as well."

"Why, is he rich?"

"His son-in-law is, but then his daughter cherishes him as she does the apple of her eye, and—well, when the Lord of the World wishes to give a man happiness he gives him good children, don't you know."

He rattled on, betraying his envy of the venerable-looking man in various ways and telling me all he knew about him—that he was a widower named Even, that he had been some years in America, and that his daughter furnished him all the money he needed and a good deal more, so that "he lived like a monarch." Even would not live in his daughter's house, however, because her kitchen was not conducted according to the laws of Moses, and everything else in it was too modern. So he roomed and boarded with pious strangers, visiting her far less frequently than she visited him and never eating at her table.

"He is a very proud man," my informant said. "One must not approach him otherwise than on tiptoe."

I threw a glance at Even. His dignified singsong seemed to confirm my interlocutor's characterization of him

"Perhaps you will ask me how his son-in-law takes it all?" the voluble Talmudist went on. "Well, his daughter is a beautiful woman and well favored." The implication was that her husband was extremely fond of her and let her use his money freely. "They are awfully rich and they live like veritable Gentiles, which is a common disease among the Jews of America. But then she observes the commandment, 'Honor thy father.' That she does."

Again he tried to read his book and again the temptation to gossip was too much for him. He returned to Even's pride, dwelling with considerable venom upon his love of approbation and vanity.

"May the Uppermost not punish me for my evil words, but to see him take his roll of bills out of his pocket and pay his contribution to the synagogue one would think he was some big merchant and not a poor devil sponging on his son-in-law."

A few minutes later he told me admiringly how Even often "loaned" him a half-dollar to enable him to do some reading at the house of God.

"I tell my virago of a wife I have sold fifty cents' worth of goods," he explained to me, sadly

After a while the man with the Thackeray face closed his book, kissed it, and rose to go. On his way out he unceremoniously paused in front of me, a silver snuff-box in his left hand, and fell to scrutinizing me. He had the appearance of a well-paid rabbi of a large, prosperous town. "He is going to say, 'A green one,'" I prophesied to myself, all but shuddering at the prospect. And, sure enough, he did, but he took his time about it, which made the next minute seem a year to me. He took snuff with tantalizing deliberation. Next he sneezed with great zest and then he resumed sizing me up. The suspense was insupportable. Another second and I might have burst out, "For mercy's sake say 'A green one,' and let us be done with it." But at that moment he uttered it of his own accord: "A green one, I see. Where from?" And grasping my hand he added in Hebrew, "Peace be to ye."

His first questions about me were obsequiously answered by the man with the forked beard, whereupon my attention was attracted by the fact that he addressed him by his Gentile name—that is, as "Mr. Even," and not by his Hebrew name, as he would have done in our birthplace. Surely America did not seem to be much of a God-fearing country

When Mr. Even heard of my Talmud studies he questioned me about the tractates I had recently read and even challenged me to explain an apparent discrepancy in a certain passage, for the double purpose of testing my "Talmud brains" and flaunting his own. I acquitted myself creditably, it seemed, and I felt that I was making a good impression personally as well.

Anyhow, he invited me to supper in a restaurant.

On our way there I told him of my mother's violent death, vaguely hoping that it would add to his interest in me. It did—even more than I had expected. To my pleasant surprise, he proved to be familiar with the incident. It appeared that because our section lay far outside the region of pogroms, or anti-Jewish riots, the killing of my mother by a Gentile mob had attracted considerable attention. I was thrilled to find myself in the lime-light of world-wide publicity. I almost felt like a hero

"So you are her son?" he said, pausing to look me over, as though I had suddenly become a new man. "My poor orphan boy!" He caused me to recount the incident in every detail. In doing so I made it as appallingly vivid as I knew how. He was so absorbed and moved that he repeatedly made me stop in the middle of the sidewalk so as to look me in the face as he listened

"Oh, but you must be hungry," he suddenly interrupted me. "Come on." Arrived at the restaurant, he ordered supper for me. Then he withdrew, commending me to the care of the proprietress until he should return.

He had no sooner shut the door behind him than she took to questioning me: Was I a relative of Mr. Even? If not, then why was he taking so much interest in me? She was a vivacious, well-fed young matron with cheeks of a flaming red and with the consciousness of business success all but spurting from her black eyes. From what she, assisted by one of the other customers present, told me about my benefactor I learned that his son-in-law was the owner of the tenement-house in which the restaurant was located, as well as of several other buildings. They also told me of the landlord's wife, of her devotion to her father, and of the latter's piety and dignity. It appeared, however, that in her filial reverence she would draw the line upon his desire not to spare the rod upon her children, which was really the chief reason why he was a stranger at her house

I had been waiting about two hours and was growing uneasy, when Mr. Even came back, explaining that he had spent the time taking his own supper and finding lodgings for me

He then took me to store after store, buying me a suit of clothes, a hat, some underclothes, handkerchiefs (the first white handkerchiefs I ever possessed), collars, shoes, and a necktie. He spent a considerable sum on me. As we passed from block to block he kept saying, "Now you won't look green," or, "That will make you look American." At one point he added, "Not that you are a bad-looking fellow as it is, but then one must be presentable in

America." At this he quoted from the Talmud an equivalent to the saying that one must do in Rome as the Romans do

When all our purchases had been made he took me to a barber shop with bathrooms in the rear

"Give him a hair-cut and a bath," he said to the proprietor. "Cut off his side-locks while you are at it. One may go without them and yet be a good Jew."

He disappeared again, but when I emerged from the bathroom I found him waiting for me. I stood before him, necktie and collar in hand, not knowing what to do with them, till he showed me how to put them on

"Don't worry. David," he consoled me. "When I came here I, too, had to learn these things." When he was through with the job he took me in front of a looking-glass. "Quite an American, isn't he?" he said to the barber, beamingly. "And a good-looking fellow, too."

When I took a look at the mirror I was bewildered. I scarcely recognized myself

I was mentally parading my "modern" make-up before Matilda. A pang of yearning clutched my heart. It was a momentary feeling. For the rest, I was all in a flutter with embarrassment and a novel relish of existence. It was as though the hair-cut and the American clothes had changed my identity. The steamer, Gitelson, and the man who had snatched him up now appeared to be something of the remote past. The day had been so crowded with novel impressions that it seemed an age

He took me to an apartment in a poor tenement-house and introduced me to a tall, bewhiskered, morose-looking, elderly man and a smiling woman of thirty-five, explaining that he had paid them in advance for a month's board and lodging. When he said, "This is Mr. Levinsky," I felt as though I was being promoted in rank as behooved my new appearance. "Mister" struck me as something like a title of nobility. It thrilled me. But somehow it seemed ridiculous, too. Indeed, it was some time before I could think of myself as a "Mister" without being tempted to laugh.

"And here is some cash for you," he said, handing me a five-dollar bill, and some silver, in addition. "And now you must shift for yourself. That's all I can do for you. Nor, indeed, would I do more if I could. A young man like you must learn to stand on his own legs. Understand? If you do well, come to see me. Understand?"

111

There was an eloquent pause which said that if I did not do well I was not to molest him. Then he added, aloud: "There is only one thing I want you to promise me. Don't neglect your religion nor your Talmud. Do you promise that, David?"

I did. There was a note of fatherly tenderness in the way this utter stranger called me David. It reminded me of Reb Sender. I wanted to say something to express my gratitude, but I felt a lump in my throat

He advised me to invest the five dollars in dry-goods and to take up peddling. Then, wishing me good luck, he left

My landlady, who had listened to Mr. Even's parting words with pious nods and rapturous grins, remarked that one would vainly search the world for another man like him, and proceeded to make my bed on a lounge

The room was a kitchen. The stove was a puzzle to me. I wondered whether it was really a stove.

"Is this used for heating?" I inquired

"Yes, for heating and cooking," she explained, with smiling cordiality. And she added, with infinite superiority, "America has no use for those big tile ovens."

When I found myself alone in the room the feeling of desolation and uncertainty which had tormented me all day seized me once again

I went to bed and began to say my bed-prayer. I did so mechanically. My mind did not attend to the words I was murmuring. Instead, it was saying to God: "Lord of the Universe, you have been good to me so far. I went out of that grocery-store in the hope of coming upon some good piece of luck and my hope was realized. Be good to me in the future as well. I shall be more pious than ever, I promise you, even if America is a godless country."

I was excruciatingly homesick. My heart went out to my poor dead mother.

Then I reflected that it was my story of her death that had led Even to spend so much money on me. It seemed as if she were taking care of me from her grave. It seemed, too, as though she had died so that I might arouse sympathy and make a good start in America. I thought of her and of all Antomir, and my pangs of yearning for her were tinged with pangs of my unrequited love for Matilda

# CHAPTER III

MY landlady was a robust little woman, compact and mobile as a billiard-ball, continually bustling about, chattering and smiling or laughing. She was a good-natured, silly creature, and her smile, which automatically shut her eyes and opened her mouth from ear to ear, accentuated her kindliness as well as her lack of sense. When she did not talk she would hum or sing at the top of her absurd voice the then popular American song "Climbing Up the Golden Stairs." She told me the very next day that she had been married less than a year, and one of the first things I noticed about her was the pleasure it gave her to refer to her husband or to quote him. Her prattle was so full of, "My husband says, says my husband," that it seemed as though the chief purpose of her jabber was to parade her married state and to hear herself talk of her spouse. The words, "My husband," were music to her ears. They actually meant, "Behold, I am an old maid no longer!"

She was so deeply impressed by the story of my meeting with Mr. Even, whose son-in-law was her landlord, and by the amount he had spent on me that she retailed it among her neighbors, some of whom she invited to the house in order to exhibit me to them

Her name was Mrs. Dienstog, which is Yiddish for Tuesday. Now Tuesday is a lucky day, so I saw a good omen in her, and thanked God her name was not Monday or Wednesday, which, according to the Talmud, are unlucky

One of the first things I did was to make up a list of the English words and phrases which our people in this country had adopted as part and parcel of their native tongue. This, I felt, was an essential step toward shedding one's "greenhornhood," an operation every immigrant is anxious to dispose of without delay. The list included, "floor," "ceiling," "window," "dinner," "supper," "hat," "business," "job," "clean," "plenty," "never," "ready," "anyhow," "never mind," "hurry up," "all right," and about a hundred other words and phrases

I was quick to realize that to be "stylishly" dressed was a good investment, but I realized, too, that to use the Yiddish word for "collar" or "clean" instead of their English correlatives was worse than to wear a dirty collar

I wrote down the English words in Hebrew characters and from my landlady's dictation, so that "never mind," for example, became "nevermine."

When I came home with a basket containing my first stock of wares, Mrs.

Dienstog ran into ecstasies over it. She took to fingering some of my collar-buttons and garters, and when I protested she drew away, pouting

Still, the next morning, as I was leaving the house with my stock, she wished me good luck ardently; and when I left the house she ran after me, shouting: "Wait, Mr. Levinsky. I'll buy something of you 'for a lucky start.'" She picked out a paper of pins, and as she paid me the price she said, devoutly, "May this little basket become one of the biggest stores in New York."

My plan of campaign was to peddle in the streets for a few weeks—that is, until my "greenness" should wear off—and then to try to sell goods to tenement housewives. I threw myself into the business with enthusiasm, but with rather discouraging results. I earned what I then called a living, but made no headway. As a consequence, my ardor cooled off. It was nothing but a daily grind. My heart was not in it. My landlord, who was a truck-driver, but who dreamed of business, thought that I lacked dash, pluck, tenacity; and the proprietor of the "peddler supply store" in which I bought my goods seemed to be of the same opinion, for he often chaffed me on the smallness of my bill. On one occasion he said: "If you want to make a decent living you must put all other thoughts out of your mind and think of nothing but your business."

Only my smiling little landlady was always chirping words of encouragement, assuring me that I was not doing worse than the average beginner. This and her cordial, good-natured manner were a source of comfort to me. We became great friends. She taught me some of her broken English; and I let her talk of her husband as long as she wanted. One of her weaknesses was to boast of holding him under her thumb, though in reality she was under his.

Ceaselessly gay in his absence, she would become shy and reticent the moment he came home. I never saw him talk to her save to give her some order, which she would execute with feverish haste. Still, in his surly, domineering way he was devoted to her

I was ever conscious of my modern garb, and as I walked through the streets I would repeatedly throw glances at store windows, trying to catch my reflection in them. Or else I would pass my fingers across my temples to feel the absence of my side-locks. It seemed a pity that Matilda could not see me now

One of the trifles that have remained embedded in my memory from those days is the image of a big, florid-faced huckster shouting at the top of his husky voice: "Strawberri-i-ies, strawberri-i-ies, five cents a quart!"

I used to hear and see him every morning through the windows of my lodging; and to this day, whenever I hear the singsong of a strawberry-peddler I scent the odors of New York as they struck me upon my arrival, in 1885, and I experience the feeling of uncertainty, homesickness, and lovesickness that never left my heart at that period

I often saw Antomir in my dreams

The immigrants from the various Russian, Galician, or Roumanian towns usually have their respective synagogues in New York, Philadelphia, Boston, or Chicago. So I sought out the house of worship of the Sons of Antomir

There were scores, perhaps hundreds, of small congregations on the East Side, each of which had the use of a single room, for the service hours on Saturdays and holidays, in a building rented for all sorts of gatherings—weddings, dances, lodge meetings, trade-union meetings, and the like. The Antomir congregation, however, was one of those that could afford a whole house all to themselves. Our synagogue was a small, rickety, frame structure

It was for a Saturday-morning service that I visited it for the first time.

I entered it with throbbing heart. I prayed with great fervor. When the devotions were over I was disappointed to find that the congregation contained not a single worshiper whom I had known or heard of at home.

playing that cardagam, hmm?

Indeed, many of them did not even belong to Antomir. When I told them about my mother there was a murmur of curiosity and sympathy, but their interest in me soon gave way to their interest in the information I could give each of them concerning the house and street that had once been his home

Upon the advice of my landlord, the truck-driver, and largely with his help, I soon changed the character of my business. I rented a push-cart and tried to sell remnants of dress-goods, linen, and oil-cloth. This turned out somewhat better than basket peddling; but I was one of the common herd in this branch of the business as well

Often I would load my push-cart with cheap hosiery collars, brushes, hand-mirrors, note-books, shoe-laces, and the like, sometimes with several of these articles at once, but more often with one at a time. In the latter case I would announce to the passers-by the glad news that I had struck a miraculous bargain at a wholesale bankruptcy sale, for instance, and exhort them not to miss their golden opportunity. I also learned to crumple up new underwear, or even to wet it somewhat, and then shout that I could sell it "so cheap" because it was slightly damaged

standing on his own feet

I earned enough to pay my board, but I developed neither vim nor ardor for the occupation. I hankered after intellectual interest and was unceasingly homesick. I was greatly tempted to call on Mr. Even, but deferred the visit until I should make a better showing.

I hated the constant chase and scramble for bargains and I hated to yell and scream in order to create a demand for my wares by the sheer force of my lungs. Many an illiterate dolt easily outshouted me and thus dampened what little interest I had mustered. One fellow in particular was a source of discouragement to me. He was a half -witted, hideous-looking man, with no end of vocal energy and senseless fervor. He was a veritable engine of imbecile vitality. He would make the street ring with deafening shrieks, working his arms and head, sputtering and foaming at the mouth like a madman. And it produced results. His nervous fit would have a peculiar effect on the pedestrians. One could not help pausing and buying something of him. The block where we usually did business was one of the best, but I hated him so violently that I finally moved my push-cart to a less desirable locality

I came home in despair

"Oh, it takes a blockhead to make a success of it," I complained to Mrs.

Dienstog

"Why, why," she consoled me, "it is a sin to be grumbling like that. There are lots of peddlers who have been years in America and who would be glad to earn as much as you do. It'll be all right. Don't worry, Mr. Levinsky."

It was less than a fortnight before I changed my place of business once again. The only thing by which these few days became fixed in my memory was the teeth of a young man named Volodsky and the peculiar tale of woe he told me. He was a homely, commonplace-looking man, but his teeth were so beautiful that their glistening whiteness irritated me somewhat. They were his own natural teeth, but I thought them out of place amid his plain features, or amid the features of any other man, for that matter. They seemed to be more suited to the face of a woman. His push-cart was next to mine, but he sold—or tried to sell—hardware, while my cart was laden with other goods; and as he was, moreover, as much of a failure as I was, there was no reason why we should not he friends. So we would spend the day in heart-to-heart talks of our hard luck and homesickness. His chief worry was over the "dower money" which he had borrowed of his sister, at home, to pay for his passage

"She gave it to me cheerfully," he said, in a brooding, listless way. "She thought I would send it back to her at once. People over there think treasure can really be had for the picking in America. Well, I have been over two years here, and have not been able to send her a cent. Her letters make holes in my heart. She has a good marriage chance, so she says, and unless I send her the money at once it will be off. Her lamentations will drive me into the grave."

*[handwritten annotations:]*

How sad!

• Mrs. Dienstog (landlady) likes to talk about her husband + changes moods in front of D / Mr. D.
  ⌐D, lively/energetic   ⌐Mr. D, shy

• went to a synagogue
• seemed to play sympathy card again
• advancing in peddler business

# CHAPTER IV

I SOON had to move from the Dienstogs' to make room for a relative of the truck-driver's who had arrived from England. My second lodgings were an exact copy of my first, a lounge in a kitchen serving me as a bed. To add to the similarity, my new landlady was incessantly singing. Only she had three children and her songs were all in Yiddish. Her ordinary speech teemed with oaths like: "Strike me blind," "May I not be able to move my arms or my legs," "May I spend every cent of it on doctor's bills," "May I not be able to get up from this chair."

A great many of our women will spice their Yiddish with this kind of imprecations, but she was far above the average in this respect

The curious thing about her was that her name was Mrs. Levinsky, though we were not related in the remotest degree

Whatever enthusiasm there was in me found vent in religion. I spent many an evening at the Antomir Synagogue, reading Talmud passionately. This would bring my heart in touch with my old home, with dear old Reb Sender, with the grave of my poor mother. It was the only pleasure I had in those days, and it seemed to be the highest I had ever enjoyed. At times I would feel the tears coming to my eyes for the sheer joy of hearing my own singsong, my old Antomir singsong. It was like an echo from the Preacher's Synagogue. My former self was addressing me across the sea in this strange, uninviting, big town where I was compelled to peddle shoe-black or oil-cloth and to compete with a yelling idiot. I would picture my mother gazing at me as I stood at my push-cart. I could almost see her slapping her hands in despair

As for my love, it had settled down to a chronic dull pain that asserted itself on special occasions only

I was so homesick that my former lodging in New York, to which I had become used, now seemed like home by comparison. I missed the Dienstogs keenly, and I visited them quite often

I wrote long, passionate letters to Reb Sender, in a conglomeration of the Talmudic jargon, bad Hebrew, and good Yiddish, referring to the Talmud studies I pursued in America and pouring out my forlorn heart to him. His affectionate answers brought me inexpressible happiness

But many of the other peddlers made fun of my piety and it could not last long. Moreover, I was in contact with life now, and the daily surprises it had in store for me dealt my former ideas of the world blow after blow. I saw the cunning and the meanness of some of my customers, of the tradespeople of whom I bought my wares, and of the peddlers who did business by my side. Nor was I unaware of certain unlovable traits that were unavoidably developing in my own self under these influences. And while human nature was thus growing smaller, the human world as a whole was growing larger, more complex, more heartless, and more interesting. The striking thing was that it was not a world of piety. I spoke to scores of people and I saw tens of thousands. Very few of the women who passed my push-cart wore wigs, and men who did not shave were an exception. Also, I knew that many of the people with whom I came in daily contact openly patronized Gentile restaurants and would not hesitate even to eat pork

The orthodox Jewish faith, as it is followed in the old Ghetto towns of Russia or Austria, has still to learn the art of trimming its sails to suit new winds. It is exactly the same as it was a thousand years ago. It does not attempt to adopt itself to modern conditions as the Christian Church is continually doing. It is absolutely inflexible. If you are a Jew of the type to which I belonged when I came to New York and you attempt to bend your religion to the spirit of your new surroundings, it breaks. It falls to pieces. The very clothes I wore and the very food I ate had a fatal effect on my religious habits. A whole book could be written on the influence of a starched collar and a necktie on a man who was brought up as I was. It was inevitable that, sooner or later, I should let a barber shave my sprouting beard

"What do you want those things for?" Mrs. Levinsky once said to me, pointing at my nascent whiskers. "Oh, go take a shave and don't be a fool. It will make you ever so much better-looking. May my luck be as handsome as your face will then be."

"Never!" I retorted, testily, yet blushing

She gave a sarcastic snort. "They all speak like that at the beginning," she said. "The girls will make you shave if nobody else does."

"What girls?" I asked, with a scowl, but blushing once again

"What do I know what girls?" she laughed. "That's your own lookout, not mine."

I did not like her. She was provokingly crafty and cold, and she had a mean smile and a dishonest voice that often irritated me. She was ruddy-faced and bursting with health, taller than Mrs. Dienstog, yet too short for her great breadth of shoulder and the enormous bulk of her bust. I thought she looked absurdly dumpy. What I particularly hated in her was her laughter, which sounded for all the world like the gobble of a turkey

She was constantly importuning me to get her another lodger who would share her kitchen lounge with me

"Rent is so high, I am losing money on you. May I have a year of darkness if I am not," she would din in my ears

She was intolerable to me, but I liked her cooking and I hated to be moving again, so I remained several months in her house

It was not long before her prediction as to the fate of my beard came true.

I took a shave. What actually decided me to commit so heinous a sin was a remark dropped by one of the peddlers that my down-covered face made me look like a "green one." It was the most cruel thing he could have told me. I took a look at myself as soon as I could get near a mirror, and the next day I received my first shave. "What would Reb Sender say?" I thought. When I came home that evening I was extremely ill at ease. Mrs. Levinsky noticed the change at once, but she also noticed my embarrassment, so she said nothing, but she was continually darting furtive glances at me, and when our eyes met she seemed to be on the verge of bursting into one of her turkey laughs. I could have murdered her

# BOOK VI

# A GREENHORN NO LONGER

# CHAPTER I

I BOUGHT my goods in several places and made the acquaintance of many peddlers. One of these attracted my attention by his popularity among the other men and by his peculiar talks of women. His name was Max Margolis. We used to speak of him as Big Max to distinguish him from a Little Max, till one day a peddler who was a good chess-player and was then studying algebra changed the two names to "Maximum Max" and "Minimum Max," which the other peddlers pronounced "Maxie Max" and "Minnie Max."

Some of the other fellows, too, were addicted to obscene story-telling, but these mostly made (or pretended to make) a joke of it. The man who had changed Max's sobriquet, for instance, never tired of composing smutty puns, while another man, who had a married daughter, was continually hinting, with merry bravado, at his illicit successes with Gentile women. Maximum Max, on the other hand, would treat his lascivious topics with peculiar earnestness, and even with something like sadness, as though he dwelt on them in spite of himself, under the stress of an obsession

Otherwise he was a jovial fellow

He was a tall, large-boned man, loosely built. His lips were always moist and when closed they were never in tight contact. He had the reputation of a liar, and, as is often the case with those who suffer from that weakness, people liked him. Nor, indeed, were his fibs, as a rule, made out of whole cloth. They usually had a basis of truth. When he told a story and he felt that it was producing no effect he would "play it up," as newspapermen would put it, often quite grotesquely. Altogether he was so inclined to overemphasize and embellish his facts that it was not always easy to say where truth ended and fiction began. Somehow it seemed to me as though the moistness and looseness of his lips had something to do with his mendacity

He was an ignorant man, barely able to write down an address

Max was an instalment peddler, his chief business being with frequenters of dance-halls, to whom he sold clothing, dress-goods, jewelry, and—when there was a marriage among them—furniture. Many a young housewife who had met her "predestined one" in one of these halls wore a marriage ring, and had her front room furnished with a "parlor set," bought of Max Margolis. He was as popular among the dancers as he was among the men he met at the stores. He was married, Max, yet it was as much by his interest in the dancers as by his business interest that he was drawn to the dance-halls. He took a fancy to me and he often made me listen to his discourses on women

The youngest married man usually appealed to me as being old enough to be my father, and as Maximum Max was not only married, but eleven years my senior, there seemed to be a great chasm between us. That he should hold this kind of conversations with an unmarried youngster like myself struck me as something unnatural, doubly indecent. As I listened I would feel awkward, but would listen, nevertheless

One day he looked me over, much as an expert in horseflesh would a colt, and said, with the utmost seriousness: "Do you know, Levinsky, you have an awfully fine figure. You are a good-looking chap all around, for that matter. A fellow like you ought to make a hit with women. Why don't you learn to dance?"

The compliment made me wince and blush. Perhaps, if he had put it in the form of a jest I should even have liked it. As it was, I felt like one stripped in public. Still, I recalled with pleasure that Matilda had said similar things about my figure

"Why don't you learn to dance, Levinsky?" he repeated

I laughed, waving the suggestion aside as a joke

On another occasion he said, "Every woman can be won, absolutely every one, provided a fellow knows how to go about it."

As he proceeded to develop his theory he described various types of women and the various methods to be used with them

"Of course, the man must not be repulsive to her," he said

That evening, when Mrs. Levinsky's husband, their three children, and myself sat around the table and she was serving us our supper she appeared in a new light to me. She was nearly twice my age and I hated her not only for her meanness and low cunning, but also for her massive, broad-shouldered figure and for her turkey laugh, but she was a full-blooded, healthy female, after all. So, as I looked at her bustling between the table and the stove, Max's rule came back to me. I could almost hear his voice, "Every woman can be won, absolutely every one. Mrs. Levinsky's oldest child was a young man of nearly my age, yet I looked her over lustfully and when I found that her florid skin was almost spotless, her lips fresh, and her black hair without a hint of gray, I was glad. Presently, while removing my plate, she threw the trembling bulk of her great, firm bust under my very eyes. I felt disturbed. "Some morning when we are alone," I said to myself, "I shall kiss those red lips of hers."

From that moment on she was my quarry

As her husband worked in a sweatshop, while I peddled, he usually got up at least an hour before me. And it was considered perfectly natural that Mrs.

Levinsky should be hovering about the kitchen while I was sleeping or lying awake on the kitchen lounge. Also, that after her husband left for the day I should go around half-naked, washing and dressing myself, in the same crowded little room in which she was then doing her work, as scantily clad as I was and with the sleeves of her flimsy blouse rolled up to her armpits.

I had never noticed these things before, but on the morning following the above supper I did. As I opened my eyes and saw her bare, fleshy arms held out toward the little kerosene-stove I thought of my resolve to kiss her

She was humming something in a very low voice. To let her know that I was awake I stretched myself and yawned audibly. Her voice rose. It was a song from a well-known Jewish play she was singing

"Good mornings Mrs. Levinsky," I greeted her, in a familiar tone which she now heard for the first time from me. "You seem to be in good spirits this morning."

She was evidently taken aback. I was the last man in the world she would have expected to address a remark of this kind to her

"How can you see it?" she asked, with a side-glance at me

"Have I no ears? Don't I hear your beautiful singing?"

"Beautiful singing!" she said, without looking at me

After a considerable pause I said, awkwardly, "You know, Mrs. Levinsky, I dreamed of you last night!"

"Did you?"

"Aren't you interested to know something more about it?" "I dreamed of telling you that you are a good-looking lady," I pursued, with fast-beating heart

"What has got into that fellow?" she asked of the kerosene-stove. "He is a greenhorn no longer, as true as I am alive." "You won't deny you are good-looking, will you?"

"What is that to you?" And again addressing herself to the kerosene-stove: "What do you think of that fellow? A pious Talmudist indeed! Strike me blind if I ever saw one like that." And she uttered a gobble-like chuckle

I saw encouragement in her manner. I went on to talk of her songs and the Jewish theater, a topic for which I knew her to have a singular weakness.

The upshot was that I soon had her telling me of a play she had recently seen. As she spoke, it was inevitable that she should come up close to the lounge. As she did so, her fingers touched my quilt, her bare, sturdy arms paralyzing my attention. The temptation to grasp them was tightening its grip on me. I decided to begin by taking hold of her hand. I warned myself that it must be done gently, with romance in my touch. "I shall just caress her hand," I decided, not hearing a word of what she was saying

I brought my hand close to hers. My heart beat violently. I was just about to touch her fingers, but I let the opportunity pass. I turned the conversation on her husband, on his devotion to her, on their wedding. She mocked my questions, but answered them all the same

"He must have been awfully in love with you," I said

"What business is that of yours? Where did you learn to ask such questions? At the synagogue? Of course he loved me! What would you have? That he should have hated me? Why did he marry me, then? Of course he was in love with me! Else I would not have married him, would I? Are you satisfied now?" She boasted of the rich and well-connected suitors she had rejected

I felt that I had side-tracked my flirtation. Touching her hand would have been out of place now

A few minutes later, when I was saying my morning prayers, I carefully kept my eyes away from her lest I should meet her sneering glance.

When I had finished my devotions and had put my phylacteries into their little bag I sat down to breakfast. "I don't like this woman at all," I said to myself, looking at her. "In fact, I abhor her. Why, then, am I so crazy to carry on with her?" It was the same question that I had once asked myself concerning my contradictory feelings for Red Esther, but my knowledge of life had grown considerably since then

In those days I had made the discovery that there were "kisses prompted by affection and kisses prompted by Satan." I now added that even love of the flesh might be of two distinct kinds: "There is love of body and soul, and there is a kind of love that is of the body only," I theorized. "There is love and there is lust."

I thought of my feeling for Matilda. That certainly was love

Various details of my relations with Matilda came back to me during these days

One afternoon, as I was brooding over these recollections, while passively awaiting customers at my cart, I conjured up that night scene when she sat on the great green sofa and I went into ecstasies speaking of my prospective studies for admission to a Russian university. I recalled how she had been irritated with me for talking too loud and how, calling me "Talmud student," or ninny, she had abruptly left the room. I had thought of the scene a hundred times before, but now a new interpretation of it flashed through my mind. It all seemed so obvious. I certainly had been a ninny, an idiot. I burst into a sarcastic titter at Matilda's expense and my own

"Of course I was a ninny," I scoffed at myself again and again

I saw Matilda from a new angle. It was as if she had suddenly slipped off her pedestal. Instead of lamenting my fallen idol, however, I gloated over her fall. And, instead of growing cold to her, I felt that she was nearer to me than ever, nearer and dearer

→ Good. She told him – however, that is not the end of it – she's going to allow him...

# CHAPTER II

ONE morning, after breakfast, when I was about to leave the house and Mrs.

Levinsky was detaining me, trying to exact a promise that I should get somebody to share the lounge with me, I said: "I'll see about it. I must be going. Good-by!" At this I took her hand, ostensibly in farewell

"Good-by," she said, coloring and trying to free herself

"Good-by," I repeated, shaking her hand gently and smiling upon her

She wrenched out her hand. I took hold of her chin, but she shook it free

"Don't," she said, shyly, turning away

"What's the matter?" I said, gaily.

She faced about again. "I'll tell you what the matter is," she said. "If you do that again you will have to move. If you think I am one of those landladies—you know the kind I mean—you are mistaken."

She uttered it in calm, rather amicable accents. So I replied: "Why, why, of course I don't! Indeed you are the most respectable and the most sweet-looking woman in the world!"

I stepped up close to her and reached out my hand to seize hold of her bare arm

"None of that, mister!" she flared up, drawing back. "Keep your hands where they belong. If you try that again I'll break every bone in your body. May both my hands be paralyzed if I don't!"

"'S-sh," I implored. Which only added fuel to her rage

"'S-sh nothing! I'll call in all the neighbors of the house and tell them the kind of pious man you are. Saying his prayers three times a day, indeed!"

I sneaked out of the house like a thief. I was wretched all day, wondering how I should come to supper in the evening. I wondered whether she was going to deliver me over to the jealous wrath of her husband. I should have willingly forfeited my trunk and settled in another place, but Mrs. Levinsky had an approximate knowledge of the places where I was likely to do business and there was the danger of a scene from her. Maximum Max's theory did not seem to count for much. But then he had said that one must know "how to go about it." Perhaps I had been too hasty. *Yeah...w/a married woman*

Late in the afternoon of that day Mrs. Levinsky came to see me. Pretending to be passing along on some errand, she paused in front of my cart, accosting me pleasantly

"I'll bet you are angry with me," she said, smiling broadly

"I am not angry at all," I answered, with feigned moroseness. "But you certainly have a tongue. Whew! And, well, you can't take a joke."

"I did not mean to hurt your feelings, Mr. Levinsky. May my luck be as good as is my friendship for you. I certainly wish you no evil. May God give me all the things I wish you. I just want you to behave yourself. That's all. I am so much older than you, anyhow. Look for somebody of your own age. You are not angry at me, are you?" she added, suavely *why is she apologizing?*

She simply could not afford to lose the rent I paid her *— ok*

Since then she held herself at a respectful distance from me

I called on smiling Mrs. Dienstog, my former landlady, in whose house I was no stranger. I timed this visit at an hour when I knew her to be alone

In this venture I met with scarcely any resistance at first. She let me hold her hand and caress it and tell her how soft and tender it was.

"Do you think so?" she said, coyly, her eyes clouding with embarrassment. "I don't think they are soft at all. They would be if I did not have so much washing and scrubbing to do." Then she added, sadly: "America has made a servant of me. A land of gold, indeed! When I was in my father's house I did not have to scrub floors."

I attempted to raise her wrist to my lips, but she checked me. She did not break away from me, however. She held me off, but she did not let go of the index finger of my right hand, which she clutched with all her might, playfully. As we struggled, we both laughed nervously. At last I wrenched my finger from her grip, and before she had time to thwart my purpose she was in my arms. I was aiming a kiss at her lips, but she continued to turn and twist, trying to clap her hand over my mouth as she did so, and my kiss landed on one side of her chin

"Just one more, dearest," I raved. "Only one on your sweet little lips, my dove. Only one. Only one."

She yielded. Our lips joined in a feverish kiss. Then she thrust me away from her and, after a pause, shook her finger at me with a good-natured gesture, as much as to say, "You must not do that, bad boy, you."

I went away in high feather

I called on Mrs. Dienstog again the very next morning. She received me well, but the first thing she did after returning my greeting was to throw the door wide open and to offer me a chair in full view of the hallway

"Oh, shut the door," I whispered, in disgust. "Don't be foolish."

She shook her head

"Just one kiss," I begged her. "You are so sweet."

She held firm

I came away sorely disappointed, but convinced that her inflexibility was a mere matter of practical common sense

I kept these experiences and reflections to myself. Nor did an indecent word ever cross my lips. In the street, while attending to my business, I heard uncouth language quite often. The other push-cart men would utter the most revolting improprieties in the hearing of the women peddlers, or even address such talk to them, as a matter of course. Nor was it an uncommon incident for a peddler to fire a volley of obscenities at a departing housewife who had priced something on his cart without buying it. These things scandalized me beyond words. I could never get accustomed to them

"Look at Levinsky standing there quiet as a kitten," the other peddlers would twit me. "One would think he is so innocent he doesn't know how to count two. Shy young fellows are the worst devils in the world."

They were partly mistaken, during the first few weeks of our acquaintance, at least. For the last thread that bound me to chastity was still unbroken.

It was rapidly wearing away, though.   T. M. I.


- Mrs. L turned down D's advances
- Mrs. L allows him to stay.
- D visits the Dienstags'
- Kisses Mrs. D → moves on fast, doesn't he?

# CHAPTER III

THE last thread snapped. It was the beginning of a period of unrestrained misconduct. Intoxicated by the novelty of yielding to Satan, I gave him a free hand and the result was months of debauchery and self-disgust. The underworld women I met, the humdrum filth of their life, and their matter-of-fact, business-like attitude toward it never ceased to shock and repel me. I never left a creature of this kind without abominating her and myself, yet I would soon, sometimes during the very same evening, call on her again or on some other woman of her class

Many of these women would simulate love, but they failed to deceive me. I knew that they lied and shammed to me just as I did to giy customers, and their insincerities were only another source of repugnance to me. But I frequented them in spite of it all, in spite of myself. I spent on them more than I could afford. Sometimes I would borrow money or pawn something for the purpose of calling on them

The fact that these wretched women were not segregated as they were in my native town probably had something to do with it. Instead of being confined to a fixed out-of-the-way locality, they were allowed to live in the same tenement-houses with respectable people, beckoning to men from the front steps, under open protection from the police. Indeed, the police, as silent partners in the profits of their shame, plainly encouraged this vice traffic. All of which undoubtedly helped to make a profligate of me, but, of course, it would be preposterous to charge it all, or even chiefly, to the police

My wild oats were flavored with a sense of my failure as a business man, by my homesickness and passion for Matilda. My push-cart bored me. I was hungry for intellectual interest, for novel sensations. I was restless. Sometimes I would stop from business in the middle of the day to plunge into a page of Talmud at some near-by synagogue, and sometimes I would lay down the holy book in the middle of a sentence and betake myself to the residence of some fallen woman In my loneliness I would look for some human element in my acquaintance with these women. I would ply them with questions about their antecedents, their family connections, as my mother had done the girl from "That" Street

As a rule, my questions bored them and their answers were obvious fabrications, but there were some exceptions

One of these, a plump, handsome, languid-eyed female named Bertha, occupied two tiny rooms in which she lived with her ten-year-old daughter. One of the two rooms was often full of men, some of them with heavy beards, who would sit there, each awaiting his turn, as patients do in the reception-room of a physician, and whiling their time away by chaffing the little girl upon her mother's occupation and her own future. Some of the questions and jokes they would address to her were of the most revolting nature, whereupon she would reply, "Oh, go to hell!" or stick out her tongue resentfully

One day I asked Bertha why she was giving her child this sort of bringing up

"I once tried to keep her in another place, with a respectable family," she replied, ruefully. "But she would not stay there. Besides, I missed her so much I could not stand it."

Another fallen woman who was frank with me proved to be a native of Antomir.

When she heard that I was from the same place she flushed with excitement

"Go away!" she shouted. "You're fooling me."

We talked of the streets, lanes, and yards of our birthplace, she hailing every name I uttered with outbursts of wistful enthusiasm

I wondered whether she knew of my mother's sensational death, but I never disclosed my identity to her, though she, on her part, told me with impetuous frankness the whole story of her life

"You are a Talmudist, aren't you?" she asked

"How do you know?"

"How do I know! As if it could not be seen by your face." A little later she said: "I am sorry you came here. Honest. You should have stayed at home and stuck to your holy books. It would have been a thousand times better than coming to America and calling on girls like myself. Honest."

She was known as Argentine Rachael

It was from her that I first heard of the relations existing between the underworld and the police of New York. But then my idea of the Russian police had always been associated in my mind with everything cruel and dishonest, so the cormption of the New York police did not seem to be anything unusual

One day she said to me: "If you want a good street corner for your cart I can fix it for you. I know Cuff-Button Leary."

"Who is he?"

"Why, have you never heard about him?' "Is he a big police officer?"

"Bigger. The police are afraid of him."

"Why?"

"Because he is the boss. He is the district leader. What he says goes."

She went on to explain that he was the local chieftain of the dominant "politician party," as she termed it

"What is a politician party?" I asked

She tried to define it and, failing in her attempt, she said, with a giggle: "Oh, you are a boob. You certainly are a green one. Why, it's an organization, a lot of people who stick together, don't you know."

She talked on, and the upshot was that I formed a conception of political parties as of a kind of competing business companies whose specialty it was to make millions by ruling some big city, levying tribute on fallen women, thieves, and liquor-dealers, doing favors to friends and meting out punishment to foes. I learned also that District-Leader Leary owed his surname to a celebrated pair of diamond cuff-buttons, said to have cost him fifteen thousand dollars, from which he never was separated, and by the blaze of which he could be recognized at a distance. "Well, shall I speak to him about you?" she asked. I gave her an evasive answer

"Why, don't you want to have favors from a girl like me?" she laughed

I colored, whereupon she remarked, reflectively: "I don't blame you, either."

She never tired talking of our birthplace.

"Aren't you homesick?" she once demanded

"Not a bit," I answered, with bravado

"Then you have no heart. I have been away five times as long as you, yet I am homesick."

"Really?"

"Honest."

She was as repellent to me as the rest of her class. I could never bring myself to accept a cup of tea from her hands. And yet I could not help liking her spirit. She was truthful and affectionate. This and, above all, her yearning for our common birthplace appealed to me strongly. I was very much inclined to think that in spite of the horrible life she led she was a good girl. To hold this sort of opinion about a woman of her kind seemed to be an improper thing to do. I knew that according to the conventional idea concerning women of the street they were all the most hideous creatures in the world in every respect. So I would tell myself that I must consider her, too, one of the most hideous creatures in the world in every respect. But I did not. For I knew that at heart she was better than some of the most respectable people I had met. It was one of the astonishing discrepancies I had discovered in the world. Also, it was one of the things I had found to be totally different from what people usually thought they were. I was gradually realizing that the average man or woman was full of all sorts of false notions

- sow his wild oats to harlots
- met Bertha (one of them) who had a daughter
- Argentine Rachael (another) came from his home town
  - Letters to get him a new corner
  - LD is impress w/ her, believing her to be truthful and affectionate

# CHAPTER IV

I ENROLLED in a public evening school. I threw myself into my new studies with unbounded enthusiasm. After all, it was a matter of book-learning, something in which I felt at home. Some of my classmates had a much better practical acquaintance with English than I, but few of these could beast the mental training that my Talmud education had given me. As a consequence, I found things irksomely slow. Still, the teacher—a young East Side dude, hazel-eyed, apple-faced, and girlish of feature and voice—was a talkative fellow, with oratorical proclivities, and his garrulousness was of great value to me. He was of German descent and, as I subsequently learned from private conversations with him, his mother was American-born, like himself, so English was his mother-tongue in the full sense of the term. He would either address us wholly in that tongue, or intersperse it with interpretations in labored German, which, thanks to my native Yiddish, I had no difficulty in understanding. His name was Bender. At first I did not like him. Yet I would hang on his lips, striving to memorize every English word I could catch and watching intently, not only his enunciation, but also his gestures, manners, and mannerisms, and accepting it all as part and parcel of the American way of speaking Sign language, which was the chief means of communication in the early days of mankind, still holds its own. It retains sway over nations of the highest culture with tongues of unlimited wealth and variety. And the gestures of the various countries are as different as their spoken languages. The gesticulations and facial expressions with which an American will supplement his English are as distinctively American as those of a Frenchman are distinctively French. One can tell the nationality of a stranger by his gestures as readily as by his language. In a vague, general way I had become aware of this before, probably from contact with some American-born Jews whose gesticulations, when they spoke Yiddish, impressed me as utterly un-Yiddish. And so I studied Bender's gestures almost as closely as I did his words

Even the slight lisp in his "s" I accepted as part of the "real Yankee" utterance. Nor, indeed, was this unnatural, in view of the "th" sound, that stumbling-block of every foreigner, whom it must needs strike as a full-grown lisp. Bender spoke with a nasal twang which I am now inclined to think he paraded as an accessory to the over-dignified drawl he affected in the class-room. But then I had noticed this kind of twang in the delivery of other Americans as well, so, altogether, English impressed me as the language of a people afflicted with defective organs of speech. Or else it would seem to me that the Americans had normal organs of speech, but that they made special efforts to distort the "t" into a "th" and the "v" into a "w."

One of the things I discovered was the unsmiling smile. I often saw it on Bender and on other native Americans—on the principal of the school, for instance, who was an Anglo-Saxon. In Russia, among the people I knew, at least, one either smiled or not. here I found a peculiar kind of smile that was not a smile. It would flash up into a lifeless flame and forthwith go out again, leaving the face cold and stiff. "They laugh with their teeth only," I would say to myself. But, of course, I saw "real smiles," too, on Americans, and I instinctively learned to discern the smile of mere politeness from the sort that came from one's heart. Nevertheless, one evening, when we were reading in our school-book that "Kate had a smile for everybody," and I saw that this was stated in praise of Kate, I had a disagreeable vision of a little girl going around the streets and grinning upon everybody she met

I abhorred the teacher for his girlish looks and affectations, but his twang and "th" made me literally pant with hatred. At the same time I strained every nerve to imitate him in these very sounds. It was a hard struggle, and when I had overcome all difficulties at last, and my girlish-looking teacher complimented me enthusiastically upon my 'thick" and "thin." my aversion for him suddenly thawed out

Two of my classmates were a grizzly, heavy-set man and his sixteen-year-old son, both trying to learn English after a long day's work. On one occasion, when it was the boy's turn to read and he said "bat" for "bath," the teacher bellowed, imperiously: "Stick out the tip of your tongue! This way."

The boy tried, and failed

"Oh, you have the brain of a horse!" his father said, impatiently, in Yiddish. "Let me try, Mr. Teacher." And screwing up his bewhiskered old face, he yelled, "Bat-t-t!" and then he shot out half an inch of thick red tongue

The teacher grinned, struggling with a more pronounced manifestation of his mirth

"His tongue missed the train," I jested, in Yiddish

One of the other pupils translated it into English, whereupon Bender's suppressed laughter broke loose, and I warmed to him still more.

Election Day was drawing near. The streets were alive with the banners, transparencies, window portraits of rival candidates, processions, fireworks, speeches. I heard scores of words from the political jargon of the country. I was continually asking questions, inquiring into the meaning of the things I saw or heard around me. Each day brought me new experiences, fresh impressions, keen sensations. An American day seemed to be far richer in substance than an Antomir year. I was in an everlasting flutter. I seemed to be panting for breath for the sheer speed with which I was rushing through life

What was the meaning of all this noise and excitement? Everybody I spoke to said it was "all humbug." People were making jokes at the expense of all politicians, irrespective of parties. "One is as bad as the other," I heard all around me. "They are all thieves." Argentine Rachael's conception of politics was clearly the conception of respectable people as well

Rejoicing of the Law is one of our great autumn holidays. It is a day of picturesque merrymaking and ceremony, when the stringent rule barring women out of a synagogue is relaxed. On that day, which was a short time before Election Day, I saw an East Side judge, a Gentile, at the synagogue of the Sons of Antomir. He was very short, and the high hat he wore gave him droll dignity. He went around the house of worship kissing babies in their mothers' arms and saying pleasant things to the worshipers. Every little while he would instinctively raise his hand to his high hat and then, reminding himself that one did not bare one's head in a synagogue, he would feverishly drop his hand again

This part of the scene was so utterly, so strikingly un-Russian that I watched it open-mouthed

"A great friend of the Jewish people, isn't he?" the worshiper who stood next to me remarked, archly

"He is simply in love with us," I chimed in, with a laugh, by way of showing off my understanding of things American. "It's Jewish votes he is after."

"Still, he's not a bad fellow," the man by my side remarked. "If you have a trial in his court he'll decide it in your favor."

"How is that?" I asked, perplexed. "And how about the other fellow? He can't decide in favor of both, can he?"

"There is no 'can't' in America," the man by my side returned, with a sage smile

I pondered the riddle until I saw light. "I know what you mean," I said. "He does favors only to those who vote for his party."

"You have hit it, upon my word! You're certainly no longer a green one." *turning point*

"Voting alone may not be enough, though," another worshiper interposed. "If you ever happen to have a case in his court, take a lawyer who is close to the judge. Understand?"

All such talks notwithstanding, the campaign, or the spectacular novelty of it, thrilled me.

Bender delivered a speech to our class, but all I could make of it was that it dealt with elections in general, and that it was something solemn and lofty, like a prayer or a psalm

Election Day came round. I did not rest. I was continually snooping around, watching the politicians and their "customers," as we called the voters.

Traffic in votes was quite an open business in those days, and I saw a good deal of it, on a side-street in the vicinity of a certain polling-place, or even in front of the polling-place itself, under the very eyes of policemen.

I saw the bargaining, the haggling between buyer and seller; I saw money passed from the one to the other; I saw a heeler put a ballot into the hand of a man whose vote he had just purchased (the present system of voting had not yet been introduced) and then march him into a polling-place to make sure that he deposited the ballot for which he had paid him. I saw a man beaten black and blue because he had cheated the party that had paid him for his vote. I saw Leary, blazing cuff-buttons and all. He was a broad-shouldered man with rather pleasing features. I saw him listening to a whispered report from one of the men whom I had seen buying votes

There was no such thing as political life in the Russia of that period. The only political parties in existence there were the secret organizations of revolutionists, of people for whom government detectives were incessantly searching so that they might be hanged or sent to Siberia. As a consequence a great many of our immigrants landed in America absolutely ignorant of the meaning of citizenship, and the first practical instrnctors on the subject into whose hands they fell were men like Cuff-Button Leary or his political underlings. These taught them that a vote was something to be sold for two or three dollars, with the prospect of future favors into the bargain, and that a politician was a specialist in doing people favors. Favors, favors, favors! I heard the word so often, in connection with politics, that the two words became inseparable in my mind. A politician was a "master of favors," as my native tongue would have it

I attended school with religious devotion. This and the rapid progress I was making endeared me to Bender, and he gave me special attention. He taught me grammar, which I relished most keenly. The prospect of going to school in the evening would loom before me, during the hours of boredom or distress I spent at my cart, as a promise of divine pleasure

Some English words inspired me with hatred, as though they were obnoxious living things. The disagreeable impression they produced on me was so strong that it made them easy to memorize, so that I welcomed them in spite of my aversion or, rather, because of it. The list of these words included "satisfaction," "think," and "because."

At the end of the first month I knew infinitely more English than I did Russian

One evening I asked Bender to tell me the "real difference" between "I wrote" and "I have written." He had explained it to me once or twice before, but I was none the wiser for it

"What do you mean by 'real difference'?" he demanded. "I have told you, haven't I, that 'I wrote' is the perfect tense, while 'I have written' is the imperfect tense." This was in accordance with the grammatical terminology of those days

"I know," I replied in my wretched English, "but what is the difference between these two tenses? That's just what bothers me."

"Well," he said, grandly, "the perfect refers to what was, while the imperfect means something that has been."

"But when do you say 'was' and when do you say 'has been'? That's just the question." "You're a nuisance, Levinsky," was his final retort

I was tempted to say, "And you are a blockhead." But I did not, of course.

At the bottom of my heart I had a conviction that one who had not studied the Talmud could not be anything but a blockhead

The first thing he did the next evening was to take up the same subject with me, the rest of the class watching the two of us curiously. I could see that his performance of the previous night had been troubling him and that he was bent upon making a better showing. He spent the entire lesson of two hours with me exclusively, trying all sorts of elucidations and illustrations, all without avail. The trouble with him was that he pictured the working of a foreigner's mind, with regard to English, as that of his own. It did not occur to him that people born to speak another language were guided by another language logic, so to say, and that in order to reach my understanding he would have to impart his ideas in terms of my own linguistic psychology. Still, one of his numerous examples gave me a glimmer of light and finally it all became clear to me. I expressed my joy so boisterously that it brought a roar of laughter from the other men

He made a pet of me. I became the monitor of his class (that is, I would bring in and distribute the books), and he often had me escort him home, so as to talk to me as we walked. He was extremely companionable and loquacious. He had a passion for sharing with others whatever knowledge he had, or simply for hearing himself speak. Upon reaching the house in which he lived we would pause in front of the building for an hour or even more.

Or else we would start on a ramble, usually through Grand Street to East River and back again through East Broadway. His favorite topics during these walks were civics, American history, and his own history

"Dil-i-gence, perr-severance, tenacity!" he would drawl out, with nasal dignity. "Get these three words engraved on your mind, Levinsky. Diligence, perseverance, tenacity."

And by way of illustration he would enlarge on how he had fought his way through City College, how he had won some prizes and beaten a rival in a race for the presidency of a literary society; how he had obtained his present two occupations—as custom-house clerk during the day and as school-teacher in the winter evenings—and how he was going to work himself up to something far more dignified and lucrative. He unbosomed himself to me of all his plans; he confided some of his intimate secrets in me, often dwelling on "my young lady," who was a first cousin of his and to whom he had practically been engaged since boyhood

All this, his boasts not excepted, were of incalculable profit to me. It introduced me to detail after detail of American life. It accelerated the process of "getting me out of my greenhornhood" in the better sense of the phrase

Bender was an ardent patriot. He was sincerely proud of his country. He was firmly convinced that it was superior to any other country, absolutely in every respect. One evening, in the course of one of those rambles of ours, he took up the subject of political parties with me. He explained the respective principles of the Republicans and the Democrats. Being a Democrat himself, he eulogized his own organization and assailed its rival, but he did it strictly along the lines of principle and policy

"The principles of a party are its soul," he thundered, probably borrowing the phrase from some newspaper. And he proceeded to show that the Democratic soul was of superior quality

He went into the question of State rights, of personal liberty, of "Jeffersonian ideals." It was all an abstract formula, and I was so overwhelmed by the image of a great organization fighting for lofty ideals that the concrete question of political baby-kissing, of Cuff-Button Leary's power, and of the scenes I had witnessed on Election Day escaped me at the moment. I merely felt that all I had heard about politics and political parties from Argentine Rachael and from other people was the product of untutored brains that looked at things from the special viewpoint of the gutter

Presently, however, the screaming discrepancy between Cuff-Button Leary's rule and "Jeffersonian ideals" did occur to me. I conveyed my thoughts to Bender as well as I could

He flared up. "Nonsense," he said, "Mr. Leary is the best man in the city.

He is a friend of mine and I am proud of it. Ask him for any favor and he will do it for you if he has to get out of bed in the middle of the night.

He spends a fortune on the poor. He has the biggest heart of any man in all New York, I don't care who he is. He helps a lot of people out of trouble, but he can't help everybody, can he? That's why you hear so many bad things about him. He has a lot of enemies. But I love him just for the enemies he has made."

"People say he collects bribes from disreputable women," I ventured to urge.

"It's a lie. It's all rumors," he shouted, testily

"On Election Day I saw a man who was buying votes whisper to him."

"Whisper to him! Whisper to him! Ha-ha, ha-ha! Well, is that all the evidence you have got against Mr. Leary? I suppose that's the kind of evidence you have about the buying of votes, too. I am afraid you don't quite understand what you see, Levinsky."

His answers were far from convincing. I was wondering what interest he had to defend Leary, to deny things that everybody saw. But he disarmed me by the force of his irritation

Bender himself was a clean, honest fellow. In his peculiar American way, he was very religious, and I knew that his piety was not a mere affectation.

Which was another puzzle to me, for all the educated Jews of my birthplace were known to be atheists. He belonged to a Reformed synagogue, where he conducted a Bible class

One evening he expanded on the beauty of the English translation of the Old Testament. He told me it was the best English to be found in all literature

"Study the Bible, Levinsky! Read it and read it again."

The suggestion took my fancy, for I could read the English Bible with the aid of the original Hebrew text. I began with Psalm

104, the poem that had thrilled me when I was on shipboard. I read the English version of it before Bender until I pronounced the words correctly. I thought I realized their music. I got the chapter by heart. When I recited it before Bender he was joyously surprised and called me a "corker."

"What is a corker?" I asked, beamingly

"It's slang for 'a great fellow.'" With which he burst into a lecture on slang

I often sat up till the small hours, studying the English Bible. I had many a quarrel with Mrs. Levinsky over the kerosene I consumed. Finally it was arranged that I should pay her five cents for every night I sat up late. But this merely changed the bone of contention between us. Instead of quarreling over kerosene, we would quarrel over hours—over the question whether I really had sat up late or not

To this day, whenever I happen to utter certain Biblical words or names in their English version, they seem to smell of Mrs. Levinsky's lamp

- enrolled in evening school
- Teacher, Bender, → D didn't like him at first but they gradually became friends
- experienced Election Day
  └ stranger noticed his greenhornness was less
- got a lesson of politics from Bender
- started to study the Bible

# CHAPTER V

EVENING school closed in April. The final session was of a festive character. Bender, excited and sentimental, distributed some presents

"Promise me that you will read this glorious book from beginning to end, Levinsky," he said, solemnly, as he handed me a new volume of Dombey and Son and a small dictionary. "We may never meet again. So you will have something to remind you that once upon a time you had a teacher whose name was Bender and who tried to do his duty."

I wanted to thank him, to say something handsome, but partly because I was overcome by his gift, partly because I was at a loss for words, I merely kept saying, sheepishly, "Thank you, thank you, thank you, thank you."

That volume of Dickens proved to be the ruin of my push-cart business and caused m.e some weeks of the blackest misery I had ever experienced

As I started to read the voluminous book I found it an extremely difficult task. It seemed as though it was written in a language other than the one I had been studying during the past few months. I had to turn to the dictionary for the meaning of every third word, if not more often, while in many cases several words in succession were Greek to me. Some words could not be found in my little dictionary at all, and in the case of many others the English definitions were as much of an enigma to me as the words they were supposed to interpret. Yet I was making headway. I had to turn to the dictionary less and less often

It was the first novel I had ever read. The dramatic interest of the narrative, coupled with the poetry and the humor with which it is so richly spiced, was a revelation to me. I had had no idea that Gentiles were capable of anything so wonderful in the line of book-writing. To all of which should be added my self-congratulations upon being able to read English of this sort, a state of mind which I was too apt to mistake for my raptures over Dickens. It seemed to me that people who were born to speak this language were of a superior race

I was literally intoxicated, and, drunkard-like, I would delay going to business from hour to hour. The upshot was that I became so badly involved in debt that I dared not appear with my push-cart for fear of scenes from my creditors. Moreover, I scarcely had anything to sell. Finally I disposed of what little stock I still possessed for one-fourth of its value, and, to my relief as well as to my despair, my activities as a peddler came to an end

I went on reading, or, rather, studying, Dombey and Son with voluptuous abandon till I found myself literally penniless.

I procured a job with a man who sold dill pickles to Jewish grocers. From his description of my duties—chiefly as his bookkeeper—I expected that they would leave me plenty of leisure, between whiles, to read my Dickens. I was mistaken. My first attempt to open the book during business hours, which extended from 8 in the morning to bedtime, was suppressed. My employer, who had the complexion of a dill pickle, by the way, proved to be a severe taskmaster, absurdly exacting, and so niggardly that I dared not take a decent-looking pickle for my lunch.

I left him at the end of the second week, obtaining employment in a prosperous fish-store next door. My new "boss" was a kinder and pleasanter man, but then the malodorous and clamorous chaos of his place literally sickened me

I left the fishmonger and jumped my board at Mrs. Levinsky's to go to a New Jersey farm, where I was engaged to read Yiddish novels to the illiterate wife of a New York merchant, but my client was soon driven from the place by the New Jersey mosquitoes and I returned to New York with two dollars in my pocket. I worked as assistant in a Hebrew school where the American-born boys mocked my English and challenged me to have an "American fight" with them, till—on the third day—I administered a sound un-American thrashing to one of them and lost my job

Maximum Max got the proprietor of one of the dance-halls in which he did his instalment business to let me sleep in his basement in return for some odd jobs. While there I earned from two to three dollars a week in tips and a good supper every time there was a wedding in the place, which happened two or three times a week. I had plenty of time for Dickens (I was still burrowing my way through Dombey and Son) while the "affairs" of the hall—weddings, banquets, balls, mass meetings—were quite exciting. I felt happy, but this happiness of mine did not last long. I was soon sent packing.

This is the way it came about. It was in the large ballroom of the establishment in question that I saw a "modern" dance for the first time in my life. It produced a bewitching effect on me. Here were highly respectable young women who would let men encircle their waists, each resting her arm on her partner's shoulder, and then go spinning and hopping with him, with a frank relish of the physical excitement in which they were joined. As I watched one of these girls I seemed to see her surrender much of her womanly reserve. I knew that the dance—an ordinary waltz—was considered highly proper, yet her pose and his struck me as a public confession of unseemly mutual interest. I almost blushed for her. And for the moment I was in love with her. As this young woman went round and round her face bore a faint smile of embarrassed satisfaction. I knew that it was a sex smile. Another woman danced with grave mien, and I knew that it was the gravity of sex

To watch dancing couples became a passion with me. One evening, as I stood watching the waltzing members of a wedding party, a married sister of the bride's shouted to me in Yiddish: "What are you doing here? Get out. You're a kill-joy."

This was her way of alluding to my unpresentable appearance. When the proprietor heard of the incident he sent for me. He told me that I was a nuisance and bade me find another "hang-out" for myself

The following month or two constitute the most wretched period of my life in America. I slept in the cheapest lodging-houses on the Bowery and not infrequently in some express-wagon. I was constantly borrowing quarters, dimes, nickels.

Maximum Max was very kind to me. As I could not meet him at the stores, where I dared not face my creditors, I would waylay him in front of his residence

"I tell you what, Levinsky," he once said to me. "You ought to learn some trade. It's plain you were not born to be a business man.

The black dots [meaning the words in books] take up too much room in your head."

Finally I owed him so many quarters, and even half-dollars, that I had not the courage to ask him for more

Hunger was a frequent experience. I had been no stranger to the sensation at Antomir, at least after the death of my mother; but, for some reason, I was now less capable of bearing it. The pangs I underwent were at times so acute that I would pick up cigarette stubs in the street and smoke them, without being a smoker, for the purpose of having the pain supplanted by dizziness and nausea. Sometimes, too, I would burn my hand with a match or bite it as hard as I could. Any kind of suffering or excitement was welcome, provided it made me forget my hunger

When famished I would sometimes saunter through the streets on the lower East Side which disreputable creatures used as their market-place. It was mildly exciting to watch women hunt for men and men hunt for women: their furtive glances, winks, tacit understandings, bargainings, the little subterfuges by which they sought to veil their purpose from the other passers-by; the way a man would take stock of a passing woman to ascertain whether she was of the approachable class; the timidity of some of the men and the matter-of-fact ease of others; the mutual spying of two or three rivals aiming at the same quarry; the pretended abstraction of the policemen, and a hundred and one other details of the traffic. Many a time I joined in the chase without having a cent in my pocket, stop to discuss terms with a woman in front of some window display, or around a corner, only soon to turn away from her on the pretense that I had expected to be taken to her residence while she proposed going to some hotel. Thus, held by a dull, dogged fascination, I would tramp around, sometimes for hours, until, feeling on the verge of a fainting-spell with hunger and exhaustion, I would sit down on the front steps of some house

I often thought of Mr. Even, but nothing was further from my mind than to let him see me in my present plight. One morning I met him, face to face, on the Bowery, but he evidently failed to recognize me

One afternoon I called on Argentine Rachael. "Look here, Rachace," I said, in a studiously matter-of-fact voice, "I'm dead broke to-day. I'll pay you in a day or two." Her face fell. "I never trust. Never," she said, shaking her head mournfully. "It brings bad luck, anyhow."

I felt like sinking into the ground. "All right, I'll see you some other time," I said, with an air of bravado

She ran after me. "Wait a moment. What's your hurry?"

By way of warding off "bad luck," she offered to lend me three dollars in cash, out of which I could pay her. I declined her offer. She pleaded and expostulated. But I stood finn, and I came away in a state of the blackest wretchedness and self-disgust

I could never again bring myself to show my face at her house

A little music-store was now my chief resort. It was kept by a man whom I had met at the synagogue of the Sons of Antomir, a former cantor who now supplemented his income from the store by doing occasional service as a wedding bard. The musicians, singers, and music-teachers who made the place their headquarters had begun by taking an interest in me, but the dimes and nickels I was now unceasingly "borrowing" of them had turned me into an outcast in their eyes. I felt it keenly. I would sulk around the store, anxious to leave, and loitering in spite of myself. There was a piano in the store, upon which they often played. This, their talks of music, and their venomous gossip had an irresistible fascination for me

I noticed that morbid vanity was a common disease among them. Some of them would frankly and boldly sing their own panegyrics, while others, more discreet and tactful, let their high opinions of themselves be inferred. Nor could they conceal the grudges they bore one another, the jealousies with which they were eaten up. I thought them ludicrous, repugnant, and yet they lured me. I felt that some of those among them who were most grotesque and revolting in their selfishness had something in their make-up—certain interests, passions, emotions, visions—which placed them above the common herd. This was especially true of a spare, haggard-looking violinist, boyish of figure and cat-like of manner, with deep dark rings under his insatiable blue eyes. He called himself Octavius. He was literally consumed by the blaze of his own conceit and envy. When he was not in raptures over the poetry, subtlety, or depth of his own playing or compositions, he would give way to paroxysms of malice and derision at the expense of some other musician, from his East Side rivals all the way up to Sarasate, who was then at the height of his career and had recently played in New York. Wagner was his god, yet no sooner would somebody else express admiration for Wagner music than he would offer to show that all the good things in the works of the famous German were merely so many paraphrased plagiarisms from the compositions of other men. He possessed a phenomenal memory. He seemed to remember every note in every opera, symphony, oratorio, or concerto that anybody ever mentioned, and there was not a piece of music by a celebrated man but he was ready to "prove" that it had been stolen from some other celebrated man

His invective was particularly violent when he spoke of those Jewish immigrants in the musical profession whose success had extended beyond the East Side. He could never mention without a jeer or some coarse epithet the name of a Madison Street boy, a violinist, who was then attracting attention in Europe and who was booked for a series of concerts before the best audiences in the United States

He was a passionate phrase-maker. Indeed, it would have been difficult to determine which afforded him more pleasure—his self-laudations or the colorful, pungent, often preposterous language in which they were clothed

"I am writing something with hot tears in it," I once heard him brag.

"They'll be so hot they'll scald the heart of every one who hears it, provided he has a heart."

He had given me some nickels, yet his boasts would fill me with disgust. On the occasion just mentioned I was so irritated with my poverty and with the whole world that I was seized with an irresistible desire to taunt him. As he continued to eulogize his forthcoming masterpiece I threw out a Hebrew quotation: "Let others praise thee, but not thine own mouth."

He took no heed of my thrust. But since then he never looked at me and I never dared ask him for a nickel again

He had a ferocious temper. When it broke loose it would be a veritable volcano of revolting acrimony, his thin, firm opening and snapping shut in a peculiar fashion, as though he were squirting venom all over the floor. He was as sensual as Maximum Max, only his voluptuous talks of women were far more offensive in form. But then his lewd drivel was apt to glitter with flashes of imagination. I do not remember ever seeing him in good humor

- evening school ended
- Bender gave him a book by Dickens, his 1st gift in Am.
  └ first novel he ever read

Jobs

Peddler (debt)
↓
Pickle seller (boss = severe taskmaster)
↓
fish monger (chaos sickened him—not to mention the smell)
↓
reader to illiterate wife in NY (moved to woman NJ)
↓
assistant in Hebrew school ("Am fight"— lost his job)

- Max helped him move into a dance hall, ⟶ became fascinated by it
- hung out at music store
- became more desperate to have a woman

# BOOK VII

## MY TEMPLE

# CHAPTER I

ONE Friday evening in September I stood on Grand Street with my eyes raised to the big open windows of a dance-hall on the second floor of a brick building on the opposite side of the lively thoroughfare. Only the busts of the dancers could be seen. This and the distance that divided me from the hall enveloped the scene in mystery. As the couples floated by, as though borne along on waves of the music, the girls clinging to the men, their fantastic figures held me spellbound. Several other people were watching the dancers from the street, mostly women, who gazed at the appearing and disappearing images with envying eyes

Presently I was accosted by a dandified-looking young man who rushed at me with an exuberant, "How are you?" in English. He was dressed in the height of the summer fashion. He looked familiar to me, but I was at a loss to locate him

"Don't you know me? Try to remember!"

It was Gitelson, my fellow-passenger on board the ship that had brought me to America, the tailor who clung to my side when I made my entry into the New World, sixteen months before

The change took my breath away

"You didn't recognize me, did you?" he said, with a triumphant snicker, pulling out his cuffs so as to flaunt their gold or gilded buttons

He asked me what I was doing, but he was more interested in telling me about himself. That cloak-contractor who picked him up near Castle Garden had turned out to be a skinflint and a slave-driver. He had started him on five dollars a week for work the market price of which was twenty or thirty. So Gitelson left him as soon as he realized his real worth, and he had been making good wages ever since. Being an excellent tailor, he was much sought after, and although the trade had two long slack seasons he always had plenty to do. He told me that he was going to that dance-hall across the street, which greatly enhanced his importance in my eyes and seemed to give reality to the floating phantoms that I had been watching in those windows.

He said he was in a hurry to go up there, as he had "an appointment with a lady" (this in English), yet he went on describing the picnics, balls, excursions he attended

Thereupon I involuntarily shot a look at his jaunty straw hat, thinking of his gray forelock. I did so several times. I could not help it. Finally my furtive glances attracted his attention

"What are you looking at? Anything wrong with my hat?" he asked, baring his head. His hair was freshly trimmed and dudishly dressed. As I looked at the patch of silver hair that shone in front of a glossy expanse of brown, he exclaimed, with a laugh: "Oh, you mean that! That's nothing. The ladies like me all the same

He went on boasting, but he did it in an inoffensive way. He simply could not get over the magic transformation that had come over him. While in his native place his income had amounted to four rubles (about two dollars) a week, his wages here were now from thirty to forty dollars. He felt like a peasant suddenly turned to a prince. But he spoke of his successes in a pleasing, soft voice and with a kindly, confiding smile that won my heart.

Altogether he made the impression of an exceedingly unaggressive, good-natured fellow, without anything like ginger in his make-up

After he had bragged his fill he invited me to have a glass of soda with him. There was a soda-stand on the next corner, and when we reached it I paused, but he pulled me away

"Come on," he said, disdainfully. "We'll go into a drug-store, or, better still, let's go to an ice-cream parlor."

This I hesitated to do because of my shabby clothes. When he divined the cause of my embarrassment he was touched

"Come on!' he said, with warm hospitality, uttering the two words in English. "When I say 'Come on' I know what I am talking about."

"But your lady is waiting for you." "She can wait. Ladies are never on time, anyhow."

"But maybe she is."

"If she is she can dance with some of the other fellows. I wouldn't be jealous. There are plenty of other ladies. I should not take fifty ladies for this chance of seeing you. Honest."

He took me into a little candy-store, dazzlingly lighted and mirrored and filled with marble-topped tables

We seated ourselves and he gave the order. He did so ra.ther swaggeringly, but his manner to me was one of affectionate and compassionate respectfulness

"Oh, I am so glad to see you," he said. "You remember the ship?"

"As if one could ever forget things of that kind."

"I have often thought of you. 'I wonder what has become of him,' I said to myself." He did not remember my name, or perhaps he had never known it, so I had to introduce myself afresh. The contrast between his flashy clothes and my frowsy, wretched-looking appearance, as I saw ourselves in the mirrors on either side of me, made me sorely ill at ease. The brilliancy of the gaslight chafed my nerves. It was as though it had been turned on for the express purpose of illuminating my disgrace. I was longing to go away, but Gitelson fell to questioning me about my affairs once more, and this time he did so with such unfeigned concern that I told him the whole cheerless story of my sixteen months' life in America

He was touched. In his mild, unemphatic way he expressed heartfelt sympathy

"But why don't you learn some trade?" he inquired. "You don't seem to be fit for business, anyhow" (the last two words in mispronounced English)

"Everybody is telling me that."

"There you are. You just listen to me, Mr. Levinsky. You won't be sorry for it." He proposed machine-operating in a cloak-shop, which paid even better than tailoring and was far easier to learn. Finally he offered to introduce me to an operator who would teach me the trade, and to pay him my tuition fee

He went into details. He continued to address me as Mr. Levinsky and tried to show me esteem as his intellectual superior, but, in spite of himself, as it were, he gradually took a respectfully contemptuous tone with me

"Don't be a lobster, Mr. Levinsky." ("Lobster" he said in English.) "This is not Russia. Here a fellow must be no fool. There is no sense in living the way you do. Do as Gitelson tells you, and you'll live decently, dress decently, and lay by a dollar or two. There are lots of educated fellows in the shops." He told me of some of these, particularly of one young man who was a shopmate of his. "He never comes to work without some book" he said.

"When there is not enough to do he reads. When he has to wait for a new 'bundle,' as we call it, he reads. Other fellows carry on, but he is always reading. He is so highly educated he could read any kind of book, and I don't believe there is a book in the world that he has not read. He is saving up money to go to college."

On parting he became fully respectful again. "Do as I tell you, Mr.

Levinsky," he said. "Take up cloak-making."

He made me write down his address. He expected that I would do it in Yiddish. When he saw me write his name and the name of the street in English he said, reverently: "Writing English already! There is a mind for you! If I could write like that I could become a designer. Well, don't lose the address. Call on me, and if you make up your mind to take up cloak-making just say the word and I'll fix you up. When Gitelson says he will, he will." The image of that cloak-operator reading books and laying by money for a college education haunted me. Why could I not do the same? I pictured myself working and studying and saving money for the kind of education which Matilda had dinned into my ears

I accepted Gitelson's offer. Cloak-making or the cloak business as a career never entered my dreams at that time. I regarded the trade merely as a stepping-stone to a life of intellectual interests

• meets Gitelson again in the street
• G made something out of himself, looking fancy
• G insists D should take up cloak-making as his trade
   ↳ D gradually accepts

# CHAPTER II

THE operator to whom Gitelson apprenticed me was a short, plump, dark-complexioned fellow named Joe. I have but a dim recollection of his features, though I distinctly remember his irresistible wide-eyed smile and his emotional nature

He taught me to bind seams, and later to put in pockets, to stitch on "under collars," and so forth. After a while he began to pay me a small weekly wage, he himself being paid, for our joint work, by the piece. The shop was not the manufacturer's. It belonged to one of his contractors, who received from him "bundles" of material which his employees (tailors, machine - operators, pressers, and finisher girls) made up into cloaks or jackets. The cheaper goods were made entirely by operators; the better grades partly by tailors, partly by operators, or wholly by tailors; but these were mostly made "inside," in the manufacturer's own establishment. The designing, cutting, and making of samples were "inside" branches exclusively. Gitelson, as a skilled tailor, was an "inside" man, being mostly employed on samples

My work proved to be much harder and the hours very much longer than I had anticipated. I had to toil from six in the morning to nine in the evening.

(Joe put in even more time. I always found him grinding away rapturously when I came to the shop in the morning, and always left him toiling as rapturously when I went home in the evening.) Ours is a seasonal trade. All the work of the year is crowded into two short seasons of three and two months, respectively, during which one is to earn enough to last him twelve months (only sample-makers, high-grade tailors like Gitelson, were kept busy throughout the year). But then wages were comparatively high, so that a good mechanic, particularly an operator, could make as much as seventy-five dollars a week, working about fifteen hours a day. However, during the first two or three weeks I was too much borne down by the cruelty of my drudgery to be interested in the luring rewards which it held out. Not being accustomed to physical exertion of any kind, I felt like an innocent man suddenly thrown into prison and put at hard labor. I was shocked. I was crushed. I was continually looking at the clock, counting the minutes, and when I came home I would feel so sore in body and spirit that I could not sleep. Studying or reading was out of the question

Moreover, as a peddler I seemed to have belonged to the world of business, to the same class as the rich, the refined, while now, behold! I was a workman, a laborer, one of the masses. I pitied myself for a degraded wretch. And when some of my shopmates indulged in coarse pleasantry in the hearing of the finisher girls it would hurt me personally, as a confirmation of my disgrace. "And this is the kind of people with whom I am doomed to associate!" I would lament. In point of fact, there were only four or five fellows of this kind in a shop of fifty. Nor were some of the peddlers or music-teachers I had known more modest of speech than the worst of these cloak-makers. What was more, I felt that some of my fellow-employees were purer and better men than I. But that did not matter. I abhorred the shop and everybody in it as a well-bred convict abhors his jail and his fellow-inmates

When the men quarreled they would call one another, among other things, "bundle-eaters." This meant that they accused one another of being ever hungry for bundles of raw material, ever eager to "gobble up all the work in the shop." I wondered how one could be anxious for physical toil. They seemed to be a lot of savages

The idea of leaving the shop often crossed my mind, but I never had the courage to take it seriously. I had tried my hand at peddling and failed.

Was I a failure as a mechanic as well? Was I unfit for anything? The other fellows at the shop had a definite foothold in life, while I was a waif, a ne'er-do-well, nearly two years in America with nothing to show for it.

Thoughts such as these had a cowing effect on me. They made me feel somewhat like the fresh prisoner who has been put to work at stone-breaking to have his wild spirit broken. I dared not give up my new occupation. I would force myself to work hard, and as I did so the very terrors of my toil would fascinate me, giving me a sense of my own worth. As the jackets that bore my stitches kept piling up, the concrete result of my useful performance would become a source of moral satisfaction to me. And when I received my first wages—the first money I had ever earned by the work of my hands—it seemed as if it were the first money I had ever earned honestly

By little and little I got used to my work and even to enjoy its processes.

Moreover, the thinking and the dreaming I usually indulged in while plying my machine became a great pleasure to me. It seemed as though one's mind could not produce such interesting thoughts or images unless it had the rhythmic whir of a sewing-machine to stimulate it

I now ate well and slept well. I was in the best of health and in the best of spirits. I was in an uplifted state of mind. No one seemed to be honorable who did not earn his bread in the sweat of his brow as I did. Had I then chanced to hear a Socialist speech I might have become an ardent follower of Karl Marx and my life might have been directed along lines other than those which brought me to financial power

The girls in the shop, individually, scarcely interested me, but their collective presence was something of which I never seemed to be quite unconscious. It was as though the workaday atmosphere were scented with the breath of a delicate perfume—a perfume that was tainted with the tang of my yearning for Matilda

Two girls who were seated within a yard from my machine were continually bandying secrets. Now one and then the other would look around to make sure that the contractor was not watching, and then she would bend over and whisper something into her chum's ear. This would set my blood tingling with a peculiar kind of inquisitiveness. It was reasonable to suppose that their whispered conferences mostly bore upon such innocent matters as their work, earnings, lodgings, or dresses. Nevertheless, it seemed to me that their whispers, especially when accompanied by a smile, a giggle, or a wink, conveyed some of their intimate thoughts of men. They were homely girls, with pinched faces, yet at such moments they represented to me all that there was fascinating and disquieting in womanhood

The jests of the foul-mouthed rowdies would make me writhe with disgust. As a rule they were ostensibly addressed to some of the other fellows or to nobody in particular, their real target being the nearest girls. These would receive them with gestures of protest or with an exclamation of mild repugnance, or—in the majority of cases—pass them unnoticed, as one does some unavoidable discomfort of toil. There was only one girl in the shop who received these jests with a shamefaced grin or even with frank appreciation, and she was a perfectly respectable girl like the rest. There were some finisher girls who could not boast an unsullied reputation, but none of them worked in our shop, and, indeed, their number in the entire trade was very small

One of the two girls who sat nearest to my machine was quite popular in the shop, but that was because of her sweet disposition and sound sense rather than for her looks. She was known to have a snug little account in a savings-bank. It was for a marriage portion she was saving; but she was doing it so strenuously that she stinted herself the expense of a decent dress or hat, or the price of a ticket to a ball, picnic, or dancing-class.

The result was that while she was pinching and scrimping herself to pave the way to her marriage she barred herself, by this very process, from contact with possible suitors. She was a good soul. From time to time she would give some of her money to a needy relative, and then she would try to make up for it by saving with more ardor than ever. Her name was Gussie

Joe, the plump, dark fellow who was teaching me the trade, was one of the several men in the shop who were addicted to salacious banter. One of his favorite pranks was to burlesque some synagogue chant from the solemn service of the Days of Awe, with disgustingly coarse Yiddish in place of the Hebrew of the prayer. But he was not a bad fellow, by any means. He was good-natured, extremely impressionable, and susceptible of good influences.

A sad tune would bring a woebegone look into his face, while a good joke would make him laugh to tears. He was fond of referring to himself as my "rabbi," which is Hebrew for teacher, and that was the way I would address him, at first playfully, and then as a matter of course

One day, after he had delivered himself of a quip that set my teeth on edge, I said to him, appealingly: "Why should you be saying these things, rabbi?"

"If you don't like them you can stop your God-fearing ears," he fired back, good-naturedly

I retorted that it was not a matter of piety, but of common decency, and my words were evidently striking home, but the girls applauded me, which spoiled it all

"If you want to preach sermons you're in the wrong place," he flared up.

"This is no synagogue."

"Nor is it a pigsty," Gussie urged, without raising her eyes from her work

A month or two later he abandoned these sallies of his own accord. The other fellows twitted him on his burst of "righteousness" and made efforts to lure him into a race of ribald punning, but he stood his ground

By and by it leaked out that he was engaged and madly in love with his girl.

I warmed to him.

The young woman who had won his heart was not an employee of our shop.

Indeed, love-affairs between working-men and working-girls who are employed in the same place are not quite so common as one might suppose. The factory is scarcely a proper setting for romance. It is one of the battle-fields in our struggle for existence, where we treat woman as an inferior being, whereas in civilized love-making we prefer to keep up the chivalrous fiction that she is our superior. The girls of our shop, hard-worked, disheveled, and handled with anything but chivalry, aroused my sympathy, but it was not the kind of feeling that stimulates romantic interest. Still, collectively, as an abstract reminder of their sex, they flavored my sordid environment with poetry

# CHAPTER III

THE majority of the students at the College of the City of New York was already made up of Jewish boys, mostly from the tenement-houses. One such student often called at the cloak-shop in which I was employed, and in which his father—a tough-looking fellow with a sandy beard, a former teamster—was one of the pressers. A classmate of this boy was supported by an aunt, a spinster who made good wages as a bunch-maker in a cigar-factory.

To make an educated man of her nephew was the great ambition of her life.

All this made me feel as though I were bound to that college with the ties of kinship. Two of my other shopmates had sons at high school. The East Side was full of poor Jews—wage-earners, peddlers, grocers, salesmen, insurance agents—who would beggar themselves to give their children a liberal education. Then, too, thousands of our working-men attended public evening school, while many others took lessons at home. The Ghetto rang with a clamor for knowledge

To save up some money and prepare for college seemed to be the most natural thing for me to do. I said to myself that I niust begin to study for it without delay. But that was impossible, and it was quite some time before I took up the course which the presser's boy had laid out for me. During the first three months I literally had no time to open a book. Nor was that all.

My work as a cloak-maker had become a passion with me, so much so that even on Saturdays, when the shop was closed, I would scarcely do any reading.

Instead, I would seek the society of other cloak-makers with whom I might talk shop

I was developing speed rather than skill at my sewing-machine, but this question of speed afforded exercise to my brain. It did not take me long to realize that the number of cloaks or jackets which one turned out in a given length of time was largely a matter of method and system. I perceived that Joe, who was accounted a fast hand, would take up the various parts of a garment in a certain order calculated to reduce to a minimum the amount of time lost in passing from section to section. So I watched him intently, studying his system with every fiber of my being. Nor did I content myself with imitating his processes. I was forever pondering the problem and introducing little improvements of my own. I was making a science of it. It was not merely physical exertion. It was a source of intellectual interest as well. I was wrapped up in it. If I happened to meet a cloak-operator who was noted for extraordinary speed I would feel like an ambitious musician meeting a famous virtuoso. Some cloak-operators were artists. I certainly was not one of them. I admired their work and envied them, but I lacked the artistic patience and the dexterity essential to workmanship of a high order. Much to my chagrin, I was a born bungler. But then I possessed physical strength, nervous vitality, method, and inventiveness—all the elements that go to make up speed

I was progressing with unusual rapidity. Joe criticized my work severely, often calling me botcher, but I knew that this was chiefly intended to veil his satisfaction at the growing profits that my work was yielding him

I now earned about ten dollars a week, of which I spent about five, saving the rest for the next season of idleness

At last that season set in. There was not a stroke of work in the shop. I was so absorbed in my new vocation that I would pass my evenings in a cloak-makers' haunt, a café on Delancey Street, where I never tired talking sleeves, pockets, stitches, trimmings, and the like. There was a good deal of card-playing in the place, but somehow I never succumbed to that temptation.

But then, under the influence of some of the fellows I met there, I developed a considerable passion for the Jewish theater. These young men were what is known on the East Side as "patriots," that is, devoted admirers of some actor or actress and members of his or her voluntary claque. Several of the other frequenters were also interested in the stage, or at least in the gossip of it; so that, on the whole, there was as much talk of plays and players as there was of cloaks and cloak-makers. Our shop discussions certainly never reached the heat that usually characterized our debates on things theatrical

The most ardent of the "patriots" was a young contractor named Mindels. He attended nearly every performance in which his favorite actor had a part, selling dozens of tickets for his benefit performances and usually losing considerable sums on these sales, loading him with presents and often running his errands. I once saw Mindels in a violent quarrel with a man who had scoffed at his idol

Mindels's younger brother, Jake, fascinated me by his appearance, and we became great chums. He was the handsomest fellow I ever had seen, with a fine head of dark-brown hair, classic features, and large, soft-blue eyes; too soft and too blue, perhaps. His was a manly face and figure, and his voice was a manly, a beautiful basso; but this masculine exterior contained an effeminate psychology. In my heart I pronounced him "a calf," and when I had discovered the English word "sissy," I thought that it just fitted him.

Yet I adored him, and even looked up to him, all because of his good looks

He was a Talmudist like myself, and we had much in common, also, regarding our dreams of the future

"Oh, I am so glad I have met you," I once said to him

"I am glad, too," he returned, flushing

I found that he blushed rather too frequently, which confirmed my notion of him as a sissy. Like most handsome men, he bestowed a great deal of time on his personal appearance. He never uttered a foul word nor a harsh one. If he heard a cloak-maker tell an indecent story he would look down, smiling and blushing like a girl

Formerly he had been employed in his brother's shop, while now he earned his living by soliciting and collecting for a life-insurance company

# CHAPTER LV

JAKE MINDELS was a devotee of Madame Klesmer, the leading Jewish actress of that period, which, by the way, was practically the opening chapter in the interesting history of the Yiddish stage in America. Madame Klesmer was a tragedienne and a prima donna at once-a usual combination in those days

One Friday evening we were in the gallery of her theater. The play was an "historical opera," and she was playing the part of a Biblical princess. It was the closing scene of an act. The whole company was on the stage, swaying sidewise and singing with the princess, her head in a halo of electric light in the center. Jake was feasting his large blue eyes on her. Presently he turned to me with the air of one confiding a secret. "Wouldn't you like to kiss her?" And, swinging around again, he resumed feasting his blue eyes on the princess.

"I have seen prettier women than she," I replied

"'S-sh! Let a fellow listen. She is a dear, all the same. You don't know a good thing when you see it, Levinsky."

"Are you in love with her?"

"'S-sh! Do let me listen."

When the curtain fell he made me applaud her. There were several curtain-calls, during all of which he kept applauding her furiously, shouting the prima donna's name at the top of his voice and winking to me imploringly to do the same. When quiet had been restored at last I returned to the subject: "Are you in love with her?"

"Sure," he answered, without blushing. "As if a fellow could help it. If she let me kiss her little finger I should be the happiest man in the world."

"And if she let you kiss her cheek?" "I should go crazy."

"And if she let you kiss her lips?" "What's the use asking idle questions?"

"Would you like to kiss her neck?" "You ask me foolish questions."

"You are in love with her," I declared, reflectively

"I should say I was."

It was a unique sort of love, for he wanted me also to be in love with her

"If you are not in love with her you must have a heart of iron, or else your soul is dry as a raisin." With which he took to analyzing the prima donna's charms, going into raptures over her eyes, smile, gestures, manner of opening her mouth, and her swing and step as she walked over the stage

"No, I don't care for her," I replied

"You are a peculiar fellow."

"If I did fall in love," I said, by way of meeting him halfway, "I should choose Mrs. Segalovitch. She is a thousand times prettier than Mrs.

Klesmer."

"Tut, tut!"

Mrs. Segalovitch was certainly prettier than the prima donna, but she played unimportant parts, so the notion of one's falling in love with her seemed queer to Jake

That night I had an endless chain of dreams, in every one of which Madame Klesmer was the central figure. When I awoke in the morning I fell in love with her, and was overjoyed

When I saw Jake Mindels at dinner I said to him, with the air of one bringing glad news: "Do you know, I am in love with her?"

"With whom? With Mrs. Segalovitch?" "Oh, pshaw! I had forgotten all about her. I mean Madame Kiesmer," I said, self-consciously

Somehow, my love for the actress did not interfere with my longing thoughts of Matilda. I asked myself no questions

And so we went on loving jointly, Jake and I, the companionship of our passion apparently stimulating our romance as companionship at a meal stimulates the appetite of the diners. Each of us seemed to be infatuated with Madame Klesmer. Yet the community of this feeling, far from arousing mutual jealousy in us, seemed to strengthen the ties of our friendship

We would hum her songs in duet, recite her lines, compare notes on our dreams of happiness with her. One day we composed a love-letter to her, a long epistle full of Biblical and homespun poetry, which we copied jointly, his lines alternating with mine, and which we signed: "Your two lovelorn slaves whose hearts are panting for a look of your star-like eyes. Jacob and David." We mailed the letter without affixing any address

The next evening we were in the theater, and when she appeared on the stage and shot a glance to the gallery Jake nudged me violently

"But she does not know we are in the gallery," I argued. "She must think we are in the orchestra."

"Hearts are good guessers."

"Guessers nothing."

"S-sh! Let's listen."

Madame Klesmer was playing the part of a girl in a modern Russian town. She declaimed her lines, speaking like a prophetess in ancient Israel, and I liked it extremely. I was fully aware that it was unnatural for a girl in a modern Russian town to speak like a prophetess in ancient Israel, but that was just why I liked it. I thought it perfectly proper that people on the stage should not talk as they would off the stage. I thought that this unnatural speech of theirs was one of the principal things an audience paid for. The only actor who spoke like a human being was the comedian, and this, too, seemed to be perfectly proper, for a comedian was a fellow who did not take his art seriously, and so I thought that this natural talk of his was part of his fun-making. I thought it was something like a clown burlesquing the Old Testament by reading it, not in the ancient intonations of the synagogue, but in the plain, conversational accents of every-day life

During the intermission, in the course of our talk about Madame Klesmer, Jake said: "Do you know, Levinsky, I don't think you really love her."

"I love her as much as you, and more, too," I retorted

"How much do you love her? Would you walk from New York to Philadelphia if she wanted you to do so?"

"Why should she? What good would it do her?"

"But suppose she does want it?"

"How can I suppose such nonsense?" "Well, she might just want to see how much you love her."

"A nice test, that."

"Oh, well, she might just get that kind of notion. Women are liable to get any kind of notion, don't you know." *Typ . . .*

"Well, if Madame Klesmer got that kind of notion I should tell her to walk to Philadelphia herself."

"Then you don't love her."

"I love her as much as you do, but if she took it into her head to make a fool of me I should send her to the eighty devils."

He winced. "And you call that love, don't you?" he said, with a sneer in the corner of his pretty mouth. "As for me, I should walk to Boston, if she wanted me to."

"Even if she did not promise to let you kiss her?"

"Even if she did not."

"And if she did?"

"I should walk to Chicago."

"And if she promised to be your mistress?"

"Oh, what's the use talking that way?" he protested, blushing. "Aren't you shy! A regular bride-to-be, I declare." "Stop!" he said, coloring once again.

It dawned upon me that he was probably chaste, and, searching his face with a mocking look, I said: "I bet you you are still innocent." "Leave me alone, please," he retorted, softly

"I have hit it, then," I importuned him, with a great sense of my own superiority.

"Do let me alone, will you?"

"I just want you to tell me whether you are innocent or not."

"It's none of your business."

"Of course you are."

"And if I am? Is it a disgrace?" "Who says it is?"

I desisted. He became more attractive than ever to me

Nevertheless, I made repeated attempts to deprave him. His chastity bothered me. The idea of breaking it down became an irresistible temptation. I would ridicule him for a sissy, appeal to him in the name of his health, beg him as one does for a personal favor, all in vain

He spoke better English than I, with more ease, and in that pretty basso of his which I envied. He had never read Dickens or any other English author, but he was familiar with some subjects to which I was a stranger. He was well grounded in arithmetic, knew some geography, and now with a view of qualifying for the study of medicine, he was preparing, with the aid of a private teacher, for the Regents' examination in algebra, geometry, English composition, American and English history. I thought he did not study "deeply" enough, that he took more real interest in his collars and neckties, the shine of his shoes, or the hang of his trousers than he did in his algebra or history

By his cleanliness and tidiness he reminded me of Naphtali, which, indeed, had something to do with my attachment for him. My relations toward him echoed with the feelings I used to have for the reticent, omniscient boy of Abner's Court, and with the hoarse, studious young Talmudist with whom I would "famish in company." He had neither Naphtali's brains nor his individuality, yet I looked up to him and was somewhat under his influence.

I adopted many of the English phrases he was in the habit of using and tried to imitate his way of dressing. As a consequence, he would sometimes assume a patronizing tone with me, addressing me with a good-natured sneer which I liked in spite of myself

We made a compact to speak nothing but English, and, to a considerable extent, we kept it

· Madame Klesmer → actress → Jake devoted to, fancies himself in love w/ her
· D soon joins Jake's feelings for MK
· D finds J is chaste / repelled by it but J reminds him of N
· pact to speak English + only English

# CHAPTER V

A FEW weeks of employment were succeeded by another period of enforced idleness. I took up arithmetic, but reading was still a great passion with me. My mornings and forenoons during that slack season were mostly spent over Dickens or Thackeray

I now lived in a misshapen attic room which I rented of an Irish family in what was then a Gentile neighborhood. I had chosen that street for the English I had expected to hear around me. I had lived more than two months in that attic, and almost the only English I heard from my neighbors were the few words my landlady would say to me when I paid her my weekly rent.

Yet, somehow, the place seemed helpful to me, as though its very atmosphere exuded a feeling for the language I was so eager to master. I made all sorts of advances to the Irish family, all sorts of efforts to get into social relations with them, all to no purpose. Finally, one evening I had a real conversation with one of my landlady's sons. My window gave me trouble and he came up to put it in working order for me. We talked of his work and of mine. I told him of my plans about going to college. He was interested and I thought him charmingly courteous and sociable. He remained about an hour and a half in my room. When he had departed I was in high spirits. I seemed to feel the progress my English had made in that hour and a half

My bed was so placed that by lying prone, diagonally across it, my head toward the window and my feet suspended in the air, I would get excellent daylight. So this became my favorite posture when I read in the daytime.

Thus, lying on my stomach, with a novel under my eyes and the dictionary by my side, I would devour scores of pages. In a few weeks, often reading literally day and night, I read through Nicholas Nickleby and Vanity Fair.

Thackeray's masterpiece did not strike me as being in the same class with anything by Dickens. It seemed to me that anybody in command of bookish English ought to be able to turn out a work like Vanity Fair, where men and things were so simple and so natural that they impressed me like people and things I had known. Indeed, I had a lurking feeling that I, too, could do it, after a while at least. On the other hand, Nicholas Nickleby and Dombey and Son were so full of extraordinary characters, unexpected wit, outbursts of beautiful rhetoric, and other wonderful things, that their author appealed to me as something more than a human being. And yet deep down in my heart I enjoyed Thackeray more than I did Dickens, It was at the East Side branch of the Young Men's Hebrew Association that I obtained my books. It was a sort of university settlement in which educated men and women from up-town acted as "workers." The advice these would give me as to my reading, their kindly manner, their native English, and, last but not least, the flattering way in which they would speak of my intellectual aspirations, led me to spend many an hour in the place. The great thing was to hear these American-born people speak their native tongue and to have them hear me speak it. It was the same as in the case of the chat I had with the son of my Irish landlady. Every time I had occasion to spend five or ten minutes in their company I would seem to be conscious of a perceptible improvement in my English

Some days I would be so carried away by my reading that I never opened my arithmetic. At other times I would drift into an arithmetical mood and sit up all night doing problems

When I happened to be in raptures over some book I would pester Jake with lengthy accounts of it, dwelling on the chapters I had read last and trying to force my exaltation upon him. As a rule, he was bored, but sometimes he would become interested in the plot or in some romantic scene.

One evening, as we were discussing love in general, I said: "Love is the greatest thing in the world."

"Sure it is," he answered. "But if you love and are not loved in return it is nothing but agony."

"Even then it is sweet," I rejoined, reflectively, the image of Matilda before me.

"How can pain be sweet?"

"But it can."

"If you were really in love with Madame Klesmer you wouldn't think so

"I love her as much as you do."

"You are always saying you do, but you don't."

"Yes, I do." And suddenly lapsing into a confidential tone, I questioned him: "By the way, Jake, is this the first time you have ever been in love?"

"Why?"

"I just want to know. Is it?"

"What difference does it make? Have you ever been in love before?"

"What difference does that make? If you answer my question I shall answer yours." "Well, then, I have never been in love before."

"And I have."

He was intensely interested, and I confided my love story in him, which served to strengthen our friendship still further. When I concluded my narrative he said, thoughtfully: "Of course you don't love Madame Klesmer. I tell you what, Levinsky, you are still in love with Matilda."

I made no answer

"Anyhow, you don't love Madame Klesmer."

This time he said it without reproach. Once I was in love with somebody else I was excused.

The next "season" came around. I was a full-fledged helper now, and, according to the customary arrangement, I received thirty per cent. of what Joe received for my work. This brought me from twenty to twenty-five dollars a week, quite an overwhelming sum, according to my then standard of income and expenditures. I saved about fifteen dollars a week. I shall never forget the day when my capital reached the round figure of one hundred dollars. I was in a flutter. When I looked at the passers-by in the street I would say to myself, "These people have no idea that I am worth a hundred dollars."

Another thing I was ever conscious of was the fact that I had earned the hundred dollars by my work. There was a touch of solemnity in my mood, as though I had performed some feat of valor or rendered some great service to the community. I was impelled to convey this feeling to Jake, but when I attempted to put it into words it was somehow lost in a haze and what I said was something quite prosaic

"Guess how much I have in the savings-bank?" I began

"I haven't any idea. How much?"

"Just one hundred."

"Really?"

"Honest. But, then, what does it amount to, after all? Of course, it is pleasant to feel that you have a trade and that you know how to keep a dollar, don't you know."

So far from endearing me to the cloak trade, as might have been expected, the hundred dollars killed at one stroke all the interest I had taken in it.

It lent reality to my vision of college. Cloak-making was now nothing but a temporary round of dreary toil, an unavoidable stepping-stone to loftier occupations

Another year and I should be a fully developed mechanic, working on my own hook—that is, as the immediate employee of some manufacturer or contractor.

"I shall soon be earning forty or fifty dollars a week," I would muse. "At that rate I shall save up plenty of money in much less time than I expected.

I shall spend as little as possible and study as hard as possible."

The Regents' examinations were not exacting in those days. I could have prepared to qualify for admission to a school of medicine, law, or civil engineering in a very short time. But I aimed higher. I knew that many of the professional men on the East Side, and, indeed, everywhere else in the United States, were people of doubtful intellectual equipment, while I was ambitious to be a cultured man "in the European way." There was an odd confusion of ideas in my mind. On the one hand, I had a notion that to "become an American" was the only tangible form of becoming a man of culture (for did not I regard the most refined and learned European as a "greenhorn"?); on the other hand, the impression was deep in me that American education was a cheap machine-made product

# CHAPTER VI

COLLEGE! The sound was forever buzzing in my ear. The seven letters were forever floating before my eyes. They were a magic group, a magic whisper.

Matilda was to hear of me as a college man. What would she say? "What do you want City College for?" Jake would argue. "Why not take up medicine at once?"

"Once I am to be an educated man I want to be the genuine article," I would reply

Every bit of new knowledge I acquired aroused my enthusiasm. I was in a continuous turmoil of exultation

My plan of campaign was to keep working until I had saved up six hundred dollars, by which time I was to be eligible to admission to the junior class of the College of the City of New York, commonly known as City College, where tuition is free. The six hundred dollars was to last me two years—that is, till graduation, when I might take up medicine, engineering, or law. During the height of the cloak season I might find it possible to replenish my funds by an occasional few days at the sewing-machine, or else it ought not to be difficult to support myself by joining the army of private instructors who taught English to our workingmen at their homes

The image of the modest college building was constantly before me. More than once I went a considerable distance out of my way to pass the corner of Lexington Avenue and Twenty-third Street, where that edifice stood. I would pause and gaze at its red, ivy-clad walls, mysterious high windows, humble spires; I would stand watching the students on the campus and around the great doors, and go my way, with a heart full of reverence, envy, and hope, with a heart full of quiet ecstasy

It was not merely a place in which I was to fit myself for the battle of life, nor merely one in which I was going to acquire knowledge. It was a symbol of spiritual promotion as well. University-bred people were the real nobility of the world. A college diploma was a certificate of moral as well as intellectual aristocracy

My old religion had gradually fallen to pieces, and if its place was taken by something else, if there was something that appealed to the better man in me, to what was purest in my thoughts and most sacred in my emotions, that something was the red, church-like structure on the southeast corner of Lexington Avenue and Twenty-third Street

It was the synagogue of my new life. Nor is this merely a figure of speech: the building really appealed to me as a temple, as a House of Sanctity, as we call the ancient Temple of Jerusalem. At least that was the term I would fondly apply to it, years later, in my retrospective broodings upon the first few years of my life in America

I was impatiently awaiting the advent of the slack season, and when it came at last I applied myself exclusively to the study of subjects required for admission to college. To accelerate matters I engaged, as my instructor in mathematics and geography, the son of our tough-looking presser. I paid him twenty-five cents an hour.

My geography lessons were rapidly dispelling the haze that had enshrouded the universe from me. I beheld the globe hanging in space, a vast independent world and yet a mere speck among countless myriads of other worlds. Its rotations were so vivid in my mind that I seemed to hear it hum as it spun round and round its axis. The phenomena producing day and night and the four seasons were as real to me as the things that took place in my restaurant. The earth was being disclosed to my mental vision as a whole and in detail. Order was coming out of chaos. Continents, seas, islands, mountains, rivers, countries, were defining themselves out of a misty jumble of meaningless names. Light was breaking all around me. Life was becoming clearer. I was broadening out. I was overborne by a sense of my growing perspicacity

My keenest pleasure was to do geometrical problems, preferably such as contained puzzles in construction. On one occasion I sat up all night and far into the following day over a riddle of this kind.

It was about 2 o'clock when I dressed and went to lunch, which was also my breakfast. The problem was still unsolved. I hurried back home as soon as I had finished my meal, went at the problem again, and did not let go until it surrendered.

Odd as it may seem, I found a certain kind of similarity between the lure of these purely mental exercises and the appeal of music. In both cases I was piqued and harassed by a personified mystery. If a tune ran in my mind it would appear as though somebody, I knew not who, was saying something, I knew not what. What was he saying? Who was he? What had happened to him? Was he reciting some grievance, bemoaning some loss, or threatening vengeance? What was he nagging me about? Questions such as these would keep pecking at my heart, and this pain, this excruciating curiosity, I would call keen enjoyment

In like manner every difficult mathematical problem seemed to shelter some unknown fellow who took pleasure in teasing me and daring me to find him. It was the same mischievous fellow, in fact, who used to laugh in my face when I had a difficult bit of Talmud to unravel

"Why, geometry is even deeper than Talmud," I once exclaimed to Jake

"Do you think so?" he answered, indifferently

"I think an interesting geometrical problem is more delicious than the best piece of meat."

"Why don't you live on problems, then? Why spend money on dinners?"

"Smart boy, aren't you?"

"Is doing problems as sweet as being in love?" he demanded, with sheepish earnestness

"You are in love with Madame Klesmer. You ought to know."

He made no answer

On the day when I began these studies I had thirty-six dollars besides the hundred which I kept in the savings-bank. Of this I was now spending, including tuition fees, less than six dollars a week. Every time I changed a dollar my heart literally sank within me. Finally, when my cash was all gone, I borrowed some money of Joe, my "rabbi" at the art of cloak-making.

Breaking the round sum total of my savings-bank account was out of the question. Joe advanced me money more than cheerfully. He was glad to have me in his debt as a pledge of my continuing to work for him. His motive was obvious, and yet I went on borrowing of him rather than draw upon my bank account

One day it crossed my mind that it would be a handsome thing if I looked up Gitelson and paid him the ten dollars I owed him. It was sweet to picture myself telling him how much his ten dollars had done and was going to do for me. I was impatient to call on him, and so I borrowed ten dollars of Joe and betook myself to the factory where I had visited Gitelson several times before. As he was a sample-maker, his work knew no seasons. When I called at that factory I found that he had given up his job there, that he had married and established a small custom-tailor shop somewhere up-town, nobody seemed to know where. Joe had not even heard of his marriage. Meanwhile, my enthusiasm for paying him his debt was gone, and I was rather glad that I had not found him

It was the middle of July. The great "winter season" was developing. I felt perfectly competent to make a whole garment unaided. It was doubtful, however, whether I should be readily accepted as an independent mechanic in the shop where I was employed now and where one was in the habit of regarding me as a mere apprentice. So I was determined to seek employment elsewhere. Joe was suspicious. Not that I betrayed my plans in any way. He took them for granted. And so he visited me every day, on all sorts of pretexts, dined me and wined me (if the phrase may be applied to a soda-water dinner), and watched my every step

Finally I wearied of it all, and one afternoon, as we were seated in the restaurant, I picked a quarrel with him

"I don't want your dinners," I burst out, "and I don't want to be watched by you as if I were a recruit in the Russian army and you were my 'little uncle.' I'll pay you what I owe you and leave me alone."

"As if I were uneasy about those few dollars!" he said, ingratiatingly

"I know you are not. That's just it."

He took fire. "What am I after, then? You think I get rich on your work, don't you?"

Our altercation waxed violent. At one point he was about to lapse into a conciliatory tone again, but his dignity prevailed

"I would not keep you if you begged me," he declared. "I hate to deal with an ingrate. But I want my money at once." "I shall pay it to you when work begins."

"No, sirrah. I want it at once." An ugly scene followed. He seized me by my coat lapels and threatened to have me arrested.

Finally the restaurant-keeper and Gussie, the homely finisher girl whom we all respected, made peace between us, and things were arranged more or less amicably

I obtained employment in an "inside" place, a factory owned by twin brothers named Manheimer

I was in high feather. My sense of advancement and independence reminded me of the days when I had just been graduated from the Talmudic Academy and went on studying as an "independent scholar." I had not, however, begun to work in my new place when a general strike of the trade was declared

- plan to save $600 for college / enter Junior class at City College
- wanted to learn more / more
  └ paid a person to give him lessons in geography ...etc
- began borrowing money from Joe
  └ Joe held it over his head
- determined to pay ⑥ back, but didn't
  └ determined to get another job
      ↓
      got one in a factory owned by Manheimer twin brothers.

# CHAPTER VII

THE Cloak-makers' Union had been a weak, insignificant organization, but at the call for a general strike it suddenly burst into life. There was a great rush for membership cards. Everybody seemed to be enthusiastic, full of fight. To me, however, the strike was a sheer calamity. I laid it all to my own hard luck. It seemed as though the trouble had been devised for the express purpose of preventing me from being promoted to full pay; for the express purpose of upsetting my financial calculations in connection with my college plans. Everybody was saying that prices were outrageously low, that the manufacturers were taking advantage of the weakness of the union, and that they must be brought to terms. All this was lost upon me. The question of prices did not interest me, because the wages I was going to receive were by far the highest I had ever been paid. But the main thing was that I looked upon the whole business of making cloaks as a temporary occupation.

My mind was full of my books and my college dreams. All I wanted was to start the "season" as soon as possible, to save up the expected sum, and to reach the next period of freedom from physical toil, when I should be able to spend day and night on my studies again. But going to work as a strike-breaker was out of the question. A new kind of Public Opinion had suddenly sprung up among the cloak-makers: a man who did not belong to the union was a traitor, worse than an apostate, worse than the worst of criminals

And so, feeling like a school-boy in Antomir when he is made to furnish the very rod with which he is to be chastised, I went to the headquarters of the union, paid my initiation fee, and became a member. It was on a Friday afternoon. The secretaries of the organization were seated at a long table in the basement of a meeting-room building on Rivington Street. The basement and the street outside were swarming with cloak-makers. A number of mass meetings had been arranged to take place in several halls, with well-known Socialists for speakers, but I had not even the curiosity to attend them.

When some of my shopmates reproached me for my indifference I said, sullenly: "I've joined the union. What more do you want?"

One of them, a Talmudist like myself, spoke of capital and labor, of the injustice of the existing economic order. He had recently, through the strike, been converted to Socialism. He made a fiery appeal to me. He spoke with the exaltation of a new proselyte. But his words fell on deaf ears. I had no mind for anything but my college studies

"Do you think it right that millions of people should toil and live in misery so that a number of idlers might roll in luxury?" he pleaded

"I haven't made the world, nor can I mend it," was my retort

The manufacturers yielded almost every point. The "season" began with a rush

My pay-envelope for the first week contained thirty-two dollars and some cents. I knew the union price, of course, and I had figured out the sum before I received it, yet when I beheld the two figures on the envelope the blood surged to my head. Thirty-two dollars! Why, that meant sixty-four rubles! I was tempted to write Naphtali about it

The next week brought me an even fatter envelope. I worked sixteen hours a day. Reading and studying had to be suspended till October. I lived on five dollars a week. My savings, and with them my sense of my own importance in the world, grew apace. As there was no time to go to the savings-bank, I had to carry what I deemed a great sum on my person (in a money-belt that I had improvised for the purpose). This was a constant source of anxiety as well as of joy. No matter how absorbed I might have been in my work or in thought, the consciousness of having that wad of paper money with me was never wholly absent from my mind. It loomed as a badge of omnipotence. I felt in the presence of Luck, which was a living spirit, a goddess. I was mostly grave. The frivolities of the other men in the factory seemed so fatuous, so revolting. A great sense of security and self-confidence swelled my heart. When I walked through the American streets I would feel at home in them, far more so than I had ever felt before. At the same time danger was constantly hovering about me-the danger of the street crowds seizing that magic wad from me.

The image of the college building loomed as a bride-elect of mine. But that, somehow, did not seem to have anything to do with my money-belt, as though I expected to go to college without encroaching upon my savings—a case of eating the cake and having it

The cloak makers were so busy they had no time to attend meetings, and being little accustomed to method and discipline, they suffered their organization to melt away. By the time the "season" came to a close the union was scarcely stronger than it had been before the strike. As there was no work now, and no prices to fix, one did not miss its protection

The number of men employed in the trade in those years did not exceed seven thousand. The industry was still in its infancy

I resumed my studies with a passion amounting to a frenzy. I would lay in a supply of coarse rye bread, cheese, and salmon to last me two or even three days, and never leave my lair during that length of time. I dined at the Delancey Street restaurant every third or fourth day, and did not go to the theater unless Jake was particularly insistent. But then I religiously attended Felix Adler's ethical-culture lectures, at Chickering Hall, on Sunday mornings. I valued them for their English rather than for anything else, but their spirit, reinforced by the effect of organ music and the general atmosphere of the place, would send my soul soaring. These gatherings and my prospective alma mater appealed to me as being of the same order of things, of the same world of refined ways, new thoughts, noble interests

If I came across a street faker and he spoke with a foreign accent I would pass on; if, however, his English struck me as that of a "real American," I would pause and listen to his "lecture," sometimes for more than an hour.

People who were born to speak English were superior beings. Even among fallen women I would seek those who were real Americans

# CHAPTER VIII

I WAS reading Pendennis. The prospect of returning to work was a hideous vision. The high wages in store for me had lost their magnetism. I often wondered whether I might not be able to secure some pupils in English or Hebrew, and drop cloak-making at once. I dreamed of enlisting the interest of a certain Maecenas, a German-American Jew who financed many a struggling college student of the Ghetto. Thoughts of a "college match" would flash through my mind—that is, of becoming engaged to some girl who earned good wages and was willing to support me through college. This form of matrimonial arrangement, which has been mentioned in an earlier chapter, is not uncommon among our immigrants. Alliances of this sort naturally tend to widen the intellectual chasm between the two parties to the contract, and often result in some of the tragedies or comedies that fill the swift-flowing life of American Ghettos. But the ambition to be the wife of a doctor, lawyer, or dentist is too strong in some of our working-girls to be quenched by the dangers involved

One of the young women I had in mind was Gussie, the cloak-finisher mentioned above, who saved for a marriage portion too energetically to make a marriage. She was a good girl, and no fool, either, and I thought to myself that she would make me a good wife, even if she was plain and had a washed-out appearance and was none too young. I was too passionately in love with my prospective alma mater to care whether I could love my fiancée or not

"I have a fellow for you," I said to Gussie, under the guise of pleasantry, meeting her in the street one day. "Something fine."

"Who is it—yourself?" she asked, quickly

"You have guessed it right."

"Have I? Then tell your fellow to go to all the black devils."

"Why?"

"Because."

"If I could go to college—"      *smart girl.*

"You want me to pay your bills, do you?"

"Wouldn't you like to be the wife of a doctor? You would take rides in my carriage—"

"You mean the other way around: you would ride in my carnage and I should have to start a breach-of-promise case against 'Dr. Levinsky.' You'll have to look for a bigger fool than I," she concluded, with a smile

It was an attractive smile, full of good nature and common sense. A smile of this kind often makes a homely face pretty. Gussie's did not. The light it shed only served to publish her ugliness. But I did not care. The infatuation I had brought with me from Antomir had not yet completely faded out, anyhow. And so I harbored vague thoughts that some day, when I saw fit to press my suit, Gussie might yield

I was getting impatient. The idea of having to go back to work became more hateful to me every day. I was in despair. Finally I decided to consider my career as a cloak-maker closed; to cut my expenses to the veriest minimum, to live on my savings, look for some source of income that would not interfere with my studies, take the college examination as soon as I was ready for it, and let the future take care of itself

In the heart of the Jewish neighborhood I found an attic for half of what I was paying the Irish family. Moreover, it was a neighborhood where everything was cheaper than in any other part of New York, the only one in which it was possible for a man to have a "room" to himself and live on four dollars a week. So I moved to that attic, a step for which, as I now think of it, I cannot but be thankful to fate, for it brought me in touch with a quaint, simple man who is my warm friend to this day, perhaps the dearest friend I have had in America

The house was a rickety, two-story frame structure, the smallest and oldest-looking on the block. Its ground floor was used as a tailoring shop by the landlord himself, a white-headed giant of a man whom I cannot recall otherwise than as smiling wistfully and sighing. His name was Esrah Nodelman. His wife, who was a dwarf beside him, ruled him with an iron hand

185

Mrs. Nodelman gave me breakfasts, and I soon felt like one of the family.

She was a veritable chatter-box, her great topic of conversation being her son Meyer, upon whom she doted, and his American-born wife, whose name she scarcely ever uttered without a malediction. She told me how she, Meyer's mother, her sister, and a niece had turned out their pockets and pawned their jewelry to help Meyer start in business as a clothing-manufacturer

"He's now worth a hundred thousand dollars—may no evil eye hit him," she said. "He's a good fellow, a lump of gold. If God had given him a better wife (may the plague carry off the one he has) he would be all right. She has a meat-ball for a face, the face of a murderess. She always was a murderess, but since Meyer became a manufacturer there is no talking to her at all. The airs she is giving herself! And all because she was born in America, the frog that she is."

I soon made Meyer's acquaintance. He was a dark man of forty, with Oriental sadness in his eyes. To lend his face capitalistic dignity he had recently grown a pair of side-whiskers, but one day, a week or two after I met him, he saw a circus poster of "Jo Jo, the human dog," and then he hastened to discard them

"I don't want to look like a man-dog," he explained, gaily, to his mother, who was unpleasantly surprised by the change.

"Man-dog nothing," she protested, addressing herself to me. "He was as handsome as gold in those whiskers. He looked like a regular monarch in them." And then to him: "I suppose it was that treasure of a wife you have who told you to have them taken off. It's a lucky thing she does not order you to have your foolish head taken off."

"You better shut up, mamma," he said, sternly. And she did

He called to see his parents quite frequently, sometimes with some of his children, but never with his wife, at least not while I lived there.

Crassly illiterate save for his ability to read some Hebrew, without knowing the meaning of the words, he enjoyed a considerable degree of native intellectual alertness, and in his crude, untutored way was a thinker

One evening he took to quizzing me on my plans, partly in Yiddish and partly in broken English, which he uttered with a strong Cockney accent, a relic of the several years he had spent in London.

"And what will you do after you finish (he pronounced it "fiendish") college?" he inquired, with a touch of derision

"I shall take up some higher things," I rejoined, reluctantly

"And what do you call 'higher things'?" he pursued in his quizzical, browbeating way. "Are you going to be a philosopher?"

"Yes, I shall be a doctor of philosophy," I answered, frostily

"What's that? You want to be both a doctor and a philosopher? But you know the saying, 'Many trades—few blessings.'"

"I am not going to be a doctor and a philosopher, but a doctor of philosophy," I said, with a sneer

"And how much will you make?"

"Oh, let him alone, Meyer," his mother intervened. "He is an educated fellow, and he doesn't care for money at all."

"Doesn't care for money, eh?" the younger Nodelman jeered

"Do you think money is really everything?" I shot back. "One might be able to find a thing or two which could not be bought with it."

"Not even at Ridley's," [note] he jested, but he was manifestly beginning to resent my attitude and to take our passage at arms rather seriously

"Not even at Ridley's. You can't get brains there, can you?"

"Well, I never learned to write, but I have a learned fellow in my office.

He's chuck full of learning and that sort of thing. Yet who is working for whom—I for him or he for me? So much for education—for the stuff that's in a man's head. And now let's take charity—the stuff that's in a man's heart.

I don't care what you say, but of what use is a good heart unless he has some jinglers [note] to go with it? You can't shove your hand into your heart and pull out a few dollars for a poor friend, can you? You can help him out of your pocket, though—that is, provided it is not empty."

My bewigged little landlady was feasting her eyes on her son

Meyer went on with his argument: "What is a man without capital? Nothing! Nobody cares for him. He is like a beast. A beast can't talk, and he can't.

'Money talks,' as the Americans say."

His words and manner put me in a socialist mood. He was hateful to me. I listened in morose silence. He felt piqued, and he wilted. The ginger went out of his voice. My taciturnity continued, until, gradually, he edged over to my side of the controversy, taking up the cudgels for education and spiritual excellence with the same force with which he had a short while ago tried to set forth their futility

"Of course it's nice to be educated," he said. "A man without writing is just like a deaf mute. What's the difference? The man who can't write has speech in his mouth, but he is dumb with his fingers, while the deaf mute he can't talk with his mouth, but he can do so with his fingers. Both should be pitied. I do like education. Of course I do. Don't I send my boy to college? I am an ignorant boor myself, because my father was poor, but my children shall have all the wisdom they can pile in. We Jews have too many enemies in the world. Everybody is ready to shed our blood. So where would we be if many of our people were not among the wisest of the wise? Why, they would just crush us like so many flies. When I see an educated Jew I say to myself, 'That's it!'"

When he heard of my ambition to give lessons he said: "I tell you what. I'll be your first pupil. I mean it." he added, seriously.

My heart gave a leap. "Very well. I'll try my best," I replied

"Mind you, I don't want to be a philosopher. I just want you to fix me up in reading, writing, and figuring a little bit. That's all. You don't think it's too late, do you?"

"Too late!" I chuckled, hysterically. "Why?"

"I can sign or indorse a check, and, thank God, for a good few dollars, too—but when it comes to fixing in the stuffing, there is trouble. I know how to write the figures, but not the words. I can write almost any number.

If I was worth all the money I can put down in figures I should be richer than Vanderbilt."

To insure secrecy I was to give him his lessons in my attic room

"I don't want my kids to know their pa is learning like a little boy, don't you know," he explained. "American kids have not much respect for their fathers, anyhow."

As a preliminary to his initial lesson Nodelman offered to show me what he could do. When I brought pen and ink and some paper he cleared his throat, screwed up a solemn mien, and took hold of the pen. In trying to shake off some of the ink he sent splashes all over the table. At last he proceeded to write his name. He handled the pen as he would a pitchfork. It was quite a laborious proceeding, and his first attempt was a fizzle, for he reached the end of the paper before he finished the "in" in Nodelman. He tried again, and this time he was successful, but it was three minutes before the task was completed. It left him panting and wiping his ink-stained fingers on his hair

"A man who has to work as hard as that over his signature has no business to be seen among decent people," he said, with sincere disgust. "I ought to be a horse-driver, not a manufacturer."

So speaking, he submitted his signature for my inspection, without, however, letting go of the sheet

"Tell me how rotten it is," he said, bashfully

When I protested that it was not "rotten" at all he grunted something to the effect that once I was to instruct him he would expect to pay me, not for empty compliments, but for the truth. At this he lighted a match and applied it to the sheet of paper containing his signature

"A signature is no joke," he explained, as he watched it burn. "Put a few words and some figures on top of it and it is a note, as good as cash. When a fellow is a beggar he has nothing to fear, but when he is in business he had better be careful."

When he asked me how much I was going to charge him and I said twenty-five cents an hour, he smiled

"I'll pay you more than that. You just try your best for me, will you?"

At the end of the first week he handed me two dollars for three lessons

I was the happiest man in New York that day. If I had had to choose between earning ten dollars a week in tuition fees and a hundred dollars as wages or profits I should, without the slightest hesitation, have decided in favor of the ten dollars, and now, behold! that coveted source of income seemed nearer at hand than I had dared forecast. Once a start had been made, I might expect to procure other pupils, even if they could not afford to pay so lavish a price as two dollars for three lessons

But alas! My happiness was not to last long.

I was giving Nodelman his fifth lesson. We were spelling out some syllables in a First Reader. Presently he grew absent-minded and then, suddenly pushing the school-book from him, said: "Too late! Too late! Those black little dots won't get through my forehead.

It has grown too hard for them, I suppose."

I attempted to reassure him, but in vain

When the next cloak season came I slunk back to work. I felt degraded. But I earned high wages and my good spirits soon returned. I firmly made up my mind, come what might, to take the college-entrance examination the very next fall. I expected to have four hundred dollars by then, but I was determined to enter college even if I had much less. "I sha'n't starve," I said to myself. "And, if I don't get enough to eat, hunger is nothing new to me."

The very firmness of my purpose was a source of encouragement and joy [note: Ridley's]: A well-known department store in those days [note: jingler]: Coin, money

• contemplating marriage
  └ pos. Gussie,
  moved into an apartment
  └ Mr. Nodelman / his wife
  └ teaching him to write / to sign

# BOOK VIII

# THE DESTRUCTION OF MY TEMPLE

# CHAPTER I

AN unimportant accident, a mere trifle, suddenly gave a new turn to the trend of events changing the character of my whole life.

It was the middle of April. The spring season was over, but Manheimer Brothers, the firm by which I was employed, had received heavy duplicate orders for silk coats, and, considering the time of the year, we were unusually busy. One day, at the lunch hour, as I was opening a small bottle of milk, the bottle slipped out of my hand and its contents were spilled over the floor and some silk coats

Jeff Manheimer, one of the twins, happened to be near me at the moment, and a disagreeable scene followed. But first a word or two about Jeff Manheimer

He was the "inside man" of the firm, having charge of the mechanical end of the business as well as of the offices. He was of German parentage, but of American birth. Bald-headed as a melon and with a tendency to corpulence, he had the back of a man of forty-five and the front of a man of twenty-five.

He was a vivacious fellow, one of those who are indefatigable in abortive attempts at being witty, one of his favorite puns being that we "Russians were not rushin' at all," that we were a "slow lot." Altogether he treated us as an inferior race, often lecturing us upon our lack of manners

I detested him

When he saw me drop the bottle of milk he flew into a rage

"Eh!" he shouted, "did you think this was a kitchen? Can't you take better care of things?" As he saw me crouching and wiping the floor and the coats with my handkerchief he added: "You might as well take those coats home. The price will be charged against you.

That 'll make you remember that this is not a barn, but a factory. Where were you brought up? Among Indians?"

Some of my shopmates tittered obsequiously, which encouraged Manheimer to further sarcasm.

"Why, he doesn't even know how to handle a bottle of milk. Did you ever see such a lobster?"

At this there was an explosion of merriment.

"A lobster!" one of the tailors repeated, relishingly

I could have murdered him as well as Manheimer.

My head was swimming. I was about to say something insulting to my employer, to get up and leave the place demonstratively. But I said to myself that I should soon be through with this kind of life for good, and I held myself in leash.

Two or three minutes later I sat at a machine, eating my milkless lunch. I was trying to forget the incident, trying to think of something else, but in vain. Manheimer's derision, especially the word "lobster," was ringing in my ear.

He passed out of the shop, but ten or fifteen minutes later he came back, and as I saw him walk down the aisle I became breathless with hate. The word "lobster" was buzzing in my brain amid vague, helpless visions of revenge

Presently my eye fell upon Ansel Chaikin, the designer, and a strange thought flashed upon me.

He was a Russian, like myself. He was an ignorant tailor, as illiterate as Meyer Nodelman, but a born artist in his line. It was largely to his skill that the firm, which was doing exceedingly well, owed the beginning of its success. It was the common talk among the "hands" of the factory that his Americanized copies of French models had found special favor with the buyer of a certain large department store and that this alone gave the house a considerable volume of business. Jeff Manheimer, who superintended the work, was a commonplace man, with more method and system than taste or initiative.

Chaikin was the heart and the actual master of the establishment. Yet all this really wonderful designer received was forty-five dollars a week. He knew his value, and he saw that the two brothers were rapidly getting rich, but he was a quiet man, unaggressive and unassuming, and very likely he had not the courage to ask for a raise

∟passive

As I now looked at him, with my heart full of rancor for Manheimer, I exclaimed to myself, "What a fool!"

He appeared to me in a new light, as the willing victim of downright robbery. It seemed obvious that the Manheimers could not do without him, that he was in a position to dictate terms to them, even to make them accept him as a third partner. And once the matter had presented itself to me in that light it somehow began to vex me. It got on my nerves, as though it were an affair of my own. I complimented myself upon my keen sense of justice, but in reality this was my name for my disgust with Chaikin's passivity and for the annoyance and the burning ill-will which the rapid ascent of the firm aroused in me. I begrudged them—or, rather, Jeff—the money they were making through his efficiency

"The idiot!" I soliloquized. "He ought to start on his own hook with some smart business man for a partner. Let Jeff try to do without that 'lobster' of a Russian."

The idea took a peculiar hold upon my imagination. I could not look at Ansel Chaikin, or think of him, without picturing him leaving the Manheimers in a lurch and becoming a fatal competitor of theirs. I beheld their downfall. I gloated over it

But Chaikin lacked gumption and enterprise. What he needed was an able partner, some man of brains and force. And so, unbeknown to Chaikin, the notion was shaping itself in my mind of becoming his manufacturing partner.

thought of Meyer Nodelman's humble beginnings and of the three hundred-odd dollars I had in my savings-bank whispered encouragement into my ear. I had heard of people who went into manufacturing with even less than that sum.

Moreover, it was reasonable to expect that Chaikin had laid up some money of his own. Our precarious life among unfriendly nations has made a thrifty people of us, and for a man like Chaikin forty-five dollars a week, every week in the year, meant superabundance

The Manheimers were relegated to the background. It was no longer a mere matter of punishing Jeff. It was a much greater thing.

I visioned myself a rich man, of course, but that was merely a detail. What really hypnotized me was the venture of the thing. It was a great, daring game of life

I tried to reconcile this new dream of mine with my college projects. I was again performing the trick of eating the cake and having it. I would picture myself building up a great cloak business and somehow contriving, at the same time, to go to college

The new scheme was scarcely ever absent from my mind. I would ponder it over my work and during my meals. It would visit me in my sleep in a thousand grotesque forms. Chaikin became the center of the universe. I was continually eying him, listening for his voice, scrutinizing his look, his gestures, his clothes

He was an insignificant-looking man of thirty-two, with almost a cadaverous face and a very prominent Adam's apple. He was not a prepossessing man by any means, but his bluish eyes had a charming look, of boy-like dreaminess, and his smile was even more child-like than his look. He was dressed with scrupulous neatness and rather pretentiously, as behooved his occupation, but all this would scarcely have prevented one from telling him for a tailor from some poor town in Russia

Now and then my project struck me as absurd. For Chaikin was in the foremost ranks of a trade in which I was one of the ruck. Should he conceive the notion of going into business on his own account, he would have no difficulty in forming a partnership with considerable capital. Why, then, should he take heed of a piteous schemer of my caliber? But a few minutes later I would see the matter in another light

• spilled milk on coats, JM angry, D hates his employer
• advises a scheme of opening his own cloak-shop w/ a passive man named Ansel Chaikin

# CHAPTER II

ONE Sunday morning in the latter part of May I betook myself to a certain block of new tenement-houses in the neighborhood of East 110th Street and Central Park, then the new quarter of the more prosperous Russian Jews.

Chaikin had recently moved into one of these houses, and it was to call on him that I had made my way from down-town. I found him in the dining-room, playing on an accordion, while his wife, who had answered my knock at the door, was busy in the kitchen

He scarcely knew me. To pave the way to the object of my visit I began by inquiring about designing lessons. As teaching was not in his line, we soon passed to other topics related to the cloak trade. I found him a poor talker and a very uninteresting companion. He answered mostly in monosyllables, or with mute gestures, often accompanied by his child-like grin or by a perplexed stare of his bluish eyes

Gradually I gave the conversation a more personal turn. When, somewhat flushed, I finally hinted at my plan, he shrank with an air of confusion

At this juncture his wife made her appearance, followed by her eight-year-old boy. Chaikin looked relieved

"I hear you are talking business," she said, summarily taking possession of the situation. "What is it all about?"

Completely taken aback by her domineering manner, I sought escape in embarrassed banter.

"You have scared me so," I said, "I can't speak. I'll tell you everything.

That's just what brings me here. Only let me first catch my breath and take a look at your stalwart little man of a boy."

Her grave face relaxed into an involuntary smile

What struck me most in her was the startling resemblance she bore to her husband. The two looked like brother and sister rather than like husband and wife

"You must be relatives," I observed, for something pleasant to say, and put my foot in it

"Not at all," she replied, with a frown

To win back her good graces I proceeded to examine Maxie, her boy, in spelling. The stratagem had the desired effect

We got down to business again. When she heard my plan she paused to survey me. I felt a sinking at the heart. I interpreted her searching look as saying, "The nerve this snoozer has!" But I was mistaken. Her pinched, sallow face grew tense with excitement, and she said, with coy eagerness: "How can we tell if your plan amounts to anything? If you gave us an idea of how much you could put up—"

"It would not require a million," I hazarded

"A million! Who talks of millions! Still, it would take a good deal of capital to start a factory that should be something like."

"There'll be no trouble about money," I parried, fighting shy of the more imposing term "capital," which made my paltry three hundred still paltrier

"There is money and money," she answered, with furtive glances at me. "A nickel is also money."

"I am not speaking of nickels, of course."

"I should say not. It's a matter of many thousands of dollars."

I was dumfounded, but instantly rallied. "Of course," I assented. "At the same time it depends on many things."

"Still, you ought to give us some idea how much you could put in. Is it—is it, say, fifteen thousand?"

That she should not deem it unnatural for a young man of my station to be able to raise a sum of this size was partly due to her utter lack of experience and partly to an impression prevalent among people of her class that "nothing is impossible in the land of Columbus."

I pretended to grow thoughtful, with an effect of making computations. I even produced a piece of paper and a pencil and indulged in some sham figuring. At last I said: "Well, I can't as yet tell you exactly how much. As I have said, it depends on certain things, but it'll be all right. Besides, money is really not the most important part in a scheme of this kind. A man of brains and a hustler will make a lot of money, while a fool will lose a lot. There are others who want to go into business with me. Only I know Mr. Chaikin is an honest man, and that's what I value more than anything else. I hate to take up with people of whom I can't be sure, don't you know—"

"You forget the main thing," she could not forbear to break in. "Mr. Chaikin is the best designer in New York."

"Everybody knows that," I conceded, deeming it best to flatter her vanity.

"That's just what makes it ridiculous that he should work for others, make other people rich instead of trying to do something for himself. I have sóme plans by which the two of us—Mr. Chaikin taking charge of the manufacturing and I of the business outside— would do wonders. We would simply do wonders.

There is another fine designer who is anxious to form a partnership with me, but I said to myself, 'I must first see if I could not get Mr. Chaikin interested.'"

Mrs. Chaikin tried to guess who that other designer was, but I pleaded, mysteriously, certain circumstances that placed the seal of discretion on my lips

"I won't tell anybody," she assured me, in a flutter of curiosity

"I know you won't, but I can't. Honest."

"But, I tell you, I won't say a word to anybody. Strike me dumb if I do!"

"I can't, Mrs. Chaikin," I besought her

"Don't bother," her husband put in, good-naturedly. "A woman will be a woman."

I went on to describe the "wonders" that the firm of Chaikin & Levinsky would do. Mrs. Chaikin's eyes glittered. I held her spellbound. Her husband, who had hitherto been a passive listener, as if the matter under discussion was one in which he was not concerned, began to show signs of interest. It was the longest and most eloquent speech I had ever had occasion to deliver.

It seemed to carry conviction

Children often act as a barometer of their mother's moods. So when I had finished and little Maxie slipped up close to me and tactily invited me to fondle him I knew that I had made a favorable impression on his mother

I was detained for dinner. I played with Maxie, gave him problems in arithmetic, went into ecstasies over his "cuteness." I had a feeling that the way to Mrs. Chaikin's heart was through Maxie, but I took good care not to over-play my part

We are all actors, more or less. The question is only what our aim is, and whether we are capable of a "convincing personation." At the time I conceived my financial scheme I knew enough of human motive to be aware of this

- met w/ Mr. Chaikin in his home
- wife loved the idea, has a son Maxie
- scheme seems to be working
  └ Chaikin & Levinsky

# CHAPTER III

IT was a sultry, sweltering July afternoon in May, one of those escapades of the New York climate when the population finds itself in the grip of midsummer discomforts without having had time to get seasoned to them. I went into the Park. I had come away from the Chaikins' under the impression that if I could raise two or three thousand dollars I might be able, by means of perseverance and diplomacy, to achieve my purpose. But I might as well have set myself to raise two or three millions

I thought of Meyer Nodelman, of Mr. Even and his wealthy son-in-law, of Maximum Max. But the idea of approaching them with my venture could not be taken seriously. The images of Gitelson and of Gussie crossed my mind almost simultaneously. I rejected them both. Gitelson and I might, perhaps, start manufacturing on a small scale, leaving Chaikin out. But Chaikin was the very soul of my project. Without him there was no life to it. Besides, where was he, Gitelson? Was it worth while hunting for him? As for Gussie, the notion of marrying her for her money seemed a joke, even if she were better-looking and younger. That her dower was anywhere near three thousand dollars was exceedingly doubtful. However, the image of her washed-out face would not leave my mind. Her hoarding might amount to over one thousand, and in my despair the sum was tempting. "She is a good girl, the best of all I know," I defended myself before the "Good Spirit" in me.

"Also she is a most sensible girl. Just the kind of wife a business man needs." In addition I urged the time-honored theory that a homely wife is less likely to flirt with other men and to neglect her duties than a good-looking one.

I took the car down-town and made my way to Gussie's lodgings that very afternoon. I did so before I had made up my mind that I was prepared to marry her. "I'll call on her, anyhow,"

I decided. "Then we shall see. There can be no harm in speaking to her."

I was impelled by the adventure of it more than by anything else

In spite of the unbearable heat, I almost felt sure that I should find her at home. Going out of a Sunday required presentable clothes, which she did not possess. She was saving for her dower with her usual intensity

I was not mistaken. I found her on the stoop in a crowd of women and children

"I must speak to you, Gussie," I said, as she descended to the sidewalk to meet me. "Let's go somewhere. I have something very important I want to say to you."

"Is it again something about your studying to be a smart man at my expense?" she asked, rather good-naturedly

"No, no. Not at all. It's something altogether different, Gussie."

The nervous emphasis with which I said it piqued her interest. Without going up-stairs for her hat she took me to the Grand Street dock, not many blocks away. The best spots were already engaged, but we found one that suited our purpose better than the water edge would have done. It was a secluded nook where I could give the rein to my eloquence

I told her of my talk with the Chaikins, omitting names, but inventing details and bits of "local color" calculated to appeal to my listener's imagination and business sense. She followed my story with an air of stiff aloofness, but this only added fuel to the fervor with which I depicted the opportunity before me

"So you have thrown that college of yours out of your mind, haven't you?" she said in a dry, non-committal way

I felt the color mounting to my face. "Well, not entirely," I answered

"Not entirely?"

"I mean—Well, anyhow, what do they do at college? They read books. Can't I read them at home? One can find time for everything." Returning to my new project, I said: "It's a great chance, Gussie. It would be an awful thing if I had to let it slip out of my hand."

That what I wanted was her dower (with herself as an unavoidable appendage) went without saying. It was implied, as a matter of course

"How much would your great designer want you to invest?" she asked, with an air of one guided by mere curiosity, and with a touch of irony to boot

"A couple of thousand dollars might do, I suppose."

"A couple of thousand!" she said, lukewarmly. "Tell your great designer he is riding too high a horse."

"Still, in order to start a decent business—" I said, throwing a covert glance at her

"Cloak-factories have been started with a good deal less," she snapped back

"On Division Street, perhaps."

"And what do you fellows expect to do—start on Broadway?"

"Well, it takes some money to get started even on Division Street."

"Not two thousand. It has been done for a good deal less."

"I know; but still—I am sure a fellow must have some money

"It depends on what you call 'some.'" It was the same kind of fencing contest as that which I had had with Mrs.

Chaikin. I was sounding Gussie's purse as the designer's wife had mine.

Finally she took me in hand for a severe cross-examination. She was obviously interested. I contradicted myself in some minor points, but, upon the whole, I stood the test well

"If it is all as you say," she finally declared, "there seems to be something in it."

"Gussie "I said, tremulously, "there is a great chance for us—"

"Wait," she interrupted me, suddenly bethinking herself of a new point. "If he is as great a designer as you say he is, and he works for a big firm, how is it, then, that he can't find a partner with big money?"

"He could, any number of them, but he has confidence in me. He says he would much rather start with me on two thousand than with somebody else on twenty.

He thinks I should make an excellent business man, and that between the two of us we should make a great success of it. Money is nothing—so he says—money can be made, but with a fool of an outside man even more than twenty thousand dollars might go up in smoke." "That's so," Gussie assented, musingly. There was a pause

"Well, Gussie?" I mustered courage to demand

"You don't want me to give you an answer right off, do you? Things like that are not decided in a hurry."

We went on to discuss the project and some indifferent topics. It was rapidly growing dark and cool. Looming through the thickening dusk, somewhat diagonally across the dock from us, was the figure of a young fellow with his head reclining on the shoulder of a young woman. A little further off and nearer to the water I could discern a white shirt-waist in the embrace of a dark coat. A song made itself heard. It was "After the Ball is Over," one of the sentimental songs of that day. "Tara-ra-boom-de-aye" followed, a tune usually full of joyous snap and go, but now performed in a subdued, brooding tempo, tinged with sadness. It rang in a girlish soprano, the rest of the crowd listening silently. By this time the gloom was so dense that the majority of us could not see the singer, which enhanced the mystery of her melody and the charm of her young voice. Presently other voices joined in, all in the same meditative, somewhat doleful rhythm. Gayer strains would have sounded sacrilegiously out of tune with the darkling glint of the river, with the mysterious splash of its waves against the bobbing bulkheads of the pier, with the starry enchantment of the passing ferry-boats, with the love-enraptured solemnity of the spring night.

I had not the heart even to think of business, much less to talk it. We fell silent, both of us, listening to the singing. Poor Gussie! She was not a pretty girl, and she did not interest me in the least. Yet at this moment I was drawn to her. The brooding, plaintive tones which resounded around us had a bewitching effect on me. It filled me with yearning; it filled me with love. Gussie was a woman to me now. My hand sought hers. It was an honest proffer of endearment, for my soul was praying for communion with hers

She withdrew her hand. "This should not be done in a hurry, either," she explained, pensively

"Gussie! Dear Gussie!" I said, sincerely, though not unaware of the temporary nature of my feeling

"Don't!" she implored me

There was something in her plea which seemed to say: "You know you don't care for me. It's my money that has brought you here. Alas! It is not my lot to be loved for my own sake."

Her unspoken words broke my heart

"Gussie! I swear to you you're dear to me. Can't you believe me?"

The singing night was too much for her. She yielded to my arms. Urged on by the chill air, we clung together in a delirium of love-making. There were passionate embraces and kisses. I felt that her thin, dried-up lips were not to my taste, but I went on kissing them with unfeigned fervor.

The singing echoed dolefully. We remained in that secluded nook until the growing chill woke us from our trance. I took her home. When we reached a tiny square jammed with express-wagons we paused to kiss once more, and when we found ourselves in front of her stoop, which was now deserted, the vigorous hand-clasp with which I took my leave was symbolic of another kiss.

I went away without discovering the size of her hoard. I was to call on her the next evening.

As I trudged along through the swarming streets on my way home the predominant feeling in my heart was one of physical distaste. Poor thing! I felt that marrying her was out of the question — *see*!

Nevertheless, the next evening I went to see her as arranged. I found her out. Her landlady handed me a letter. It was in Yiddish:

> Mr. Levinsky [it read], I do not write this myself, for I cannot write, and I do not want you to think that I want to make believe that I can. A man is writing it for me for ten cents. I am telling him the words and he is writing just as I tell him. It was all a mistake. You know what I mean. I don't care to marry you. You are too smart for me and too young, too. I am afraid of you. I am a simple girl and you are educated. I must look for my equal. If I married you, both of us would be sorry for it.

*Why do I get the feeling this is not the final woman in his life? Oh — b/c the book isn't even halfway finished*

Excuse me, and I wish you well. Please don't come to see me any more

GUSSIE

The message left me with a feeling of shame, sadness, and commiseration.

During that evening and the forenoon of the following day I was badly out of spirits

There was nothing to do at the shop, yet I went there just to see Chaikin, so as to keep up his interest in my scheme. He was glad to see me. He had a message from his wife, who wanted me to call in the evening. Gussie's letter was blotted out of my memory. I was once more absorbed in my project

I spent the evening at the designer's house. Mrs. Chaikin made new attempts at worming out the size of my fortune and, in addition, something concerning its origin

"Is it an inheritance?" she queried.

"An inheritance? Why, would you like me to get one?" I said, playfully, as though talking to a child

She could not help laughing. "Well, then, is it from a rich brother or a sister, or is it your own money?" she pursued, falling in with the facetious tone that I was affecting

"Any kind of money you wish, Mrs. Chaikin. But, seriously, there will be no trouble about cash. The main point is that I want to go into manufacturing and that I should prefer to have Mr. Chaikin for my partner. There is plenty of money in cloaks, and I am bent upon making heaps, great heaps, of it—for Mr. Chaikin and myself. Really, isn't it maddening to think that he should be making other people rich, while all he gets is a miserable few dollars a week? It's simply outrageous."

So speaking, I worked Mrs. Chaikin up to a high sense of the absurdity of the thing. I was rapidly gaining ground with her

And so, pending that mysterious something to which I was often alluding as the source of my prospective fortune, I became a frequent visitor at her house. Sometimes she would invite me to supper; once or twice we spent Sunday together. As for little Maxie, he invariably hailed me with joy. I was actually fond of him, and I was glad of it

# CHAPTER IV

THE time I speak of, the late '80's and the early '90's, is connected with an important and interesting chapter in the history of the American cloak business. Hitherto in the control of German Jews, it was now beginning to pass into the hands of their Russian co-religionists, the change being effected under peculiar conditions that were destined to lead to a stupendous development of the industry. If the average American woman is to-day dressed infinitely better than she was a quarter of a century ago, and if she is now easily the best-dressed average woman in the world, the fact is due, in a large measure, to the change I refer to

The transition was inevitable. While the manufacturers were German Jews, their contractors, tailors, and machine operators were Yiddish-speaking immigrants from Russia or Austrian Galicia. Although the former were of a superior commercial civilization, it was, after all, a case of Greek meeting Greek, and the circumstances were such that just because they represented a superior commercial civilization they were doomed to be beaten

The German manufacturers were the pioneers of the industry in America. It was a new industry, in fact, scarcely twenty years old. Formerly, and as late as the '70's, women's cloaks and jackets were little known in the United States. Shawls were worn by the masses. What few cloaks were seen on women of means and fashion were imported from Germany. But the demand grew.

So, gradually, some German-American merchants and an American shawl firm bethought themselves of manufacturing these garments at home. The industry progressed, the new-born great Russian immigration—a child of the massacres of 1881 and 1882—bringing the needed army of tailors for it. There was big money in the cloak business, and it would have been unnatural if some of these tailors had not, sooner or later, begun to think of going into business on their own hook. At first it was a hard struggle. The American business world was slow to appreciate the commercial possibilities which these new-comers represented, but it learned them in course of time

It was at the beginning of this transition period that my scheme was born in my mind. Schemes of that kind were in the air

Meyer Nodelman, the son of my landlady, had not the remotest inkling of my plans, yet I had consulted him about them more than once. Of course, it was all done in a purely abstract way. Like the majority of our people, he was a talkative man so I would try to keep him talking shop. By a system of seemingly casual questioning I would pump him on sundry details of the clothing business, on the differences and similarities between it and the cloak trade, and, more especially, on how one started on a very small capital

He bragged and blustered, but oftentimes he would be carried away by the sentimental side of his past struggles. Then he would unburden himself of a great deal of unvarnished history. On such occasions I would obtain from him a veritable treasure of information and suggestions.

Some of the generalizations of this homespun and quaint thinker, too, were interesting. Talking of credit, for example, he once said: "When a fellow is a beginner it's a good thing if he has a credit face."

I thought it was some sort of commercial term he was using, and when I asked him what it meant he said: "Why, some people are just born with the kind of face that makes the woolen merchant or the bank president trust them. They are not more honest than some other fellows. Indeed, some of them are plain pickpockets, but they have a credit face, so you have got to trust them. You just can't help it."

"And if they don't pay?"

"But they do. They get credit from somebody else and pay the jobber or the banker. Then they get more credit from these people and pay the other fellows. People of this kind can do a big business without a cent of capital. In Russia a fellow who pays his bills is called an honest man, but America is miles ahead of Russia. Here you can be the best pay in the world and yet be a crook. You wouldn't say that every man who breathes God's air is honest, would you? Well, paying your bills in America is like breathing.

If you don't, you are dead."

Chaikin, too, often let fall, in his hesitating, monosyllabic way, some observation which I considered of value. Of the purely commercial side of the industry he knew next to nothing, but then he could tell me a thing or two concerning the psychology of popular taste, the forces operating behind the scenes of fashion, the methods employed by small firms in stealing styles from larger ones, and other tricks of the trade.

At last I resolved to act. It was the height of the season for winter orders, and I decided to take time by the forelock

One day when I called at the designer's, and Mrs. Chaikin asked me for news (alluding to the thousands I was supposed to be expecting), I said: "Well, I have rented a shop."

"Rented a shop?"

"That's what I did. It's no use missing the season. If a fellow wants to do something, there is nothing for it but to go to work and do it, else he is doomed to be a slave all his life."

When I added that the shop was on Division Street her face fell

"But what difference does it make where it is?" I argued, with studied vehemence. "It's only a place to make samples in—for a start."

"Mr. Chaikin is not going into a wee bit of a business like that. No, sir."

In the course of our many discussions it had often happened that after overruling me with great finality she would end by yielding to my point of view. I hoped this would be the case in the present instance

"Don't be so hasty, Mrs. Chaikin," I said, with a smile. "Wait till you know a little more about the arrangement."

And dropping into the Talmudic singsong, which usually comes back to me when my words assume an argumentative character, I proceeded "In the first place, I don't want Mr. Chaikin to leave the Manheimers—not yet. All I want him to do is to attend to our shop evenings. Don't be uneasy: the Manheimers won't get wind of it. Leave that to me. Well, all I want is some samples to go around the stores with. The rest will come easy.

We'll make things hum. See if we don't. When we have orders and get really started we'll move out of Division Street. Of course we will. But would it not be foolish to open up on a large scale and have Mr. Chaikin give up his job before we have accomplished anything? I think it would. Indeed, it's my money that's going to be invested. Do you blame me for being careful, at the beginning at least? I neither want Mr. Chaikin to risk his job nor myself to risk big money."

"But you haven't even told me how much you can put in," she blurted out, excitedly.

"As much as will be necessary. But what's the use dumping a big lot at once? Many a big business has failed, while firms who start in a modest way have worked themselves up. Why should Mr. Chaikin begin by risking his position? Why? Why?"

The long and short of it was that Mrs. Chaikin became enthusiastic for my Division Street shop, and the next day her husband took two hours off to accompany me to a nondescript woolen-store on Hester Street, where we bought fifty dollars' worth of material

The rent for the shop was thirty dollars a month. One month's rent for two sewing-machines was two dollars. A large second-hand table for designing and cutting and some old chairs cost me twelve dollars more, leaving me a balance of over two hundred dollars

Before I went to rent the premises for our prospective shop I had withdrawn my money from the savings-bank and deposited it in a small bank where I opened a check account

"Once I am to play the part of a manufacturer it would not do to pay bills in cash," I reflected. "I must pay in checks, and do so like one to the manner born."

At this the magic word "credit" loomed in letters of gold before me. I was aware of the fascination of check-books, so, being armed with one, I expected to be able to buy things, in some cases, at least, without having to pay for them at once. Besides, my bank might be induced to grant me a loan. Then, too, one might issue a check before one had the amount and thereby gain a day's time. There seemed to be a world of possibilities in the long, narrow book in my breast pocket. I was ever conscious of its presence. I have a vivid recollection of the elation with which I drew and issued my first check (in payment of thirty dollars, the first month's rent for our prospective cloak-factory). Humanity seemed to have become divided into two distinct classes—those who paid their obligations in cash and those who paid them in checks. I still have that first check-book of mine

- a history lesson
- Using Meyer Nodelman; talking of trade
- paying bills is key in America (boy, is that true!)
- rented a shop on Division St, 1st Mrs. C upset but then gradually lighten up
- D Learning the value of Am money.

# CHAPTER V

CHAIKIN made up half a dozen sample garments. I took them to the department store to which the Manheimer Brothers catered, but the buyer of the cloak department would not so much as let me untie my bundle. He was a middle-aged man (women buyers were rare in those days), an Irish-American of commanding figure. After sweeping me with a glance of cold curiosity, he waved me aside. My Russian name and my appearance were evidently against me. I tried the other department stores—with the same result. The larger business world of the city had not yet learned to take the Russian Jew seriously as a factor in advanced commerce. The buyer of the cloak department in the last store I visited was an American Jew, a fair-complexioned little fellow, all aglitter with neatness. At first he took an amused interest in me. When I had unpacked my goods and was about to show him one of Chaikin's jackets he checked me

"Suppose we gave you an order for five hundred," he said, with a smile; "five hundred jackets to be delivered at a certain date."

"I would deliver it," I answered, boldly. "Why not?"

"I don't know why. Maybe you would, maybe you wouldn't. How can we be sure you would?" Before I had time to answer he asked me how long I had been in the country.

When I told him, he complimented me on my English. I was sure it meant business. I was thrilled

"Have you got a shop?" he further questioned. "How many hands do you employ?"

"Seventy-five."

He sized me up. "Where is your place?"

"On Division Street."

"Well, well! What is your rating?" I did not know what he meant. So, for an answer, I made a new attempt to submit the contents of my bundle for his inspection. At this he made a gesture of disgust and withdrew. A cold sweat broke out on my forehead

I had heard of the existence of small department stores in various sections of the city, so I went in search of them

I found myself in the vicinity of the City College. As I passed that corner I studiously looked away. I felt like a convert Jew passing a synagogue

It was a warm day. My pack seemed to grow heavier with every block I walked, and so did my heart. I was perspiring freely; my collar wilted. All of which did anything but make me look as "a man who paid his bills in checks." At last, walking up Third Avenue I came across a place where there was quite a large display of jackets in the windows. Upon my opening the door and announcing my mission, two jaunty young fellows invited me in with elaborate courtesy, almost with anxiety. My heart leaped for joy. I fell to opening my bundle. The two young men inspected every jacket, went into ecstasies over each of them, and then asked me all sorts of irrelevant questions until it dawned upon me that I was being made game of. It appeared that the father of the two young men, the proprietor of the store, manufactured his own goods, for wholesale as well as for retail trade

I received much better treatment in a store on Avenue B, but my goods proved too high for that neighborhood. As if to atone for this, the proprietor of this store, a kindly Galician Jew, gave me a list of the minor department stores I was looking for, and some valuable suggestions in addition

My dinner that day consisted of two ring-shaped rolls which I bought in a Jewish grocery-store and which I ate on a bench in Tompkins Square

The day passed most discouragingly. It was about 7 o'clock when, disheartened to the point of despair, I dragged my wearied limbs in the direction of my "factory." When I got there I found my partner waiting for me—not alone, but in the company of his wife

"Well?" she shrieked, jumping to meet me

"Splendid!" I replied, with enthusiasm. "It looks even better than I expected. I could have got good orders at once, but a fellow must not be too hasty. You have got to look around first—find out who is who, you know."

Mrs. Chaikin looked crestfallen. "So you did not get any orders at all?"

"What's your hurry?" her husband said, pleadingly. "Levinsky is right. You can't sell goods unless you know who you deal with."

The following two days were as barren of results as the first. Mrs. Chaikin had lost all confidence in the venture. She was becoming rather hard to handle

"I don't want Ansel to bother any more," she said, peevishly. "You know what the Americans say, 'Time is money.' Pay Ansel for his work and let us be 'friends at a distance.'"

"Very well," I said, and, producing my check-book, I asked, "How much is it?"

The sight of my check-book acted like a charm. The situation suddenly assumed brighter colors in Mrs. Cbaikin's eyes

"Look at him! He thought I really meant it," she grinned, sheepishly

Every night I would go to bed sick at heart and with my mind half made up to drop it all, only to wake in the morning more resolute and hopeful than ever. Hopeful and defiant. It was as though somebody—the whole world—were jeering at my brazen-faced, piteous efforts, and I was bound to make good, "just for spite."

I learned of the existence of "purchasing offices" where the buyers of several department stores, from so many cities, made their headquarters in New York. Also, I discovered that in order to keep track of the arrivals of these buyers I must follow a daily paper called Hotel Reporter (the ordinary newspapers did not furnish information of this character in those days). A man who manufactured neckties in the same ramshackle building in which I hoped to manufacture cloaks volunteered to let me look at his Reporter every day. This man was naturally inclined to be neighborly, but I had found that an occasional quotation or two from the Talmud was particularly helpful in obtaining a small favor from him

I knocked about among the purchasing offices with bulldog tenacity, but during the first few days my efforts in this direction were as futile as in the case of the New York stores. Meanwhile, time was pressing. So far as out-of-town buyers were concerned, the "winter season" was drawing to a close. All I could see were some belated stragglers. One of these was a man from the Middle West, a stout, fleshy American with quick, nervous movements which contradicted his well-fed, languid-looking face

He shot a few glances at my samples, just to get rid of me, but he liked the designs, and I could see that he found my prices tempting

"How soon will you be able to deliver five hundred?" he snarled

"In three weeks."

"Very well—go ahead!" And speaking in his jerky, impatient way, he went on to specify how many cloaks he wanted of each kind

I left him with my heart divided between unutterable triumph and black despair. Five hundred cloaks! How would I raise the money for so much raw material? It almost looked like another practical joke

By this time I was more than sure that the Chaikins had a considerable little pile, but to turn to them for funds was impossible. It would have let my cat out of the bag. I sought credit at Claflin's and at half a dozen smaller places, but all in vain. I could not help thinking of Nodelman's "credit face." Ah, if that kind of a face had fallen to my lot! But it had not, it seemed. It looked as if there were no hope for me

Finally I took the necktie man into my confidence, the result being that he unburdened himself of his own financial straits to me

One afternoon I was moping around some of the side-streets off lower Broadway in quest of some new place where I might try to beg for credit, when I noticed the small sign-board of a commission merchant. Upon entering the place I found a fine-looking elderly American dictating something to a stenographer. When the man had heard my plea he looked me over from head to foot.

I felt like a prisoner facing the jury which is about to announce its verdict

At last he said: "Well, you look pretty reliable. I guess I'll trust you the goods for thirty days."

⌐His big break

It was all I could do to restrain myself from invoking benedictions on his head and kissing his hands as my mother would have done under similar circumstances

"So I do have a 'credit face'!" I exclaimed to myself, gleefully

When I found myself in the street again I looked at my reflection in store windows, scanning my "credit face."

The Chaikins took it for granted that I had paid for the goods on the spot

Things brightened up at our "factory." I ordered an additional sewing-machine of the instalment agent and hired two operators—poor fellows who were willing to work fourteen or fifteen hours a day for twelve dollars a week. (The union had again been revived, but it was weak, and my employees did not belong to it.) As for myself, I toiled at my machine literally day and night, snatching two or three hours' sleep at dawn, with some bundles of cut goods or half-finished cloaks for a bed. Chaikin spent every night, from 7 to 2, with me, cutting the goods and doing the better part of the other work. Mrs. Chaikin, too, lent a hand. Leaving Maxie in the care of her mother, she would spend several hours a day in the factory, finishing the cloaks

The five hundred cloaks were shipped on time. I was bursting with consciousness of the fact that I was a manufacturer—that a big firm out West (a firm of Gentiles, mind you!) was recognizing my claim to the title.

I was American enough to be alive to the special glamour of the words, "out West."

Goods in our line of business usually sold "for cash," which meant ten days.

Ten days more, then, and I should receive a big check from that firm. That would enable me to start new operations. Accordingly, I went out to look for more orders

Whether my first success had put new confidence in me, or whether my past experiences had somewhat rounded off my rough edges and enabled me to speak to business people in a more effective manner than I could have done before, the proprietor of a small department store on upper Third Avenue let me show him my samples. My prices made an impression on him. My cloaks were five dollars apiece lower than he was in the habit of paying. He looked askance at me, as though my figures seemed too good to be true, until I found it the best policy to tell him the unembellished truth.

"The big manufacturers of whom you buy have big office expenses," I explained. "They make a lot of fuss, and you've got to pay for it. My principle is not to make fuss at the retailer's expense. Our office costs us very, very little. We are plain people. But that isn't all. Your big manufacturer pays for union labor, so he takes it out of you. Now, we don't bother about these things. We get the best work done for the lowest wages.

The big men in the business wouldn't even know where hands of this kind could be got. We do."

I took my departure with an order for three hundred cloaks, expecting to begin work on them as soon as I received that check "from out West." Things seemed to be coming my way.

As I sat in an Elevated train going down-town I figured the profits on the two orders and pictured other orders coming in. I beheld our little factory crowded with machines, I heard their bewitching whir-r, whir-r. Chaikin would have to leave the Manheimers, of course

In the afternoon of the sixth day, when I called at one of the purchasing offices I have mentioned, I received the information that the firm whose check I was awaiting so impatiently had failed!

# CHAPTER VI

THE failure of the Western firm seemed to nave nipped my commercial career in the bud. The large order I had received from its representative was apparently to be the death as well as the birth of my glory. In my despair, I tried to make a virtue of necessity. I was telling myself that it served me right; that I had had no business to abandon my intellectual pursuits. I was inclined to behold something like the hand of Providence in the bankruptcy of that firm. At the same time I was casting about in my mind for some way of raising new money with which to pay the kindly commission merchant, get a new bill of goods from him, and fill my new order.

When I explained the matter to Mrs. Chaikin she was on the brink of a fainting spell

"You're a liar and a thief!" she shrieked. "There never was a Western firm in the world. It's all a lie. You sold the goods for cash."

Her husband knew something about firms and credit, so I had no difficulty in substantiating my assertion to him

"It's only a matter of days when I shall get the big check that is coming to me," I assured them. I went on to spin a long yarn, to which she listened with jeers and outbursts of uncomplimentary Yiddish

One day I mustered courage and called on Mrs. Chaikin. I did so on an afternoon when her husband was sure to be at work, because I had a lurking feeling that, being alone with me, she would be easier to deal with

When she saw me she gasped. "What, you?" she said. "You have the nerve to come up here?"

"Come, come, Mrs. Chaikin," I said, earnestly. "Please be seated and let us talk it all over in a business-like manner. With your sense, and especially with your sense for business. you will understand me."

"Please don't flatter me," she demurred, sternly

But I knew that nothing appealed to her vanity so much as being thought a clever business woman, and I protested: "Flatter you! In the first place, it is a well-known fact that women have more sense than men. In the second place, it is the talk of every cloak-shop that Mr. Chaikin owes his high position to you as much as to his own ability. Everybody, everybody says so."

I talked of "unforeseen difficulties," of a "well-known landlord" whose big check I was expecting every day; I composed a story about that landlord's father-in-law agreed with Mrs. Chaikin that it had been a mistake on my part to trust the buyer of that Western firm the goods without first consulting her; and the upshot was that she made me stay to supper and that pending the arrival of Chaikin I took Maxie to the Park

The father-in-law of my story was Mr. Even, of course. I had portrayed him vividly as coming to my rescue in my present predicament, so vividly, indeed, that my own fib haunted me the next day. The result was that in the evening I made myself as presentable as I could, and repaired to the synagogue where he spent much of his time reading Talmud

I had not visited the place since that memorable day, my first day in America. I recognized it at once. I was thrilled. The four-odd years seemed twenty-four

Mr. Even was not there, but he soon came in. He had aged considerably. He was beginning to look somewhat decrepit. His dignity was tinged with the sadness of old age

"Good evening, Mr. Even. Do you know me?" I began

He scanned me closely, but failed to recognize me

"I am David Levinsky, the 'green one' you befriended four and a half years ago. Don't you remember me, Mr. Even? It was in this very place where I had the good fortune to make your acquaintance. I'm the son of the woman who was killed by Gentiles, in Antomir," I added, mournfully

"Oh yes, indeed!" he said, with a wistful smile, somewhat abashed. He took snuff, looked me over once more, and, as if his memory had been brightened by the snuff, he burst out: "Lord of the World! You are that young man! Why, I confess I scarcely recognize you. Of course I remember it all. Why, of course I remember you. Well, well! How have you been getting along in America?"

"Can't complain. Not at all. You remember that evening? After you provided me with a complete outfit, like a father fixing up his son for his wedding-day, and you gave me five dollars into the bargain, you told me not to call on you again until I was well established in life. Do you remember that?"

"Of course I do," he answered, with a beaming glance at two old Talmudists who sat at their books close by

"Well, here I am. I am running a cloak-factory."

He began to question me about my affairs with sad curiosity. I said that business was "good, too good, in fact," so that it required somewhat more capital than I possessed.

I soon realized, however, that he did not care for me now. My Americanized self did not make the favorable impression that I had made four and a half years before, when he gave me my first American hair-cut

I inquired after his daughter and his son-in-law, but my hint that the latter might perhaps be willing to indorse a note for me evoked an impatient grunt

"My son-in-law! Why, you don't even know him!" he retorted, with a suspicious look at me

I turned it off with a joke and asked about the hen-pecked man. Mr. Even had not seen him for four years. The other Talmudists present had never even known him. A man with extremely long black side-locks who spoke with a Galician accent became interested. After Mr. Even went to his wonted seat at the east wall, where he took up a book, this man said to me, with a sigh: "Oh, it is not the old home. Over there people go to the same synagogue all their lives, while here one is constantly on the move. They call it a city.

Pshaw! It is a market-place, a bazar, an inn, not a city! People are together for a day and then, behold! they have flown apart. Where to? Nobody knows. I don't know what has become of you and you don't know what has become of me."

"That's why there is no real friendship here," I chimed in, heartily.

"That's why one feels so friendless, so lonely."

220

My shop, of course, shut down, and I roamed about the streets a good deal. I was restless. I continually felt nonplussed, ashamed to look myself in the face, as it were. One forenoon I found myself walking in the direction of Twenty-third Street and Lexington Avenue. The college building was now a source of consolation. Indeed, what was money beside the halo of higher education? I paused in front of the building. There were several students on the campus, all Jewish boys. I accosted one of them. I spoke to him enviously, and left the place thrilling with a determination to drop all thought of business, to take the entrance examination, and be a college student at last. I was almost grateful to that Western firm for going into bankruptcy

And yet, even while I was tingling with this feeling, a voice exclaimed in my heart, "Ah, if that Western firm had not failed!"

The debt I owed the American commission merchant agonized me without let-up.

I couldn't help thinking of my "credit face." To disappoint him, of all men, seemed to be the most brutal thing I had ever done. I imagined myself obtaining just enough money to pay him; but, as I did so, I could not resist the temptation of extending the sum so as to go on manufacturing cloaks. I was incessantly cudgeling my brains for some "angel" who would come to my financial rescue

The spell of my college aspirations was broken once for all. My Temple was destroyed. Nothing was left of it but vague yearnings and something like a feeling of compunction which will assert itself, sometimes, to this day

The Talmud tells us how the destruction of Jerusalem and the great Temple was caused by a hen and a rooster. The destruction of my American Temple was caused by a bottle of milk

The physical edifice still stands, though the college has long since moved to a much larger and more imposing building or group of buildings. I find the humble old structure on Lexington Avenue and Twenty-third Street the more dignified and the more fascinating of the two. To me it is a sacred spot. It is the sepulcher of my dearest ambitions, a monument to my noblest enthusiasm in America

# BOOK IX

## DORA

# CHAPTER I

"HOW about it?" Mrs. Chaikin said to me, ominously

"About what? What do you mean, Mrs. Chaikin?"

"Oh, you know what I mean. It is no use playing the fool and trying to make a fool of me."

The conversation was held in our deserted shop on an afternoon. The three sewing-machines, the cutting-table, and the pressing-table looked desolate.

She spoke in an undertone, almost in a whisper, lest the secret of her husband's relations with me should leak out and reach his employers. She had been guarding that secret all along, but now, that our undertaking had apparently collapsed, she was particularly uneasy about it

"I don't believe that store in the West has failed at all. In fact, I know it has not. Somebody told me all about it."

This was her method of cross-examining me. I read her a clipping containing the news of the bankruptcy, but as she could not read it herself, she only sneered. I reasoned with her, I pleaded, I swore; but she kept sneering or nodding her head mournfully

"I don't believe you. I don't believe you," she finally said, shutting her eyes with a gesture of despair and exhaustion. "Do I believe a dog when it barks? Neither do I believe you. I curse the day when I first met you. It was the black year that brought you to us." She fell to wringing her hands and moaning: "Woe is me! Woe is me!"

Finally she tiptoed out of the room and down the stairs. In my despair I longed for somebody to whom I could unbosom myself. I thought of Meyer Nodelman. A self-made man and one who had begun manufacturing almost penniless like myself, he seemed to be just the man I needed. A thought glimmered through my mind, "And who knows but he may come to my rescue I was going to call at his warehouse, but upon second thought I realized that the seat of his cold self-interest would scarcely be a favorable setting for the interview and that I must try to entrap him in the humanizing atmosphere of his mother's home for the purpose

The next time I saw him at his mother's I took him up to my little attic and laid my tribulations before him. I told him the whole story, almost without embellishments, omitting nothing but Chaikin's name

"Is it all true?" he interrupted me at one point

I swore that it was, and went on. At the end I offered to prove it all to his satisfaction

"You don't need to prove it to me," he replied. "What do I care?" Then, suddenly, casting off his reserve, he blurted out: "Look here, young fellow! If you think I am going to lend you money you are only wasting time, for I am not." "And why not?" I asked, boldly, with studied dignity

"Why not! You better tell me why yes," he chuckled. "You have a lot of spunk. That you certainly have, and you ought to make a good business man, but I won't loan you money, for all that."

"Weren't you once hard up yourself, Mr. Nodelman? You have made a success of it, and now it would only be right that you should help another fellow get up in the world. You won't lose a cent by it, either. I take an oath on it."

"You can't have an oath cashed in a bank, can you?"

"Why did that commission merchant take a chance? If a Gentile is willing to help a Jew, and one whom he had never seen before, you should not hesitate, either."

"Well, there is no use talking about it," was his final decision

The following day I received a letter from him, inviting me to his office

His warehouse occupied a vast loft on a little street off Broadway. Arrived there, I had to pass several men, all in their shirt-sleeves, who were attacking mountains of cloth with long, narrow knives. One of these directed me to a remote window, in front of which I presently found Nodelman lecturing a man who wore a tape-measure around his neck

Nodelman kept me waiting, without offering me a scat, a good half-hour. He was in his shirt-sleeves, like the others, yet he looked far more dignified than I had ever seen him look before. It was as though the environment of his little kingdom had made another man of him

Finally, he left the man with the tape-measure and silently led me into his little private office, a narrow strip of partitioned-off space at the other end of the loft

When we were seated and the partition door was shut he said, with grave mien, "Well," and fell silent again

I gazed at him patiently

"Well," he repeated, "I have thought it over." And again he paused. At last he burst out: "I do want to help you, young fellow. You didn't expect it, did you? I do want to help you. And do you know why? Because otherwise you won't pay that Gentile and I don't want a good-hearted Gentile to think that Jews are a bad lot. That's number one. Number two is this: If you think Meyer Nodelman is a hog, you don't know Meyer Nodelman. Number three: I rather liked the way you talked yesterday. I said to myself, said I: 'An educated fellow who can talk like that will be all right. He ought to be given a lift, for most educated people are damn fools.' Well, I'll tell you what I am willing to do for you. I'll get you the goods for that order of yours, not for thirty days, but for sixty. What do you think of that? Now is Nodelman a hog or is he not? But that's as far as I am willing to go. I can only get you the goods for that Third Avenue order. See? But that won't be enough to help you out of your scrape, not enough for you to pay that good Gentile on time." He engaged in some mental arithmetic by means of which he reached the conclusion that I should need an additional four hundred dollars, and he wound up by an ultimatum: he would not furnish me the goods until I had produced that amount

"Look here, young fellow," he added; "since you were smart enough to get that Gentile and Meyer Nodelman to help you out, it ought not to be a hard job for you to get a third fellow to take an interest in you. Do you remember what I told you about those credit faces? I think you have got one."

"I have an honest heart, too," I said, with a smile

"Your heart I can't get into, so I don't know. See? Maybe there is a rogue hiding there and maybe there isn't. But your face and your talk certainly are all right. They ought to be able to get you some more cash. And if they don't, then they don't deserve that I should help you out, either. See?" He chuckled in appreciation of his own syllogism

"It's a nice piece of Talmud reasoning," I complimented him, with an enthusiastic laugh. "But, seriously, Mr. Nodelman, I shall pay you every cent. You run absolutely no risk."

I pleaded with him to grant me the accommodation unconditionally. I tried to convince him that I should contrive to do without the additional cash. But he was obdurate, and at last I took my leave

"Wait a moment! What's your hurry? Are you afraid you'll be a couple of minutes longer becoming a millionaire? There is something I want to ask you."

"What is it, Mr. Nodelman?"

"How about your studying to be a doctor-philosopher?" he asked, archly

"Oh, well, one can attend to business and find time for books, too," I answered

I came away in a new transport of expectations and in a new agony of despair at once. On the whole, however, my spirits were greatly buoyed up.

Encouraged by the result of taking Nodelman into my confidence, I decided to try a similar heart-to-heart talk on Max Margolis, better known to the reader as Maximum Max. He had some money.

I had seen very little of him in the past two years, having stumbled upon him in the street but two or three times. But upon each of these occasions he had stopped me and inquired about my affairs with genuine interest. He was fond of me. I had no doubt about it. And he was so good-natured. Our last chance meeting antedated my new venture by at least six months, and he was not likely to have any knowledge of it. I felt that he would be sincerely glad to hear of it and I hoped that he would be inclined to help me launch it. Anyhow, he seemed to be my last resort, and I was determined to make my appeal to him as effective as I knew how

As he had always seen me shabbily clad, I decided to overwhelm him with a new suit of clothes. I needed one, at any rate

After some seeking and inquiring, I found him in a Bowery furniture-store, one of the several places from which he supplied his instalment customers.

It was about 10 o'clock in the morning

"There is something I want to consult you about, Max," I said. "Something awfully important to me. You're the only man I know who could advise me and in whom I can confide," I added, with an implication of great intimacy and affection. "It's a business scheme, Max. I have a chance to make lots of money."

The conversation was held in a dusky passage of the labyrinthine store, a narrow lane running between two barricades of furniture

"What is that? A business scheme?" he asked, in a preoccupied tone of voice and straining his eyes to look me over. "You are dressed up, I see. Quite prosperous, aren't you?"

As we emerged into the glare of the Bowery he scrutinized my suit once again. I quailed. I now felt that to have come in such a screamingly new suit was a fatal mistake. I cursed myself for an idiot of a smart Aleck. But he spoke to me with his usual cordiality and my spirits rose again. However, he seemed to be busy, and so I asked him to set an hour when he could see me at leisure. We made an appointment for 3 o'clock in the afternoon. I was to meet him at the same furniture-store; but upon second thought, and with another glance at my new clothes, he said, jovially: "Why, you are rigged out like a regular monarch! It is quite an honor to invite you to the house. Come up, will you? And, as I won't have to go out to meet you, you can make it 2 o'clock, or half past."

- gets chatized for the closing of the store by Mrs. C
- talked w/ Nodelman
  └ smart Aleck

# CHAPTER II

MAX occupied the top floor of an old private house on Henry Street, a small "railroad" apartment of two large, bright rooms—a living-room and a kitchen—with two small, dark bedrooms between them. The ceiling was low and the air somewhat tainted with the odor of mold and dampness. I found Max in the general living-room, which was also a dining-room, a fat boy of three on his lap and a slender, pale girl of eight on a chair close by. His wife, a slender young woman with a fine white complexion and serious black eyes, was clearing away the lunch things

"Mrs. Margolis, Mr. Levinsky," he introduced us. "Plainly speaking, this is my wifey and this is a friend of mine."

As she was leaving the room for the kitchen he called after her, "Dvorah! Dora! make some tea, will you?"

She craned her neck and gave him a look of resentment. "It's a good thing you are telling me that," she said. "Otherwise I shouldn't know what I have got to do, should I?"

When she had disappeared he explained to me that he variously addressed her by the Yiddish or English form of her name

"We are plain Yiddish folk," he generalized, good-humoredly

A few minutes later, as Mrs. Margolis placed a glass of Russian tea before me, he drew her to him and pinched her white cheek

"What do you think of my wifey, Levinsky?"

She smiled—a grave, deprecating smile—and took to pottering about the house

"And what do you think of these little customers?" he went on. "Lucy, examine mamma in spelling. Quick! Dora, be a good girl, sit down and let Levinsky see how educated you are." ("Educated" he said in English, with the accent on the "a.") "What do you want?" his wife protested, softly. "Mr. Levinsky wants to see you on business, and here you are bothering him with all sorts of nonsense

"Never mind his business. It won't run away. Sit down, I say. It won't take long." She yielded. Casting bashful side-glances at nobody in particular, she seated herself opposite Lucy

"Well?" she said, with a little laugh

I thought her eyes looked too serious, almost angry. "Insane people have eyes of this kind," I said to myself. I also made a mental note of her clear, fresh, delicate complexion. Otherwise she did not interest me in the least, and I mutely prayed Heaven to take her out of the room

"How do you spell 'great'?" the little girl demanded

"G-r-e-a-t—great," her mother answered, with a smile

"Book?"

"B-o-o-k—book. Oh, give me some harder words."

"Laughter."

"L-a-u-g-h-t-e-r—laughter."

"Is that correct?" Margolis turned to me, all beaming. "I wish I could do as much. And nobody has taught her, either. She has learned it all by herself.

Little Lucy is the only teacher she ever had. But she will soon be ahead of her. Won't she, Lucy?"

"I'm afraid I am ahead of her already," Mrs. Margolis said, gaily, yet flushed with excitement

"You are not!" Lucy protested, with a good-natured pout

"Shut up, bad girl you," her mother retorted, again with a bashful side-glance

"Is that the way you talk to your mamma?" Max intervened. "I'll tell your teacher."

I was on pins and needles to be alone with him and to get down to the object of my visit

Finally he said, brusquely: "Well, we have had enough of that. Leave us alone, Dora. Go to the parlor and take the kids along."

She obeyed

When he heard of my venture he was interested. He often interrupted me with boisterous expressions of admiration for my subterfuges as well as for the plan as a whole. With all his boisterousness, however, there was an air of caution about him, as if he scented danger. When I finally said that all depended upon my raising four hundred dollars his face clouded

"I see, I see," he murmured, with sudden estrangement. "I see. I see." "Don't lose courage," I said to myself. "Nodelman was exactly like that at first. Go right ahead."

I portrayed my business prospects in the most alluring colors and gave Max to understand that if "somebody" advanced me the four hundred dollars he would be sure to get it back in thirty days plus any interest he might name

"It would be terrible if I had to let it all go to pieces on account of such a thing," I concluded

There was a moment of very awkward silence. It was broken by Max

"It's really too bad. What are you going to do about it?" he said. "Where can you get such a 'somebody'?"

"I don't know. That's why I came to consult you. I thought you might suggest some way. It would be a pity if I had to give it all up on account of four hundred dollars."

"Indeed it would. It would be terrible. Still, four hundred dollars is not four hundred cents. I wish I were a rich man. I should lend it to you at once. You know I should."

"I should pay you every cent of it, Max."

"You say it as if I had money. You know I have not." What I did know was that he had, and he knew that I did

He took to analyzing the situation and offering me advice. Why not go to that kindly Gentile, the commission merchant, make a clean breast of it, and obtain an extension of time? Why not apply to some money-lender? Why not make a vigorous appeal to Nodelman? He seemed to be an obliging fellow, so if I pressed him a little harder he might give me the cash as well as the goods

I was impelled to retort that advice was cheap, and he apparently read my thoughts

Presently he said, with genuine ardor: "I tell you what, Levinsky. Why not try to get your old landlady to open her stocking? From what you have told me, she ought not to be a hard nut to crack if you only go about it in the right way.

This suggestion made a certain appeal to me, but I would not betray it. I continued resentfully silent

"You just try her, Levinsky. She'll let you have the four hundred dollars, or half of it, at least."

"And if she does, her son will refuse to get me the goods," I remarked, with a sneer.

"Nonsense. If you know how to handle her, she will realize that she must keep her mouth shut until after she gets the money back."

"Oh, what's the use?" I said, impatiently. "I must get the cash at once, or all is lost."

Again he spoke of money-lenders. He went into details about one of them and offered to ascertain his address for me. He evidently felt awkward about his part in the matter and eager to atone for it in some way

"Why should a usurer trust me?" I said, rising to go

"Wait. What's your hurry? If that money-lender hears your story, he may trust you. He is a peculiar fellow, don't you know. When he takes a fancy to a man he is willing to take a chance on him. Of course, the interest would be rather high." He paused abruptly, wrinkled his forehead with an effect of pondering some new scheme, and said: "Wait. I think I have a better plan.

I'll see if I can't get you the money without a money-lender." With this he sprang to his feet and had his wife bring him his coat and hat. "I'll be back in less than half an hour," he said. "Dvorah dear, give Levinsky some more tea, will you? I am going out for a few minutes. Don't let him be downhearted." Then, shaking a finger of warning at me, he said, playfully, "Only take care that you don't fall in love with her!" And he was gone

"It's all play-acting," I thought. "He just wants me to believe he is trying to do something for me." But, of course, I was not altogether devoid of hope that I was mistaken and that he was making a sincere effort to raise a loan for me

Mrs. Margolis went into the kitchen immediately her husband departed.

Presently she came back, carrying a glass of tea on a saucer. She placed it before me with an embarrassed side-glance, brought some cookies, and seated herself at the far end of the table. I uttered some complimentary trivialities about the children

When a man finds himself alone with a woman who is neither his wife nor a close relative, both feel awkward. It is as though they heard a whisper, "There is nobody to watch the two of you."

Still, confused as I was, I was fully aware of her tempting complexion and found her angry black eyes strangely interesting. Upon the whole, however, I do not think she made any appeal to me save by virtue of the fact that she was a woman and that we were alone. I was tense with the consciousness of that fact, and everything about her disturbed me. She wore a navy-blue summer wrapper and I noticed the way it set off the soft whiteness of her neck. I remarked to myself that she looked younger than her husband, that she must be about twenty-eight or thirty, perhaps. My glances apparently caused her painful embarrassment. Finally she got up again, making a pretense of bustling about the room. It seemed to me that when she was on her feet she looked younger than when she was seated

I asked the boy his name, and he answered in lugubrious, but distinct, accents: "Daniel Margolis."

"He speaks like a grown person," I said

"She used to speak like that, too, when she was of his age," my hostess replied, with a glance in the direction of her daughter

"Did you?" I said to Lucy

The little girl grinned coyly

"Why don't you answer the gentleman's question?" her mother rebuked her, in English. "It's Mr. Levinsky, a friend of papa's."

Lucy gave me a long stare and lost all interest in me. "Don't you like me at all? Not even a little bit?" I pleaded

She soon unbent and took to plying me with questions. Where did I live? Was I a "customer peddler "like her papa? How long had I been in America? (A question which a child of the East Side hears as often as it does queries about the weather.) "Can you spell?" "No," I answered. "Not at all?"

"Not at all!"

"Shame! But my papa can't spell, neither."

"Shut up, you bad girl you!" her mother broke in with a laugh. "Vere you lea'n such nasty things? By your mamma? The gentleman will think by your mamma."

She delivered her a little lecture in English, taking pains to produce the "th" and the American "r," though her were "v's."

She urged me not to let the tea get cold. As I took hold of the tall, thin, cylindrical glass I noted that it was scrupulously clean and that its contents had a good clear color. I threw a glance around the room and I saw that it was well kept and tidy

Mrs. Margolis took a seat again. Lucy, with part of a cooky in her mouth, stepped over to her and seated herself on her lap, throwing her arm around her. She struck me as the very image of her mother. Presently, however, I discovered that she resembled her father quite as closely. It seemed as though the one likeness lay on the surface of her face, while the other loomed up from underneath, as the reflection of a face does from under the surface of water. Lucy soon wearied of her mother and walked over to my side. I put her on my lap. She would not let me pat her, but she did not mind sitting on my knees.

"Are you a good speller?" I asked

"I c'n spell all the words we get at school," she answered, sagely

"How do you spell 'colonel'?"

"We never got it at school. But you can't spell it, either."

"How do you know I can't? Maybe I can. Well, let us take an easier word. How do you spell 'because'?"

She spelled it correctly, her mother joining in playfully. I gave them other words, addressing myself to both, and they made a race of it, each trying to head off or outshout the other. At first Mrs. Margolis did so with feigned gaiety, but her face soon set into a grave look and glowed with excitement

At last I asked them to spell "coefficient."

"We never got it at school," Lucy demurred

"I don't know what it means," said Mrs. Margolis, with a shrug of her shoulders.

"It means something in mathematics, in high figuring," I explained in Yiddish

Mrs. Margolis shrugged her shoulders once more

I asked Lucy to try me in spelling. She did and I acquitted myself so well that she exclaimed: "Oh, you liar you! Why did you say you didn't know how to spell?"

Once more her mother took her to task for her manners

"Is that the vay to talk to a gentleman? Shame! Vere you lea'n up to be such a pig? Not by your mamma!"

beginning

When Max came back Lucy hastened to inform him that I could spell "awful good." To which he replied in Yiddish that he knew I was a smart fellow, that I could read and write "everything," and that I had studied to go to college and "to be a doctor, a lawyer, or anything."

His wife looked me over with bashful side-glances. "Really?" she said

Max told me a lame story about his errand and promised to let me know the "final result." It was clearer than ever to me that he was making a fool of me

'finally see Dora (Dvorah)
  └ Talker w/ her
  └ Is she a married woman or single?
        /
     wasn't sure

# CHAPTER III

WHEN I hear a new melody and it makes an appeal to me its effect usually lasts only as long as I hear it, but it is almost sure to reassert itself later on. I scarcely ever think of it during the first two, three, or four days, but then, all of a sudden, it will pop up in my brain and haunt me a few days in succession, humming itself and nagging me like a living thing.

This was precisely what happened to me with regard to Mrs. Margolis. During the first two days after I left her house I never gave her a thought, but on the third her shy side-glances suddenly loomed up in my mind and would not leave it. Just her black, serious eyes and those shy looks of theirs gleaming out of a white, strikingly interesting complexion. Her face in general was a mere blur in my memory

I was incessantly racking my brain over my affairs. I was so low-spirited and worried that I was unconscious of the food I ate or of the streets through which I passed, yet her manner of darting embarrassed glances out of the corner of her eye and her complexion were never absent from my mind. I felt like seeing her once more. However, the prospect of calling at her house was now anything but alluring. I could almost see the annoyed air with which her husband would receive me — I wonder why!,

I sought out two usurers and begged each of them to grant me the loan, but they unyieldingly insisted on more substantial security than the bare story or my venture. I made other efforts to raise the money. I approached several people, including the proprietor of the little music-store. All to no purpose

One afternoon, eight or ten days after my call at the Margolises', when I came to my "factory" I found under the door a closed envelope bearing the name of that Western firm. It contained a typewritten letter and a check in full payment of my bill. Also a circular explaining that the firm had been reorganized with plenty of capital, and naming as one of its new directors a man who, from the tone of the circular, seemed to be of high standing in the financial world

My head was in a whirl. The desolate-looking sewing-machines of my deserted shop seemed to have suddenly brightened up. I looked at the check again and again. The figure on it literally staggered me. It seemed to be part of a fairy tale

I rushed over to Nodelman's office, but found him gone for the day. The next thing on my program was to carry the glad news to the Chaikins and to discuss plans for the immediate future with my partner. But Chaikin never came home before 7. So I first dropped in on the Margolises to flash my check in Max's face and, incidentally, to see his wife

I found him playing with his fat boy

"Hello, Max! I have good news!" I shouted, excitedly. Which actually meant: "Don't be uneasy, Max. I am not going to ask you for a loan again."

When he had examined the check he said, sheepishly: "Now you are all right. Why, something told me all along that you would get it." His wife came in, apparently from the kitchen. She returned my "Good evening" with free and easy amiability, without any shyness or side-glances, and disappeared again. I felt annoyed. I was tempted to call after her to come back and let me take a good look at her

"Say, Levinsky, you must have thought I would not trust you for the four hundred dollars," Max said. "May I have four hundred days of distress if I have a cent. What few dollars I do have is buried in the business. So help me, God! Let a few of my customers stop paying and I would have to go begging. It's the real truth I am telling you. Honest."

"I know, I know," I said, awkwardly. "Well, it was as if the check had dropped from heaven. Thank God! Now I can begin to do things."

I went over the main facts of my venture, this time with a touch of bluster.

And he listened with far readier attention and more genuine interest than he had done on the previous occasion. We discussed my plans and my prospects.

At one point, when I referred to the Western check, he asked to see it again, just for curiosity's sake, and as I watched him look it over I could almost see the change that it was producing in his attitude toward me. I do not know to what extent he had previously believed my story, if at all. One thing was clear: the magic check now made it all real to him. As he handed me back the strip of paper he gave me a look that seemed to say: "So you are a manufacturer, you whom I have always known as a miserable ragamuffin."

Mrs. Margolis reappeared. Her husband told her of my great check and she returned some trivialities. As we thus chatted, I made a mental note of the fascinating feminine texture of her flesh

He made me stay to supper. It was a cheery repast. As though to make amends for his failure to respond when I knocked at his door, Max overwhelmed me with attention

We were eating cold sorrel soup, prepared in the old Ghetto way, with cream, bits of boiled egg, cucumber, and scallions

"How do you like it?" he asked

"Delicious! And the genuine article, too."

"'The genuine article'!" he mocked me. "What's the use praising it when you eat it like a bird? What's the matter with you? Are you bashful? Fire away, old man!" Then to his wife: "Why do you keep quiet, Dvorah? Why don't you tell him to eat like a man and not like a bird?"

"Maybe he doesn't care for my cooking," she jested, demurely

"Why, why," I replied. "The sorrel soup is fit for a king."

"You mean for a president," Max corrected me. "We are in America, not in Europe."

"How do you know the President of the United States would care for a plate of cold sorrel soup?"

"And how do you know a king would?" "If you care for it, I am satisfied," the hostess said to me

"I certainly do. I haven't eaten anything like it since I left home," I replied

"Feed him well, Dvorah. Now is your chance. He will soon be a millionaire, don't you know. Then he won't bother about calling on poor people like us."

"But I have said the sorrel soup is fit for a king, and a king has many millions," I rejoined. "I shall always be glad to come, provided

Lucy and Dannie have no objection." "You remember their names, don't you?" Mrs. Margolis said, beamingly. "You certainly have a good memory."

"Who else should have one?" her husband chimed in. "I have told you he was going to study to be a doctor or a lawyer. Lucy, did you hear what uncle said? If you let him in he will come to see us even when he is worth a million. What do you say? Will you let him in?"

Lucy grinned childishly

Max did most of the talking. He entertained me with stories of some curious weddings which he said had recently been celebrated in his dance-halls, and, as usual, it was not easy to draw a line of demarkation between fact and fiction. Of one bridegroom, who had agreed to the marriage under threats of violence from the girl's father, he said: "You should have seen the fellow! He looked like a man going to the electric chair. They were afraid he might bolt, so the bride's father and brother, big, strapping fellows both, stuck to him like two detectives. 'You had better not make monkey business,' they said to him. 'If you don't want a wedding, you'll have a funeral.' That's exactly what they said to him. I was standing close to them and I heard it with my own ears. May I not live till to-morrow if I did not." Mrs. Margolis looked down shamefacedly. She certainly was not unaware of her husband's failing, and she obviously took anything but pride in it. As I glanced at her face at this moment it struck me as a singularly truthful face. "Those eyes of hers do not express anger, but integrity," I said to myself. And the more I looked at her, watched her gestures, and listened to her voice, the stronger grew my impression that she was a senous-minded, ingenuous woman, incapable of playing a part. Her mannerisms were mostly her version of manners, and those that were not were frankly affected, as it were

The meal over and the dishes washed, Mrs. Margolis caused Lucy to bring her school reader and began to read it aloud, Lucy or I correcting her pronunciation where it was faulty. She was frankly parading her intellectual achievements before me, and I could see that she took them quite seriously.

She was very sensitive about the mistakes she made. She accepted our corrections, Lucy's and mine, with great earnestness, often with a gesture of annoyance and mortification at the failure of her memory

When I bade them good night Max said, heartily, in English, "Call again, Levinsky." And he added, in a mixture of English and Yiddish, "Don't be a stranger, even if you are a manufacturer."

"Call again," his wife echoed, affably

"Call again!" shouted Dannie, in his funereal voice

I left with the comfortable feeling of having spent an hour or two in a house where I was sincerely welcome

"It's a good thing to have real friends," I soliloquized in a transport of good spirits, on my way to the Elevated station. "Now I sha'n't feel all alone in the world. There is at least one house where I can call and feel at home."

I beheld Mrs. Margolis's face and her slender figure and I was conscious of a remote desire to see her again

I was in high feather. While the Elevated train was carrying me up-town I visioned an avalanche of new orders for my shop and a spacious factory full of machines and men. I saw myself building up a great business. An ugly thought flashed through my mind: Why be saddled with a partner? Why not get rid of Chaikin? I belittled the part which his samples had played in my successful start, and it seemed to be a cruel injustice to myself to share my fortune with a man who had no more brains than a cat. But I instantly saw the other side of the situation: It was Chaikin's models that had made the Manheimers what they were, and if I clung to him until he could afford to let me announce him as my partner the very news of it would be a tremendous boost for my factory. And then I had a real qualm of compunction for having entertained that thought even for a single moment. My heart warmed to Chaikin and his family. "I shall be faithful to them," I vowed inwardly.

"They have been so good to me. We must be absolutely devoted to each other.

Their house, too, will be like a home to me. Oh, it is so sweet to have friends, real friends."

It was close upon 10 o'clock when I reached the Chaikins' flat in Harlem. I had barely closed the door behind me when I whipped out the check, and, dangling it before Mrs. Chaikin, I said, radiantly: "Good evening. Guess what it is!" "The check you expected from your uncle or cousin or whatever he is to you.

Is it?" she conjectured

"No. It's something far better," I replied. "It's a check from the Western company, and for the full amount, too." And, although I was fairly on the road to atheism, I exclaimed, with a thrill of genuine pity, "Oh, God has been good to us, Mrs. Chaikin!"

I let her see the figures, which she could scarcely make out. Then her husband took a look at the check. He did know something about figures, so he read the sum out aloud

Instead of hailing it with joy, as I had expected her to do, she said to me, glumly: "And how do we know that you did not receive more?"

"But that was the bill," her husband put in

"I am not asking you, am I?" she disciplined him

"But it is the amount on the bill," I said, with a smile

"And how do we know that it is?" she demanded. "It's you who write the bills, and it's you who get the checks. What do we know?"

"Mrs. Chaikin! Mrs. Chaikin!" I remonstrated. "Why should you be so suspicious? Can't you see that I am the most devoted friend you people ever had? God has blessed us; we are making a success of our business so we must be devoted to one another, while here you imagine all kinds of nonsense."

"A woman will be a woman," Chaikin muttered, with his sheepish smile

The unfeigned ardor of my plea produced an impression on Mrs. Chaikin.

Still, she insisted upon receiving her husband's share of the profits at once in spot cash. I argued again

"Why, of course you are going to get your share of the profits," I said, genially. "Of course you are. Only we must first pay for the goods of those five hundred coats and for some other things. Mustn't we? Then, too, there is that other order to fill. We need more goods and cash for wages and rent and other expenses.

"But you said you were going to get it all yourself, and now you want us to pay for it. You think you are smart, don't you?"

Her husband opened his mouth, but she waved it shut before she had any idea what he wanted to say

"Anybody could fool you," she said. "'When a fool goes shopping there is rejoicing among the shopkeepers.'"

With our joint efforts we finally managed to placate her, however, and the next evening our shop was the scene of feverish activity

- To answer my question earlier, Dora is married
- stayed w/ Dora + her husband + child
  └ can't get her out of his mind (again)
- check came in for full amount
  └ back in business

# CHAPTER IV

I FILLED my Third Avenue order and went on soliciting other business. The season was waning, but I obtained a number of small orders and laid foundations for future sales. Our capital was growing apace, but we often lacked working cash

After I paid the debt I owed Meyer Nodelman I obtained other favors from him. He took a sponsorial interest in my business and often offered me the benefit of his commercial experience in the form of maxims

"Don't bite off more than you can chew, Levinsky," he would tell me.

"Finding it easy to get people to trust you is not enough. You must also find it easy to pay them."

Some of his other rules were: "Be pleasant with the man you deal with, even if he knows you don't mean it.

He likes it, anyway."

"Take it from me, Levinsky: honesty is the best policy. There is only one line of business in which dishonesty pays: the burglar business, provided the burglar does not get caught. If I thought lying could help my business, I should lie day and night. But I have learned that it hurts far more than it helps. Be sure that the other fellow believes what you say. If you have his confidence you have him by the throat."

It was not always easy to comply with Meyer's tenets, however. The inadequacy of my working capital often forced me to have recourse to subterfuges that could not exactly be called honorable. One day, when we had some bills to meet two days before I could expect to obtain the cash, I made out and signed checks, but inclosed each of them in the wrong envelope—this supposed act of inadvertence gaining me the needed two days of grace. On another occasion I sent out a number of checks without my signature, which presumably I had forgotten to affix. There were instances when I was so hard pressed for funds that the fate of our factory hinged on seventy-five or a hundred dollars. In one of these crises I bought two gold watches on the instalment plan, for the express and sole purpose of pawning them for fifty dollars. I bought the watches of two men who did not know each other, and returned them as soon as I could spare the cash to redeem them, forfeiting the several weekly payments which I had made on the pretended purchases.

There were instances, too, when I had to borrow of my employees a few dollars with which to buy cotton. Needless to say that all this happened in the early stages of my experience as a manufacturer. I have long since been above and beyond such methods. Indeed, business honor and business dignity are often a luxury in which only those in the front ranks of success can indulge. But then there are features of the game in which the small man is apt to be more honorable and less cruel than the financial magnate

I was continually consulting Max on my affairs. Not that I needed his advice or expected to act upon it. These confidential talks seemed to promote our intimacy and to enhance the security of the welcome I found in his house. A great immigrant city like New York or Chicago is full of men and women who are alone amid a welter of human life. For these nothing has a greater glamour than a family in whose house they might be made to feel at home. I was one of these desolate souls. I still missed my mother. The anniversary of her death was still a feast of longing agony and spiritual bliss to me. I scarcely ever visited the synagogue of the Sons of Antomir these days, but on that great day I was sure to be there. Forgetful of my atheism, I would place a huge candle for her soul, attend all the three services, without omitting a line, and recite the prayer for the dead with sobs in my heart. I had craved some family who would show me warm friendship. The Margolises were such a family (Meyer Nodelman never invited me to his house). They were a godsend to me

Max was essentially a hospitable man, and really fond of me. As for his wife, who received me with the same hearty welcome as he, her liking for me was primarily based, as she once put it herself in the presence of her husband, upon my intellectual qualifications

"It's good to have educated people come to the house," she remarked. "It's good for the children and for everybody else." "I knew she would like you," Max said to me. "She would give her head for education. Only better look out, you two. See that you don't fall in love with each other. Ha, ha!"

Sometimes there were other visitors in the house—some of Max's friends, his and her fellow-townspeople, her relatives, or some neighbor. Dora's great friend was a stout woman with flaxen hair and fishy eyes, named Sadie, or Mrs. Shornik, whose little girl, Beckie, was a classmate of Lucy's, the acquaintance and devoted intimacy of the two mothers having originated in the intimacy of the two school-girls. Sadie lived several blocks from the Margolises, but she absolutely never let a day pass without calling on her, if it were only for just time enough to kiss her. She was infatuated with Dora, and Beckie was infatuated with Lucy

"They just couldn't live without one another," Max said, after introducing me to Sadie and explaining the situation

"Suppose Lucy and Beckie had not happened to be in the same school," I jested, addressing myself to the two women. "What would you have done then?"

"This shows that we have a good God in heaven," Sadie returned, radiantly.

"He put the children in the same school so that we might meet."

"'A providential match,'" I observed.

"May it last for many, many years," Sadie returned, devoutly

"Say, women!" Max shouted, "you have been more than five minutes without kissing. What's the matter with you?"

At this, Sadie, with mock defiance, walked up to Mrs. Margolis, threw her arms around her, and gave her a luscious smack on the lips

"Bravo! And now you, kids!" Max commanded

With a merry chuckle the two little girls flew into each other's arms and kissed. Lucy had dark hair like Dora's, and Beckie flaxen hair like Sadie's, so when their heads were close together they were an amusing reduced copy of their mothers as these had looked embracing and kissing a minute before

Max often dropped in to see me at my factory, and when I was not busy we would talk of my cloaks, of his instalment business, or of women. Women were his great topic of conversation, as usual. But then these talks of his no longer found a ready listener in me. Now, that I knew his wife, they jarred on me. A decided change had come over me in this respect. I remember it vividly. It was as if his lewd discourses desecrated her name and thereby offended me. It may be interesting to note, however, that he never took up this kind of topics when we were in his house, not even when his wife was out

Sometimes I would have supper at his house. More often, however—usually on Monday, when Max seldom went to the dance-halls—I would come after supper and spend the rest of the evening there. Sometimes the Shorniks would drop in—Sadie, her husband, and Beckie. Ben Shornik and Max would play a game of pinochle, while I, who never cared for cards, would chat with the women or entertain them by entertaining the children. Ben—as I came into the habit of calling him—was a spare little man with an extremely high forehead. He was an insurance-collector and only one degree less illiterate than Max; but because he had the "forehead of a learned man," and because it was his business to go from house to house with a long, thick book under his arm, he affected longish hair, flowing black neckties, and a certain pomposity of manner. One of his ways of being tremendously American was to snap his fingers ferociously and to say, "I don't care a continental!" or, "One, two, three, and there you are!" The latter exclamation he would be continually murmuring to himself when he was absorbed in pinochle

- paid off debt to Nodelman
- aniversary of mother's death
- seem to be jealous of Max / Dan's marriage or relationship
  L Lucy (M/D) + Beckie (Sadie + Ben) = friends

# CHAPTER V

ONE evening, when the Shorniks and I were at Max's house, and Max and Ben were having their game of pinochle, the conversation between the women and myself turned upon Dora's efforts to obtain education through her little daughter. Encouraged by Sadie and myself, Dora let herself loose and told us much of Lucy's history, or, rather, of her own history as Lucy's mother. In her crude, lumbering way and with flushed cheeks she talked with profound frankness and quaint introspective insight, in the manner of one touching upon things that are enshrined in innermost recesses of one's soul

She depicted the thrills of joyous surprise with which she had watched Lucy, in her infancy, master the beginnings of speech. Sometimes her delight would be accompanied by something akin to fright. There had been moments when it all seemed unreal and weird

"The little thing seemed to be a stranger to me," she said. "Or else, she did not seem to be a human being at all."

The next moment she would recognize her, as it were, and then she would kiss and yearn over her in a mad rush of passion

The day when she took Lucy to school—about two years before—was one of the greatest days in Dora's life. She would then watch her learn to associate written signs with spoken words as she had once watched her learn to speak.

But that was not all. She became jealous of the child. She herself had never been taught to read even Hebrew or Yiddish, much less a Gentile language, while here, lo and behold! her little girl possessed a Gentile book and was learning to read it. She was getting education, her child, just like the daughter of the landlord of the house in Russia in which Dora had grown up

"C-a-t—cat," Lucy would spell out. "R-a-t—rat. M-a-t—mat."

And poor Dora would watch the performance with mixed joy and envy and exclamations like: "What do you think of that snip of a thing! Did you ever?"

Lucy's school-reader achievements stirred a novel feeling of rivalry in Dora's breast. When the little girl could spell half a dozen English words she hated herself for her inferiority to her

"The idea of that kitten getting ahead of me! Why, it worried the life out of me!" she said. "You may think it foolish, but I couldn't help it. I kept saying to myself, 'She'll grow up and be an educated American lady and she'll be ashamed to walk in the street with me.' Don't we see things like that? People will beggar themselves to send their children to college, only to be treated as fools and greenhorns by them. I call that terrible. Don't you? Well, I am not going to let my child treat me like that. Not I. I should commit suicide first. I want my child to respect me, not to look down on me. If she reads a book she is to bear in mind that her mother is no ignorant slouch of a greenhorn, either."

A next-door neighbor, a woman who could read English, would help Lucy with her spelling lesson of an evening. This seemed to have established special relations between the child and that woman from which Dora was excluded

She made up her mind to learn to read. If Lucy could manage it, she, her mother, could. So she caused the child to teach her to spell out words in her First Reader. At first she pretended to treat it as a joke, but inwardly she took it seriously from the very outset, and later, under the intoxicating effect of the progress she was achieving, these studies became the great passion of her life. Whenever Lucy recited some new lines, learned at school, she would not rest until she, too, had learned them by heart.

Here are two "pieces" which she proudly recited to us: "The snow is white, The sky is blue, The sun is bright, And so are you."

"Our ears were made to hear, Our tongues were made to talk, Our eyes were made to see, Our feet were made to walk."

Her voice, as she declaimed the lines, attracted Lucy's attention, so she sent her and Beckie into the kitchen

"She doesn't know what a treasure she is to me," she said to us. Then, after she finished the two verses, she remarked, wistfully, "Well, my own life is lost, but she shall be educated."

"Why? Why should you talk like that, Dora?" Sadie protested, her fishy eyes full of tragedy. "Why, you are only beginning to live."

"Of course she is," I chimed in.

"Well," Dora rejoined, "anyhow, I am afraid I love her too much. Sometimes it seems to me I am going crazy over her. I love Dannie, too, of course.

When he happens to hurt a finger or to hit his dear little head against something I can't sleep. Is he not my flesh and blood like Lucy? Still, Lucy is different." She paused and then rose from her seat, saying, with a smile: "Wait. I am going to show you something." She went into the kitchen and came back, holding a tooth-brush in either hand. "Guess what it is."

"Two tooth-brushes," I answered, with perplexed gaiety

"Aren't you smart! I know they are not shoe-brushes, but what kind of tooth-brushes? How did I come by them? That's the question. Did I use a tooth-brush in my mother's house?"

*Huh?*

She then told me how Lucy, coming from school one day, had announced an order from the teacher that every girl in the class must bring a tooth-brush the next morning

Sadie nodded confirmation

"Of course, I went to work and bought, not one brush, but two," Dora pursued. "I am as good as Lucy, am I not? If she is worth twelve cents, I am. And if she is American lady enough to use a tooth-brush, I am."

*adaptation/submission*

Lucy is not a usual name on the East Side. It was, in fact, the principal of the school who had recommended it, at Dora's solicitation. The little girl had hitherto been called Lizzie, the commonplace East Side version of Leah, her Hebrew name. Dora never liked it. It did not sound American enough, for there were Lizzies or Lizas in Europe, too. Any "greenhorn" might bear such a name. So she called on Lizzie's principal and asked her to suggest some "nicer name" for her daughter

"I want a real American one," she said

The principal submitted half a dozen names beginning with "L," and the result was that Lizzie became Lucy

Dora went over every spelling lesson with the child. It was so sweet to be helpful to her in this way. Lucy, on her part, had to reciprocate by hearing her mother spell the same words, and often they would have a spelling-match.

All of which, as I could see, had invested Lucy with the fascination of a spiritual companion

The child had not been at school many weeks when she began to show signs of estrangement from her mother-tongue. Her Yiddish was rapidly becoming clogged with queer-sounding "r's" and with quaintly twisted idioms. Yiddish words came less and less readily to her tongue, and the tendency to replace them with their English equivalents grew in persistence. Dora would taunt her on her "Gentile Yiddish," yet she took real pride in it. Finally, Lucy abandoned her native tongue altogether. She still understood her parents, of course, but she now invariably addressed them or answered their Yiddish questions in English. As a result, Dora would make efforts to speak to her in the language that had become the child's natural means of expression. It was a sorry attempt at first; but she was not one to give up without a hard struggle. She went at it with great tenacity, listening intently to Lucy's English and trying to repeat words and phrases after her. And so, with the child's assistance, conscious or unconscious, she kept adding to her practical acquaintance with the language, until by the end of Lucy's first school year she spoke it with considerable fluency

Dora tried her hand at writing, but little Lucy proved a poor penmanship-teacher, and she was forced to confine herself to reading. She forged ahead of her, reading pages which Lucy's class had not yet reached.

To take Lucy to school was one of the keen joys of Dora's existence. Very often they would fall in with Lucy's bosom friend

"Good morning, Lucy."

"Good morning, Beckie."

As she described the smiling, childishly lady-like way in which the little girls exchanged their greetings and then intertwined their little arms as they proceeded on their way together, Sadie's fishy eyes filled with tears

"Oh, how sweet it is to be a mother!" Dora said

"I should say it was," her chum and follower echoed, wiping her tears and laughing at once

251

There was a curious element of superstition in Dora's attitude toward her little girl. She had taken it into her head that Lucy had been playing the part of a mascot in her life

"I was a bag of bones until she was born," she said. "Why, people who are put into the grave look better than I did. But my birdie darling came, and, well, if I don't look like a monkey now, I have her to thank. It was after her birth that I began to pick up." She had formed the theory that the child was born to go to school for her mother's sake as well as her own—a little angel sent down from heaven to act as a messenger of light to her

Her story made a strong impression on me. "Max is not worthy of her," I reflected. I wondered whether she was fully aware what manner of man he was

*here we go again...*

- Dora jealous of her daughter's education
  - afraid
- adaptation into Am society
- D fancies himself in love w/ Dora
  ...sand familiar?

# CHAPTER VI

SOMETIMES we would go to the Jewish theater together, Max, Dora, and I, the children being left at Sadie's house. Once, when Max's lodge had a benefit performance and he had had some tickets for sale, we made up a party of five: the two couples and myself. On that occasion I met Jake Mindels at the playhouse. He was now studying medicine at the University Medical College, and it was a considerable time since I had last seen him. To tell the truth, I had avoided meeting him. I hated to stand confessed before him as a traitor to my dreams of a college education, and I begrudged him his medical books.

I took Max and Dora to see an American play. He did not understand much of what he saw and was bored to death. As for her, she took in scarcely more than did her husband, though she understood many of the words she heard, but then she reverently followed the good manners of the "real Americans" on the stage, and the sound of their "educated" English seemed to inspire her with mixed awe and envy

Once, on a Monday evening, when I called on the Margolises, I found Max out.

Dora seemed to be ill at ease in my company, and I did not stay long. It seemed natural to fear that Max, who gave so much attention to the relations between the sexes, should view visits of this kind with misgivings. His playful warnings that we should beware of falling in love with each other seemed to be always in the air, and on that evening when he was away and we found ourselves alone I seemed to hear their echo more distinctly than ever.

It had a disquieting effect on me, that echo, and I decided never to call unless Max was sure to be at home. I enjoyed their hospitality too much to hazard it rashly. Moreover, Max and Dora lived in peace and I was the last man in the world to wish to disturb it

To my surprise, however, he did not seem to be jealous of me in the least.

Quite the contrary. He encouraged my familiarities with her, so much so that I soon drifted into the habit of addressing her as Dora

The better I knew her the greater was the respect with which she inspired me. I thought her an unusual woman, and I looked up to her

It became a most natural thing that I should propose myself as a boarder.

Thousands of families like the Margolises kept boarders to lighten the burden of rent-day

The project had been trailing in my mind for some time and, I must confess, the fact that Max stayed out till the small hours four or five nights a week had something to do with it

"You would be alone with her," Satan often whispered. Still, there was nothing definitely reprehensible in this reflection. It was the prospect of often being decorously alone with a woman who inspired me with respect and interested me more and more keenly that tempted me. Vaguely, however, I had a feeling that I was on the road to falling in love with her

One evening, as I complained of my restaurant meals and of certain inconveniences of my lodgings, Max said: "Nothing like being married, Levinsky. Take my advice and get you a nice little wifey. One like mine, for instance."

"Like yours! The trouble is that there is only one such, and you have captured her." "Don't worry," Dora broke in. "There are plenty of others, and better ones, too."

"I have a scheme," I said, seriously. "Why shouldn't you people let me board with you?"

Natural as the suggestion was, it took them by surprise. For a second or two Max gazed at his wife with a perplexed air. Then he said: "That would not he a bad idea. Would it, Dora?"

"I don't know, I am sure," she answered, with a shrug and an embarrassed smile. "We have never kept boarders."

"You will try to keep one now, then," I urged

"If there were room in the house, I should be glad. Upon my health and strength I should." "Oh, you can make room," I said.

"Of course you can," Max put in, warming to the plan somewhat. "He could have the children's bedroom, and they could sleep in this room."

She held to her veto

"Oh, you don't know what an obstinate thing she is," Max said. "Let her say that white is black, and black it must be, even if the world turned upside down."

"What do you want of me?" she protested. "Levinsky may think I really don't care to have him. Let us move to a larger apartment and I'll be but too glad to give him a room."

The upshot was a compromise. For the present I was to content myself with having my luncheons and dinners or suppers at their house, Dora charging me cost price

"Get him to move to one of those new houses with modern improvements," she said to me, earnestly; "to an apartment of five light rooms, and I shall give you a room at once. The rent would come cheaper than it is now. But Max would rather pay more and have the children grow in these damp rooms than budge."

"Don't bother me. By and by we shall move out of here. All in due time.

Don't bother. Meanwhile see that your dinners and suppers are all right.

Levinsky thinks you a good cook. Don't disappoint him, then. Don't run away with the idea it's on your own account he wants to board with us. It is on account of your cooking. That's all. Isn't it, Levinsky?"

"It's a good thing to know that I am not a bad cook, at least," she returned

"But how about the profits you are going to make on him? I'll deduct them from your weekly allowance, you know," he chaffed her

"Oh no. I am just going to save them and buy a house on Fifth Avenue."

"You ought to allow me ten per cent. for cash," I said. "She does not want cash," Max replied. "Your note is good enough."

I had been taking my meals with them a little over a month when they moved into a new apartment, with me as their roomer and boarder. The apartment was on the third floor of a corner house on Clinton Street, one of a row of what was then a new type of tenement buildings. It consisted of five rooms and bath, all perfectly light, and it had a tiny private corridor or vestibule, a dumb-waiter, an enameled bath-tub, electric and gas light, and an electric door-bell. There was a rush for these apartments and Dora paid a deposit on the first month's rent before the builder was quite through with his work.

My room opened into the vestibule, its window looking out upon a side-street. The rent for the whole apartment was thirty-two dollars, my board being five and a half dollars a week, which was supposed to include a monthly rental of six dollars for my room

The Shorniks moved into the same house

*wow!*

- Like I said, D is on the brink of falling in love w/ Dora
- manages to move in w/ them as a boarder... sly dog...

# CHAPTER VII

MY growing interest in Dora burst into flame all at once, as it were. It happened at a moment which is distinctly fixed in my mind. At least I distinctly remember the moment when I became conscious of it

It was on an afternoon, four days after the Margolises had taken possession of the new place. The family was fully established in it, while I had just moved in. I had seen my room, furniture and all, several times before, but I had never seen it absolutely ready for my occupancy as I did now. It was by far the brightest, airiest, best-furnished, and neatest room that I had ever had all to myself. Everything in it, from the wall-paper to the little wash-stand, was invitingly new. I can still smell its grateful odor of freshness. When I was left to myself in it for the first time and I shut its door the room appealed to me as a compartment in the nest of a family of which I was a member. My lonely soul had a sense of home and domestic comfort that all but overpowered me. The sight of the new quilt and of the fresh white pillow, coupled with the knowledge that it was Dora whose fingers had prepared it all for me, sent a glow of delight through my heart

Dora's name was whispering itself in my mind. I paused at the window, an enchanted man

A few minutes later, when I re-entered the living-room, where she was counting some freshly ironed napkins, her face seemed to have acquired a new meaning. I felt that a great change had come in my attitude toward her

"Well, is everything all right?" she inquired

"First rate," I answered, in a voice that sounded unnatural to myself

Max was fussing with the rug in the parlor. The children were gamboling from room to room, testing the faucets, the dumb-waiter

"Get avey from there!" Dora shouted. "You'll hurt yourself. Max, tell Lucy not to touch the dumb-vaiter, vill you?"

"Children! Children! What's a madder vitch you?" he called out from the parlor, in English, with a perfunctory snarl. Presently he came into the living-room. "Well, are you satisfied with your new palace?" he addressed me in Yiddish. And for the hundredth time he proceeded to make jokes at the various modern "improvements," at the abundance of light, and at my new rank of "real boarder."

It is one of the old and deep-rooted customs of the Ghetto towns of Europe for a young couple to live with the parents of the bride for a year or two after the wedding. So Max gaily dubbed me his "boarding son-in-law

"Try to behave, boarding son-in-law," he bantered me. "If you don't your mother-in-law will starve you."

The pleasantry grated on me

Dora's ambition to learn to read and spell English was a passion, and the little girl played a more important part in the efforts she made in this direction than Dora was willing to admit. Lucy would tell her the meaning of new words as she had heard it at school, but it often happened that the official definition she quoted was incomprehensible to both. This was apt to irritate Dora or even lead to a disagreeable scene

If I happened to be around I would explain things to her, but she seemed to accept my explanations with a grain of salt. She bowed before my intellectual status in a general way, but since she had good reason to doubt the quality of my English enunciation, she doubted my Yiddish interpretations as well. Indeed, she doubted everything that did not bear the indorsement of Lucy's school. Whatever came from that sacred source was "real Yankee"; everything else was "greenhorn." If she failed to grasp some of the things that Lucy brought back from school, she would blame it on the child.

"Oh, you didn't understand what your teacher said," she would scold her.

"You must have twisted it all up, you stupid."

One afternoon, when business was slow and there did not seem to be anything to preclude my staying at home and breathing the air that Dora breathed, I witnessed a painful scene between them. It was soon after Lucy returned from school. Her mother wanted her to go over her last reading-lesson with her, and the child would not do so, pleading a desire to call on Beckie

"Stay where you are and open your reader," Dora commanded

Lucy obeyed, whimperingly. "Read!" "I want to go to Beckie."

"Read, I say." And she slapped her hand

"Don't," I remonstrated. "Let the poor child go enjoy herself." But it only spoiled matters

"Read!" she went on, with grim composure, hitting her on the shoulder

"I don't want to! I want to go down-stairs," Lucy sobbed, defiantly

"Read!" And once more she hit her.

My heart went out to the child, but I dared not intercede again

Dora did not relent until Lucy yielded, sobbingly

I left the room in disgust. The scene preyed upon my mind all that afternoon. I remained in my room until supper-time. Then I found Dora taciturn and downcast and I noticed that she treated Lucy with exceptional, though undemonstrative, tenderness

"Must have given her a licking," Max explained to me, with a wink

I kept my counsel

She beat her quite often, sometimes violently, each scene of this kind being followed by hours of bitter remorse on her part. Her devotion to her children was above that of the average mother. Lucy had been going to school for over two years, yet she missed her every morning as though she were away to another city; and when the little girl came back, Dora's face would brighten, as if a flood of new sunshine had burst into the house.

On one occasion there was a quarrel between mother and daughter over the result of a spelling-match between them which I had umpired and which Lucy had won. Dora took her defeat so hard that she was dejected all that evening

I have said that despite her passionate devotion to Lucy she was jealous of her. She was jealous not only of the school education she was receiving, but also of her American birth

She was feverishly ambitious to bring up her children in the "real American syle," and the realization of her helplessness in this direction caused her many a pang of despair. She was thirstily seeking for information on the subject of table manners, and whatever knowledge she possessed of it she would practise, and make Lucy practise, with amusing pomp and circumstance.

"Don't reach out for the herring, Lucy!" she would say, sternly. "How many times must I tell you about it? What do you say?"

"Pass me the herring, mamma, please." "Not 'mamma.'"

"Pass me the herring, mother, please."

The herring is passed with what Dora regards as a lady-like gesture

"Thank you, ma'am," says Lucy

"There is another way," Dora might add in a case of this kind. "Instead of saying, 'Pass me the herring or the butter,' you can say—What is it, Lucy?"

"May I trouble you for the herring, mother?"

I asked her to keep track of my table etiquette, too, and she did. Whenever I made a break she would correct my error solemnly, or with a burst of merriment, or with a scandalized air, as if she had caught me in the act of committing a felony. This was her revenge for my general intellectual superiority, which she could not help admitting and envying

"You just let her teach you and she will make a man of you," Max would say to me.

Sometimes, when I mispronounced an English word with which she happened to be familiar, or uttered an English phrase in my Talmudic singsong, she would mock me gloatingly. On one such occasion I felt the sting of her triumph so keenly that I hastened to lower her crest by pointing out that she had said "nice" where "nicely" was in order

"What do you mean?" she asked, perplexedly

My reply was an ostentatious discourse on adjectives 2 and adverbs, something which I knew to be utterly beyond her depth. It had the intended effect. She listened to my explanation stupidly, and when I had finished she said, with resignation: "I don't understand what you say. I wish I had time to go to evening school, at least, as you did. I haven't any idea of these things. Lucy will be educated for both of us, for herself and for her poor mamma. If my mother had understood as much as I do it would have been different." She uttered a sigh, fell silent, and then resumed: "But I can't complain of my mother, either. She was a diamond of a woman, and she was wise as daylight. But Russia is not America. No, I can't complain of my parents. My father was a poor man, but ask Max or some of our fellow-townspeople and they will tell you what a fine name he had."

She was talkative and somewhat boastful like the average woman of her class, but there was about her an elusive effect of reserve and earnestness that kept me at a distance from her. Moreover, the tireless assiduity and precision which she brought to her housework and, above all, the grim passion of her intellectual struggles created an atmosphere of physical and spiritual tidiness about her that inspired me with something like reverence.

Living in that atmosphere seemed to be making a better man of me

Attempting a lark with her, as I had done with Mrs. Dienstog and Mrs.

Levinsky, my first two landladies in New York, was out of the question.

Needless to explain that this respectful distance did not prevent my eyes and ears from feasting upon her luxurious complexion, her clear, honest voice, and all else that made me feel both happy and forlorn in her company. Nor would she, aware as she undoubtedly was of the meaning of my look or smile, hesitate to respond to them by some legitimate bit of coquetry. In short, we often held converse in that language of smiles, glances, blushes, pauses, gestures, which is the gesture language of sex across the barrier of decorum.

These speechless flirtations cost me many an hour which I should have otherwise spent at my shop or soliciting trade. When away from the magnetic force of her presence I would attend to business with unabated intensity.

Her image visited my brain often, but it did not disturb me. Rather, it was the image of some customer or creditor or of some new style of jacket or cloak that would interfere with my peace of mind. My brain was full of prices, bills, notes, checks, fabrics, color effects, "lines." Not infrequently, while walking in the street or sitting in a street-car, I would catch myself describing some of those garment lines in the air.

And yet, through all these preoccupations I seemed to be constantly aware that something unusual had happened to me, giving a novel tinge to my being; that I was a changed man

- Dora/Max found a new apartment, bigger for their boarders, David one of them
- Dora is becoming ceaselessly jealous of her daughter, Lucy's, education
  Lwants to learn how to be a "real American"
- flirtations w/ Dora
  L "changed man"

# CHAPTER VIII

MAX saw nothing. His wife was a very womanly woman with a splendid, almost a gorgeous snow-white womanly complexion, and I was a young man in whom, according to his own dictum, women ought to be interested; yet he never seemed to feel anything like apprehension about us. This man who plumed himself upon his knowledge of women and love and who actually had a great deal of insight in these matters, this man, I say, was absolutely blind to his wife's power over me. He suspected every man and every woman under the sun, yet he was the least jealous of men so far as his wife was concerned, though he loved and was proud of her. From time to time he would chaff Dora and myself on the danger of our falling in love with each other, but that was never more than a joke and, at any rate, I heard it from him far less often than that other joke of his—about my being his and Dora's son-in-law

"Look out, mother-in-law," he would say to her. "If you don't treat your son-in-law right you'll lose him."

I have said that he was proud of her. One evening, while she stood on a chair struggling with a recalcitrant window-shade, he drew my attention to her efforts admiringly

"Look at her!" he said under his breath. "Another woman would make her husband do it. Not she. I can't kick. She is not a lazy slob, is she?"

"Certainly not," I asserted

We watched her take the shade down, wind up the spring, fit the pins back into their sockets, and then test the flap. It was in good working order now

"No, she is not a slob," he repeated, exultantly. "And she is not a gossiping sort, either. She just minds her own business."

At this point Dora came over to the table where we sat. "Move along!" he said, gaily. "Don't disturb us. I am telling Levinsky what a bad girl you are. Run along."

She gave us a shy side-glance like those that had carried the first germ of disquiet into my soul, and moved away

"No, she is no slob, thank God," he resumed. He boasted of her tidiness and of the way she had picked up her English and learned to read and spell, with little Lucy for her teacher. He depicted the tenacity and unflagging ardor with which she had carried on her mental pursuits ever since Lucy began to go to school. "Once she makes up her mind to do something she will stick to it, even if the world went under. That's the kind of woman she is. And she is no mean, foxy thing, either. When she says something you may be sure she means it, if I do say so. You ought to know her by this time. Have you ever heard her say things that are not so? Or have you heard her talk about the neighbors as other women-folk will do? Have you, now? Just tell me," he pressed me

"Of course I have not," I answered, awkwardly. "There are not many women like her." _— there's a double meaning in that!_

"I know there are not. And, well, if she is not devoted tc her hubby, I don't know who is," he added, sheepishly

_· Max is blind to the flirtation that is going on between his wife + D_
_· M praises Dora for her hard work around the house_

# CHAPTER IX

IT was during this period that I received my first baptism of dismay as patron of a high-class restaurant. The occasion was a lunch to which I had invited a buyer from Philadelphia. The word "buyer" had a bewitching sound for me, inspiring me with awe and enthusiasm at once. The word "king" certainly did not mean so much to me. The august person to whom I was doing homage on the occasion in question was a man named Charles M. Eaton, a full-blooded Anglo-Saxon of New England origin, with a huge round forehead and small, blue, extremely genial eyes. He was a large, fair-complexioned man, and the way his kindly little eyes looked from under his hemispherical forehead, like two swallows viewing the world from under the eaves of a roof, gave him a striking appearance. The immense restaurant, with its high, frescoed ceiling, the dazzling whiteness of its rows and rows of table-cloths, the crowd of well-dressed customers, the glint and rattle of knives and forks, the subdued tones of the orchestra, and the imposing black-and-white figures of the waiters struck terror into my Antomir heart.

The bill of fare was, of course, Chinese to me, though I made a pretense of reading it. The words swam before me. My inside pocket contained sufficient money to foot the most extravagant bill our lordly waiter was likely to present, but I was in constant dread lest my treasure disappear in some mysterious way; so, from time to time, I felt my breast to ascertain whether it was still there

The worst part of it all was that I had not the least idea what I was to say or do. The occasion seemed to call for a sort of table manners which were beyond the resources not only of a poor novice like myself, but also of a trained specialist like Dora

Finally my instinct of self-preservation whispered in my ear, "Make a clean breast of it." And so, dropping the bill of fare with an air of mock despair, I said, jovially: "I'm afraid you'll have to tell me what to do, Mr. Eaton. It's no use bluffing. I have never been in such a fine restaurant in my life. I am scared to death, Mr. Eaton. Take pity."

The Philadelphian, who was a slow-spoken, slow-witted, though shrewd, man, was perplexed at first

"I see," he said, coloring, and looking confusedly at me. The next minute he seemed to realize the situation and to enjoy it, too, but even then he was apparently embarrassed. I cracked another joke or two at my own expense, until finally he burst into a hearty laugh and cheerfully agreed to act as master of ceremonies. Not only did he do the ordering, explaining things to me when the waiter was not around, but he also showed me how to use my napkin, how to eat the soup, the fish, the meat, what to do with the finger-bowl, and so forth and so on, to the minutest detail

"I am afraid one lesson won't be enough," I said. "You must give me another chance."

how nice!
✱ "With pleasure," he replied. "Only the next 'lesson' will be on me." And then he had to tell me what "on me" meant

He took a fancy to me and that meant orders, not only from him, but also from some people of his acquaintance, buyers from other towns

I sought to dress like a genteel American, my favorite color for clothes and hats being (and still is) dark brown. It became my dark hair well, I thought. The difference between taste and vulgar ostentation was coming slowly, but surely, I hope. I remember the passionate efforts I made to learn to tie a four-in-hand cravat, then a recent invention. I was forever watching and striving to imitate the dress and the ways of the well-bred American merchants with whom I was, or trying to be, thrown. All this, I felt, was an essential element in achieving business success; but the ambition to act and look like a gentleman grew in me quite apart from these motives

Now, Dora seemed to notice these things in me, and to like them. So I would parade my newly acquired manners before her as I did my neckties or my English vocabulary

After that lecture I gave her on adverbs she no longer called my English in question. To be educated and an "American lady" had, thanks to Lucy's influence, become the great passion of her

266

life. It almost amounted to an obsession. She thought me educated and a good deal of an American, so she looked up to me and would listen to my harangues reverently

- went to dinner w/ a Mr. Eaton
- becoming more "educated" in "American ways"
  └ Dora opening up more towards him
        └ shame!!! ?

# CHAPTER X

ONE Saturday evening she said to me: "Lord! you are so educated. I wish I had a head like yours."

"Why, you have an excellent head, Dora," I replied. "You have no reason to complain."

She sighed

"I wish I had not gone into business," I resumed

I had already told her, more than once, in fact, how I had been about to enter college when an accident had led me astray; so I now referred to those events, dwelling regretfully upon the sudden change I had made in my life plans

"It was the devil that put it in my head to become a manufacturer," I said, bitterly, yet with relish in the "manufacturer." "Well, one can be a manufacturer and educated man at the same time," she consoled me

"Of course. That's exactly what I always say," I returned, joyously. "Still, I wish I had stuck to my original plan. There was a lady in Antomir who advised me to prepare for college. She was always speaking to me about it."

It was about 10 o'clock. Max was away to his dancing-schools. The children were asleep. We were alone in the living-room

I expected her to ask who that Antomir lady was, but she did not, so I went on speaking of Matilda of my own accord. I sketched her as an "aristocratic" young woman, the daughter of one of the leading families in town, accomplished, clever, pretty, and "modern."

"It was she, in fact, who got me the money for my trip to America," I said, lowering my voice, as one will when a conversation assumes an intimate character

"Was it?" Dora said, also in a low voice

"Yes. It is a long story. It is nearly five years since I left home, but I still think of it a good deal. Sometimes I feel as if my heart would snap unless I had somebody to tell about it."

This was my way of drawing Dora into a flirtation, my first attempt in that direction, though in my heart I had been making love to her for weeks

I told her the story of my acquaintance with Matilda. She listened with non-committal interest, with an amused, patronizing glimmer of a smile

"You did not fall in love with her, did you?" she quizzed me as she might Lucy

"That's the worst part of it," I said, gravely

"Is it?" she asked, still gaily, but with frank interest now

I recounted the episode at length. To put it in plain English, I was using my affair with Matilda (or shall I say her affair with me?) as a basis for an adventure with Dora. At first I took pains to gloss over those details in which I had cut an undignified figure, but I soon dropped all embellishments. The episode stood out so bold in my memory. its appeal to my imagination was so poignant, that I found an intoxicating satisfaction in conveying the facts as faithfully as I knew how. To be telling a complete, unvarnished truth is in itself a pleasure. It is as though there were a special sense of truth and sincerity in our make-up (just as there is a sense of musical harmony, for example), and the gratification of it were a source of delight.

*always using David, always!*

Nor was this my only motive for telling Dora all. I had long since realized that the disdain and mockery with which Matilda handled me had been but a cloak for her interest in my person. So when I was relating to Dora the scenes of my ignominy I felt that the piquant circumstances surrounding them were not unfavorable to me

Anyhow, I was having a singularly intimate talk with Dora and she was listening with the profoundest interest, all the little tricks she employed to disguise it notwithstanding

In depicting the scene of the memorable night when Matilda came to talk to me at my bedside I emphasized the fact that she had called me a ninny

"I did not know what she meant," I said.

Dora tittered, looking at the floor shamefacedly. "The nasty thing!" she said

"What do you mean?" I inquired, dishonestly

"I mean just what I say. She is a nasty thing, that grand lady of yours." And she added another word—the East Side name for a woman of the streets—that gave me a shock

"Don't call her that," I entreated. "Please don't. You are mistaken about her. I assure you she is a highly respectable lady. She has a heart of gold," I added, irrelevantly

"Well, well! You are still in love with her, aren't you?"

I was tempted to say: "No. It is you I now love." But I merely said, dolefully: "No. Not any more."

She contemplated me amusedly and broke into a soft laugh

The next time we were alone in the house I came back to it. I added some details. I found a lascivious interest in dwelling on our passionate kisses, Matilda's and mine. Also, it gave me morbid pleasure to have her behold me at Matilda's feet, lovelorn, disdained, crushed, yet coveted, kissed, triumphant

Dora listened intently. She strove to keep up an amused air, as though listening to some childish nonsense, but the look of her eye, tense or flinching, and the warm color that often overspread her cheeks, betrayed her      —Oh crap!

- Had a talk w/ Dora, using Matilda as a way of flirting w/ her
  L I swear he uses women like someone uses tissues for a runny nose.
- Dora asked him if he still loved Matilda, he replied no
  L He mentioned kissing + she blushed ... my sentiments are "Oh crap! Not again"

# CHAPTER XI

WE talked about my first love-affair for weeks. She asked me many questions about Matilda, mostly with that pretended air of amused curiosity. Every time I had something good to say about Matilda she would assail her brutally *jealous of Matilda, is she?*

The fact that Dora never referred to my story in the presence of her husband was a tacit confession that we had a secret from him. Outwardly it meant that the secret was mine, not hers; that she had nothing to do with it; but then there was another secret—the fact that she was my sole confidante in a matter of this nature—and this secret was ours in common

On one occasion, in the course of one of these confabs of ours, she said, with ill-concealed malice: "Do you really think she cared for you? Not that much," marking off the tip of her little finger

"Why should you say that? Why should you hurt my feelings?" I protested

"It still hurts your feelings, then, does it? There is a faithful lover for you! But what would you have me say? That she loved you as much as you loved her?"

At this Dora jerked her head backward, with a laugh that rang so charmingly false and so virulent that I was impelled both to slap her face and to kiss it

"But tell me," she said, with a sudden affectation of sedate curiosity, "was she really so beautiful?"

"I never said she was 'so beautiful,' did I? You are far more beautiful than she." "Oh, stop joking, please! Can't you answer seriously?"  *Trap! Don't listen Dora!*

"I really mean it."

"Mean what?"

"That you are prettier than Matilda." "Is that the way you are faithful to her?"

"Oh, that was five years ago. Now there is somebody else I am faithful to."

She was silent. Her cheeks glowed

"Why don't you ask who that somebody is?"

"Because I don't care. What do I care? And please don't talk like that. I mean what I say. You must promise me never to talk like that," she said, gravely

During the following few days Dora firmly barred all more or less intimate conversation. She treated me with her usual friendly familiarity, but there was something new in her demeanor, something that seemed to say, "I don't deny that I enjoy our talks, but that's all the more reason why you must behave yourself."

The story of my childhood seemed legitimate enough, so she let me tell her bits of it, and before she was aware of it she was following my childish love-affair with the daughter of one of my despotic school-teachers, my struggles with Satan, and my early dreams of marriage. Gradually she let me draw her out concerning her own past.

One evening, while Lucy was playing school-teacher, with Dannie for the class, Dora told me of an episode connected with her betrothal to Max

"Was that a love match?" I asked, with a casual air, when she had finished

She winced. "What difference does it make?" she said, with an annoyed look.

"We were engaged as most couples are engaged. Much I knew of the love business in those days."

"You speak as though you married when you were a mere baby. You certainly knew how you felt toward him."

"I don't think I felt anything," she answered

"Still," I insisted, "you said to yourself, 'This man is going to be my husband; he will kiss me, embrace me.' How did you feel then?"

"You want to know too much, Levinsky," she said, coloring. "You know the saying, 'If you know too much you get old too quick.' Well, I don't think I gave him any thought at all. I was too busy thinking of the wedding and of the pretty dress they were making for me. Besides. I was so rattled and so shy. Much I understood. I was not quite nineteen."

It called to my mind that in the excitement following my mother's death I was so overwhelmed by the attentions showered on me that it was a day or two before I realized the magnitude of my calamity

"Anyhow, you certainly knew that marriage is the most serious thing in life," I persisted

"Oh, I don't think I knew much of anything."

"And after the wedding?"

"After the wedding I knew that I was a married woman and must be contented," she parried

"But this is not love," I pressed her

"Oh, let us not talk of these things, pray! Don't ask me questions like that," she said in a low, entreating voice. "It isn't right."

"I don't know if it is right or wrong," I replied, also in a low voice. "All I do know is that I am interested in everything that ever happened to you

Silence fell. She was the first to break it. She tried to talk of trivialities. I scarcely listened. She broke off again

"Dora!" I said, amorously. "My heart is so full."

"Don't," she whispered, with a gesture of pained supplication. "Talk of something else, pray."

"I can't. I can't talk of anything else. Nor think of anything else, either."

"You mustn't, you mustn't, you mustn't," she said, with sudden vehemence, though still with a beseeching ring in her voice. "I won't let you. May I not live to see my children again if I will. Do you hear, Levinsky? Do you hear? Do you hear? I want you to understand it. Be a man. Have a heart, Levinsky. You must behave yourself. If you don't you'll have to move. There can't be any other way about it. If you are a real friend of mine, not an enemy, you must behave yourself." She spoke with deep, solemn earnestness, somewhat in the singsong of a woman reading the Yiddish Commentary on the Five Books of Moses or wailing over a grave. She went on: "Why should you vex me? You are a respectable man. You don't want to do what is wrong. You don't want to make me miserable, do you? So be good, Levinsky. I beg of you.

I beg of you. Be good. Be good. Be good. Let us never have another talk like this. Do you promise?"

I was silent

"Do you promise, Levinsky? You must. You must. Do you promise me never to come back to this kind of talk?"

"I do," I said, like a guilty school-boy

She was terribly in earnest. She almost broke my heart. I could not thwart her will

She was in love with me

Days passed. There was no lack of unspoken tenderness between us. That she was tremulously glad to see me every time I came home was quite obvious, but she bore herself in such a manner that I never ventured to allude to my feeling, much less to touch her hand or sit close to her.

"It is as well that I should not," I often said to myself. "Am I not happy as it is? Is it not bliss enough to have a home—her home? It would be too awful to forfeit it." I registered a vow to live up to the promise she had exacted from me, but I knew that I would break it

She was in love with me. She had an iron will, but I hoped that this, too, would soon be broken. — so comfident David

There were moments when I would work myself up to an exalted, religious kind of mood over it. "I should be a vile creature if I interfered with the peace of this house," I would exhort myself, passionately. "Max has been a warm friend to me. Oh, I will be good."

Dora talked less than usual. She, too, seemed to be a changed person. She was particularly taciturn when we happened to be alone in the house, and then it would be difficult for us to look each other in the face. Such tête-à-têtes occurred once or twice a week, quite late in the evening. I was very busy at the shop and I could never leave it before 10, 11, or even 12, except on Sabbath eve (Friday night), when it was closed. On those evenings when Max stayed out very late I usually found her alone in the little dining-room, sewing, mending, or—more often—poring over Lucy's school reader or story-book

After exchanging a few perfunctory sentences with her, each of us aware of the other's embarrassment, I would take a seat a considerable distance from her and take up a newspaper or clipping from one, while she went on with her work or reading. Lucy had begun to take juvenile books out of the circulating library of the Educational Alliance, so her mother would read them also. The words were all short and simple and Dora had not much difficulty in deciphering their meaning. Anyhow, she now never sought my assistance for her reading. I can still see her seated at the table, a considerable distance from me, moving her head from word to word and from line to line, and silently working her lips, as though muttering an incantation. I would do her all sorts of little services (though she never asked for any), all silently, softly, as if performing a religious rite

I have said that on such occasions I would read my newspaper or some clipping from it. In truth I read little else in those days. Editorials of the daily press interested me as much as the most sensational news, and if some of the more important leading articles in my paper had to be left unread on the day of their publication I would clip them and glance them over at the next leisure moment, sometimes days later

The financial column was followed by me with a sense of being a member of a caste for which it was especially intended, to the exclusion of the rest of the world. At first the jargon of that column made me feel as though I had never learned any English at all. But I was making headway in this jargon, too, and when I struck a recondite sentence I would cut the few lines out and put them in my pocket, on the chance of coming across somebody who could interpret them for me. Often, too, I would clip and put away a paragraph containing some curious piece of information or a bit of English that was an addition to my knowledge of the language. My inside pocket was always full of all sorts of clippings

- still talked of Matilda but Dora always "assailed her brutally" (271) + they stopped
- Dora wants to be some distance between them b/c according to David, she loves him + she is a married woman — before D asks Dora about her marriage, if it was a love match, Dora gave him the cold shoulder about it.

↳ uncomfortable/embarrassed w/ each other

275

# CHAPTER XII

It was about this time that I found myself confronted with an unexpected source of anxiety in my business affairs. There were several circumstances that made it possible for a financial midget like myself to outbid the lions of the cloak-and-suit industry. Now, however, a new circumstance arose which threatened to rob me of my chief advantage and to undermine the very foundation of my future

The rent of my loft, which was in the slums, was, comparatively speaking, a mere trifle, while my overhead expense amounted to scarcely anything at all.

I did my own bookkeeping, and a thirteen-year-old girl, American-born, school-bred, and bright, whose bewigged mother was one of my finishers, took care of the shop while I was out, helped me with my mail, and sewed on buttons between-whiles— all for four dollars a week. Another finisher, a young widow, saved me the expense of a figure woman. To which should be added that I did business on a profit margin far beneath the consideration of the well-known firms. All this, however, does not include the most important of all the items that gave me an advantage over the princes of the trade. That was cheap labor

Three of my men were excellent tailors. They could have easily procured employment in some of the largest factories, where they would have been paid at least twice as much as I paid them. They were bewhiskered, elderly people, strictly orthodox and extremely old-fashioned as to dress and habits. They felt perfectly at home in my shop, and would rather work for me and be underpaid than be employed in an up-to-date factory where a tailor was expected to wear a starched collar and necktie and was made the butt of ridicule if he covered his head every time he took a drink of water. These, however, were minor advantages. The important thing, the insurmountable obstacle which kept these three skilled tailors away from the big cloak-shops, was the fact that one had to work on Saturdays there, while in my place one could work on Sunday instead of Saturday

My pressers were of the same class as my tailors. As for my operators, who were younger fellows and had adopted American ways, my shop had other attractions for them. For example, my operations were limited to a very small number of styles, and, as theirs was piece-work, it meant greater earnings. While the employee of a Broadway firm (or of one of its contractors) was engaged on a large variety of garments, being continually shifted from one kind of work to another, a man working for me would be taken up with the same style for many days in succession, thus developing a much higher rate of speed and a fatter pay-envelope

Altogether, I always contrived to procure the cheapest labor obtainable, although this, as we have seen, by no means implied that my "hands" were inferior mechanics. The sum and substance of it all was that I could afford to sell a garment for less than what was its cost of production in the best-known cloak-houses

My business was making headway when the Cloak and Suit Makers' Union sprang into life again, with the usual rush and commotion, but with unusual portents of strength and stability. It seemed as if this time it had come to stay. My budding little establishment was too small, in fact, to be in immediate danger. It was one of a scattered number of insignificant places which the union found it difficult to control. Still, cheap labor being my chief excuse for being, the organization caused me no end of worry

"Just when a fellow is beginning to make a living all sorts of black dreams will come along and trip him up," I complained to Meyer Nodelman, bitterly.

"A bunch of good-for-nothings, too lazy to work, will stir up trouble, and there you are."

"Oh, it won't last long," Meyer Nodelman consoled me. "Don't be excited, anyhow. Business does not always go like grease, you know. You must be ready for trouble too."

He told me of his own experiences with unions and he drifted into a philosophic view of the matter. "You and I want to make as much money as possible, don't we?" he said. "Well, the working-men want the same. Can you blame them? We are fighting them and they are fighting us. The world is not a wedding-feast, Levinsky. It is a big barn-yard full of chickens and they are scratching one another, and scrambling over one another. Why? Because there are little heaps of grain in the yard and each chicken wants to get as much of it as possible. So let us try our best. But why be mad at the other chickens? Scratch away, Levinsky, but what's the use being excited?"

He gave a chuckle, and I could not help smiling, but at heart I was bored and wretched.

The big manufacturers could afford to pay union wages, yet they were fighting tooth and nail, and I certainly could not afford to pay high wages.

If I had to, I should have to get out of business.

Officially mine had become a union shop, yet my men continued to work on non-union terms. They made considerably more money by working for non-union wages than they would in the places that were under stringent union supervision. They could work any number of hours in my shop, and that was what my piece-workers wanted. To toil from sunrise till long after sunset was what every tailor was accustomed to in Antomir, for instance. Only over there one received a paltry few shillings at the end of the week. while I paid my men many dollars

So far, then, I had been successful in eluding the vigilance of the walking delegates and my shop was in full blast from 5 in the morning to midnight, whereas in the genuine union shops the regular workday was restricted to ten hours, and overtime to three, which, coupled with the especial advantage accruing from a limited number of styles handled, made my shop a desirable place to my "hands."

A storm broke. All cloak-manufacturers formed a coalition and locked out their union men. A bitter struggle ensued. As it was rich in quaint "human-nature" material, the newspapers bestowed a good deal of space upon it

I made a pretense of joining in the lockout, my men clandestinely continuing to work for me. More than that, my working force was trebled, for, besides filling my own orders, I did some of the work of a well-known firm which found it much more difficult to procure non-union labor than I did. What was a great calamity to the trade in general seemed to be a source of overwhelming prosperity to me. But the golden windfall did not last long.

The agitation and the picketing activities of the union, aided by the Arbeiter Zeitung, a Yiddish socialist weekly, were spreading a spell of enthusiasm (or fear) to which my men gradually succumbed. My best operator, a young fellow who exercised much influence over his shopmates and who had hitherto been genuinely devoted to me, became an ardent convert to union principles and led all my operatives out of the shop. I organized a shop elsewhere, but it was soon discovered

Somebody must have reported to the editor of the Arbeiter Zeitung that at one time I had been a member of the union myself, for that weekly published a scurrilous paragraph, branding me as a traitor  — What?! ?

I read the paragraph with mixed rage and pain, and yet the sight of my name in print flattered my vanity, and when the heat of my fury subsided I became conscious of a sneaking feeling of gratitude to the socialist editor for printing the attack on me. For, behold! the same organ assailed the Vanderbilts, the Goulds, the Rothschilds, and by calling me "a fleecer of labor" it placed me in their class. I felt in good company. I felt, too, that while there were people by whom "fleecers" were cursed, there were many others who held them in high esteem, and that even those who cursed them had a secret envy for them, hoping some day to be fleecers of labor like them

The only thing in that paragraph that galled me was the appellation of "cockroach manufacturer" by which it referred to me. I was going to parade the "quip" before Max and Dora, but thought better of it. The notion of Dora hearing me called "cockroach" made me squirm

But Max somehow got wind of the paragraph, and one evening as I came home for supper he said, good-naturedly: "You got a spanking, didn't you? I have seen what they say in the Arbeiter Zeitung about you."

"Oh. to the eighty black years with them!" I answered, blushing, and hastened to switch the conversation to the lockout and strike in general.

"Oh, we'll get all the men we want," I said. "It's only a matter of time.

We'll teach these scoundrels a lesson they'll never forget."

"If only you manufacturers stick together."

"You bet we will. We can wait. We are in no hurry. We can wait till those tramps come begging for a job," I said. For the benefit of Dora I added a little disquisition on the opportunities America offered to every man who had brains and industry, and on the grudge which men like myself were apt to arouse in lazy fellows. "Those union leaders have neither brains nor a desire to work. That's why they can't work themselves up," I said. "Yes, and that's why they begrudge those who can. All those scoundrels are able to do is to hatch trouble."

I spoke as if I had been a capitalist of the higher altitudes and of long standing. That some of the big cloak firms had promised to back me with funds to keep me from yielding to the union I never mentioned

- His business was making headway
- coalition of cloak-manufacturers.
  └ someone reported his name to the paper, claiming him to be a traitor
    └ mix of awe + anger
- "cockroach" = "David"

# CHAPTER XIII

MY shop being practically closed, I was at home most of the time, not only in the evening, but many a forenoon or afternoon as well. Dora and I would hold interminable conversations. Our love was never alluded to. A relationship on new terms seemed to have been established between us. It was as if she were saying: "Now, isn't this better? Why can't we go on like this forever?"

Sometimes I would watch her read with Lucy. Or else I would take up a newspaper or a book and sit reading it at the same table. Dora was making rapid headway in her studies. It was July and Lucy was free from school, so she would let her spend many an hour in the street, but she caused her to spend a good deal of time with her, too. If she did not read with her she would talk or listen to her. I often wondered whether it was for fear of being too much thrown into my company that she would make the child stay indoors. At all events, her readings, spelling contests, or talks with Lucy bore perceptible fruit. Her English seemed to be improving every day, so much so that we gradually came to use a good deal of that language even when we were alone in the house; even when every word we said had an echo of intimacy with which the tongue we were learning to speak seemed to be out of accord

One evening mother and daughter sat at the open parlor window. While I was reclining in an easy-chair at the other end of the room Lucy was narrating something and Dora was listening, apparently with rapt attention. I watched their profiles. Finally I said: "She must be telling you something important, considering the interest you are taking in it."

"Everything she says is important to me," Dora answered

"What has she been telling you?"

"Oh, about her girls, about their brothers and their baseball games, about lots of things," she said, with a far-away tone in her voice. "I want to know everything about her. Everything. I wish I could get right into her. I wish I could be a child like her. Oh, why can't a person be born over again?"

Her longing ejaculation had perhaps more to do with her feelings for me than with her feelings for her child. Anyhow, what she said about her being interested in everything that Lucy had to say was true. And, whether she listened to the child's prattle or not, it always seemed to me as though she absorbed every English word Lucy uttered and every American gesture she made. The American school-girl radiated a subtle influence, a spiritual ozone, which her mother breathed in greedily

"My own life is lost, but she shall be educated"—these words dropped from her lips quite often. On one occasion they came from her with a modification that lent them unusual meaning. It was on a Friday evening. Max was out, as usual, and the children were asleep. "My own life is lost, but Lucy shall be happy," she said

"Why?" I said, feelingly. "Why should you think yourself lost? I can't bear it, Dora."

She made no answer. I attempted to renew the conversation, but without avail. She answered in melancholy monosyllables and my voice had a constrained note

At last I burst out, in our native tongue: "Why do you torture me, Dora? Why don't you let me talk and pour my heart out?"

"'S-sh! You mustn't," she said, peremptorily, also in Yiddish. "You'll get me in trouble if you do. It'll be the ruin of me and of the children, too.

You mustn't."

"But you say your life is lost," I retorted, coming up close to the chair on which she sat. "Do you think it's easy for me to hear it? Do you think my heart is made of iron?"

"'S-sh! You know everything without my speaking," she said, slowly rising and drawing back. "You know well enough that I am not happy. Can't you rest until you have heard me say so again and again? Must you drink my blood? All right, then. Go ahead. Here. I am unhappy, I am unhappy, I am unhappy. Max is a good husband to me. I can't complain. And we get along well, too. And I shall be true to him. May I choke right here, may darkness come upon me, if I ever cease to be a faithful wife to him. But you know that my heart has never been happy. Lucy will be happy and that will be my

282 why do I have this feeling she will become unfaithful?

happiness, too. She shall go to college and be an educated American lady, and, if God lets me live, I shall see to it that she doesn't marry unless she meets the choice of her heart. She must be happy. She must make up for her mother's lost life, too. If my mother had understood things as I do, I, too, should have been happy. But she was an old-fashioned woman and she would have me marry in the old-fashioned way, as she herself had married: without laying her eyes on her 'predestined one' until the morning after the wedding." She laughed bitterly. "Of course I did see Max before the wedding, but it made no difference. I obeyed my mother, peace upon her soul. I thought love-marriages were something which none but educated girls could dream of.

My mother—peace upon her soul—told me to throw all fancies out of my mind, that I was a simple girl and must get married without fuss. And I did. In this country people have dlfferent notions. But I am already married and a mother. All I can do now is to see to it that Lucy shall be both educated and happy, and, well, I beg of you, I beg of you, I beg of you, Levinsky, never let me talk of these things again. They must be locked up in my heart and the key must be thrown into the river, Levinsky. It cannot be otherwise, Levinsky. Do you hear?"

*off - limits David!*

- *a relationship buds between David | Dora*
- *Dora says it can't work between them*
  *└ she's off-limits, David! stop it!*

# CHAPTER XIV

THE situation could not last. One morning about three weeks subsequent to the above conversation Max left town for a day. One of his debtors, a dancing-master, had disappeared without settling his account and Max had recently discovered that he was running a dance-hall and meeting-rooms in New Haven; so he went there to see what he could do toward collecting his bill. His absence for a whole day was nothing new, and yet the house seemed to have assumed a novel appearance that morning. When, after breakfast, Lucy ran out into the street I felt as though Dora and I were alone for the first time, and from her constraint I could see that she was experiencing a similar feeling. I hung around the house awkwardly. She was trying to keep herself busy. Finally I said: "I think I'll be going. Maybe there is some news about the lockout."

I rose to go to the little corridor for my hat, but on my way thither, as I came abreast of her, I paused, and with amorous mien I drew her to me.

She made but a perfunctory attempt at resistance, and when I kissed her she responded, our lips clinging together hungrily. It all seemed to have happened in a most natural way. When our lips parted at last her cheeks were deeply flushed and her eyes looked filmed

"Dearest," I whispered

"I must go out," she said, shrinking back, her embarrassed gaze on the floor. "I have some marketing to do."

"Don't. Don't go away from me, Dora. Please don't," I said in Yiddish, with the least bit of authority. "I love thee. I love thee, Dora," I raved, for the first time addressing her in the familiar pronoun

"You ought not to speak to me like that," she said, limply, with frank happiness in her voice. "It's terrible. What has got into me?"

I strained her to me once again, and again we abandoned ourselves to a transport of kisses and hugs

"Dost thou love me, Dora? Tell me. I want to hear it from thine own lips."

She slowly drew me to her bosom and clasped me with all her might. That was her answer to my question. Then, with a hurried parting kiss on my forehead, she said: "Go. Attend to business, dearest." As I walked through the street I was all but shouting to myself: "Dora has kissed me! Dora dear is mine!" My heart was dancing with joy over my conquest of her, and at the same time I felt that I was almost ready to lay down my life for her. It was a blend of animal selfishness and spiritual sublimity. I really loved her

I attended to my affairs (that is, to some of the affairs of the Manufacturers' Organization) that day; but while thus engaged I was ever tremulously conscious of my happiness, ever in an uplifted state of mind. I was bubbling over with a desire to be good to somebody, to everybody—except, of course, the Cloak-makers' Union. My membership in the Manufacturers' Association flattered my vanity inordinately, and I always danced attendance upon the other members, the German Jews, the big men of the trade; now, however, I ran their errands with an alacrity that was not mere servility

I was constantly aware of the fact that this was my second love-affair, as if it were something to be proud of. My love for Matilda was remote as a piece of art, while my passion for Dora was a flaming reality. "Matilda only tortured me," I said to myself, without malice. "She treated me as she would a dog, whereas Dora is an angel. I would jump into fire for her. Dora dear! Sweetheart mine!" I had not the patience to wait until evening. I ran in to see her in the middle of the day

She flung herself at me and we embraced and kissed as if we had been separated for years. Then, holding me by both hands, she gave me a long look full of pensive bliss and clasped me to her bosom again. When she had calmed down she smoothed my hair, adjusted my necktie, told me she did not like it and offered to get me one more becoming

"Do you love me? Do you really?" she asked, with deep earnestness

"I do, I do. Dora mine, I am crazy for you," I replied. "Now I know what real love means."

She sighed, and after a pause her grave, strained mien broke into a smile

"So all you told me about Matilda was a lie, was it?" she said, roguishly.

"There is no such person in the world, is there?"

"Don't talk about her, pray. You don't understand me. I never was happy before. Never in my life."

"Never at all?" she questioned me, earnestly

"Never, Dora dearest. Anyhow, let bygones be bygones. All I know is that I love you, that I am going crazy for you. Oh, I do love you." "And nobody else?"

"And nobody else."

"And you are not lying?"

"Lying? Why should you talk like that, dearest?"

"Why, have you forgotten Matilda so soon?"

"Do you call that soon? It's more than five years."

"But you told me that you had been in love with her a considerable time after you came to this country. Will you forget me so soon, too?"

I squirmed, I writhed. "Don't be tormenting me, dearest," I implored, my voice quavering with impatience. "I love thee and nobody else."

She fell into a muse. Then she said, with a far-away look in her eyes: "I don't know where this will land me. It seems as if a great misfortune had befallen me. But I don't care. I don't care. I don't care. Come what may. I can't help it. At last I know what it means to be happy. I have been dreaming of it all my life. Now I know what it is like, and I am willing to suffer for it. Yes, I am willing to suffer for you, Levinsky." She spoke with profound, even-voiced earnestness, with peculiar solemnity, as though chanting a prayer. I was somewhat bored. Presently she paused, and, changing her tone, she asked. "Matilda talked to you of education. She wanted you to be an educated man, did she? Yes, but what did she do for you? She drank your blood, the leech, and when she got tired of it she dropped you. A woman like that ought to be torn to pieces. May every bit of the suffering she caused you come back to her a thousandfold. May her blood be shed as she shed yours." Suddenly she checked herself and said: "But, no, I am not going to curse her. I don't want you to think badly of her. Your love must be sacred, Levinsky. If you ever go back on me and love somebody else, don't let her curse me. Don't let anybody say a cross word about me." Max came home after midnight and I did not see him until the next evening.

When we met at supper (Dora was out at that moment) I had to make an effort to meet his eye. But he did not seem to notice anything out of the usual, and my awkwardness soon wore off

Nor, indeed, was there any change in my feelings toward him. I had expected that he would now be hateful to me. He was not. He was absolutely the same man as he had always been, except, perhaps, that I vaguely felt like a thief in his presence. Only I hated to think of Dora while I looked at him

Presently Dora made her appearance. My embarrassment returned, more acute than ever. The consciousness of her confusion and, above all, the consciousness of the three of us being together, was insupportable. It was a terrible repast, though Max was absolutely unaware of anything unnatural in our demeanor. I retired to my room soon after supper

I had a what-not half filled with books, so I drew a volume from it. I found it difficult to get my mind on it. My thoughts were circling round Dora and Max, round my precarious happiness, round the novelty of carrying on a romantic conspiracy with a married woman. Dora was so dear to me. I seemed to be vibrating with devotion to her. Regardless of the fact that she was somebody else's wife and a mother of two children, my love impressed me as something sacred. I seemed to accept the general rule that a wife-stealer is a despicable creature, a thief, a vile, immoral wretch. But now, that I was not facing Max, that rule, somehow, did not apply to my relations with Dora.

Simultaneously with this feeling I had another one which excused my conduct on the theory that everybody was at the bottom of his heart likewise ready to set that rule at defiance and to make a mistress of his friend's wife, provided it could be done with absolute secrecy and safety. Max in my place would certainly not have scrupled to act as I did. But then I hated to think of him in this connection. I would brush all thoughts of him aside as I would a vicious fly. I was too selfish to endure the pain even of a moment's compunction. I treated myself as a doting mother does a wayward son

The book in my hands was the first volume of Herbert Spencer's Sociology. My interest in this author and in Darwin was of recent origin. It had been born of my hatred for the Cloakmakers' Union, in fact. This is how I came to discover the existence of the two great names and to develop a passion for the ideas with which they are identified

In my virulent criticism of the leaders of the union I had often characterized them as so many good-for-nothings, jealous of those who had succeeded in business by their superior brains, industry, and efficiency.

One day I found a long editorial in my newspaper, an answer to a letter from a socialist. The editorial derived its inspiration from the theory of the Struggle for Existence and the Survival of the Fittest. Unlike many of the other editorials I had read, it breathed conviction. It was obviously a work of love. When the central idea of the argument came home to me I was in a turmoil of surprise and elation. "Why, that's just what I have been saying all these days!" I exclaimed in my heart. "The able fellows succeed, and the misfits fail. Then the misfits begrudge those who accomplish things." I almost felt as though Darwin and Spencer had plagiarized a discovery of mine. Then, as I visualized the Struggle for Existence, I recalled Meyer Nodelman's parable of chickens fighting for food, and it seemed to me that, between the two of us, Nodelman and I had hit upon the whole Darwinian doctrine. Later, however, when I dipped into Social Statics, I was over-borne by the wondrous novelty of the thing and by a sense of my own futility, ignorance, and cheapness. I felt at the gates of a great world of knowledge whose existence I had not even suspected. I had to read the Origin of Species and the Descent of Man, and then Spencer again. I sat up nights reading these books. Apart from the purely intellectual intoxication they gave me, they flattered my vanity as one of the "fittest." It was as though all the wonders of learning, acumen, ingenuity, and assiduity displayed in these works had been intended, among other purposes, to establish my title as one of the victors of Existence

A working-man, and every one else who was poor, was an object of contempt to me—a misfit, a weakling, a failure, one of the ruck

# CHAPTER XV

IT was August. In normal times this would have been the beginning of the great "winter season" in our trade. As it was, the deadlock continued. The stubbornness of the men, far from showing signs of wilting under the strain of so many weeks of enforced idleness 'and suffering, seemed to be gathering strength, while our own people, the manufacturers, were frankly weakening.

The danger of having the great season pass without one being able to fill a single order overcame the fighting blood of the most pugnacious among them.

One was confronted with the risk of losing one's best customers. The trade threatened to pass from New York to Philadelphia and Chicago. If you called the attention of a manufacturer to the unyielding courage of the workmen, the reply invariably was, first, that it was all mere bravado; and, second, that, anyhow, the poor devils had nothing to lose, while the manufacturers had their investments to lose

The press supported the strikers. It did so, not because they were working-people, but because they were East-Siders. Their district was the great field of activity for the American University Settlement worker and fashionable slummer. The East Side was a place upon which one descended in quest of esoteric types and "local color," as well as for purposes of philanthropy and "uplift" work. To spend an evening in some East Side café was regarded as something like spending a few hours at the Louvre so much so that one such café, in the depth of East Houston Street, was making a fortune by purveying expensive wine dinners to people from up-town who came there ostensibly to see "how the other half lived," but who only saw one another eat and drink in freedom from the restraint of manners. Accordingly, to show sympathy for East Side strikers was within the bounds of the highest propriety. It was as "correct" as belonging to the Episcopal Church. And so public opinion was wholly on the side of the Cloak-makers' Union. This hastened the end. We succumbed. A settlement was patched up. We were beaten.

But even this did not appease the men. They repudiated the agreement between their organization and ours, branding it as a trap, and the strike was continued. Then the manufacturers yielded completely, acceding to every demand of the union

I became busy. I continued to curse the union, but at the bottom of my heart I wished it well, for the vigor with which it enforced its increased wage scale in all larger factories gave me greater advantages than ever. I was still able to get men who were willing to trick the organization. Every Friday afternoon these men received pay-envelopes which bore figures in strict conformity with the union's schedule, but the contents of which were considerably below the sum marked outside. Subsequently this proved to be a risky practice to pursue, for the walking delegates were wide awake and apt to examine the envelopes as the operatives were emerging from the shop.

Accordingly, I adopted another system: the men would receive the union pay in full, but on the following Monday each of them would pay me back the difference between the official and the actual wage. The usual practice was for the employee to put the few dollars into his little wage-book, which he would then place on my desk for the ostensible purpose of having his account verified

By thus cheating the union I could now undersell the bigger manufacturers more easily than I had been able to do previous to the lockout and strike. I had more orders than I could fill. Money was coming in in floods

The lockout and the absolute triumph of the union was practically the making of me

I saw much less of Dora than I had done during the five months of the lockout, and our happiness when we managed to be left alone was all the keener for it. Our best time for a tê-à-tˆte were the hours between 10 and 12 on the evenings, when Max was sure to be away at his dancing-schools, but then it often happened that those were among my busiest hours at the shop.

Sometimes I would snatch half an hour from my work in the middle of a busy day to surprise her with my caresses. If a week passed without my doing so she would punish me with mute scenes of jealousy, of which none but she and I were aware. She would avoid looking at me, and I would press my hand to my heart and raise a pleading gaze at her, which said: "I couldn't get away, dearest. Honest, I couldn't."

One evening I bought her some roses. As I carried them home I was thrilled as much by the fact that I, David of Abner's Court, was taking flowers to a lady as I was by visioning the moment when I should hand them to Dora. When I came home and put my offering into her hand she was in a flurry of delight over it, but she was scared to death lest it should betray our secret. After giving way to bursts of admiration for the flowers and myself, and smelling her fill, and covering me with kisses, she burned the bouquet in the stove and forbade me to use this method of showing her attention again

"Your dear eyes are the best flowers you can bring me," she said

Her love burned with a steady flame, bright and even. It manifested itself in a thousand little things which she did for the double purpose of ministering to my comfort and keeping me in mind of herself. I felt it in the taste of the coffee I drank, in the quality of my cup and saucer, in the painstaking darning on my socks, in the frequency with which my room was swept, my towel changed, my books dusted

"Did you notice the new soap-dish on your wash-stand?" she asked me, one morning. "Do you deserve it? Do you know how often I am in your room every day? Just guess."

"A million times a day."

"To you it's a joke. But if you loved as I do you would not be up to joking."

"Very well, I'll cry." And I personated a boy crying. "Don't. It breaks my heart," she said, earnestly. "I can't see you crying even for fun." She kissed my eyes. "No, really, I go to your room twenty times a day, perhaps.

When I am there it seems to me that I am nearer to you. I kiss the pillow on which you sleep. I pat the blanket, the pitcher, every book of yours—everything your dear little hands touch. I want you to know it. I want you to know how I love you. I knew that love was sweet, but I never knew that it was so sweet. Oh, my loved one!"

She would pour out all sorts of endearments on me, some of them rather of a fantastic nature, but "my loved one" became her favorite appellation, while I found special relish in calling her "my bride" or "bridie mine."

I can almost feel her white fingers as they played with my abundant dark hair or rested on my shoulders while she looked into my eyes and murmured, yearningly: "My loved one! My loved one! My loved one!"

The set of my shoulders was a special object of her admiration. She would shake them tenderly, call me monkey, and ask me if I realized how much she loved me and if I deserved it all, bad boy that I was

She held me in check with an iron hand. Whenever my caresses threatened to overstep the bounds of what she termed "respectable love" she would stop them. With clouded eyes she would slap my hand and then kiss it, saying: "Be a gentleman, Levinsky. Be a gentleman. Can't you be a gentleman?"

"Oh, you don't love me," I would grunt

"I don't? I don't? I wish you would love me half as much," with a sigh. "If you did you would not behave the way you do. That's all your love amounts to—behaving like that. All men are hogs, after all." With which she would take to lecturing me and pouring out her infatuated heart in that solemn singsong of hers, which somewhat bored me

If she thought my kisses unduly passionate and the amorous look of my eye dangerous she would move away from me

"Don't be angry at me, sweetheart," she would say, cooingly

"I am not angry, but you don't love me."

"Why should you hurt my feelings like that? Why should you shed my blood? Am I not yours, heart and soul? Am I not ready to cut myself to pieces to please you? Why should you torture me?"

"What are you afraid of? He won't know any more than he does now," I once urged.

She blushed, looking at the floor. After a minute's silence she said, dolefully: "It isn't so much on account of that as on account of the children. How could I look Lucy in the face?"

Her eyes grew humid. My heart went out to her.

"I understand. You are right," I yielded

The scene repeated itself not many days after. It occurred again and again at almost regular intervals. She fought bravely

Many months passed, and still she was able "to look Lucy in the face."

At first, for a period of six or seven weeks, my moral conduct outside the house was immaculate. Then I renewed my excursions to certain streets. I made rather frequent calls at the apartment of a handsome Hungarian woman who called herself Cleo. Once, in a frenzy, I tried to imagine that she was Dora, and then I experienced qualms of abject compunction and self-loathing

Sometimes Lucy would arouse my jealous rancor, as a living barrier between her mother and myself. But she was really dear to me. I revered Dora for her fortitude, and Lucy appealed to me as the embodiment of her mother's saintliness

I would watch Lucy. She was an interesting study. Her manner of speaking, her giggle, her childish little affectations seemed to grow more American every day. She was like a little foreigner in the house

Dora was watching and studying her with a feeling akin to despair, I thought. It was as though she was pursuing the little girl, with outstretched arms, vainly trying to overtake her

- met w/ Dora in secret, stealing kisses and carresses
- gave her flowers but Dora burned them to destroy the evidence of their affair
- D was jealous of Lucy, only b/c the child could express her love for her mother freely

# CHAPTER XVI

I WAS rapidly advancing on the road to financial triumphs. I was planning to move my business to larger quarters, in the same modest neighborhood. Mrs.

Chaikin, my partner's wife, failed to realize the situation, however. She could not forgive me the false representations I had made to her regarding my assets

"And where is the treasure you were expecting?" she would twit me. "You never tell a lie, do you? You simply don't know how to do it. Poor thing!"

When we were in the midst of an avalanche of lucrative orders promising a brilliant winter season she took it into her head to withdraw her husband from the firm, in which he was a silent partner. Her decision was apparently based on the extreme efforts she had once seen me making to raise five hundred dollars. As a matter of fact, this was due to the rapidity of our growth. I lacked capital. But then my credit was growing, too, and altogether things were in a most encouraging condition

"What is the use worrying along like that?" she said. "You deceived me from the start. You made me believe you had a lot of money, while you were really a beggar. Yes, you are a beggar, and a beggar you are bound to stay. A beggar and a swindler—that's what you are. You have fooled me long enough.

You can't fool me any longer. So there!"

Her husband was still employed by the German firm, attending to the needs of our growing little factory surreptitiously every evening and on Sundays. The day seemed near when it would pay him to give all his time to our shop. And he was aware of it, too; to some extent, at least. But Mrs. Chaikin ordained otherwise

I attempted to present the actual state of affairs to her, but broke off in the middle of a sentence. It suddenly flashed upon my mind that it might all be to my advantage. "A designer can be hired," I said to myself. "The business is progressing rapidly. To make him my life partner is too high a price to pay for his skill. Besides, having him for a partner actually means having his nuisance of a wife for a partner. It will be a good thing to get rid of her." I consulted Max, as I did quite often now. Not that I thought myself in need of his advice, or anybody else's, for that matter. Success had made me too self-confident for that. I played the intimate and ardent friend, and this was simply part of my personation. To flatter his vanity I would make him think his suggestions had been acted upon and that they had brought good results. As a consequence, he was developing the notion that my success was largely due to his guidance, a notion which jarred on me, but which I humored, nevertheless

"Do you know what's the matter?" he said, sagely. "Mrs. Chaikin must have found another partner for her husband. Some fellow with big money, I suppose."

"You are right, Max," I said, sincerely. "How stupid I am."

"Why, of course they have got another partner. Of course they have," he repeated, with elation. "So much the better for you. Let them go to the eighty black years. Don't run after him. Just do as I tell you and you'll be all right, Levinsky. My advice has never got you in trouble, has it?"

"Indeed not. Indeed not," I answered

Max's blindness to what was going on between Dora and myself was a riddle to which I vainly sought a solution. That this cynic who charged every man and woman with immorality should, in the circumstances, be so absolutely undisturbed in his confidence regarding his wife seemed nothing short of a miracle. When I now think of the riddle I see its solution in a modified version of the old rule concerning the mote in thy neighbor's eye and the beam in thine own eye. Your worst pessimist is, after all, an optimist with regard to himself. We are quick to recognize the gravity of ill health in somebody else, yet we ourselves may be on the very brink of death without realizing it. It is a special phase of selfishness. We are loath to connect the idea of a catastrophe with our own person. Max, who saw a mote in the eye of everybody else's wife, failed to perceive the beam in the eye of his own

→ Watch, he's gonna die thinking he was the only one

As for Sadie, who lived in the same house now, and who visited Dora's apartment at all hours, she was too silly and too deeply infatuated with her friend to suspect her of anything wrong

I idolized Dora. It seemed to me that I adored her soul even more than I did her body. I was under her moral influence, and the firmness with which she maintained the distance between us added to my respect for her. And yet I never ceased to dream of and to seek her moral downfall

I had extended my canvassing activities to a number of cities outside New York, my territory being a semicircle with a radius of about a hundred and fifty miles. I had long since picked up some of the business jargon of the country and I was thirstily drinking in more and more

"What do you think of this number, Mr. So-and-so?" I would say, self-consciously, to a merchant, as I dangled a garment in front of him.

"You can make a run on it. It's the kind of suit that gives the wearer an air of distinction."

If I heard a bit of business rhetoric that I thought effective I would jot it down and commit it to memory. In like manner I would write down every new piece of slang, the use of the latest popular phrase being, as I thought, helpful in making oneself popular with Americans, especially with those of the young generation. But somehow a slang phrase would be in general use for a considerable time before it attracted my attention. The Americans I met were so quick to discern and adopt these phrases it seemed as if they were born with a special slang sense which I, poor foreigner that I was, lacked.

That I was not born in America was something like a physical defect that asserted itself in many disagreeable ways—a physical defect which, alas! no surgeon in the world was capable of removing

Other things that I would enter in my note-book were names of dishes on the bills of fare of the better restaurants, with explanations of my own. I would describe the difference between Roquefort cheese and Liederkranz cheese, between consommé Celestine and consommé princesse; I would make a note of the composition of macaroni au gratin, the appearance and taste of potatoes Lyonnaise, of various salad-dressings. But I gradually picked up this information in a practical way and really had no need of my culinary notes. I had many occasions to eat in high-class restaurants and I was getting to feel quite at home in them

Max's conjecture regarding Chaikin was borne out. The talented designer had given up his job at the Manheimer Brothers' and opened a cloak-and-suit house with a man who had made considerable money as a cloak salesman, and as a landlord for a partner. When Max heard of it he was overjoyed

"I tell you what, Levinsky," he said, half in jest and half in earnest. "Let the two of us make a partnership of it. I could put some money into the business."

I reflected that when I approached him for a loan of four hundred dollars, on my first visit at his house, he had pleaded poverty

"I could do a good deal of hustling, too," he added, gravely. "Between the two of us we should make a great success of it."

I gave him an evasive answer. I must have looked annoyed, for he exclaimed: "Look at him! Look at him, Dora! Scared to death, isn't he?" And to me: "Don't be uneasy, old chap! I am not going to snatch your factory from you.

But you are a big hog, all the same. I can tell you that. How will you manage all alone? Who will take care of your business when you go traveling?"

"Oh, I'll manage it somehow," I answered, making an effort to be pleasant.

"Chaikin was scarcely ever in the shop, anyhow."

• business booming, wanted to have Mr. Chaikin as a partner, but wife always in the way.

• Max blind to what is under his nose

└ thinks his advice is helping D's bus.

# CHAPTER XVII

I TRAVELED quite often, sometimes staying away from New York for two or three days, but more frequently for only one day. On one occasion, however, I was detained on the road for five days in succession. It was the beginning of June, a little over a year since the Margolises moved into the Clinton Street flat with myself as their boarder. I was homesick. I missed Dora acutely. I loved her passionately, tenderly, devotedly. I now felt it with special force. Her face and figure loomed up a hundred times a day.

"Dora dear! Bridie mine!" I would whisper, all but going to pieces with tenderness and yearning

One afternoon, after closing an unexpectedly large sale in a department store, I went to the jewelry department of the same firm and paid a hundred and twenty dollars for a bracelet. I knew that she would not be able to wear it, yet I was determined to make her accept it

"Let her keep it in some hiding-place," I thought. "Let her steal an occasional look at it. I don't care what she does with it. I want her to know that I think of her, that I am crazy for her."

It was Friday evening when I returned to New York, having been on the road since the preceding Monday morning. I first went to my place of business and then to a restaurant for supper. I would not make my appearance at the house until half past 10, when the coast was sure to be clear. With thrills of anticipation that verged on physical pain I was looking forward to the moment when I should close the bracelet about her slender white wrist

At the fixed minute I was at the door of the Clinton Street apartment. I pulled the bell. I expected an excited rush, a violent opening of the door, a tremulous: "My loved one! My loved one!"

There was a peculiar disappointment in store for me. She received me icily, not letting me come near her

"Why, what's the matter? What's up?" "Nothing," she muttered

When we reached the light of the Sabbath candles in the dining-room I noticed that she looked worn and haggard

"What has happened?" I asked, greatly perplexed. "I have something for you," I said, producing the blue-velvet box containing the bracelet and opening it. "Here, my bride!"

"How dare you call me 'bride,' you hypocrite?" she gasped. "Away with you, your present and all!"

"Why? Why? What does it all mean?" I asked, between mirth and perplexity

For an answer she merely continued: "You thought you could bribe me by this present of yours, did you? You can fool me no longer. I have found you out.

You have fallen into your own trap. You have. How dare you buy me presents?"

At this she tore the bracelet out of my hand and flung it into the little corridor. She was on the verge of a fit of hysterics. I fetched her a glass of water, but she dashed it out of my hand. Then, frightened and sobered by the crash, she first tiptoed to the bedroom to ascertain if Lucy was not awake and listening, and then went to the little corridor, picked up the bracelet and slipped it into my pocket

"If you have decided to get married, I can't stop you, of course," she began, in a ghastly undertone, as she crouched to gather up the fragments of the glass and to wipe the floor.

"Decided to get married?" I interrupted her. "Where on earth did you get that? What 'trap' are you talking about, Dora?"

She made no answer. I continued to protest my innocence. Finally, when she had removed the broken glass, she said: "It's no use pretending you don't know anything about it. It won't do you any good. You have been very foxy about it, but you made a break, and there you are! You think you are very clever. If you were you wouldn't let your shadchen [note] know where you live—"

Oh, I see," I said, with a hearty laugh. "Has he been here?" And I gave way to another guffaw

Shadchen was a conspiracy name for a man who would bring an employer together with cloak-makers who were willing to cheat the union. The one who performed these services for me was one of my own "hands." He was thoroughly dishonest, but he possessed a gentle disposition and a certain gift of expression. This gave him power over his shopmates. He was their "shop chairman" and a member of their "price committee." He was the only man in my employ who actually received the full union price. In addition to this, I paid him his broker's commission for every new man he furnished me, and various sums as bribes pure and simple

I explained it all to Dora. The ardor with which I spoke and the details of my dealings with the shadchen must have made my explanation convincing, for she accepted it at once

"You're not fooling me, are you?" she asked, piteously, yet in a tone of immense relief.

"Strike me dumb if—"

"'S-sh! Don't curse yourself," she said, clapping her hand over my mouth. "I can't bear to hear it. I believe you. If you knew what I have gone through!"

"Poor, poor child!" I said, kissing her soft white fingers tenderly. "Poor, poor baby! How could you think of such a thing! There is only one bride for me in all the world, and that is my own Dora darling."

Her face shone with a wan, beseeching kind of light

Again I drew forth the bracelet

"Foolish child!" I said, examining it. "Thank God, it isn't damaged. Not a bit."

I took her by the hand, opened the bracelet, and closed it over her wrist.

She instantly took it off again, with an instinctive side-glance at the door. Then, holding it up to the light admiringly, she said: "Oh! Oh! Must have cost a pile of money! Why did you spend so much? I can't wear it, anyway. Better return it."

"Never! It's yours, my sweetheart. Do whatever you like with it. Put it away somewhere. If you wear it for one minute every week I shall be happy. If you only look at it once in a while I shall be happy."

"I am afraid to keep it. Somebody may come across it some day. Better return it, my loved one! I am happy as it is. It would make me nervous to have it in the house."

She made me take it back

"Thank God it wasn't a real shadchen! I thought I was going to commit suicide," she said

I seized her in my arms. She abandoned herself to a transport of gratitude and happiness in which her usual fortitude melted away

The next morning she had the appearance of one doomed to death. Her eyes avoided everybody, not only her husband and Lucy, but myself as well. She pleaded indisposition

Max left for the synagogue, as he always did on Saturday morning _____ to business _____ car. Instead _____ ning to be al _____

"I _____ you are to m _____ who were ha _____ the parlor, _____ er to me and _____

Sh _____ ran back to _____

I _____

La _____ nd I rushed _____

" _____

" _____ with shame _____

[handwritten marginal note:]
• missed Dora, bought her a bracelet
• D got upset, thinking D was briding her b/c he found a single woman to marry
  └ whole ch. about calming her down

"Do you hate me?"

"Hate you! I wish I could," she answered, with a sad smile, still looking down.

"Why this new way, then?" I said, rather impatiently. "You are dearer than ever to me, Levinsky. Tell me to jump into fire, and I will. But—can't we love each other and be good?"

"What are you talking about, Dora? What has got into you? Do you know what you are to me now?" I demanded, melodramatically

I made another attempt at kissing her, but was repulsed again

"Not now, anyway, my loved one," she said, entreatingly. "Let a few days pass. You don't want me to feel bad, do you, dearest?"

I looked sheepish. I was convinced that it was merely a passing mood [note: shadchen]: Marriage broker, match-maker

# CHAPTER XVIII

NEXT Monday, when I was ready to go to my place of business, Dora left the house, pitcher in hand, before I rose from the breakfast-table. She was going for milk, but a side-glance which she cast at the floor in my direction as she turned to shut the door behind her told me that she wanted to see me in the street. After letting some minutes pass I put on my overcoat and hat, bade Max a studiously casual good-by, and departed

I awaited her on the stoop. Presently she emerged from the .grocery in the adjoining building

"Could you be free at 4 o'clock this afternoon?" she asked, ascending the few steps, and pausing by my side. "I want to have a talk with you.

Somewhere else. Not at home."

"Why not at home, in the evening?" "No. That won't do," she overruled me, softly. "Somebody might come in and interrupt me. I'll wait for you in the little park on Second Avenue and Fifteenth Street. You know the place, don't you?"

She meant Stuyvesant Park, which the sunny Second Avenue cuts in two, and she explained that our meeting was to take place on the west side of the thoroughfare

"Will you come?" she asked, nervously

"I will, I will. But what's up? Why do you look so serious? Dora! Dora mine!"

"'S-sh! You had better go. When we meet I'll explain everything. At 4 o'clock, then. Don't forget. As you come up the avenue, going up-town, it is on the left-hand side. Write it down."

To insure against any mistakes on my part she made me repeat it and then jot it down. As she turned to go upstairs she said, in a melancholy whisper: "Good-by, dearest."

When I reached the appointed place the brass hands of the clock on the steeple high overhead indicated ten minutes of 4. It was June, but the day was a typical November day, mildly warm, clear, and charged with the exhilarating breath of a New York autumn. Dora had not yet arrived. The benches in the little park were for the most part occupied by housewives or servant-girls who sat gossiping in front of baby-carriages, amid the noise of romping children. Here and there an elderly man sat smoking his pipe broodingly. They were mostly Germans or Czechs. There were scarcely any of our people in the neighborhood at the period in question, and that was why Dora had selected the place

I stood outside the iron gate, gazing down the avenue. The minutes were insupportably long.

At last her womanly figure came into dim view. My heart leaped. I was in a flutter of mixed anxiety and joyous anticipation. "Oh, she'll back down," I persuaded myself

She was walking fast, apparently under the impression that she was late. Her face was growing more distinct every moment. The blue hat she wore and the parasol she carried gave her a new aspect. I had more than once seen her leave the house in street array, but watching her come up the street thus formally attired somehow gave her a different appearance

She looked so peculiarly dignified and so exquisitely lady-like she almost seemed to be a stranger. This, added to her romantic estrangement from me and to the clandestine nature of our tryst, produced a singular effect upon me.

"Am I very late?" she asked

"No. Not at all, Dora!" I said, yearningly

She made no answer

We could not find an empty bench, and to let Germans overhear our Yiddish, which is merely a German dialect, would have been rather risky. So she delivered her message as we walked round and round, both of us eying the asphalt all the while. Her beautiful complexion and our manner attracted much attention. The people on the benches apparently divined the romantic nature of our interview. One white-haired little man with a terrier face never took his eyes off her

"First of all I want to tell you that this is one of the most important days in my life," she began. "It is certainly not a happy day. It's Yom Kippur [note] with me. I want to say right here that I am willing to die for you, Levinsky. I am terribly in love with you, Levinsky. Yes—"

Her voice broke. She was confused and agitated, but she soon regained her self-mastery. She spoke in sad, solemn, quietly passionate tones, and gradually developed a homespun sort of eloquence which I had never heard from her before. But then the gift of homely rhetoric is rather a common talent among Yiddish-speaking women

The revolting sight of the dog-faced old fellow who was ogling Dora so fascinated me that it interfered with my listening. I made a point of looking away from him every time we came round to his bench, but that only kept me thinking of him instead of listening to Dora. Finally we confined our walk to the farther side of the little park, giving him a wide berth

"I love you more than I can tell you, Levinsky," she resumed. "But it is not my good luck to be happy. I dreamed all my life of love, and now that it is here, right here in my heart, I must choke it with my own hands." "Why? Why?" I said, with vehemence. "Why must you?"

"Why!" she echoed, bitterly. "Because the Upper One brought you to me only to punish me, to tease me. That's all. That's all. That's all."

"Why should you take it that way?" "Don't interrupt me, Levinsky," she said, chanting, rather than speaking. As she proceeded, her voice lapsed into a quaint, doleful singsong, not unlike the lament of our women over a grave. "No, Levinsky. It is not given to me to be happy. But I ask no questions of the Upper One. I used to live in peace. I was not happy, but I lived in peace. I did not know what happiness was, so I did not miss it much. I only dreamed of it. But the Lord of the World would have me taste it, so that I might miss it and that my heart might be left with a big, big wound. I want you to know exactly how I feel.

Oh, if I could turn this poor heart of mine inside out! Then you could see all that is going on there. Listen, Levinsky. If it were not for my children, my dear children, my all in all in the world, I should not live with Margolis another day. If he gave me a divorce, well and good; if not, then I don't know what I might do. I shouldn't care. I love you so and I want to be happy. I do, I do, I do."

A sob rang through her voice as she repeated the words. "You do, and yet you are bound to make both of us miserable," I said

"Can I help it?"

"If you would you could," I said, grimly. "Get a divorce and let us be married and have it over."

She shook her head sadly

"Thousands of couples get divorced." She kept shaking her head

"Then what's the use pretending you love me?"

"Pretending! Shall I turn my heart inside out to show you how hard it is to live without you? But you can't understand. No, Levinsky. I have no right to be happy. Lucy shall be happy. She certainly sha'n't marry without love. Her happiness will be mine, too. That's the only kind I am entitled to. She shall go to college. She shall be educated. She shall marry the loved one of her heart. She shall not be buried alive as her mother was. Let her profit by what little sense I have been able to pick up."

A bench became vacant and we occupied it. The momentary interruption and the change in her physical attitude broke the spell. The solemnity was gone out of her voice. She resumed in a distracted and somewhat listless manner, but she soon warmed up again

"What would you have me do? Let Lucy find out some day that her mother was a bad woman? I should take poison first."

"A bad woman!" I protested. "A better woman could not be found anywhere in the world. You are a saint, Dora."

"No, I am not. I am a bad, wicked, nasty woman. I hate myself."

"'S-sh! You mustn't speak like that," I said, stopping my ears. "I cannot bear it."

"Yes, that's what I am, a nasty creature. I used to be pure as gold. There was not a speck on my soul, and now, woe is me, pain is me! What has come over me?"

When she finally got down to the practical side of her resolution it turned out that she wanted me to move out of her house and never to see her again

I was shocked. I flouted the idea of it. I argued, I poured out my lovelorn heart. But she insisted with an iron-clad finality. I argued again, entreated, raved, all to no purpose

"I'll never come close to you. All I want is to be able to see you, to live in the same house with you."

"Don't be tearing my heart to pieces," she said. "It is torn badly enough as it is. Do as I say, Levinsky." "Don't you want to see me at all?" "Oh, it's cruel of you to ask questions like that. You have no heart, Levinsky. It's just because I am crazy to see you that you have got to move."

"Don't you want me even to call at your house?" I asked, with an ironical smile, as though I did not take the matter seriously

"Well, that would look strange. Call sometimes, not often, though, and never when Margolis is out."

"Oh, I shall commit suicide," I snarled

"Oh, well. It isn't as bad as all that."

"I will. I certainly will," I said, knowing that I was talking nonsense

"Don't torment me, Levinsky. Don't sprinkle salt over my wound. Take pity on me. Do as I wish and let the tooth be pulled out with as little pain as possible."

I accompanied her down the avenue as far as Houston Street, where she insisted upon our parting. Before we did, however, she indulged in another outburst of funereal oratory, bewailing her happiness as she would a dead child. It was apparently not easy for her to take leave of me, but her purpose to make our romance a thing of the past and to have me move to other lodgings remained unshaken

"This is the last time I shall ever speak to you of my love, Levinsky," she said. "I must tear it out of my heart, even if I have to tear out a piece of my heart along with it. Such is my fate. Good-by, Levinsky. Good luck to you. Be good. Be good. Be good. Remember you have a good head. Waste no time. Study as much as you can. God grant you luck in your business, but try to find time for your books, too. You must become a great man. Do you promise me to read and study a lot?"

"I do. I do. But I won't move out. I can't live without you. We belong to each other, and all you say is nothing but a woman's whim. It's all bosh," I concluded, with an air of masculine superiority. "I won't move out."

"You shall, dearest. Good-by. Good-by."

She broke into a fit of sobbing, but checked it, shook my hand vehemently and hastened away

[note: Yom Kippur] Day of Atonement; figuratively, a day of anguish and tears

- Dora spots D + arranges a meeting time to talk
  - met in the park
  - Dora spilling out her feelings for D and breaks off the affair
  - of course, D doesn't get it and I wouldn't expect him too,
    Don't worry, Dora, I understand,

# CHAPTER XIX

I HOPED she would yield, but she did not. I found myself in the grip of an iron will and I did as I was bidden

When I set out in quest of a furnished room I instinctively betook myself to the neighborhood of Stuyvesant Park. That park had acquired a melancholy fascination for me. As though to make amends for my agonies, I determined to move into a good, spacious room, even if I had to pay three or four times as much as I had been paying at the Margolises'. I found a sunny front room with two windows in an old brown-stone house on East Nineteenth Street, between Second Avenue and First, a short distance from the little park and near an Elevated station. The curtains, the carpet, the huge, soft arm-chair, and the lounge struck me as decidedly "aristocratic." To cap the climax of comfort and "swellness," the landlady—a gray little German-American—had, at my request, a bookcase placed between the mantelpiece and one of the windows. It was a "regular" bookcase, doors and all, not a mere "what-not," and the sight of it swelled my breast

"I shall forget all my troubles here," I thought. "I am going to buy a complete set of Spencer and some other books. Won't the bookcase look fine! I shall read, read, read."

When I reported to Dora that I was ready to move, her face clouded

"You seem to be glad to," she said, with venom, dropping her eyes

"Glad? Glad? Why, I am not going to move, then. May I stay here, darling mine? May I?"

"Are you really sorry you have to move?" she asked, fixing a loving glance at me. "Do you really love me?"

There were tears in her eyes. I attempted to come close to her, to kiss her, but she held me back

"No, dearest," she said, shaking her head. "Move out to-morrow, will you? Let's be done with it."

"And what will Max say?" I asked, sardonically. Will nothing seem strange to him nothing at all?"

"Never mind that."

She never mentioned Max to me now, not even by pronoun

"Then you must know him to be an idiot." Now I hated Max with all my heart.

"Don't," she implored

"Oh, I see. He's dear to you now," I laughed

"Have a heart, Levinsky. Have a heart. Must you keep shedding my blood? Have you no pity at all?"

"But it is all so ridiculous. It will look strange," I argued, seriously.

"He is bound to get suspicious."

"I have thought it all out. Don't be uneasy. I'll say we had a quarrel over your board bill."

"A nice dodge, indeed! It may fool Dannie, not him."

"Leave it all to me. Better tell me what sort of lodgings you have got. Is it a decent room? Plenty of air and sunshine? But, no. Don't tell me anything. I mustn't know." I sneered

She was absorbed in thought, flushed, nervous.

Presently she said, with an effect of speaking to herself: "It's sweet to suffer for what is right." — interesting words

I moved out according to her program. I came home at io the first evening.

My double room, with its great arm-chair, carpets, bookcase, imposing lace curtains, and the genteel silence of the street outside, was a prison to me.

I attempted to read, but there was a lump in my throat and the lines swam before me

I went out, roamed about the streets, dropped in at a Hungarian café, took another ramble, and returned to my room

I tossed about on my great double bed. I sat up in front of one of my two windows, gazing at a street-lamp. It was not solely Dora, but also Lucy and Dannie that I missed. Only the image of Max now aroused hostile feelings in me

Max called at my shop the very next day. The sight of him cut me to the quick. I received him in morose silence

"What's the matter? What's the matter?" he inquired, with pained amazement.

"What did you two quarrel about?"

I made no answer. His presence oppressed me. My surly reticence was no mere acting. But I knew that he misinterpreted it into grim resentment of Dora's sally, as though I said, "Your wife's conduct had better be left undiscussed."

"What nonsense! She charged you too much, did she? Is that the way it all began? Did she insult you? Well, women-folk are liable to flare up, you know. Tell me all about it. I'll straighten it out between you. The children miss you awfully. Come, don't be a fool, Levinsky. Who ever took the words of a woman seriously? What did she say that you should take it so hard?"

"You had better ask her," I replied, with a well-acted frown

"Ask her! She gets wild when I do. I never saw her so wild. She thinks you insulted her first. Well, she is a woman, but you aren't one, are you? Come to the house this evening, will you?"

"That's out of the question."

"Then meet me somewhere else. I want to have a talk with you. It's all so foolish." I pleaded important other engagements, but he insisted that I should meet him later in the evening, and I had to make the appointment. I promised to be at a Canal Street café on condition that he did not mention the disagreeable episode nor offer to effect a reconciliation between Dora and myself

"You're a tough customer. As tough as Dora," he said

When I came to the café, at about 11, I found him waiting for me. He kept his promise about avoiding the subject of Dora, but he talked of women, which jarred on me inordinately now. His lecherous fibs and philosophy made him literally unbearable to me. To turn the conversation I talked shop, and this bored him.

About a week later he called on me again. He informed me that Dora had taken a new apartment up in Harlem, where the rooms were even more modern and cheaper than on Clinton Street

"I wouldn't mind staying where we are," he observed. "But you know how women are. Everybody is moving up-town, so she must move, too."

My face hardened, as if to say: "Why will you speak of your wife? You know I can't bear to hear of her." At the same time I said to myself: "Poor Dora! She must have found it awful to live in the old place, now that I am no longer there."

His next visit at my shop took place after a lapse of three or four weeks.

He descanted upon his new home and the Harlem dwellings in general, and I made an effort to show him cordial attention and to bear myself generally as though there were no cause for estrangement between us, but I failed

At last he said, resentfully: "What's the matter with you? Why are you so sour? If you and Dora have had a falling out, is that any reason why you and I should not be good friends?" "Why, why?" I protested. "Who says I am sour?" └ He doesn't know the half of that

We parted on very friendly terms. But it was a long time before I saw him again, and then under circumstances that were a disagreeable surprise to me

- He moved out of the apartment like he promised and got another one
- Met w/ Max → Max was trying to figure out what happened between them but to no avail
  └ I feel sorry for Max b/c he thinks he knows women but he doesn't even know his wife.
- Max / Dora are moving up-town

# BOOK X

# ON THE ROAD

# CHAPTER I

WEEKS went by. My desolation seemed to be growing in excruciating intensity.

From time to time, when I chanced to recall some trait or trick of Dora's, her person would come back to me with special vividness, smiting me with sudden cruelty. The very odor of her flesh would grip my consciousness. At such moments my agony would be so great that I seemed to be on the brink of a physical collapse. During intervals there was a steady gnawing pain. It was as though the unrelenting tortures of a dull toothache had settled somewhere in the region of my heart or stomach, I knew not exactly where. I recognized the pang as an old acquaintance. It had the same flavor as the terrors of my tantalizing love for Matilda

My shop had lost all meaning to me. I vaguely longed to flee from myself

There was plenty to do in the shop and all sorts of outside appointments to keep, not to speak of my brief trips as traveling salesman. To all of which I attended with automatic regularity, with listless doggedness. The union was a constant source of worry. In addition, there was a hitch in my relations with the "marriage broker." But even my worrying seemed to be done automatically

Having forfeited the invaluable services of Chaikin, who now gave all his time to his newly established factory, I filled the gap with all sorts of makeshifts and contrivances. An employee of one of the big shops, a tailor, stole designs for me. These were used in my shop by a psalm-muttering old tailor with a greenish-white beard full of snuff, who would have become a Chaikin if he had been twenty years younger. Later I hired the services of a newly graduated cloak-designer who would drop in of an afternoon. Officially the old man was my foreman, but in reality he acted as

*[handwritten in right margin: knowing you, I'm not worried.]*

a guiding spirit to that designer and one of my sample-makers, as well as foreman

I was forming new connections, obtaining orders from new sources. Things were coming my way in spite of myself, as it were. There was so much work and bustle that it became next to impossible to manage it all single-handed.

The need of a bookkeeper, at least, was felt more keenly every day. But I simply lacked the initiative to get one

While I was thus cudgeling my brains, hovering about my shop, meeting people, signing checks, reading or writing letters, that dull pain would keep nibbling, nibbling, nibbling at me. At times, during some of those violent onslaughts I would seek the partial privacy of my second-hand desk for the express purpose of abandoning myself to the tortures of my helpless love. There is pleasure in this kind of pain. It was as though I were two men at once, one being in the toils of hopeless love and the other filled with the joy of loving, all injunctions and barriers notwithstanding

One October evening as I passed through the Grand Central station on my way from an Albany train I was hailed with an impulsive, "Hello, Levinsky!"

It was Bender, my old-time evening-school instructor. I had not seen him for more than three years, during which time he had developed a pronounced tendency to baldness, though his apple face had lost none of its roseate freshness. He looked spruce as ever, his clothes spick and span, his "four-in-hand" tastefully tied, his collar and cuffs immaculate. His hazel eyes, however, had a worn and wistful look in them.

"Quite an American, I declare," he exclaimed, with patronizing admiration and pride, as who should say, "My work has borne fruit, hasn't it?"

"Well, how is the world treating you?" he questioned me, after having looked me over more carefully. "You seem to be doing well."

When he heard that I was "trying to manufacture cloaks and suits" he surveyed me once again, with novel interest

"Are you really? That's good. Glad to hear you're getting on in the world."

"Do you remember the two books you gave me—Dombey and Son and the little dictionary?"

I told him how much good they had done me and he complimented me on my English

He wanted to know more about my business, and I sketched for him my struggles during the first year and the progress I was now making. My narrative was interspersed with such phrases as, "my growing credit," "my "in my desk," "dinner with a buyer from Ohio," all of which I uttered with great self-consciousness. He congratulated me upon my success and upon my English again. Whereupon I exuberantly acknowledged the gratitude I owed him for the special pains he had taken with me when I was his pupil

He still taught evening school during the winter months. When I asked about his work at the custom-house, which had been his chief occupation three years before, he answered evasively. By little and little, however, he threw off his reserve and told, at first with studied flippancy and then with frank bitterness, how "the new Republican broom swept clean," and how he had lost his job because of his loyalty to the Democratic party. He dwelt on the civil-service reform of President Cleveland, charging the Republicans with "offensive partisanship," a Cleveland phrase then as new as four-in-hand neckties. And in the next breath he proceeded to describe certain injustices (of which he apparently considered himself a victim) within the fold of his own party. His immediate ambition was to obtain a "permanent appointment" as teacher of a public day school

He was a singular surprise to me. Formerly I had looked up to him as infinitely my superior, whereas now he struck me as being piteously beneath me

"Can't you think of something better?" I said, with mild contempt. Then, with a sudden inspiration, I exclaimed: "I have a scheme for you, Mr.

Bender! Suppose you try to sell cloaks? There's lots of money in it."

The outcome of our conversation was that he agreed to spend a week or two in my shop preparatory to soliciting orders for me, at first in the city and then on the road

Our interview lasted a little over an hour, but that hour produced a world of difference in our relations. He had met me with a patronizing, "Hello, Levinsky." When we parted there was a note of gratitude and of something like obsequiousness in his voice

# CHAPTER II

ON a Friday afternoon, during the first week of Bender's connection with my establishment, as he and I were crossing a side-street on our way from luncheon, I ran into the loosely built, bulky figure of Max Margolis. Max and I paused with a start, both embarrassed. I greeted him complaisantly

"And how are you?" he said, looking at the lower part of my face

I introduced my companion and after a brief exchange of trivialities we were about to part, when Max detained me

"Wait. What's your hurry?" he said. "There is something I want to speak to you about. In fact, it was to your shop I was going."

His manner disturbed me. "Were you? Come on, then," I said

"Hold on. What's your hurry? We might as well talk here."

Bender tipped his hat to him and moved away, leaving us to ourselves

"What is it?" I repeated, with studied indifference

"Well, I should like to have a plain, frank talk with you, Levinsky," he answered. "There is something that is bothering my mind. I never thought I should speak to you about it, but at last I decided to see you and have it out. I was going to call on you and to ask you to go out with me, because you have no private office."

There was a nervous, under-dog kind of air about him. His damp lips revolted me

"But what is it? What are all these preliminaries for? Come to the point and be done with it. What is it?" Then I asked, with well-simulated indignation, "Your wife has not persuaded you that I have cheated her out of some money, has she?"

"Why, no. Not at all," he answered, looking at the pavement. "It isn't that at all. The thing is driving me mad."

"But what is it?" I shouted, in a rage

"'S-sh!" he said, nervously. "If you are going to be excited like that it's no use speaking at all. Perhaps you are doing it on purpose to get out of it."

Get out of what? What on earth are you prating about?" I demanded, with a fine display of perplexity and sarcasm

We were attracting attention. Bystanders were eying us. An old woman, leading a boy by the hand, even paused to watch us, and then her example was followed by some others

"Come on, for God's sake!" he implored me. "All I want is a friendly talk with you. We might talk in your shop, but you have no private office."

"Whether I have one or not is none of your business" I retorted, with irrelevant resentment

We walked on. He proposed to take me to one of the ball and meeting-room places in which he did business, and I acquiesced

A few minutes later we were seated on a long cushion of red plush covering one of the benches in a long, narrow meeting-hall. We were close to the window, in the full glare of daylight. A few feet off the room was in semi-darkness which, still farther off, lapsed into night. As the plush cushions stretched their lengths into the deepening gloom their live red died away. There was a touch of weirdness to the scene, adding to the oppressiveness of the interview

"I want to ask you a plain question," he began, in a strange voice. "And I want you to answer it frankly. I assure you I sha'n't be angry. On the contrary, I shall be much obliged to you if you tell me the whole truth.    ⌐→ Finally !!

Tell me what happened between you and Dora." I was about to burst into laughter, but I felt that it would not do. Before I knew how to act he added, with a sort of solemnity: "She has confessed everything."

"Confessed everything!" I exclaimed, with a feigned compound of hauteur, indignation, and amusement, playing for time

"That's what she did."

A frenzy of hate took hold of me. I panted to be away from him, to be out of this room, semi-darkness, red cushions, and all, and let the future take care of itself. And so, jumping to my feet, I said, in a fury: "You always were a liar and an idiot. I don't want to have anything to do with you." With which I made for the door

See ?.

"Oh, don't be excited. Don't go yet, Levinsky dear, please," he implored, hysterically, running after me. "I have the best of feelings for you. May the things that I wish you come to me. Levinsky! Dear friend! Darling!"

"What do you want of me?" I demanded, with quiet rancor, pausing at the door and half opening it, without moving on

"If you tell me it isn't true I'll believe you, even if she did confess. I don't know if she meant what she said. If only you were not excited! I want to tell you everything, everything."

I laughed sardonically. My desire to escape the ordeal gave way to strange curiosity. He seemed to be aware of it, for he boldly shut the door. lie begged me to take a seat again, and I did, a short distance from the door, where the gloom was almost thick enough to hide our faces from each other's view

"Why, you are simply crazy, Max!" I said. "You probably bothered the life out of her and she 'confessed' to put an end to it all. You might as well have made her confess to murder."

"That's what she says now. But I don't know. When she confessed she confessed. I could see it was the truth."

"You are crazy, Max! It is all nonsense. Ab-solutely."

"Is it?" he demanded, straining to make out the expression of my face through the dusk. "Do assure me it is all untrue. Take pity, dear friend. Do take pity."

"How can I assure you, seeing that you have taken that crazy notion into your head and don't seem to be able to get rid of it? Come, throw that stuff out of your mind!" I scolded him, mentorially. "It's enough to make one sick. Come to reason. Don't be a fool. I am no saint, but in this case you are absolutely mistaken. Why, Dora is such an absolutely respectable woman, a fellow would never dare have the slightest kind of fun with her. The idea!"—with a little laugh. "You are a baby, Max. Upon my word, you are.

Dora and I had some words over my bill and—well, she insulted me and I wouldn't take it from her. That's all there was to it. Why, look here, Max.

why is he lying?
—committing a sin
old David wouldn't dare

With your knowledge of men and women, do you mean to say that something was going on under your very nose and you never noticed anything? Don't you see how ridiculous it is?"

"Well, I believe you, Levinsky," he said, lukewarmly. "Now that you assure me you don't know anything about it, I believe you. I know you are not an enemy of mine. I have always considered you a true friend. You know I have.

That's why I am having this talk with you. I am feeling better already. But you have no idea what I have been through the last few weeks. She is so dear to me. I love her so." His voice broke

I was seized with a feeling of mixed abomination and sympathy

"You are a child," I said, taking him by the hand. As I did so every vestige of hostility faded out of me. My heart went out to him. "Come, Max, pull yourself together! Be a man!"

"I have always known you to be my friend. I believe all you say. I first began to think of this trouble a few days after you moved out. But at first I made no fuss about it. I thought she was not well. I came to see you a few times and you did not behave like a fellow who was guilty."

I gave a silent little laugh

He related certain intimate incidents which had aroused his first twinge of suspicion. He was revoltingly frank

"I spoke to her plainly," he said. "'What's the matter with you, Dora?' I asked her. 'Don't you like me any more?' And she got wild and said she hated me like poison. She never talked to me like that before. It was a different Dora. She was always downhearted, cranky. The slightest thing made her yell or cry with tears. It got worse and worse. Oh, it was terrible! We quarreled twenty times a day and the children cried and I thought I was going mad.

Maybe she was just missing you. You were like one of the family, don't you know. And, well, you are a good-looking fellow, Levinsky, and she is only a woman."

"Nonsense!" I returned, the hot color mounting to my cheeks. "I am sure Dora had not a bad thought in her mind—"

"But she confessed," he interrupted me. "She said she was crazy for you and I could do as I pleased."

"But you know she did not mean it. She said it just for spite, just to make you feel bad, because you were quarreling with her."

He quoted a brutal question which he had once put to her concerning her relations with me, and then he quoted Dora as answering: "Yes, yes, yes! And if you don't like it you can sue me for divorce."

I laughed, making my merriment as realistic as I could. "It's all ridiculous nonsense, Max," I said. "You made life miserable to her and she was ready to say anything. She may have been worried over something, and you imagined all sorts of things. Maybe it was something about her education that worried her. You know how ambitious she is to be educated, and how hard she takes these things."

Max shook his head pensively

"I am sure it is as I say," I continued. "Dora is a peculiar woman. The trouble is, you judge her as if she were like the other women you meet. Hers is a different character."

This point apparently interested him

"She is always taken up with her thoughts," I pursued. "She is not so easy to understand, anyway. I lived over a year in your house, and yet I'll be hanged if I know what kind of woman she is. Of course you're her husband, but still—can you say you know what she is thinking of most of the time?"

"There is something in what you say," he assented, half-heartedly

As we rose to go he said, timidly: "There is only one more question I want to ask of you, Levinsky. You won't be angry, will you?" "What is it?" I demanded, with a good-natured laugh. "What is bothering your head?"

"I mean if you meet her now, sometimes?"

"Now, look here, Max. You are simply crazy," I said, earnestly. "I swear to you by my mother that I have not seen Dora since I moved out of your house, and that all your suspicions are nonsense" (to keep the memory of my mother from desecration I declared mutely that my oath referred to the truthful part of my declaration only—that is, exclusively to the fact that I no longer met Dora)

"I believe you, I believe you, Levinsky," he rejoined. We parted more than cordially, Max promising to call on me again and to spend an evening with me

I was left in a singular state of mind. I was eaten up with compunction, and yet the pain of my love reasserted itself with the tantalizing force of two months before

Max never called on me again

- saw Max again
  └ Max said Dora confessed her feelings about D
- D panicked + denied it
  └ Max believed him

# CHAPTER III

AS a salesman Bender proved a dismal failure, but I retained him in my employ as a bookkeeper and a sort of general supervisor. I could offer him only ten dollars a week, with a promise to raise his salary as soon as I could afford it, and he accepted the job "temporarily." As general supervisor under my orders he developed considerable efficiency, although he lacked initiative and his naïveté was a frequent cause of annoyance to me. I found him spotlessly honest and devoted

I quickly raised his salary to fifteen dollars a week

He was the embodiment of method and precision and he often nagged me for my deficiency in these qualities. Sometimes these naggings of his or some display of poor judgment on his part would give rise to a tiff between us.

Otherwise we got along splendidly. We were supposed to be great chums. In reality, however, I would freely order him about, while he would address me with a familiarity which had an echo of respectful distance to it

With him to take care of my place when I was away, it became possible for me gradually to extend my territory as traveling salesman till it reached Nebraska and Louisiana. Thus, having failed as a drummer himself, he made up for it by enabling me to act as one

He had been less than a year with me when his salary was twenty dollars

Charles Eaton, the Pennsylvanian of the hemispherical forehead and bushy eyebrows who had given me my first lesson in restaurant manners, was now my sponsor at the beginning of my career as a full-fledged traveling salesman.

He took a warm interest in me. Having spent many years on the road himself, more particularly in the Middle West and Canada, he had formed many a close friendship among retailers, so he now gave me some valuable letters of intro duction to merchants in several cities

When I asked him for suggestions to guide me on the road he looked perplexed

"Oh, well, I guess you'll do well," he said

"Still, you have had so much experience, Mr. Eaton."

"Well, I really don't know. It's all a matter of common sense, I guess. And, after all, the merchandise is the thing, the merchandise and the price."

He added a word or two about the futility of laying down rules, and that was all I could get out of him. That a man of few words like him should have succeeded as a salesman was a riddle to me. I subsequently realized that his reticence accentuated an effect of solidity and helped to inspire confidence in the few words which he did utter. But at the time in question I was sure that the "gift of the gab" was an indispensable element of success in a salesman.

Indeed, one of my faults as a drummer, during that period at least, was that I was apt to talk too much. I would do so partly for the sheer lust of hearing myself use the jargon of the market, but chiefly, of course, from eagerness to make a sale, from over-insistence. I was too exuberant in praising my own goods and too harsh in criticising those of my competitors.

Altogether there was more emphasis than dignity in my appeal.

One day, as I was haranguing the proprietor of a small department store in a Michigan town, he suddenly interrupted me by placing a friendly hand on my shoulder. His name was Henry Gans. He was a stout man of fifty, with the stamp of American birth on a strong Jewish face

"Let me give you a bit of advice, young man," he said, with paternal geniality. "You won't mind, will you?"

I uttered a perplexed, "Why, no"; and he proceeded: "If you want to make good as a salesman, observe these two rules: Don't knock the other fellow and don't talk too much."

For a minute I stood silent, utterly nonplussed. Then, pulling myself together, I said, with a bow: "Thank you, sir. Thank you very much. I am only a beginner, and only a few years in the country. I know I have still a great deal to learn. It's very kind of you to point out my mistakes to The gay light of Gans's eye gave way to a look of heart-to-heart earnestness

"It ain't nice to run down your competitor," he said. "Besides, it don't pay. It makes a bad impression on the man you are trying to get an order from."

We had a long conversation, gradually passing from business to affairs of a personal nature. He was interested in my early struggles in America, in my mode of living, in the state of my business, and I told him the whole story.

He seemed to be well disposed toward me, but it was evident that he did not take my "one-horse" establishment seriously, and I left his store without an order. I was berating myself for having revealed the true size of my business. Somehow my failure in this instance galled me with special poignancy. I roamed around the streets, casting about for some scheme to make good my mistake

Less than an hour after I left Gans's store I re-entered it, full of fresh spirit and pluck.

"I beg your pardon for troubling you again, Mr. Gans," I began, stopping him in the middle of an aisle. "You've been so kind to me. I should like to ask you one more question. Only one. I trust I am not intruding?"

"Go ahead," he said, patiently

"I shall do as you advise me. I shall never knock the other fellow," I began, with a smile. "But suppose his merchandise is really good, and I can outbid him. Why should it not be proper for me to say so? If you'll permit me"—pointing at one of the suits displayed in the store, a brown cheviot trimmed with velvet. "Take that suit, for instance. It's certainly a fine garment. It has style and dash. It's really a beautiful garment. I haven't the least idea how much you pay for it, of course, but I do know that I could make you the identical coat for a much smaller price. So why shouldn't it be right for me to say so?"

He contemplated me for a moment, broke into a hearty laugh, and said: "You're a pretty shrewd fellow. Why, of course, there's nothing wrong in selling cheaper than your competitor. That's what we're all trying to do.

That's the game, provided you really can sell cheaper than the other man, and there are no other drawbacks in doing business with you."

What I said about the brown suit piqued him. He had his bookkeeper show me the bill, and defied me to sell him a garment of exactly the same material, cut, and workmanship for less. I accepted the challenge, offering to reduce the price by four dollars and a half before I had any idea whether I could afford to do so. I was ready to lose money on the transaction, so long as I got a start with this man

Gans expressed doubt of my ability to make good my offer. I proceeded to explain the special conditions under which I ran my business. I waxed eloquent

"Doing business on a gigantic scale is not always an advantage, Mr. Gans," I sang out, with an affected Yankee twang. "There are exceptions. And the cloak-and-suit industry is one of these exceptions, especially now that the Cloak-makers' Union has come to stay. By dealing with a very big firm you've got to pay for union labor, while a modest fellow like myself has no trouble in getting cheap labor. And when I say cheap I don't mean poor labor, but just the opposite. I mean the very best tailors, the most skilled mechanics in the country. It sounds queer, doesn't it? But it's a fact, nevertheless, Mr. Gans. It is a fact that the best ladies' tailors are old-fashioned, pious people, green in the country, who hate to work in big places, and who keep away from Socialists, anarchists, unionists, and their whole crew. They need very little, and they love their work. They willingly stay in the shop from early in the morning till late at night."

"They are dead stuck on it, hey?" Gans said, quizzically. "They are used to it," I explained. "In Russia a tailor works about fourteen hours a day. Of course, I don't let them overwork themselves. I treat them as if they were my brothers or uncles. We get along like a family, and they earn twice as much as the strict union people, too."

"I see. They get low wages and don't work too much and are ahead of the game, after all. Is that it? Well, well. But you're a smart fellow, just the same."

I explained to him why my men earned more than they would in the big shops, and the upshot was an order for a hundred suits. Twenty of these were to be copies of the brown-cheviot garment which was the subject of his challenge, I buying that suit of him, so as to use it as a sample

On my way home I exhibited that suit to merchants in other cities, giving it out for my own product. It was really an attractive garment and it brought me half a dozen additional sales.

I developed into an excellent salesman. If I were asked to name some single element of my success on the road I should mention the enthusiasm with which I usually spoke of my merchandise. It was genuine, and it was contagious.

Retailers could not help believing that I believed in my goods

temp.
- kept Bender as an employee even if he +most of the time - annoyed D
- started bad mouthing his competition until a Mr Henry Gans told him it was bad business
  I offered to make a suit at a cheaper price → Gans accepted
- Believed in his product.

# CHAPTER IV

THE road was a great school of business and life to me. I visited scores of cities. I met hundreds of human types. I saw much of the United States.

Every time I returned home I felt as though, in comparison with the places which I had just visited, New York was not an American city at all, and as though my last trip had greatly added to the "real American" quality in me

Thousands of things reminded me of my promotion in the world. I could not go to bed in a Pullman car, walk over the springy "runner" of a hotel corridor, unfold the immense napkin of a hotel dining-room, or shake down my trousers upon alighting from a boot-black's chair, without being conscious of the difference between my present life and my life in Antomir

I was full of energy, full of the joy of being alive, but there was usually an undercurrent of sadness to all this. While on the road I would feel homesick for New York, and at the same time I would feel that I had no home anywhere, that my mother was dead and I was all alone in the world.

I missed Dora many months after she made me move from her house. As for Max, the thought of him, his jealousy and the way he groveled before me the last time I had seen him, would give me a bad taste in the mouth. I both pitied and despised him, and I hated my guilty conscience; so I would try to keep him out of my mind. What I missed almost as much as I did Dora was her home.

There was no other to take its place. There was not a single family in New York or in any other American town who would invite me to its nest and make me feel at home there. I saw a good deal of Meyer Nodelman, but he never asked me to the house. And so I was forever homesick, not for Antomir—for my native town had become a mere poem—but for a home

I did some reading on the road. There was always some book in my hand-bag—some volume of Spencer, Emerson, or Schopenhauer (in an English translation), perhaps. I would also read articles in the magazines, not to mention the newspapers. But I would chiefly spend my time in the smoker, talking to the other drummers or listening to their talk. There was a good deal of card-playing in the cars, but that never had any attraction for me.

I tried to learn poker, but found it tedious.

The cigarette stumps by which I had sought to counteract my hunger pangs at the period of my dire need had developed the cigarette habit in me. This had subsequently become a cigar habit. I had discovered the psychological significance of smoking "the cigar of peace and good will." I had realized the importance of offering a cigar to some of the people I met. I would watch American smokers and study their ways, as though there were a special American manner of smoking and such a thing as smoking with a foreign accent. I came to the conclusion that the dignity of smoking a cigar lasted only while the cigar was still long and fresh. There seemed to be special elegance in a smoker taking a newly lighted cigar out of his mouth and throwing a glance at its glowing end to see if it was smoking well.

Accordingly, I never did so without being conscious of my gestures and trying to make them as "American" as possible

The other cloak salesmen I met on the road in those days were mostly representatives of much bigger houses than mine. They treated me with ill-concealed contempt, and I would retaliate by overstating my sales. One of the drummers who were fond of taunting me was an American by birth, a fellow named Loeb

"Well, Levinsky," he would begin. "Had a big day, didn't you?"

"I certainly did," I would retort.

"How much? Twenty-five thousand?" "Well, it's no use trying to be funny, but I've pulled in five thousand dollars to-day." "Is that all?"

"Well, if you don't believe me, what's the use asking? What good would it do me to brag? If I say five thousand. it is five thousand. As a matter of fact, it 'll amount to more." Whereupon he would slap his knee and roar

He was a good-looking, florid-faced man with sparkling black eyes—a gay, boisterous fellow, one of those who are the first to laugh at their own jests. He was connected with the largest house in the cloak trade. Our relations were of a singular character. He was incessantly poking fun at me; nothing seemed to afford him more pleasure than to set a smokerful of passengers laughing at my expense. At the same time he seemed to like me.

But then he hated me, too. As for me, I reciprocated both feelings ] – Men !.

One day, on the road, he made me the victim of a practical joke that proved an expensive lesson to me. The incident took place in a hotel in Cincinnati, Ohio. He "confidentially" let me see one of his samples, hinting that it was his "leader," or best seller. He then went to do some telephoning, leaving the garment with me the while. Whereupon I lost no time in making a pencil-sketch of it, with a few notes as to materials, tints, and other details. I subsequently had the garment copied and spent time and money offering it to merchants in New York and on the road. It proved an unmitigated failure.

"You are a nice one, you are," he said to me, with mock gravity, on a subsequent trip. "You copied that garment I showed you in Cincinnati, didn't you?"

"What garment? What on earth are you talking about?" I lied, my face on fire.

"Come, come, Levinsky. You know very well what garment I mean. While I was away telephoning you went to work and made a sketch of it. It was downright robbery. That's what I call it. Well, have you sold a lot of them?" And he gave me a merry wink that cut me as with a knife

One of the things about which he often made fun of me was my Talmud gesticulations, a habit that worried me like a physical defect. It was so distressingly un-American. I struggled hard against it. I had made efforts to speak with my hands in my pockets; I had devised other means for keeping them from participating in my speech. All of no avail. I still gesticulate a great deal, though much less than I used to

One afternoon, on a west-bound train, Loeb entertained a group of passengers of which I was one with worn-out stories of gesticulating Russian Jews. He told of a man who never opened his mouth when he was out of doors and it was too cold for him to expose his hands; of another man who never spoke when it was so dark that his hands could not be seen. I laughed with the others, but I felt like a cripple who is forced to make fun of his own deformity. It seemed to me as though Loeb, who was a Jew, was holding up our whole race to the ridicule of Gentiles. I could have executed him as a traitor to his people. Presently he turned on me

"By the way, Levinsky, you never use a telephone, do you?"

"Why? Who says I don't?" I protested, timidly

"Because it's of no use to you," he replied. "The fellow at the other end of the wire couldn't see your hands, could he?" And he broke into a peal of self-satisfied mirth in which some of his listeners involuntarily joined.

"You think you're awfully smart," I retorted, in abject misery

"And you think you're awfully grammatical." And once more he roared

"You are making fun of the Jewish people," I said, in a rage. "Aren't you a Jew yourself?"

"Of course I am," he answered, wiping the tears from his laughing black eyes. "And a good one, too. I am a member of a synagogue. But what has that got to do with it? I can speak on the telephone, all right." And again the car rang with his laughter

I was aching to hurl back some fitting repartee, but could think of none, and to my horror the moments were slipping by, and presently the conversation was changed

At the request of a gay little Chicagoan who wore a skull-cap a very fat Chicagoan told a story that was rather risqué. Loeb went him one better. The man in the skull-cap declared that while he could not bring himself to tell a smutty story himself, he was "as good as any man in appreciating one." He then offered a box of cigars for the most daring anecdote, and there ensued an orgy of obscenity that kept us shouting (I could not help thinking of similar talks at the cloak-shops). Loeb suggested that the smoking-room be dubbed "smutty room" and was applauded by the little Chicagoan. The prize was awarded, by a vote, to a man who had told his story in the gravest tone of voice and without a hint of a smile

Frivolity gave way to a discussion of general business conditions. A lanky man with a gray beard, neatly trimmed, and with the most refined manners in our group, said something about competition in the abstract. I made a remark which seemed to attract attention and then I hastened to refer to the struggle for life and the survival of the fittest. Loeb dared not burlesque me. I was in high feather

Dinner was announced. To keep my traveling expenses down I was usually very frugal on the road. I had not yet seen the inside of a dining-car (while stopping at a hotel I would not indulge in a dining-room meal uuless I deemed it advisable to do so for business considerations). On this occasion, however, when most of our group went to the dining-car I could not help joining them. The lanky man, the little Chicagoan, and the fleshy Chicagoan—the three "stars" of the smoker—went to the same table, and I hastened, with their ready permission, to occupy the remaining seat at that table. I ordered an expensive dinner. At my instance the chat turned on national politics, a subject in which I felt at home, owing to my passion for newspaper editorials. I said something which met with an encouraging reception, and then I entered upon a somewhat elaborate discourse. My listeners seemed to be interested. I was so absorbed in the topic and in the success I was apparently scoring that I was utterly oblivious to the taste of the food in my mouth. But I was aware that it was "aristocratic American" food, that I was in the company of well-dressed American Gentiles, eating and conversing with them, a nobleman among noblemen. I throbbed with love for America

"Don't be excited," I was saying to myself. "Speak in a calm, low voice, as these Americans do. And for goodness' sake don't gesticulate!"

I went on to speak with exaggerated apathy, my hands so strenuously still that they fairly tingled with the effort, and, of course, I was so conscious of the whole performance that I did not know what I was talking about. This state of my mind soon wore off, however

Neither the meal nor the appointments of the car contained anything that I had not enjoyed scores of times before—in the hotels at which I stopped or at the restaurants at which I would dine and wine some of my customers; but to eat such a meal amid such surroundings while on the move was a novel experience. The electric lights, the soft red glint of the mahogany walls, the whiteness of the table linen, the silent efficiency of the colored waiters, coupled with the fact that all this was speeding onward through the night, made me feel as though I were partaking of a repast in an enchanted palace. The easy urbanity of the three well-dressed Americans gave me a sense of uncanny gentility and bliss

"Can it be that I am I?" I seemed to be wondering

The gaunt, elderly man, who was a member of a wholesale butcher concern, was seated diagonally across the table from me, but my eye was for the most part fixed on him rather than on the fat man who occupied the seat directly opposite mine. He was the most refined-looking man of the three and his vocabulary matched his appearance and manner. He fascinated me. His cultured English and ways conflicted in my mind with the character of his business. I could not help thinking of raw beef, bones, and congealed blood. I said to myself, "It takes a country like America to produce butchers who look and speak like noblemen." The United States was still full of surprises for me.

I was still discovering America

After dinner, when we were in the smoking-room again, it seemed to me that the three Gentiles were tired of me. Had I talked too much? Had I made a nuisance of myself? I was wretched

- homesick for any home
- met another drummer, Loeb
  └ didn't like him
  └ L made fun of D a lot
- still discovering the wonders of America.

# CHAPTER V

I LOST track of Loeb before the train reached Chicago, but about a fortnight later, when I was in St. Louis, I encountered him again. It was on a Monday morning. With sample-case in hand, I was crossing one of the busiest spots in the shopping district with preoccupied mien, when he hailed me: "Hello, Levinsky! How long have you been here?"

"Just arrived," I answered

"Where are you stopping?"

I named my hotel. I could see that he was taking note of the fact that I was crossing the street to the Great Bazar, one of the largest department stores in St. Louis

"I am going to tackle Huntington this morning," I said, with mild defiance

"Are you? Wish you luck," he remarked, quite gravely. "You'll find him a pretty tough customer, though." He was apparently too busy to indulge in raillery. "Wish you luck," he repeated, and was off

Huntington was the new head of the cloak-and-suit department in the Great Bazar, and in this capacity he was said to be doing wonders. It was not true that I had just arrived. I had been in the city nearly three days, and the day before I had mailed a letter to Huntington upon which I was building great hopes. I knew but too well that he was a "tough customer," my previous efforts to obtain an interview with him—in New York as well as here, in St. Louis—having proven futile. I was too small a fish for him. Nor, indeed, was the Great Bazar the only large department store in the country whose door was closed to me. Barring six or seven such stores, in as many cities, with which I was in touch largely through the good offices of Eaton, my business was almost confined to small concerns. Eaton had given me letters to many other large firms, but these had brought no result. For one thing, my Russian name was against me. As I have said before, the American business world had not yet learned to take our people seriously

And so I had written Huntington, making a special plea for a few minutes of his "most valuable time." All I asked for was an opportunity "to point out some specific conditions that enable our house to reduce the cost of production to an unheard-of level." If he had only read that letter! I had bestowed so much effort on it, and I gave myself credit for having made a fine job of it

Arriving at the big store, I made my way to the sample-rooms. I did so by a freight-elevator, the passenger-cars being denied to men carrying sample-cases. In the waiting-room of the buyers' offices I found four or five men, all of them accompanied by colored porters who carried their sample-cases for them. A neat-looking office-boy, behind a small desk, was rocking on the hind legs of his chair with an air of supreme indifference.

"Will you take it in?" I said to him, handing him my card. "I want to see Mr. Huntington."   .

"Mr. Huntington is busy," he answered, mechanically, without ceasing to rock.

"Take it in, please," I whispered, imploringly. But he took no heed of me.

Had I been the only salesman in the room, I should have offered him a bribe.

As it was, there was nothing to do but to take a seat and wait

"These office-boys treat salesmen like so many dogs," I muttered, addressing myself to the man by my side

He sized me up, without deigning an answer.

Other salesmen made their appearance, some modestly, others with a studied air of confidence, loudly greeting those they knew. The presence of so many rivals and the frigidity of the office-boy made my heart heavy. I was still a novice at the game, and the least mark of hostility was apt to have a depressing effect on my spirits, though, as a rule, it only added fuel to my ambition

Some of the other salesmen were chatting and cracking jokes, for all the world like a group of devoted friends gathered for some common purpose. The ostensible meaning of it all was that the competition in which they were engaged was a "mere matter of business," of civilized rivalry; that it was not supposed to interfere with their friendship and mutual sense of fair play. But I thought that all this was mere pretense, and that at the bottom of their hearts each of them felt like wiping the rest of us off the face of the earth — *probably true*

Presently the office-boy gathered up our cards and disappeared behind a door. He was gone quite a few minutes. They were hours to me. I was in the toils of suspense, in a fever of eagerness and anxiety. As I sat gazing at the door through which the office-boy had vanished, Mr. Huntington loomed in my imagination large and formidable, mighty and stern. To be admitted to his presence was at this moment the highest aim of my life. Running through my anxious mind were various phrases from the letter I had sent him. Some of these seemed to be highly felicitous. The epistle was bound to make an impression. "Provided he has read it," I thought, anxiously. "But why should he have bothered with it? He probably receives scores like it. No, he has not read it."

The next moment it became clear to me that the opening sentence of my plea was sure to have arrested Huntington's attention, that he had read it to the end, and would let me not only show him my samples, but explain matters as well. Of a sudden, however, it struck me, to my horror, that I had no recollection of having signed that letter of mine

A middle-aged woman with a Jewish cast of features passed through the waiting-room. I knew that she was Huntington's assistant and she was apparently going to his compartment of the sample-room. The fact that she had a Jewish face seemed encouraging. Not that the Jews I had met in business had shown me more leniency or cordiality than the average Gentile.

Nor was an assistant buyer, as a rule, in a position to do something for a salesman unless his samples had been referred to her by her superior.

Nevertheless, her Jewish features spoke of kinship to me. They softened the grimness of the atmosphere around me

*— something familiar*

Finally the office-boy came back. My heart beat violently. Pausing at his desk, with only two or three of all the cards he had taken to the potentate, he looked at them, as he called out, with great dignity: "Mr. Huntington will see Mr. Sallinger, Mr. Stewart, and Mr. Feltman."

My heart sank. I suspected that my poor card had never reached its destination, that the boy had simply thrown it away, together with some of the other cards, perhaps, on his way to Mr. Huntington's room. Indeed, I knew that this was the fate of many a salesman's card

The boy called out Sallinger's name again, this time admitting him to the inner precincts. All those whose cards had been ignored except myself—there were about a dozen of them—picked up their sample-cases or had their porters do so and passed out without ado. As for me, I simply could not bring myself to leave

"He didn't mark my card, did he?" I said to the boy

"No, sir," he snapped, with a scowl.

When I reached the street I paused for some minutes, as though glued to the sidewalk. Was it all over? Was there no hope of my seeing Huntington? My mind would not be reconciled to such an outcome. I stood racking my brains for some subterfuge by which I might be able to break through the Chinese wall that separated me from the great Mogul, and when I finally set out on my way to other stores I was still brooding over the question. I visited several smaller places that day and I made some sales, but all the while I was displaying my samples, quoting prices, arguing, cajoling, explaining, jesting, the background of my brain never ceased bothering about Huntington and devising means of getting at him

The next morning I was in Huntington's waiting-room again. I fared no better than on the previous occasion. I tried to speak to Huntington on the telephone, but I only succeeded in speaking to a telephone-girl and she told me that he was busy

"Please tell Mr. Huntington I have a job to close out, a seventeen-dollar garment for seven fifty."

"Mr. Huntington is busy."

At this moment it seemed to me that all talk of American liberty was mere cant

I asked the manager of the hotel at which I was stopping to give me a letter of introduction to him, and received a polite no for an answer. I discovered the restaurant where Huntington was in the habit of taking lunch and I went there for my next noon-hour meal for the purpose of asking him for an interview. I knew him by sight, for I had seen him twice in New York, so when he walked into the restaurant there was a catch at my heart. He was a spare little man with a face, mustache, and hair that looked as though he had just been dipped in a pail of saffron paint. He was accompanied by another man. I was determined first to let him have his lunch and then, on his way out, to accost him. Presently, lo and behold! Loeb entered the restaurant and walked straight up to Huntington's table, evidently by appointment. I nearly groaned. I knew that Loeb had a spacious sample-room at his hotel, with scores of garments hung out, and even with wire figures.

It was clear that Huntington had visited it or was going to, while I could not even get him to hear my prices. Was that fair? I saw the law of free competition, the great law of struggle and the survival of the fittest, defied, violated, desecrated

I discovered the residence of Huntington's assistant, and called on her. I had offered presents to other assistant buyers and some of them had been accepted, so I tried the same method in this case—with an unfortunate result. Huntington's assistant not only rejected my bribe, but flew into a passion to boot, and it was all my powers of pleading could do to have her promise me not to report the matter to her principal

I learned that Huntington was a member of the Elks and a frequenter of their local club-house, but, unfortunately, I was not a member of that order

I went to the Yiddish-speaking quarter of St. Louis, made the acquaintance of a man who was ready to sell me, on the instalment plan, everything under the sun, from a house lot and a lottery ticket to a divorce, and who undertook to find me (for ten dollars) somebody who would give me a "first-class introduction" to Huntington; but his eager eloquence failed to convince me. I had my coat pressed by a Jewish tailor whose place was around the corner from Huntington's residence and who pressed his suits for him. I had a shave in the barber shop at which Huntington kept his shaving-cup. I learned something of the great man's family life, of his character, ways, habits. It proved that he lived quite modestly, and that his income was somewhere between sixty and seventy dollars a week. Mine was three times as large. That I should have to rack my brains, do detective work, and be subjected to all sorts of humiliation in an effort to obtain an audience with him seemed to be a most absurd injustice

I was losing precious time, but I could not bring myself to get away from St. Louis without having had the desired interview. Huntington's name was buzzing in my mind like an insect. It was a veritable obsession

My talk with his barber led me to a bowling-alley. Being a passionate bowler, the cloak-buyer visited the place for an hour or so three or four times a week. As a consequence of this discovery I spent two afternoons and an evening there, practising a game which I had never even heard of before

My labors were not thrown away. The next evening I saw Huntington and a son of his in the place and we bowled some games together. Seen at close range, the cloak-buyer was a commonplace-looking fellow. I thought that he did not look much older than his son, and that both of them might have just stepped out from behind a necktie counter. I searched the older man's countenance for marks of astuteness, initiative, or energy, without being able to find any. But he certainly was a forcible bowler

When he made a sensational hit and there broke out a roar of admiration I surpassed all the other bystanders in exuberance. "I must not overdo it, though," I cautioned myself. "He cannot be a fool. He'll see through me." His son was apparently very proud of him, so I said to the young man: "Anybody can see your father is an energetic man."

"You bet he is," the young man returned, appreciatively. I led him on and he told me about his father's baseball record. I dropped a remark about his being "successful in business as well as in athletics" and wound up by introducing myself and asking to be introduced to his father. It was a rather dangerous venture, for the older Huntington was apt to remember my name, in which case my efforts might bring me nothing but a rebuff. Anyhow, I took the plunge and, to my great delight, he did not seem ever to have heard of me

Ten minutes later the three of us were seated over glasses of lager in the beer-garden with which the bowling-alley was connected. I told them that I was from New York and that I had come to St. Louis partly on business and partly to visit a sister who lived in their neighborhood. The elder Huntington said something of the rapid growth of New York, of its new high buildings. His English was curiously interspersed with a bookish phraseology that seemed to be traceable to the high-flown advertisements of his department in the newspapers. I veered the conversation from the architectural changes that had come over New York to changes of an ethnographic character.

"Our people, immigrants from Russia, I mean, are beginning to play a part in the business life of the city," I said

"Are you a Russian?" he asked

"I used to be," I answered, with a smile. "I am an American now."

"That's right."

"You see, we are only new-comers. The German Jews began coming a great many years ahead of us, but we can't kick, either."

"I suppose not," he said, genially.

"For one thing, we are the early bird that gets, or is bound to get, the worm. I mean it in a literal sense. Our people go to business at a much earlier hour and go home much later. There is quite a number of them in your line of business, too."

"I know," he said. "Of course, the 'hands' are mostly Russian Hebrews, but some of them have gone into manufacturing, and I don't doubt but they'll make a success of it."

"Why, they are making a success of it, Mr. Huntington."

I felt that I was treading on risky gound, that he might smell a rat at any moment; but I felt, also, that when he heard why manufacturers of my type were able to undersell the big old firms he would find my talk too tempting to cut it short. And so I rushed on. I explained that the Russian cloak-manufacturer operated on a basis of much lower profits and figured down expenses to a point never dreamed of before; that the German-American cloak-manufacturer was primarily a merchant, not a tailor; that he was compelled to leave things to his designer and a foreman, whereas his Russian competitor was a tailor or cloak-operator himself, and was, therefore, able to economize in ways that never occurred to the heads of the old houses.

"I see," Huntington said, with a queer stare at me

"Besides, our people content themselves with small profits," I pursued. "We are modest."

Here I plagiarized an epigram I had heard from Meyer Nodelman: "Our German co-religionists will spend their money before they have made it, while we try to make it first."

I expected Huntington to smile, but he did not. He was listening with sphinx-like gravity. When I paused, my face and my ears burning, he said, with some embarrassment: "What is your business, may I ask?" "I am in the same line. Cloaks." "Are you?" With another stare

Tense with excitement, I said, with daredevil recklessness: "The trouble is that successful men like yourself are so hard to get at, Mr.

Huntington."

"What do you mean?" he said, with a cryptic laugh

I made a clean breast of it

Perhaps he was flattered by my picture of him as an inaccessible magnate; perhaps he simply appreciated the joke of the thing and the energy and tenacity I had brought to it, but he let me narrate the adventure in detail.

I told him the bare truth, and I did so with conscious simple-heartedness, straining every nerve to make a favorable impression

As he listened he repeatedly broke into laughter, and when I had finished he said to his son: "Sounds like a detective story, doesn't it?"

But his demeanor was still enigmatic, and I anxiously wondered whether I impressed him as an energetic business man or merely as an adventurer, a crank, or even a crook

"All I ask for is an opportunity to show you my samples, Mr. Huntington," I said.

"Well," he answered, deliberately, "there can be no harm in that." And after a pause, "You've bagged your game so far as that's concerned."

And he merrily made me an appointment for the next morning

About a month later I came across Loeb on Broadway, New York

"By the way," he said, in the course of our brief talk, with a twinkle in his eve, "did you sell anything to Huntington?" "Huntington? St. Louis? Why, he really is a hard man to reach," I answered, glumly.

At that very moment my cutters were at work on a big order from Huntington, largely for copies from Loch's styles. I had filled a test order of his so promptly and so completely to his satisfaction, and my prices were so overwhelmingly below those in Loch's bill, that the St. Louis buyer had wired me a "duplicate" for eight hundred suits

There was a buyer in Cleveland, a bright, forceful little man who would not let a salesman quote his price until he had made a guess at it. His name was Lemmelmann. He was an excellent business man and a charming fellow, but he had a weakness for parading his ability to estimate the price of a garment "down to a cent." The salesmen naturally humored this ambition of his and every time he made a correct guess they would applaud him without stint, and I would follow their example. On one occasion I came to Cleveland with two especially prepared compliments in my mind

"Every human being has five senses," I said to the little buyer. "You have six, Mr. Lemmelmann. You were born with a price sense besides the ordinary five."

"My, but it's a good one," he returned, jovially

"Yes, you have more senses than anybody else, Mr. Lemmelmann," I added.

"You're the most sensible man in the world."

"Why—why, you can send stuff like that to Puck or Judge and get a five-dollar bill for it. How much will you charge me? Will that do?" he asked, handing me a cigar

The two compliments cemented our friendship. At least, I thought they did

Another buyer, in Atlanta, Georgia, had a truly wonderful memory. He seemed to remember every sample he had ever seen—goods, lines, trimmings, price, and all. He was an eccentric man. Sometimes he would receive a crowd of salesmen in rapid succession, inspect their merchandise and hear their prices without making any purchase. Later, sometimes on the same day, he would send out orders for the "numbers" that had taken his fancy

While showing him my samples one morning I essayed to express amazement at his unusual memory. But in this case I mistook my man

"If everybody had your marvelous memory there would be little work for bookkeepers," I jested

Whereupon he darted an impatient glance at me and growled: "Never mind my memory. You sell cloaks and suits, don't you? If you deal in taffy, you'll have to see the buyer of the candy department."

# CHAPTER VI

HUNTINGTON was a rising man and the other cloak-buyers were watchng him.

When it became known that there was a young manufacturer named Levinsky with whom he was placing heavy orders I began to attract general attention. My reputation for selling "first-rate stuff" for the lowest prices quoted spread. Buyers would call at my rookery of a shop before I had time to seek an interview with them. The appearance of my place and the crudity of my office facilities, so far from militating against my progress, helped to accelerate it. Skeptical buyers who had doubted my ability to undersell the old-established houses became convinced of it when they inspected my primitive-looking establishment.

The place became far too small for me. I moved to much larger quarters, consisting of the two uppermost floors and garret of a double tenement-house of the old type. A hall bedroom was converted into an office, the first separate room I ever had for the purpose, and I enjoyed the possession of it as much as I had done my first check-book. I had a lounge put in it, and often, at the height of the manufacturing season, when I worked from daybreak far into the night and lived on sandwiches, I would, instead of going home for the night, snatch three or four hours' sleep on it. The only thing that annoyed me was a faint odor of mold which filled my bedroom-office and which kept me in mind of the Margolises' old apartment.

There was the pain of my second love-affair in that odor, for, although I had not seen Dora nor heard of her for more than two years, I still thought of her often, and when I did her image still gave me pangs of yearning.

There was an air of prosperity and growth about my new place, but this did not interfere with the old air of skimpiness and cheapness as to running expenses and other elements that go to make up the cost of production

Bender's salary had been raised substantially, so much so that he had resigned his place as evening-school teacher, devoting himself exclusively to my shop and office. He was provokingly childish as ever, but he had learned a vast deal about the cloak business, its mechanical branch as well as the commercial end of it, and his usefulness had grown enormously

One morning I was hustling about my garret floor, vibrating with energy and self-importance, when he came up the stairs, saying: "There is a woman on the main floor who wants to see you. She says you know her." Was it Dora? I descended the stairs in a flutter

I was mistaken. It was Mrs. Chaikin. She looked haggard and more than usually frowsy. The cause of her pitiable appearance was no riddle to me. I knew that her husband's partner had made a mess of their business and that Chaikin had lost all his savings. "Does she want a loan?" I speculated

My first impulse was to take her to my little office, but I instantly realized that it would not be wise to flaunt such a mark of my advancement before her. I offered her a chair in a corner of the room in which I found her

"How is Chaikin? How is Maxie?"

"Thank God, Maxie is quite a boy," she answered, coyly. "Why don't you come to see him? Have you forgotten him? He has not forgotten you. Always asking about 'Uncle Levinsky.' Some little children have a better memory than some grown people."

Having delivered this thrust, she swept my shop with a sepulchral glance, followed by a succession of nods. Then she said, with a grin at once wheedling and malicious: "There are two more floors, aren't there? And I see you're very busy, thank God. Plenty of orders, hey? Thank God. Well, when Chaikin gets something started and there is nobody to spoil it, it's sure to go well. Isn't it?"

"Chaikin is certainly a fine designer," I replied, noncommittally, wondering what she was driving at

"A fine designer! Is that all?" she protested, with exquisite sarcasm. "And who fixed up this whole business? styles got the business started and gave it the name it has? Only 'a fine designer,' indeed! It's a good thing you admit that much at least. Well, but what's the use quarreling? I am here as a friend, not to make threats. That's not in my nature."

She gave me a propitiating look, and paused for my reply. "What do you mean, Mrs. Chaikin?" I asked, with an air of complaisant perplexity

"'What do you mean?'" she mocked me, suavely. "Poor fellow, he doesn't understand what a person means. He has no head on his shoulders, the poor thing. But what's the good beating about the bush, Levinsky? I am here to tell you that we have decided to come back and be partners again."

I did not burst into laughter. I just looked her over, and said, in the calmest and most business-like manner: "That's impossible, Mrs. Chaikin. The business doesn't need any partner."

"Doesn't need any partner! But it's ours, this business, as much as yours; even more. It is our sweat and our blood. Why, you hadn't a cent to your name when we started it, and you know it. And what did you have, pray? Did you know anything about cloaks? Could you do anything without Chaikin?"

"We won't argue about it, Mrs. Chaikin."

"Not argue about it?"

She was working herself into a rage, but she nipped it in the bud. "Now, look here, Levinsky," she said, with fresh suavity. "I have told you I haven't come here to pick a quarrel. Maxie misses you very much. He's always speaking about you." She tried a tone of persuasion. "When Chaikin and you are together again the business will go like grease. You know it will. He'll be the inside man and you'll attend to the outside business. You won't have to worry about anything around the shop, and, well, I needn't tell you what his designs will do for the business. Why, the Manheimers are just begging him to become their partner" (this was a lie, of course), "but I say: 'No, Chaikin! Better let us stick to our own business, even if it is much smaller, and let's be satisfied with whatever God is pleased to give us.'" Her protestations and pleadings proving ineffectual, she burst into another fury and made an ugly scene, threatening to retain "the biggest lawyer in the 'Nited States" and to commence action against me

I smiled

"Look at him! He's smiling!" she said, addressing herself to some of my men.

"He thinks he can swindle people and be left alone."

"Better go home, Mrs. Chaikin," I said, impatiently. "I have no time." "All right. We shall see!" she snapped, flouncing out. Before she closed the door on herself she returned and, stalking up to the chair which she had occupied a minute before, she seated herself again, defiantly. "Chase me out, if you dare," she said, with a sneer, her chin in the air. "I should just like to see you do it. Should like to see you chase me out of my own shop. It's all mine! all mine!" she shouted, her voice mounting hysterically. "All mine! Chaikin's sweat and blood. You're a swindler, a thief! I'll put you in Sing Sing."

She went off into a swoon, more or less affected, and when I had brought her to herself she shed a flood of quiet tears

"Take pity, oh, do take pity!" she besought, patting my hand. "You have a Jewish heart; you'll take pity."

There was nothing for it but to edge out of the room and to hide myself

A week later she came again, this time with Maxie, whom I had not seen for nearly three years and who seemed to have grown to double his former size.

On this occasion she threatened to denounce me to the Cloakmakers' Union for employing scab labor. Finally she made a scene that caused me to whisper to Bender to telephone for a policeman. Before complying, however, he tried persuasion.

"You had better go, madam," he said to her, meekly. "You are excited."

Partly because he was a stranger to her, but mainly, I think, because of his American appearance and English, she obeyed him at once.

The next day her husband came. He looked so worn and wretched and he was so ill at ease as he attempted to explain his errand that I could scarcely make out his words, but I received him well and my manner was encouraging, so he soon found his tongue

"Don't you care to have it in the old way again?" he said, piteously

"Why, I wish I could, Mr. Chaikin. I should be very glad to have you here. I mean what I say. But it's really impossible."

"I should try my best, you know." "I know you would."

After a pause he said: "She'll drive me into the grave. She makes my life so miserable."

"But it was she who made you get out of our partnership," I remarked, sympathetically

"Yes, and now she blames it all on me. When she heard you had moved to a larger place she fainted. Couldn't you take me back?"

He finally went to work as a designer for one of the old firms, at a smaller salary than his former employers had paid him

For the present I continued to worry along with my free-lance designer, but as a matter of fact Chaikin's wonderful feeling for line and color was, unbeknown to himself, in my service. The practice of pirating designs was rapidly becoming an open secret, in fact. Styles put out by the big houses were copied by some of their tailors, who would sell the drawing for a few dollars to some of the smaller houses in plenty of time before the new cloak or suit had been placed on the market. In this manner it was that I obtained, almost regularly, copies of Chaikin's latest designs

The period of dire distress that smote the country about this time—the memorable crisis of 1893—dealt me a staggering blow, but I soon recovered from it. The crisis had been preceded by a series of bitter conflicts between the old manufacturers and the Cloak-makers' Union, in the form of lockouts, strikes, and criminal proceedings against the leaders of the union, which had proved fatal to both. The union was still in existence, but it was a mere shadow of the formidable body that it had been three years before. And, as work was scarce, labor could be had for a song, as the phrase goes. This enabled me to make a number of comparatively large sales.

To tell the truth, the decay of the union was a source of regret to me, as the special talents I had developed for dodging it while it was powerful had formerly given me an advantage over a majority of my competitors which I now did not enjoy. Everybody was now practically free from its control.

Everybody could have all the cheap labor he wanted

Still, I was one of a minority of cloak-manufacturers who contrived to bring down the cost of production to an extraordinarily low level, and so I gradually obtained considerable business, rallying from the shock of the panic before it was well over

# CHAPTER VII

THE panic was followed by a carnival of prosperity of which I received a generous share. My business was progressing with leaps and bounds

The factory and office were moved to Broadway. This time it was a real office, with several bookkeepers, stenographers, model girls, and golden legends on the doors. These legends were always glittering in my mind

People were loading me with flattery. Everybody was telling me that I had "got there," and some were hinting, or saying in so many words, that I was a man of rare gifts, of exceptional character. I accepted it all as my due.

Nay, I regarded myself as rather underestimated. "They don't really understand me," I would think to myself. "They know that I possess brains and grit and all that sort of thing, but they are too commonplace to appreciate the subtlety of my thoughts and feelings."

Every successful man is a Napoleon in one thing at least—in believing himself the ward of a lucky star. I was no exception to this rule. I came to think myself infallible

In short, prosperity had turned my head

I looked upon poor people with more contempt than ever. I still called them "misfits," in a Darwinian sense. The removal of my business to Broadway was an official confirmation of my being one of the fittest, and those golden inscriptions on my two office doors seemed to proclaim it solemnly

At the same time I did not seem to be successful enough. I felt as though my rewards were inadequate. I was now worth more than one hundred thousand dollars, and the sum did not seem to be anything to rejoice over. My fortune was not climbing rapidly enough. I was almost tempted to stamp my foot and snarlingly urge it on. Only one hundred thousand! Why, there were so many illiterate dunces who had not even heard of Darwin and Spencer and who were worth more

There were moments, however, when my success would seem something incredible. That was usually when I chanced to think of some scene of my past life with special vividness. Could it be possible that I was worth a hundred thousand dollars, that I wore six-dollar shoes, ate dollar lunches, and had an army of employees at my beck and call? I never recalled my unrealized dreams of a college education without experiencing a qualm of regret

One day—it was a drizzly afternoon in April—as I walked along Broadway under my umbrella I came across Jake Mindels, the handsome young man who had been my companion during the period when I was preparing for City College. I had not seen him for over two years, but I had kept track of his career and I knew that he had recently graduated from the University Medical College and had opened a doctor's office on Rivington Street. His studiously dignified carriage, his Prince Albert coat, the way he wore his soft hat, the way he held his open umbrella, and, above all, the beard he was growing, betrayed a desire to look his new part. And he did look it, too. The nascent beard, the frock-coat, and the soft hat became him. He was handsomer than ever, and there was a new air of quiet, though conscious, intellectual importance about him.

The sight of him as I beheld him coming toward me gave me a pang of envy

"Levinsky! How are you? How are you?" he shouted, flinging himself at me effusively

"I hear you're practising medicine," I returned. And, looking him over gaily, I added, "A doctor every inch of you."

He blushed

"And you're a rich man, I hear."

"Vanderbilt is richer, I can assure you. I should change places with you any time." In my heart I remarked, "Yes, I am worth a hundred thousand dollars, while he is probably struggling to make a living, but I can beat him at his own intellectual game, too, even if he has studied anatomy and physiology."

"Well, you will be a Vanderbilt some day. You're only beginning to make money. People say you are a great success. I was so glad to hear of it."

"And I am glad to hear that you were glad," I jested, gratefully. "And how are things with you?"

"All right," he answered, firmly. "I can't complain. For the time I've been practising I am doing very well. Very well, indeed."

He told me of a case in which one of the oldest and most successful physicians on the East Side had made a false diagnosis, and where he, Mindels, had made the correct one and saved the patient's life

"The family wouldn't hear of another doctor now. They would give their lives for me," he said, with a simper

I took him up to my factory and showed him about. He was lavish in his expressions of surprise at the magnitude of my concern, and when I asked him to have dinner with me that evening he seemed to be more than pleased. Apart from other feelings, he was probably glad to renew acquaintance with a man who could afford to pay a decent doctor's bill, and through whom he might get in touch with other desirable patrons

Presently he wrinkled his forehead, as though he had suddenly remembered something

"Oh! Let me see!" he said. "Couldn't we postpone it? I have a confinement this evening. I expect to be called at any moment."

We changed the date, and he departed. I was left somewhat excited by the reminiscences that the meeting had evoked in me. I fell to pacing the floor of my office, ruminating upon the change which the past few years had wrought in his life and in mine. His boastful garrulity was something new in him. Was it the struggle for existence which was forcing it upon him? I wondered whether that confinement story was not a fib invented to flaunt his professional success. Thereupon I gave myself credit for my knowledge of human nature. "That's one of the secrets of my success," I thought. I complimented myself upon the possession of all sorts of talents, but my keenest ambition was to be recognized as an unerring judge of men

The amusing part of it was that in 1894, for example, I found that in 1893 my judgment of men and things had been immature and puerile. I was convinced that now at last my insight was a thoroughly reliable instrument, only a year later to look back upon my opinions of 1894 with contempt. I was everlastingly revising my views of people, including my own self

# BOOK XI

# MATRIMONY

# CHAPTER I

ONE afternoon in January or February I was on a Lexington Avenue car going up-town. At Sixty-seventh Street the car was invaded by a vivacious crowd of young girls, each with a stack of books under one of her arms. It was evident that they were returning home from Normal College, which was on that corner. Some of them preferred to stand, holding on to straps, so as to face and converse with their seated chums

I was watching them as they chattered, laughed, or whispered, bubbling over with the joy of being young and with the consciousness of their budding womanhood, when my attention was attracted to one of their number—a tall, lanky, long-necked lass of fifteen or sixteen. She was hanging on to a strap directly across the car from me. I could not see her face, but the shape of her head and a certain jerk of it, when she laughed, looked strikingly familiar to me. Presently she chanced to turn half-way around, and I recognized her. It was Lucy. I had not seen her for six years. She was completely changed and yet the same. Not yet fully formed, elongated, attenuated, angular, ridiculously too tall for her looks, and not quite so pretty as she had been at nine or ten, but overflowing with color, with light, with blossoming life, she thrilled me almost to tears. I was aching to call out her name, to hear myself say "Lucy" as I had once been wont to do, but I was not sure that it would be advisable to let her father hear of my lingering interest in his family. While I was thus debating with myself whether I should accost her, her glance fell on me. She transferred it to one of the windows, and the next moment she fell to eying me furtively.

"She has recognized me, but she won't come over to me," I thought. "She seems to be aware of her father's jealousy." It was a painful moment

Presently her fresh, youthful face brightened up. She bent over to two of her girl friends and whispered something to them, and then these threw glances at me. After some more whispering Lucy faced about boldly and stepped over to me

"I beg your pardon. Aren't you Mr. Levinsky?" she asked, with sweet, girlish shyness

"Of course I am, Lucy! Lucy dear, how are you? Quite a young lady!"

"I was wondering," she went on without answering. "At first I did not know.

You did seem familiar to me, but I could not locate your face. But then, all at once, don't you know, I said to myself, 'Why, it's Mr. Levinsky.' Oh, I'm so glad to see you."

She was all flushed and beaming with the surprise of the meeting, with consciousness of the eyes of her classmates who were watching her, and with something else which seemed to say: "I am Lucy, but not the little girl you used to play with. I am a young woman."

"And I was wondering who that tall, charming young lady was," I said. "Lord! how you have grown, Lucy!"

"Yes, I'm already taller than mother and father," she answered

"Than both together?"

"No, not as bad as all that," she giggled

For children of our immigrants to outgrow their parents, not only intellectually, but physically as well, is a common phenomenon. Perhaps it is due to their being fed far better than their parents were in their childhood and youth

I asked Lucy to take a seat by my side and she did, cheerfully. ("Maybe she does not know anything," I wondered.) "How is Danny?" I asked. "Still fat?"

"No, not very," she laughed. "He goes to school. I have a little sister, too," she added, blushing the least bit.

I winced. It was as though I had heard something revoltingly unseemly. Then a thought crossed my mind, and, seized with an odd feeling of curiosity, I asked: "How old is she?"

"Oh, a little less than a year," Lucy replied. "She's awful cute," she laughed

"And how is papa?" I inquired, to turn the conversation

"He's all right, thank you," she answered, gravely. "Only he lost a lot of money on account of the hard times. Many of his customers were out of work.

Business is picking up, though."

"And how is Becky? Are you still great friends?"

"Why, she ought to be here!" she replied, gazing around the car. "Must be in the next car."

"In another car!" I exclaimed, in mock amazement. "Not by your side?" Lucy laughed. "We are in the same class," she said

"And, of course, the families still live in the same house?" She nodded affirmatively, adding that they lived at One Hundred and Second Street near Madison Avenue, about a block and a half from the Park       .

"Come up some time, won't you?" she gurgled, with childish amiability, yet with apparent awkwardness

I wondered whether she was aware of her father's jealousy. "If she were she certainly would not invite me to the house," I reflected

I made no answer to her invitation

"Won't you come up?" she insisted.

I thought: "She doesn't seem to know anything about it. She has only heard that I had a quarrel with her mother." I shook my head, smiling affectionately

"Why, are you still angry at mother?" she pursued, shaking her head, deprecatingly, as who should say, "You're a bad boy."

I thought, "Of course she doesn't know." I smiled again. Then I said: "You're a sweet girl, all the same. And a big one, too."

"Thank you. Do come. Will you?" I shook my head

"Will you never come?" she asked, playfully. "Never? Never?"

"I have told you you're a charming girl, haven't I? What more do you want?"

The American children of the Ghetto are American not only in their language, tastes, and ambitions, but in outward appearance as well. Their bearing, gestures, the play of their features, and something in the very expression of their Semitic faces proclaim the land of their birth. All this was true of Lucy. She was fascinatingly American, and I told her so

"You're not simply a charming girl. You're a charming American girl," I said.

I wondered whether Dora had been keeping up her studies, and by questioning Lucy about the books under her arm I contrived to elicit the information that her mother had read not only such works as the Vicar of Wakefield, Washington Irving's Sketch Book, and Lamb's Shakespeare Stories, which had been part of Lucy's course during her first year at college, but that she had also read some of the works of Cooper, George Eliot, Dickens, Thackeray, Hawthorne, and all sorts of cheaper novels

"Mother is a great reader," Lucy said. "She reads more than I do. Why, she reads newspapers and magazines—everything she can lay her hands on! Father calls her Professor."

She also told me that her mother had read a good deal of poetry, that she knew the "Ancient Mariner" and "The Raven" by heart

"She's always at me because I don't care for poetry as much as she does," she laughed.

"Well, you're not taller than your mother in this respect, are you?"

"N-no," she assented, with an appreciative giggle

She left the car on the corner of One Hundred and Second Street. I was in a queer state of excitement

It flashed upon my mind that the section of Central Park in the vicinity of One Hundred and Second Street teemed with women and baby-carriages, and that it was but natural to suppose that Dora would be out every day wheeling her baby in that locality, and reading a book, perhaps. I visioned myself meeting her there some afternoon and telling her of my undying love. I even worked out the details of the plan, but I felt that I should never carry it out

I still loved Dora, but that was the Dora of six years before, an image of an enshrined past. She was a dear, sad memory scarcely anything more, and it seemed as though to disturb that sadness were sacrilege

"I shall probably run up against her some day," I said to myself, dolefully

And an echo seemed to add, "You are all alone in the world!"

# CHAPTER II

I WAS a lonely man. I was pulsating with activity and with a sense of triumph. I was receiving multitudes of new impressions and enjoying life in a multitude of ways, with no dearth of woman and song in the program. But at the bottom of my consciousness I was always lonely

There were moments when my desolation would assert itself rather violently.

This happened nearly every time I returned to New York from the road. As the train entered the great city my sense of home-coming would emphasize a feeling that the furnished two-room apartment on Lexington Avenue which was waiting to receive me was not a home

Meyer Nodelman, whom I often met in a Broadway restaurant at the lunch hour these days, would chaff or lecture me earnestly upon my unmarried state

"You don't know who you're working for," he would say, his sad, Oriental face taking on an affectionate expression. "Life is short at best, but when a fellow has nobody to bear his name after he is gone it is shorter still.

Get married, my boy. Get married." He took a lively interest in the growth of my business. He rejoiced in it as though he ascribed my successes to the loans he had given me when I struggled for a foothold. He often alluded to those favors, but he was a devoted friend, all the same. Moreover, he was a most attractive man to talk to, especially when the conversation dealt with one's intimate life. With all his illiteracy and crudity of language he had rare insight into the human heart and was full of subtle sympathy. He was the only person in America with whom I often indulged in a heart-to-heart confab. He was keenly aware of my loneliness. It seemed as though it disturbed him

"You are not a happy man, Levinsky," he once said to me. "You feel more alone than any bachelor I ever knew. You're an orphan, poor thing. You have a fine business and plenty of money and all sorts of nice times, but you are an orphan, just the same. You're still a child. You need a mother. Well, but what's the use? Your own mother—peace upon her—cannot be brought to life until the coming of the Messiah, so do the next best thing, Levinsky. Get married and you will have a mother—for your children. It isn't the same kind, but you won't feel lonesome any longer."

I laughed

"Laugh away, Levinsky. But you can't help it. And the smart books you read won't help you, either. You've got to get married whether you want it or not. This is a bill that must be paid."

I had lunch with him a day or two after my meeting with Lucy. The sight of his affectionate, melancholy face and the warmth of his greeting somehow made me think of the sentimental mood in which I had been left by that encounter

"I do feel lonesome," I said, with a smile, in the course of our chat. "I met a girl the other day—"

"Did you?" he said, expectantly.

"Oh, she is a mere child, not the kind of girl you mean, Mr. Nodelman. I once boarded in her mother's house. She was a mere child then. She is still a child, but she goes to college now, and she is taller than her mother.

When I saw her I felt old."

"Is that anything to be sad about? Pshaw! Get married, and you'll have a daughter of your own, and when she grows up you won't be sorry. Take it from me, Levinsky. There can be no greater pleasure than to watch your kids grow." And he added, in a lower tone, "I do advise you to get married."

"Perhaps I ought to," I said, listlessly. "But then it takes two to make a bargain."

"Oh, there are lots of good girls, and you can have the best piece of goods there is." "Oh, I don't know. It wouldn't be hard to find a good girl, perhaps. The question is whether she'll be good after the honeymoon is over."

"You don't want a bond and mortgage to guarantee that you'll be happy, do you? A fellow must be ready to take a chance."

There is an old story of a rabbi who, upon being asked by a bachelor whether he should marry, said: "If you do you will regret it, my son; but then if you remain single you are sure to regret it just as much; perhaps more. So get married like everybody else and regret it like everybody else." Nodelman now quoted that rabbi. I had heard the anecdote more than once before, but it seemed as though its meaning had now revealed itself to me for the first time.

"According to that rabbi, marriage is not a pleasure, but a miserable necessity," I urged

"Well, it isn't all misery, either. People are fond of saying that the best marriage is a curse. But it's the other way around. The worst marriage has some blessing in it, Levinsky."

"Oh, I don't know."

"Get married and you will. There is plenty of pleasure in the worst of homes. Take it from me,. Levinsky. When I come home and feel that I have somebody to live for, that it is not the devil I am working for, then—take it from me, Levinsky—I should not give one moment like that for all the other pleasures in the world put together."

I thought of his wife whom his mother had repeatedly described to me as a "meat-ball face" and a virago, and of his home which I had always pictured as hell. His words touched me

"It isn't that I don't want to take chances, Mr. Nodelman. It's something else. Were you ever in love, Mr. Nodelman?"

"What? Was I in love? Why?" he demanded, coloring. "What put it in your head to ask me such a funny question?"

"Funny! There's more pain than fun in it. Well, I have loved, Mr. Nodelman, and that's why it's so hard for me to think of marriage as a cold proposition. I don't think I could marry a girl I did not love."

I expected an argument against love-marriages, but Nodelman had none to offer. Instead, he had me dilate on the bliss and the agony of loving. He asked me questions and eagerly listened to my answers. I told him of my own two love-affairs, particularly of my relations with Dora. I omitted names and other details that might have pointed, ever so remotely, to Mrs.

Margolis's identity. Nodelman was interested intensely. His interrogations were of the kind that a girl of sixteen who had not yet loved might address to a bosom friend who had. How does it feel to be in doubt whether one's passion had found an echo? How did I feel when our lips were joined in our first kiss? How did she carry herself the next time I saw her? Was she shy? Did she look happy? Was she afraid of her husband? Was I afraid? The restaurant had been nearly deserted for about an hour, and we still sat smoking cigars and whispering

* Nodelman advised him to get married so he won't be lonely anymore
  └ D shared his experiences w/ women and love
  └ N was fascinated + kept asking D questions

# CHAPTER III

ONE day, as Nodelman took his seat across the table from me at the restaurant, he said: "Well, Levinsky, it's no use, you'll have to get married now. There will be no wriggling out of it. My wife has set her mind on it."

"Your wife?" I asked in surprise.

"Yes. I have an order to bring you up to the house, and that's all there is to it. Don't blame her, though. The fault is mine. I have told her so much about you she wants to know you."

"To know me and to marry me off, hey? And yet you claim to be a friend of mine."

"Well, it's no use talking. You'll have to come."

I received a formal invitation, written in English by Mrs. Nodelman, and on a Friday night in May I was in my friend's house for supper, as Nodelman called it, or "dinner," as his wife would have it

The family occupied one of a small group of lingering, brownstone, private dwellings in a neighborhood swarming with the inmates of new tenement "barracks."

"Glad to meechye," Mrs. Nodelman welcomed me. "Meyer should have broughchye up long ago. Why did you keep Mr. Levinsky away, Meyer? Was you afraid you might have reason to be jealous?"

"That's just it. She hit it right. I told you she was a smart girl, didn't I, Levinsky?"

"Don't be uneasy, Meyer. Mr. Levinsky won't even look at an old woman like me. It's a pretty girl he's fishin' for. Ainchye, Mr. Levinsky?"

She was middle-aged, with small features inconspicuously traced in a bulging mass of full-blooded flesh. This was why her mother-in-law called her "meat-ball face." She had a hoarse voice, and altogether she might have given me the impression of being drunk had there not been something pleasing in her hoarseness as well as in that droll face of hers. That she was American-born was clear from the way she spoke her unpolished English. Was Nodelman the henpecked husband that his mother advertised him to be? I wondered whether the frequency with which his wife used his first name could be accepted as evidence to the contrary

They had six children: a youth of nineteen named Maurice who was the image of his father and, having spent two years at college, was with him in the clothing business; a high-school boy who had his mother's face and whose name was Sidney—an appellation very popular among our people as "swell American"; and four smaller children, the youngest being a little girl of six.

"What do you think of my stock, Levinsky?" Nodelman asked. "Quite a lot, isn't it? May no evil eye strike them. What do you think of the baby? Come here, Beatrice! Recite something for uncle!" The command had barely left his mouth when Beatrice sprang to her feet and burst out mumbling something in a kindergarten singsong. This lasted some minutes Then she courtesied, shook her skirts, and slipped back into her seat

"She is only six and she is already more educated than her father," Nodelman said. "And Sidney he's studyin' French at high school. Sidney, talk some French to Mr. Levinsky. He'll understand you. Come on, show Mr. Levinsky you ain't going to be as ignorant as your pa."

The scene was largely a stereotyped copy of the one I had witnessed upon my first call at the Margolises'

Sidney scowled

"Come on, Sidney, be a good boy," Nodelman urged, taking him by the sleeve

"Let me alone," Sidney snarled, breaking away and striking the air a fierce backward blow with his elbow

"What do you want of him?" Mrs. Nodelman said to her husband, frigidly

My friend desisted, sheepishly

"He does seem to be afraid of his American household," I said to myself

After the meal, when we were all in the parlor again, Nodelman said to his wife, winking at me: "Poor fellow, his patience has all given out. He wants to know about the girl you've got for him. He has no strength any longer. Can't you see it, Bella? Look at him! Look at him! Another minute and he'll faint."

"What girl? Oh, I see! Why, there is more than one!" Mrs. Nodelman returned, confusedly. "I didn't mean anybody in particular. There are plenty of young ladies."

"That's the trouble. There are plenty, and no one in particular," I said

"Don't cry," Nodelman said. "Just be a good boy and Mrs. Nodelman will get you a peach of a young lady. Won't you, Bella?"

"I guess so," she answered, with a smile

"Don't you understand?" he proceeded to explain. "She first wants to know the kind of customer you are. Then she'll know what kind of merchandise to look for. Isn't that it, Bella?"

She made no answer

"I hope Mrs. Nodelman will find me a pretty decent sort of customer," I put in.

"You're all right," she said, demurely. "I'm afraid it won't be an easy job to get a young lady to suit a customer like you."

"Try your best, will you?" I said.

"I certainly will."

She was less talkative now, and certainly less at her ease than she had been before the topic was broached, which impressed me rather favorably.

Altogether she was far from the virago or "witch" her mother-in-law had described her to be. As to her attitude toward her husband, I subsequently came to the conclusion that it was a blend of affection and contempt.

Nodelman was henpecked, but not badly so

I called on them three or four times more during that spring. Somehow the question of my marriage was never mentioned on these occasions, and then Mrs. Nodelman and the children, all except Maurice, went to the seashore for the summer

\ "YOU'LL examine the merchandise, and if you don't like it nobody is going to make you buy it," said Nodelman to me one day in January of the following winter. By "merchandise" he meant a Miss Kalmanovitch, the daughter of a wealthy furniture-dealer, to whom I was to be introduced at the Nodelman residence four days later. "She is a peach of a girl, beautiful as the sun, and no runt, either; a lovely girl." "Good looks aren't everything. Beauty is skin deep, and handsome is as handsome does," I paraded my English

"Oh, she is a good girl every way: a fine housekeeper, good-natured, and educated. Gee! how educated she is! Why, she has a pile of books in her room, Bella says, a pile that high." He raised his hand above his head. "She is dead stuck on her, Bella is."

Owing to an illness in the Kalmanovitch family, the projected meeting could not take place, but Nodelman's birthday was to be celebrated in March, so the gathering was to serve as a match-making agency as well as a social function

The great event came to pass on a Sunday evening. The prospect of facing a girl who offered herself as a candidate for becoming my wife put me all in a flutter. It took me a long time to dress and I made my appearance at the Nodelmans' rather late in the evening. Mrs. Nodelman, who met me in the hall, offered me a tempestuous welcome

"Here he is! Better late than never," she shrieked, hoarsely, as I entered the hall at the head of the high stoop. "I was gettin' uneasy. Honest I was." And dropping her voice: "Miss Kalmanovitch came on time. She's a good girl. Always." And she gave me a knowing look that brought the color to my face and a coy smile into hers

Her husband appeared a minute later. After greeting me warmly he whispered into my ear: "Nobody knows anything about it, not even the young lady. Only her mother does."

But I soon discovered that he was mistaken. My appearance produced a sensation, and the telltale glances of the women from me to a large girl with black eyes who stood at the mantelpiece not only showed plainly that they knew all about "it," but also indicated who of the young women present was Miss Kalmanovitch

The spacious parlor was literally jammed. The hostess led the way through the throng, introducing me to the guests as we proceeded. There were Nodelman's father and mother among them, the gigantic old tailor grinning childishly by the side of his wife, who looked glum

"That one, with the dark eyes, by the mantelpiece," Meyer Nodelman whispered to me, eagerly

The girl pointed out was large and plump, with full ivory-hued cheeks, and a dimple in her fleshy chin. Her black eyes were large and round. That the object of my coming, and of her own, was no secret to her was quite evident.

She was blushing to the roots of her glossy black hair, and in her apparent struggle with her constraint she put her stout, long arm around the waist of a girl who stood by her side against the mantelpiece

Upon the whole, Miss Kalmanovitch impressed me more than favorably; but a minute later, when I was introduced to her and saw her double chin and shook her gently by a hand that was fat and damp with perspiration, I all but shuddered. I felt as though she exuded oil. I was introduced to her mother, a spare, hatchet-face little woman with bad teeth, who looked me over in a most business-like way, and to her father, a gray man with a goatee

Miss Kalmanovitch and I soon found ourselves seated side by side. Conscious of being the target of many eyes, I was as disconcerted as I had been twelve years before, when Matilda played her first practical joke upon my sidelocks. My would-be fiancée was the first to recover her ease. She asked me if I was related to a white-goods man named Levinsky, and when I said no she passed to other topics. She led the conversation, and I scarcely followed her. At one moment, for example, as I looked her in the face, endeavoring to listen to what she was saying about the Purim ball she had attended, I remarked to myself that the name Kalmanovitch somehow seemed to go well with her face and figure, and that she was too self-possessed for a "bridal candidate."

Presently we heard Mrs. Nodelman's hoarse voice: "Now Miss Kalmanovitch will oblige us with some music. Won't you, please, Miss Kalmanovitch?"

A swarthy, middle-aged woman, with features that somewhat resembled those of the host, whose cousin she was, and with huge golden teeth that glistened good-naturedly, took Miss Kalmanovitch by the arm, saying in a mannish voice: "Come on, Ray! Show them what you can do!"

My companion rose and, throwing gay glances at some of the other girls, she walked over to the piano and seated herself. Then, with some more smiles at the girls, she cold-bloodedly attacked the keyboard

"A nauctourrn by Chopin," her mother explained to me in an audible whisper across the room

Miss Kalmanovitch was banging away with an effect of showing how quickly she could get through the nocturne. I am not musical in the accepted meaning of the term, and in those days I was even less so than I am now, perhaps, but I was always fond of music, and had a discriminating feeling for it. At all events, I knew enough to realize that my would-be fiancée was playing execrably. But her mother, her father, the hostess, and the swarthy woman with the golden teeth, were shooting glances at me that seemed to say: "What do you think of that? Did you ever see such fast playing?" and there was nothing for it but to simulate admiration

The woman with the great golden teeth, Meyer Nodelman's cousin, was even more strenuous in her efforts to arouse my exultation than Ray's mother. She was the wife of a prosperous teamster whose moving-vans were seen all over the East Side. Gaunt, flat-chested, with a solemn masculine face, she was known for her jolly disposition and good-natured sarcasm. There was something suggestive of Meyer Nodelman in her manner of speaking as well as in her looks. She was childless and took an insatiable interest in the love-affairs and matrimonial politics of young people. Her name was Mrs.

Kaleh, but everybody called her Auntie Yetta

When Ray finished playing Auntie Yetta led the applause, for all the world like a ward heeler. When the acclaim had died down she rushed at Ray, pressed her ample bosom to her own flat one, kissed her a sounding smack on the lips, and exclaimed, with a wink to me: "Ever see such a tasty duck of a girl?"

Miss Kalmanovitch was followed by a bespectacled, anemic boy of thirteen who played something by Wieniavsky on the violin, and then Miss Kalmanovitch "obliged" us with a recitation from "Macbeth." There were four other solos on the piano and on the violin by boys and girls, children of the invited guests, the violinists having brought their instruments with them. Not that the concert was part of a preconceived program, although it might have been taken for granted. The mothers of the performers had simply seized the opportunity to display the talents of their offspring before an audience. → *pageants*

Only one boy—a curly-headed, long-necked little pianist, introduced as Bennie Saminsky—played with much feeling and taste. All the rest grated on my nerves

I beguiled the time by observing the women. I noticed, for instance, that Auntie Yetta, whose fingers were a veritable jewelry-store, now and again made a pretense of smoothing her grayish hair for the purpose of exhibiting her flaming rings. Another elderly woman, whose fingers were as heavily laden, kept them prominently interlaced across her breast. From time to time she would flirt her interlocked hands, in feigned absent-mindedness, thus flashing her diamonds upon the people around her. At one moment it became something like a race between her and Auntie Yetta. Nodelman's cousin caught me watching it, whereupon she winked to me merrily and interlaced her own begemmed fingers, as much as to say, "What do you think of our contest?" and burst into a voiceless laugh

I tried to listen to the music again. To add to my ordeal, I had to lend an ear to the boastful chatter of the mothers or fathers on the virtuosity of Bennie, Sidney, Beckie, or Sadie. The mother of the curly-headed pianist, the illiterate wife of a baker, first wore out my patience and then enlisted my interest by a torrent of musical terminology which she apparently had picked up from talks with her boy's piano-teacher. She interspersed her unsophisticated Yiddish with English phrases like "rare technique," "vonderful touch," "bee-youtiful tone," or "poeytic temperament." She assured me that her son was the youngest boy in the United States to play Brahms and Beethoven successfully. At first I thought that she was prattling these words parrot fashion, but I soon realized that, to a considerable extent, at least, she used them intelligently

She had set her heart upon making the greatest pianist in the world of Bennie, and by incessantly discussing him with people who were supposed to know something about music she had gradually accumulated a smattering acquaintance with the subject. That she was full of it there could be no doubt. Perhaps she had a native intuition for music. Perhaps, too, it was from her that her son had inherited his feeling for the poetry of sound. She certainly had imagination

"Some boys play like monkeys," she said in Yiddish. "They don't know what they are at. May I know evil if they do. My Bennie is not that sort of a pianist, thank God! He knows what he is talking about—on his piano, I mean.

You saw for yourself that he played with head and heart, didn't you?"

"Indeed, I did," I said, with ardor. "I liked his playing very much."

"Yes, it comes right from his heart," she pursued. "He has a golden temperament. The piano just talks under his fingers. I mean what I say.

People think a piano is just a row of dead pieces of bone or wood. It is not. No, sirrah. It has speech just like a human being, provided you know how to get it out of the keyboard. Bennie does."

In a certain sense this unlettered woman was being educated by her little boy in the same manner as Dora had been and still was, perhaps, by Lucy

There were at least three girls in the gathering who were decidedly pretty.

One of these was a graduate of Normal College. She was dark-eyed, like Miss Kalmanovitch, but slender and supple and full of life. Everybody called her affectionately by her first name, which was Stella. At the supper-table, in the dining-room, I was placed beside Miss Kalmanovitch, but I gave most of my attention to Stella, who was seated diagonally across the table from us.

I felt quite at home now

"What was your favorite subject at college?" I questioned Stella, facetiously.

"That's my secret," she answered.

"I can guess it, though."

"Try."

"Dancing."

"That's right," she shouted, amidst an outburst of laughter

"Well, have you learned it well?" I went on

"Why don't you ask me for a waltz and find out for yourself?"

"I wish I could, but unfortunately they did not take up dancing at my college."

"Did you go to college?" Stella asked, seriously

"I don't look like one who did, I suppose. Well, I should like to say I did, but I haven't the heart to tell you a lie."

"Never mind," Nodelman broke in. "He's an educated fellar, all the same.

He's awful educated. That's what makes him such a smart business man. By the way, Levinsky, how is the merchandise?"

"This is no place to talk shop," I replied, deprecatingly. "Especially when there are so many pretty ladies around."

"That's right!" several of the women chimed in in chorus

Mrs. Nodelman, the hostess, who stood in the doorway, beckoned to her husband, and he jumped up from the table. As he passed by my seat I seized him by an arm and whispered into his ear: "The merchandise is too heavy. I want lighter goods." With this I released him and he disappeared with Mrs. Nodelman

A few minutes later he came back

"Be a good boy. Show Ray a little more attention," he whispered into my ear.

"Do it for my sake. Will you?"

"All right."

I became aware of Mrs. Kalmanovitch's fire-flashing eyes, and my efforts to entertain her daughter were a poor performance

The Kalmanovitch family left immediately after supper, scarcely making their farewells. Portentous sounds came from the hallway. We could hear Mrs.

Kalmanovitch's angry voice. A nervous hush fell over the parlor. Auntie Yetta gave us all an eloquent wink

"There's a woman with a tongue for you," she said in an undertone. "Pitch and sulphur. When she opens her mouth people had better sound the fire-alarm." After a pause she added: "Do you know why her teeth are so bad? Her mouth is so full of poison, it has eaten them up."

Presently the younger Mrs. Nodelman made her appearance. Her ruddy "meat-ball" face was fairly ablaze with excitement. Her husband followed with a guilty air

"What's the matter with you folks?" the hostess said. "Why ainchye doin' somethin'?"

"What shall we do?" the baker's wife answered in Yiddish. "We have eaten a nice supper and we have heard music and now we are enjoying ourselves quietly, like the gentlemen and the ladies we are. What more do you want?" "Come, folks, let's have a dance. Bennie will play us a waltz. Quick, Bennie darling! Girls, get a move on you!"

I called the hostess aside. "May I ask you a question, Mrs. Nodelman?" I said, in the manner of a boy addressing his teacher

"What is it?" she asked, awkwardly.

"No, I won't ask any questions. I see you are angry at me."

"I ain't angry at all," she returned, making an effort to look me straight in the face.

"Sure?"

"Sure," with a laugh. "What is it you want to ask me about?"

And again assuming the tone of a penitent pupil, I said, "May I ask Stella to dance with me?"

"But you don't dance."

"Let her teach me, then."

"Let her, if she wants to. I ain't her mother, am I?"

"But you have no objection, have you?"

"Where do I come in? On my part, you can dance with every girl in the house."

"Oh, you don't like me this evening, Mrs. Nodelman. You are angry witn me.

Else you wouldn't talk the way you do."

She burst into a laugh, and said, "You're a hell of a fellow, you are."

"I know I misbehaved myself, but I couldn't help it. Miss Kalmanovitch is too fat, you know, and her hands perspire so."

"She's a charmin' girl," she returned, with a hearty laugh. "I wish her mother was half so good."

"Was she angry, her mother?"

"Was she! She put all the blame on me. I invited her daughter on purpose to make fun of her, she says. My, how she carried on!"

"I'm really sorry, but it's a matter of taste, you know."

"I know it is. I don't blame you at all."

"So you and I are friends again, aren't we?"

She laughed

"Well, then, you have no objection to my being sweet on Stella, have you?"

"You are a hell of a fellow. That's just what you are. But I might as well tell you it's no use trying to get Stella. She's already engaged." *obviously, like his previous affairs*

"Is she really?"

"Honest."

"Well, I don't care. I'll take her away from her fellow. That's all there is to it." "You can't do it," she said, gaily. "She is dead stuck on her intended.

They'll be married in June."

I went home a lovesick man, but the following evening I went to Boston for a day, and my feeling did not survive the trip

• The Nodelmans set D up on a "date" w/ Miss Kalmanovitch, daughter of a wealthy furniture dealer

  L D didn't like her for she was too fat and her hands sweaty

• At the party, D was enchanted w/ Stella, a dancer

  L finds she is engaged (of course, that doesn't stop him)

# CHAPTER V

THAT journey to Boston is fixed in my memory by an incident which is one of my landmarks in the history of my financial evolution and, indeed, in the history of the American cloak industry. It occurred in the afternoon of the Monday which I spent in that city, less than two days after that birthday party at the Nodelmans'. I was lounging in an easy-chair in the lobby of my hotel, when I beheld Loeb, the "star" salesman of what had been the "star" firm in the cloak-and-suit business. I had not seen him for some time, but I knew that his employers were on their last legs and that he had a hard struggle trying to make a living. Nor was that firm the only one of the old-established cloak-and-suit concerns that found itself in this state at the period in question—that is, at the time of the economic crisis and the burst of good times that had succeeded it. Far from filling their coffers from the golden flood of those few years, they were drowned in it almost to a man. The trade was now in the hands of men from the ranks of their former employees, tailors or cloak operators of Russian or Galician origin, some of whom were Talmudic scholars like myself. It was the passing of the German Jew from the American cloak industry

We did profit by the abundance of the period. Moreover, there were many among us to whom the crisis of 1893 had proved a blessing. To begin with, some of our tailors, being unable to obtain employment in that year, had been driven to make up a garment or two and to offer it for sale in the street, huckster fashion—a venture which in many instances formed a stepping-stone to a cloak-factory. Others of our workmen had achieved the same evolution by employing their days of enforced idleness in taking lessons in cloak-designing, and then setting up a small shop of their own

Newfangled manufacturers of this kind were now springing up like mushrooms.

Joe, my old-time instructor in cloak-making, was one of the latest additions to their number. They worked—often assisted by their wives and children—in all sorts of capacities and at all hours. They lived on bread and salmon and were content with almost a nominal margin of profit. There were instances when the clippings from the cutting-table constituted all the profit the business yielded them. Pitted against "manufacturers" of this class or against a fellow like myself were the old-established firms, with their dignified office methods and high profit-rates, firms whose fortunes had been sorely tried, to boot, by their bitter struggle with the union

Loeb swaggered up to me with quizzical joviality as usual. But the smug luster of his face was faded and his kindly black eyes had an unsteady glance in them that belied his vivacity. I could see at once that he felt nothing but hate for me

"Hello, Get-Rich-Quick Levinsky!" he greeted me. "Haven't seen you for an age."

"How are you, Loch?" I asked, genially, my heart full of mixed triumph and compassion

We had not been talking five minutes before he grew sardonic and venomous.

As Division Street—a few blocks on the lower East Side—was the center of the new type of cloak-manufacturing, he referred to us by the name of that street. My business was on Broadway, yet I was included in the term, "Division Street manufacturer."

"What is Division Street going to do next?" he asked. "Sell a fifteen-dollar suit for fifteen cents?"

I smiled

"That's a great place, that is. There are two big business streets in New York—Wall Street and Division." He broke into a laugh at his own joke and I charitably joined in. I endeavored to take his thrusts good-naturedly and for many minutes I succeeded, but at one point when he referred to us as "manufacturers," with a sneering implication of quotation marks over the word, I flared up

"You don't seem to like the Division Street manufacturers, do you?" I said.

"I suppose you have a reason for it." "I have a reason? Of course I have," he retorted. "So has every other decent man in the business."

"It depends on what you call decent. Every misfit claims to be more decent than the fellow who gets the business."

He grew pale. It almost looked as though we were coming to blows. After a pause he said, with an effect of holding himself in leash: "Business! Do you call that business? I call it peanuts."

*nice!*

"Well, the peanuts are rapidly growing in size while the oranges and the apples are shrinking and rotting. The fittest survives." ("A lot he knows about the theory of the survival of the fittest!" I jeered in my heart. "He hasn't even heard the name of Herbert Spencer.") "Peanuts are peanuts, that's all there's to it," he returned

"Then why are you excited? How can we hurt you if we are only peanuts?"

He made no answer

"We don't steal the trade we're getting, do we? If the American people prefer to buy our product they probably like it."

"Oh, chuck your big words, Levinsky. You fellows are killing the trade, and you know it."

He laughed, but what I said was true. The old cloak-manufacturers, the German Jews, were merely merchant. Our people, on the other hand, were mostly tailors or cloak operators who had learned the mechanical part of the industry, and they were introducing a thousand innovations into it, perfecting, revolutionizing it. We brought to our work a knowledge, a taste, and an ardor which the men of the old firms did not possess. And we were shedding our uncouthness, too. In proportion as we grew we adapted American business ways

Speaking in a semi-amicable vein, Loeb went on citing cases of what he termed cutthroat competition on our part, till he worked himself into a passion and became abusive again. The drift of his harangue was that "smashing" prices was something distasteful to the American spirit, that we were only foreigners, products of an inferior civilization, and that we ought to know our place.

"This way of doing business may be all right in Russia, but it won't do in this country," he said. "I tell you, it won't do."

"But it does do. So it seems."

As he continued to fume and rail at us, and I sat listening with a bored air, an idea flashed upon my mind, and, acting upon it on the spur of the moment, I suddenly laid a friendly hand on his arm

"Look here, Loeb," I said. "What's the use being excited? I have a scheme.

What's the matter with you selling goods for me?"

He was taken aback, but I could see that he was going to accept it

"What do you mean?" he asked, flushing

"I mean what I say. I want you to come with me. You will make more money than you have ever made before. You're a first-rate salesman, Loeb, and—well, it will pay you to make the change. What do you say?"

He contemplated the floor for a minute or two, and then, looking up awkwardly, he said: "I'll think it over. But you're a smart fellow, Levinsky. I can tell you that."

We proceeded to discuss details, and I received his answer—a favorable one—before we left our seats

To celebrate the event I had him dine with me that evening, our pledges of mutual loyalty being solemnized by a toast which we drank in the costliest champagne the hotel restaurant could furnish

It was not a year and a half after this episode that Chaikin entered my employ as designer

- saw Loeb again, L's business suffering while D's thrived
- L jealous + filled w/ more hate towards D
- had dinner together and made up their differences
  L chaikin became his designer, after all

# CHAPTER VI

I SAW other girls with a view to marriage, but I was "too particular," as my friends, the Nodelmans, would have it. I had two narrow escapes from breach-of-promise suits.

"He has too much education," Nodelman once said to his wife in my presence.

"Too much in his head, don't you know. You think too much, Levinsky. That's what's the matter. First marry, and do your thinking afterward. If you stopped to think before eating you would starve to death, wouldn't you? Well, and if you keep on thinking and figuring if this girl's nose is nice enough and if that girl's eyes are nice enough, you'll die before you get married, and there are no weddings among the dead, you know."

My matrimonial aspirations made themselves felt with fits and starts. There were periods when I seemed to be completely in their grip, when I was restless and as though ready to marry the first girl I met. Then there would be many months during which I was utterly indifferent, enjoying my freedom and putting off the question indefinitely

Year after year slid by. When my thirty-ninth birthday became a thing of the past and I saw myself entering upon my fortieth year without knowing who I worked for I was in something like a state of despair. When I was a boy forty years had seemed to be the beginning of old age. This notion I now repudiated as ridiculous, for I felt as young as I had done ten, fifteen, or twenty years before; and yet the words "forty years" appalled me. The wish to "settle down" then grew into a passion in me. The vague portrait of a woman in the abstract seemed never to be absent from my mind. Coupled with that portrait was a similarly vague image of a window and a table set for dinner. That, somehow, was my symbol of home. Home and woman were one, a complex charm joining them into

378

an inseparable force. There was the glamour of sex, shelter, and companionship in that charm, and of something else that promised security and perpetuity to the successes that fate was pouring into my lap. It whispered of a future that was to continue after I was gone

My loneliness often took on the pungence of acute physical discomfort. The more I achieved, the more painful was my self-pity

Nothing seemed to matter unless it was sanctified by marriage, and marriage now mattered far more than love

Girls had acquired a new meaning. They were not merely girls. They were matrimonial possibilities

Odd as it may appear, my romantic ideals of twenty years ago now reasserted their claim upon me. It was my ambition to marry into some orthodox family, well-to-do, well connected, and with an atmosphere of Talmudic education—the kind of match of which I had dreamed before my mother died, with such modifications as the American environment rendered natural

There were two distinct circumstances to account for this new mood in me

In the first place, my sense of approaching middle age somehow rekindled my yearning interest in the scenes of my childhood and boyhood. Memories of bygone days had become ineffably dear to me. I seemed to remember things of my boyhood more vividly than I did things that had happened only a year before

I was homesick for Antomir again

To revisit Abner's Court or the Preacher's Synagogue, to speak to Reb Sender, or to the bewhiskered old soldier, the skeepskin tailor, if they were still living, was one of my day-dreams.

Eliakim Zunzer, the famous wedding-bard whose songs my mother used to sing in her dear, sonorous contralto, had emigrated to America several years before and I had heard of it at the time of his arrival, yet I had never thought of going to see him. Now, however, I could not rest until I looked him up. It appeared that he owned a small printing-shop in a basement on East Broadway, so I called at his place one afternoon on the pretext of ordering some cards. When I saw the poet—an aged little man with a tragic, tired look on a cadaverous face—I was so unstrung that when a young man in the shop asked me something about the cards, he had to repeat the question before I understood it

"My mother used to sing your beautiful songs, Mr. Zunzer," I said to the poet some minutes later, my heart beating violently again.

"Did she? Where do you come from?" he asked, with a smile that banished the tired look, but deepened the tragic sadness of his death-like countenance

Everything bearing the name of my native place touched a tender spot in my heart. It was enough for a cloak-maker to ask me for a job with the Antomir accent to be favorably recommended to one of my foremen. A number of the men who received special consideration and were kept working in my shop in the slack seasons, when my force was greatly reduced, were fellow-townspeople of mine. This had been going on for several years, in fact, till gradually an Antomir atmosphere had been established in my shop, and something like a family spirit of which I was proud. We had formed a Levinsky Antomir Benefit Society of which I was an honorary member and which was made up, for the most part, of my own employees

All this, I confess, was not without advantage to my business interests, for it afforded me a low average of wages and safeguarded my shop against labor troubles. The Cloak-makers' Union had again come into existence, and, although it had no real power over the men, the trade was not free from sporadic conflicts in individual shops. My place, however, was absolutely immune from difficulties of this sort—all because of the Levinsky Antomir Benefit Society

If one of my operatives happened to have a relative in Antomir, a women's tailor who wished to emigrate to America, I would advance him the passage money, with the understanding that he was to work off the loan in my employ.

That the "green one" was to work for low wages was a matter of course. But then, in justice to myself, I must add that I did my men favors in numerous cases that could in no way redound to my benefit. Besides, the fiscal advantages that I did derive from the Antomir spirit of my shop really were not a primary consideration with me. I sincerely cherished that spirit for its own sake. Moreover, if my Antomir employees were willing to accept from me lower pay than they might have received in other places, their average earnings were actually higher than they would have been elsewhere. I gave them steady work. Besides, they felt perfectly at home in my shop. I treated them well. I was very democratic

Compared to the thoughts of home that had oppressed me during my first months in America, my new visions of Antomir were like the wistful lights of a sunset as compared with the glare of midday. But then sunsets produce deeper, if quieter, effects on the emotions than the strongest daylight

It was my new homesickness, then, which inclined me to an American form of the kind of marriage of which I used to dream in the days of my Talmudic studies. Another motive that led me to matrimonial aspirations of this kind lay in my new ideas of respectability as a necessary accompaniment to success. Marrying into a well-to-do orthodox family meant respectability and solidity. It implied law and order, the antithesis of anarchism, socialism, trade-unionism, strikes

I was a convinced free-thinker. Spencer's Unknowable had irrevocably replaced my God. Yet religion now appealed to me as an indispensable instrument in the great orchestra of things. From what I had seen of the world, or read about it in the daily press, I was convinced that but few people of wealth and power had real religion in their hearts. I felt sure that most of them looked upon churches or synagogues as they did upon police-courts; that they valued them primarily as safeguards of law and order and correctness, and this had become my attitude. For the rest, I felt that a vast number of the people who professed Christianity or Judaism did so merely because to declare oneself an atheist was not a prudent thing to do from a business or social point of view, or that they were in doubt and chose to be on the safe side of it, lest there should be a God, "after all," while millions of other people were not interested enough even to doubt, or to ask questions, and were content to do as everybody did. But there were some who did ask questions and did dare to declare themselves atheists. I was one of these, and yet I looked upon religion as a most important institution, and was willing to contribute to its support

My business life had fostered the conviction in me that, outside of the family, the human world was as brutally selfish as the jungle, and that it was worm-eaten with hypocrisy into the bargain. From time to time the newspapers published sensational revelations concerning some pillar of society who had turned out to be a common thief on an uncommon scale. I saw that political speeches, sermons, and editorials had, with very few exceptions, no more sincerity in them than the rhetoric of an advertisement.

I saw that Americans who boasted descent from the heroes of the Revolution boasted, in the same breath, of having spent an evening with Lord So-and-so; that it was their avowed ambition to acquire for their daughters the very titles which their ancestors had fought to banish from the life of their country. I saw that civilization was honeycombed with what Max Nordau called conventional lies, with sham ecstasy, sham sympathy, sham smiles, sham laughter

The riot of prosperity introduced the fashion of respectable women covering their faces with powder and paint in a way that had hitherto been peculiar to women of the streets, so I pictured civilization as a harlot with cheeks, lips, and eyelashes of artificial beauty. I imagined mountains of powder and paint, a deafening chorus of affected laughter, a huge heart, as large as a city, full of falsehood and mischief

The leaders of the Jewish socialists, who were also at the head of the Jewish labor movement, seemed to me to be the most repulsive hypocrites of all. I loathed them

I had no creed. I knew of no ideals. The only thing I believed in was the cold, drab theory of the struggle for existence and the survival of the fittest. This could not satisfy a heart that was hungry for enthusiasm and affection, so dreams of family life became my religion. Self-sacrificing devotion to one's family was the only kind of altruism and idealism I did not flout

I was worth over a million, and my profits had reached enormous dimensions, so I was regarded a most desirable match, and match-makers pestered me as much as I would let them, but they found me a hard man to suit

There was a homesick young man in my shop, a native of Antomir, with whom I often chatted of our common birthplace. His name was Mirmelstein. He was a little fellow with a massive head and a neck that seemed to be too slender to support it. I liked his face for its honest, ingenuous expression, but more especially because I thought his eyes had a homesick look in them. He was a poor mechanic, but I found him a steady job in my shipping department

He could furnish me no information about Reb Sender, of whom he had never heard before; he knew of the Minsker family, of course, and he told me that Shiphrah, Matilda's mother, was dead; that Yeffim, Matilda's brother, had been sent to Siberia some three years before for complicity in the revolutionary movement, and that Matilda herself had had a hair-breadth escape from arrest and was living in Switzerland

He wrote to Antomir, and a few weeks later he brought me the sad information that Reb Sender had been dead for several years, and that his wife had married again

- viewed as "too particular" in selecting a wife by the Nodelmans
  - N thought it was b/c D had too much education
- D turned 40 (wasn't he a boy of just ten years? Time goes by fast)
  - so the thought of settling down strong
- D looked up a famous wedding-bard, Eliakim Zunzer, → his mother used to sing his songs
- formed a club, Levinsky Antomir Benefit Society
- his religion replaced by facts
  - no faith at all (shame!!)
- worth over a million now
  - considered a good match; however, matchmakers found him "a hard man to suit" (382).
- found kinship w/ a young man named Mirmelstein, native of Antomir as he is
  - Mir. told him news
    - Matilda's mother dead
    - Matilda's brother soldier
    - Mat. living in switzerland
    - Reb dead / wife remarried

# CHAPTER VII

ONE day in November less than six months after I had learned of Yeffim Minsker's arrest and of Matilda's escape, as I was making the rounds of my several departments, little Mirmelstein accosted me timidly

"Yeffim Minsker and his sister are here," he said, with the smile of one breaking an interesting surprise

I paused, flushing. I feigned indifference and preoccupation, but the next moment I cast off all pretense

"Are they really?" I asked

He produced a clipping from a socialist Yiddish daily containing an advertisement of a public meeting to be held at Cooper Institute under the auspices of an organization of Russian revolutionists for the purpose of welcoming Yefflm and another man, a Doctor Gorsky, both of whom had recently escaped from Siberia. The revolutionary movement was then at its height in Russia, and the Jews were among its foremost and bravest leaders (which, by the way, accounts for the anti-Jewish riots and massacres which the Government inspired and encouraged quite openly). As was mentioned in an early chapter of this book, the then Minister of the Interior was the same man who had been Director of Police over the whole empire at the time of the anti-Jewish riots which followed the assassination of Czar Alexander II. in 1881, and which started the great emigration of Jews to America. From time to time some distinguished revolutionist would be sent to America for subscriptions to the cause. This was the mission of Doctor Gorsky and Yeffim. They were here, not as immigrants, but merely to raise funds for the movement at home

As for Matilda, it appeared that Doctor Gorsky was her husband. Whether he had married her in Russia, before his arrest, or in Switzerland, where he and her brother had spent some time after their escape from exile, Mirmelstein could not tell me. Matilda's name was not mentioned in the advertisement, but my shipping-clerk had heard of her arrival and marriage from some Antomir people.

I could scarcely do anything that day. I was in a fever of excitement. "Do I still love her?" I wondered    Stop!

I made up my mind to attend the Cooper Institute meeting. It was a bold venture, for the crowd was sure to contain some socialist cloak-makers who held me in anything but esteem. But then I had not had a strike in my shop for several years, and it did not seem likely that they would offer me an insult. Anyhow, the temptation to see Matilda was too strong. I had to go.

She was certain to be on the platform, and all I wanted was to take a look at her from the auditorium. "And who knows but I may have a chance to speak to her, too," I thought.

It was a cold evening in the latter part of November. I went to the meeting in my expensive fur coat (although fur coats were still a rare spectacle in the streets), with a secret foretaste of the impression my prosperity would make upon Matilda. It was a fatal mistake

It was twenty minutes to 8 when I reached the front door of the historical meeting-hall, but it was already crowded to overflowing, and the policemen guarding the brightly illuminated entrance turned me away with a crowd of others. I was in despair. I tried again, and this time, apparently owing to my mink coat, I was admitted. Every seat in the vast underground auditorium was occupied. But few people were allowed to stand, in the rear of the hall, and I was one of them. From the chat I overheard around me I gathered that there were scores of men and women in the audience who had been in the thick of sensational conflicts in the great crusade for liberty that was then going on in Russia. I questioned a man who stood beside me about Doctor Gorsky, and from his answers I gained the impression that Matilda's husband was considered one of the pluckiest men in the struggle. At the time of his arrest he was practising medicine

Ranged on the platform on either side of the speaker's desk were about a hundred chairs, several of which in the two front rows were kept vacant.

Presently there was a stir on the platform. A group of men and women made their appearance and seated themselves on the unoccupied chairs. They were greeted with passionate cheers and applause

One of them was Matilda. I recognized her at once. Her curly brown hair was gray at the temples, and her oval little face was somewhat bloated, and she was stouter than she had been twenty-one years before; but all this was merely like a new dress. Had I met her in the street, I might have merely felt that she looked familiar to me, without being able to trace her. As it was, she was strikingly the same as I had known her, though not precisely the same as I had pictured her, of late years, at least. Some errors had stolen into my image of her, and now, that I saw her in the flesh, I recalled her likeness of twenty-one years before, and she now looked precisely as she had done then. She was as interesting as ever. I was in such a turmoil that I scarcely knew what was happening on the platform. Did I still love her, or was it merely the excitement of beholding a living memory of my youth? One thing was certain—the feeling of reverence and awe with which I had once been wont to view her and her parents was stirring in my heart again. For the moment I did not seem to be the man who owned a big cloak-factory and was worth over a million American dollars

The chairman had been speaking for some time before I became aware of his existence. As his address was in Russian and I had long since unlearned what little I had ever known of that language, his words were Greek to me

Matilda was flanked by two men, both with full beards, one fair and the other rather dark. The one of the fair complexion and beard was Yeffim, although I recognized him by his resemblance to Matilda and more especially to her father, rather than by his image of twenty-one years ago. I supposed that the man on the other side of her, the one with the dark beard, was her husband, and I asked the man by my side about it, but he did not know

Several speakers made brief addresses of welcome. One of these spoke in Yiddish and one in English, so I understood them. They dealt with the revolution and the anti-Semitic atrocities, and paid glowing tributes to the new-comers. They were interrupted by outburst after outburst of enthusiasm and indignation. When finally Doctor Gorsky was introduced (it was the man with the dark beard) there was a veritable pandemonium of applause, cheers, and ejaculations that lasted many minutes. He spoke in Russian and he seemed to be a poor speaker. I searched his face for evidence of valor and strength, but did not seem to find any. I thought it was rather a weak face—weak and kindly and girlish-looking. His beard, which was long and thin, did not become him. I asked myself whether I was jealous of him, and the question seemed so incongruous, so remote. He made a good impression on me. The fact that this man, who was possessed of indomitable courage, had a weak, good-natured face interested me greatly, and the fact that he had gone through much suffering made a strong appeal to my sympathies (somehow his martyrdom was linked in my mind to his futility as a speaker). I warmed to him

He was followed by Yeffim, and the scene of wild enthusiasm was repeated

When Minsker had finished the chairman declared the meeting closed. There was a rush for the platform. It was quite high above the auditorium floor; unless one reached it by way of the committee-room, which was a considerable distance to the right, it had to be mounted, not without an effort, by means of the chairs in the press inclosure. After some hesitation I made a dash for one of these chairs, and the next minute I was within three or four feet from Matilda, but with an excited crowd between us. Everybody wanted to shake hands with the heroes. The jam and scramble were so great that Doctor Gorsky, Yeffim, and Matilda had to extricate themselves and to escape into the spacious committee-room in the rear of the platform

Some minutes later I stood by her side in that room, amid a cluster of revolutionists, her husband and Yeffim being each the center of another crowd in the same room

"I beg your pardon," I began, with a sheepish smile. "Do you know me."

Her glittering brown eyes fixed me with a curious look. "My name is David Levinsky," I added. "'Dovid,' the Talmudic student to whom you gave money with which to go to America."

"Of course I know you," she snapped. taking stock of my mink overcoat. "And I have heard about you, too. You have a lot of money, haven't you? I see you are wearing a costly fur coat." And she brutally turned to speak to somebody else

My heart stood still. I wanted to say something, to assure her that I was not so black as the socialists painted me. I had an impulse to offer her a generous contribution to the cause, but I had not the courage to open my mouth again. The bystanders were eying me with glances that seemed to say, "The idea of a fellow like this being here!" I was a despicable "bourgeois," a "capitalist" of the kind whose presence at a socialist meeting was a sacrilege

I slunk out of the room feeling like a whipped cur. "Why, she is a perfect savage!" I thought. "But then what else can you expect of a socialist?"

I thought of the scenes that had passed between her and myself in her mother's house and I sneered. "A socialist, a good, pure soul, indeed!" I mused, gloatingly. "That's exactly like them. A bunch of hypocrites, that's all they are."

At the same time I was nagging myself for having had so little sense as to sport my prosperity before a socialist, of all the people in the world

A few days later the episode seemed to have occurred many years before. It did not bother me. Nor did Matilda *finally over her*

- Matilda was married to Dr. Borsky
  └ test to see if he still cares
- saw her at a convention
  └ he passed the test

# CHAPTER VIII

IT was an afternoon in April. My chief bookkeeper, one of my stenographers, Bender, and myself were hard at work at my Broadway factory amid a muffled turmoil of industry. There were important questions of credit to dispose of and letters to answer. I was taking up account after account, weighing my data with the utmost care, giving every detail my closest attention. And all the while I was thus absorbed, seemingly oblivious to everything else, I was alive to the fact that it was Passover and the eve of the anniversary of my mother's death; that three or four hours later I should be solemnizing her memorial day at the new Synagogue of the Sons of Antomir; that while there I should sit next to Mr. Kaplan, a venerable-looking man to whose daughter I had recently become engaged, and that after the service I was to accompany Mr. Kaplan to his house and spend the evening in the bosom of his family, by the side of the girl that was soon to become my wife. My consciousness of all this grew keener every minute, till it began to interfere with my work.

I was getting fidgety. Finally I broke off in the middle of a sentence

I washed myself, combed my plentiful crop of dark hair, carefully brushed myself, and put on my spring overcoat and derby hat—both of a dark-brown hue

"I sha'n't be back until the day after to-morrow," I announced to Bender, after giving him some orders

"Till day after to-morrow!" he said, with reproachful amazement

I nodded

"Can't you put it off? This is no time for being away," he grumbled

"It can't be helped."

"You're not going out of town, are you?"

"What difference does it make?" After a pause I added: "It isn't on business. It's a private matter."

"Oh!" he uttered, with evident relief. Nothing hurt his pride more than to suspect me of having business secrets from him.

He was a married man now, having, less than a year ago, wedded a sweet little girl, a cousin, who was as simple-hearted and simple-minded as himself, and to whom he had practically been engaged since boyhood. His salary was one hundred and twenty-five dollars a week now. I was at home in their well-ordered little establishment, the sunshine that filled it having given an added impulse to my matrimonial aspirations

I betook myself to the new Antomir Synagogue. The congregation had greatly grown in prosperity and had recently moved from the ramshackle little frame building that had been its home into an impressive granite structure, formerly a Presbyterian church. This was my first visit to the building.

Indeed, I had not seen the inside of its predecessor, the little old house of prayer that had borne the name of my native town, years before it was abandoned. In former years, even some time after I had become a convinced free-thinker, I had visited it at least twice a year-on my two memorial days—that is, on the anniversaries of the death of my parents. I had not done so since I had read Spencer. This time, however, the anniversary of my mother's death had a peculiar meaning for me. Vaguely as a result of my new mood, and distinctly as a result of my betrothal, I was lured to the synagogue by a force against which my Spencerian agnosticism was powerless

I found the interior of the building brilliantly illuminated. The woodwork of the "stand" and the bible platform, the velvet-and-gold curtains of the Holy Ark, and the fresco paintings on the walls and ceiling were screamingly new and gaudy. So were the ornamental electric fixtures. Altogether the place reminded me of a reformed German synagogue rather than of the kind with which my idea of Judaism had always been identified. This seemed to accentuate the fact that the building had until recently been a Christian church. The glaring electric lights and the glittering decorations struck me as something unholy. Still, the scattered handful of worshipers I found there, and more particularly the beadle, looked orthodox enough, and I gradually became reconciled to the place as a house of God

The beadle was a new incumbent. Better dressed and with more authority in his appearance than the man who had superintended the old place, he comported well with the look of things in the new synagogue. After obsequiously directing me to the pew of my prospective father-in-law, who had not yet arrived, he inserted a stout, tall candle into one of the sockets of the "stand" and lit it. It was mine. It was to burn uninterruptedly for my mother's soul for the next twenty-four hours. Mr.

Kaplan's pew was in a place of honor—that is, by the east wall, near the Holy Ark. To see my memorial candle I had to take a few steps back. I did so, and as I watched its flame memories and images took possession of me that turned my present life into a dream and my Russian past into reality.

According to the Talmud there is a close affinity between the human soul and light, for "the spirit of man is the lamp of God," as Solomon puts it in his Parables. Hence the custom of lighting candles or lamps for the dead. And so, as I gazed at that huge candle commemorating the day when my mother gave her life for me, I felt as though its light was part of her spirit. The gentle flutter of its flame seemed to be speaking in the sacred whisper of a grave-yard

"Mother dear! Mother dear!" my heart was saying. And then: "Thank God, mother dear! I own a large factory. I am a rich man and I am going to be married to the daughter of a fine Jew, a man of substance and Talmud. And the family comes from around Antomir, too. Ah, if you were here to escort me to the wedding canopy!"

The number of worshipers was slowly increasing. An old woman made her appearance in the gallery reserved for her sex. At last Mr. Kaplan, the father of my fiancée, entered the synagogue—a man of sixty, with a gray patriarchal beard and a general appearance that bespoke Talmudic scholarship and prosperity. He was a native of a small town near Antomir, where his father had been rabbi, and was now a retired flour merchant, having come to America in the seventies. He had always been one of the pillars of the Synagogue of the Sons of Antomir. In the days when I was a frequenter at the old house of prayer the social chasm between him and myself was so wide that the notion of my being engaged to a daughter of

whats her name?

his would have seemed absurd. Which, by the way, was one of the attractions that his house now had for me

"Good holiday, Mr. Kaplan!" some of the other worshipers saluted him, as he made his way toward his pew

"Good holiday! Good holiday!" he responded, with dignified geniality

I could see that he was aware of my presence but carefully avoided looking at me until he should be near enough for me to greet him. He was a kindly, serious-minded man, sincerely devout, and not over-bright. He had his little vanities and I was willing to humor them

"Good holiday, Mr. Kaplan!" I called out to him

"Good holiday! Good holiday, David!" he returned, amiably. "Here already? Ahead of me? That's good! Just follow the path of Judaism and everything will be all right." "How's everybody?" I asked

"All are well, thank God."

."How's Fanny?"

"Now you're talking. That's the real question, isn't it?" he chaffed me, with dignity. "She's well, thank God."

He introduced me to the cantor—a pug-nosed man with a pale face and a skimpy little beard of a brownish hue

"Our new cantor, the celebrated Jacob Goldstein!" he said. "And this is Mr.

David Levinsky, my intended son-in-law. An Antomir man. Was a fine scholar over there and still remembers a lot of Talmud."

The newly arrived synagogue tenor was really a celebrated man, in the Antomir section of Russia, at least. His coming had been conceived as a sensational feature of the opening of the new synagogue. While "town cantor" in Antomir he had received the highest salary ever paid there. The contract that had induced him to come over to America pledged him nearly five times as much. Thus the New York Sons of Antomir were not only able to parade a famous cantor before the multitude of other New York congregations, but also to prove to the people at home that they were the financial superiors of the whole town of their birth. So far, however, as the New York end of the sensation was concerned, there was a good-sized bee in the honey. The imported cantor was a tragic disappointment. The trouble was that his New York audiences were far more critical and exacting than the people in Antomir, and he was not up to their standard. For one thing, many of the Sons of Antomir, and others who came to their synagogue to hear the new singer, people who had mostly lived in poverty and ignorance at home, now had a piano or a violin in the house, with a son or a daughter to play it, and had become frequenters of the Metropolitan Opera House or the Carnegie Music Hall; for another, the New York Ghetto was full of good concerts and all other sorts of musical entertainments, so much so that good music had become all but part of the daily life of the Jewish tenement population; for a third, the audiences of the imported cantor included people who had lived in much larger European cities than Antomir, in such places as Warsaw, Odessa, Lemberg, or Vienna, for example, where they had heard much better cantors than Goldstein. Then, too, life in New York had Americanized my fellow-townspeople, modernized their tastes, broadened them out. As a consequence, the methods of the man who had won the admiration of their native town seemed to them old-fashioned, crude, droll

Still, the trustees, and several others who were responsible for the coming of the pug-nosed singer, persisted in speaking of him as "a greater tenor than Jean de Rezske," and my prospective father-in-law was a trustee, and a good-natured man to boot, so he had compassion for him

"In the old country when we meet a new-comer we only say, 'Peace to you,'" I remarked to the cantor, gaily. "Here we say this and something else, besides. We ask him how he likes America."

"But I have not yet seen it," the cantor returned, with a broad smile in which his pug nose seemed to grow in size

I told him the threadbare joke of American newspaper reporters boarding an incoming steamer at Sandy Hook and asking some European celebrity how he likes America hours before he has set foot on its soil

"That's what we call 'hurry up,'" Kaplan remarked

"That means quick, doesn't it?" the cantor asked, with another broad smile

"You're picking up English rather fast," I jested

"He has not only a fine voice, but a fine head, too," Kaplan put in

"I know what 'all right' means, too," the cantor laughed. I thought there was servility in his laugh, and I ascribed it to the lukewarm reception with which he had met. I was touched We talked of Antomir, and although a conversation of this kind was nothing new to me, yet what he said of the streets, market-places, the bridge, the synagogues, and of some of the people of the town interested me inexpressibly

Presently the service was begun—not by the imported singer, but by an amateur from among the worshipers, the service on a Passover evening not being considered important enough to be conducted by a professional cantor of consequence

My heart was all in Antomir, in the good old Antomir of synagogues and Talmud scholars and old-fashioned marriages, not of college students, revolutionists, and Matildas

When the service was over I stepped up close to the Holy Ark and recited the Prayer for the Dead, in chorus with several other men and boys. As I cast a glance at my "memorial candle" my mother loomed saintly through its flame. I beheld myself in her arms, a boy of four, on our way to the synagogue, where I was to be taught to parrot the very words that I was now saying for her spirit

The Prayer for the Dead was at an end. "A good holiday! A merry holiday!" rang on all sides, as the slender crowd streamed chatteringly toward the door

Mr. Kaplan, the cantor, and several other men, clustering together, lingered to bandy reminiscences of Antomir, interspersing them with "bits of law."

.engaged to Mr. Kaplan's daughter

# CHAPTER IX

The Kaplans occupied a large, old house on Henry Street that had been built at a period when the neighborhood was considered the best in the city. While Kaplan and I were taking off our overcoats in the broad, carpeted, rather dimly lighted hall, a dark-eyed girl appeared at the head of a steep stairway

"Hello, Dave! You're a good boy," she shouted, joyously, as she ran down to meet me with coquettish complacency

She had regular features, and her face wore an expression of ease and self-satisfaction. Her dark eyes were large and pretty, and altogether she was rather good-looking. Indeed, there seemed to be no reason why she should not be decidedly pretty, but she was not. Perhaps it was because of that self-satisfied air of hers, the air of one whom nothing in the world could startle or stir. Temperamentally she reminded me somewhat of Miss Kalmanovitch, but she was the better-looking of the two. I was not in love with her, but she certainly was not repulsive to me

"Good holiday, dad! Good holiday, Dave!" she saluted us in Yiddish, throwing out her chest and squaring her shoulders as she reached us

She was born in New York and had graduated at a public grammar-school and English was the only language which she spoke like one born to speak it, and yet her Yiddish greeting was precisely what it would have been had she been born and bred in Antomir

Her "Good holiday, dad. Good holiday, Dave!" went straight to my heart

"Well, I've brought him to you, haven't I? Are you pleased?" her father said, with affectionate grimness, in Yiddish

"Oh, you're a dandy dad. You're just sweet," she returned, in English, putting up her red lips as if he were her baby. And this, too, went to my heart

When her father had gone to have his shoes changed for slippers and before her mother came down from her bedroom, where she was apparently dressing for supper, Fanny slipped her arm around me and I kissed her lips and eyes

A chuckle rang out somewhere near by. Standing in the doorway of the back parlor, Mefisto-like, was Mary, Fanny's twelve-year-old sister

"Shame!" she said, gloatingly

"The nasty thing!" Fanny exclaimed, half gaily, half in anger

"You're nasty yourself," returned Mary, making faces at her sister

"Shut up or I'll knock your head off."

"Stop quarreling, kids," I intervened. Then, addressing myself to Mary, "Can you spell 'eavesdropping'?"

Mary laughed

"Never mind laughing," I insisted. "Do you know what eavesdropping means? Is it a nice thing to do? Anyhow, when you're as big as Fanny and you have a sweetheart, won't you let him kiss you?" As I said this I took Fanny's hand tenderly

"She has sweethearts already," said Fanny. "She is running around with three boys."

"I ain't," Mary protested, pouting.

"Well, three sweethearts means no sweetheart at all," I remarked

Fanny and I went into the front parlor, a vast, high-ceiled room, as large as the average four-room flat in the "modern apartment-house" that had recently been completed on the next block. It was drearily too large for the habits of the East Side of my time, depressingly out of keeping with its sense of home. It had lanky pink-and-gold furniture and a heavy bright carpet, all of which had a forbidding effect. It was as though the chairs and the sofa had been placed there, not for use, but for storage. Nor was there enough furniture to give the room an air of being inhabited, the six pink-and-gold pieces and the marble-topped center-table losing themselves in spaces full of gaudy desolation

"She's awful saucy," said Fanny.

I caught her in my arms. "I have not three sweethearts. I have only one, and that's a real one," I cooed

"Only one? Really and truly?" she demanded, playfully. She gathered me to her plump bosom, planting a deep, slow, sensuous kiss on my lips

I cast a side-glance to ascertain if Mary was not spying upon us

"Don't be uneasy," Fanny whispered. "She won't dare. We can kiss all we want."

I thought she was putting it in a rather matter-of-fact way, but I kissed her with passion, all the same

"Dearest! If you knew how happy I am," I murmured

"Are you really? Oh, I don't believe you," she jested, self-sufficiently.

"You're just pretending, that's all. Let me kiss your sweet mouthie again."

She did, and then, breaking away at the sound of her mother's lumbering steps, she threw out her bosom with an upward jerk, a trick she had which I disliked

Ten minutes later the whole family, myself included, were seated around a large oval table in the basement dining-room. Besides the members already known to the reader, there was Fanny's mother, a corpulent woman with a fat, diabetic face and large, listless eyes, and Fanny's brother, Rubie, a boy with intense features, one year younger than Mary. Rubie was the youngest of five children, the oldest two, daughters, being married

Mr. Kaplan was in his skull-cap, while I wore my dark-brown derby.

Everything in this house was strictly orthodox and as old-fashioned as the American environment would permit

That there was not a trace of leavened bread in the house, its place being taken by thin, flat, unleavened "matzos," and that the repast included "matzo balls," wine, mead, and other accessories of a Passover meal, is a matter of course

Mr. Kaplan was wrapped up in his family, and on this occasion, though he presided with conscious dignity, he was in one of his best domestic moods, talkative, and affectionately facetious. The children were the real masters of his house

Watching his wife nag Rubie because he would not accept another matzo ball, Mr. Kaplan said: "Don't worry, Malkah. Your matzo balls are delicious, even if your 'only son' won't do justice to them. Aren't they, David?"

"They certainly are," I answered. "What is more, they have the genuine Antomir taste to them."

"Hear that, Fanny?" Mr. Kaplan said to my betrothed. "You had better learn to make matzo balls exactly like these. He likes everything that smells of Antomir, you know." "That's all right," said Malkah. "Fanny is a good housekeeper. May I have as good a year."

"It's a good thing you say it," her husband jested. "Else David might break the engagement."

"Let him," said Fanny, with a jerk of her bosom and a theatrical glance at me. "I really don't know how to make matzo balls, and Passover is nearly over, so there's no time for mamma to show me how to do it."

"I'll do so next year," her mother said, with an affectionate smile that kindled life in her diabetic eyes. "The two of you will then have to pass Passover with us."

"I accept the invitation at once," I said

"Provided you attend the seder, too," remarked Kaplan, referring to the elaborate and picturesque ceremony attending the first two suppers of the great festival

I had been expected to partake of those ceremonial repasts on the first and second nights of this Passover, but had been unavoidably kept away from the city. Kaplan had resented it, and even now, as he spoke of the next year's seder, there was reproach in his voice.

"I will, I will," I said, ardently.

"One mustn't do business on a seder night. It isn't right."

"Give it to him, pa!" Fanny cut in.

"I am not joking," Kaplan persisted. "One has got to be a Jew. Excuse me, David, for speaking like that, but you re going to be as good as a son of mine and I have a right to talk to you in this way."

"Why, of course, you have!" I answered, with filial docility

His lecture bored me, but it did me good, too. It was sweet to hear myself called "as good as a son" by this man of Talmudic education who was at the same time a man of substance and of excellent family

The chicken was served. My intended wife ate voraciously, biting lustily and chewing with gusto. The sight of it jarred on me somewhat, but I overruled myself. "It's all right," I thought. "She's a healthy girl. She'll make me a strong mate, and she'll bear me healthy children."

I had a temptation to take her in my arms and kiss her. "I am not in love with her, and yet I am so happy," I thought. "Oh, love isn't essential to happiness. Not at all. Our old generation is right."

Fanny's reading, which was only an occasional performance, was confined to the cheapest stories published. Even the popular novels of the day, the "best sellers," seemed to be beyond her depth. Her intellectual range was not much wider than that of her old-fashioned mother, whose literary attainments were restricted to the reading of the Yiddish Commentary on the Pentateuch. She often interrupted me or her mother; everybody except her father. But all this seemed to be quite natural and fitting. "She is expected to be a wife, a mother, and a housekeeper," I reflected, "and that she will know how to be. Everything else is nonsense. I don't want to discuss Spencer with her, do I?"

Kaplan quoted the opening words of a passage in the Talmud bearing upon piety as the bulwark of happiness. I took it up, finishing the passage for him

"See?" he said to his wife. "I have told you he remembers his Talmud pretty well, haven't I?"

"When a man has a good head he has a good head," she returned, radiantly

Rubie went to a public school, but he spent three or four hours every afternoon at an old-fashioned Talmudic academy, or "yeshivah." There were two such "yeshivahs" on the East Side, and they were attended by boys of the most orthodox families in the Ghetto. I had never met such boys before. That an American school-boy should read Talmud seemed a joke to me. I could not take Rubie's holy studies seriously. As we now sat at the table I banteringly asked him about the last page he had read. He answered my question, and at his father's command he ran up-stairs, into the back parlor, where stood two huge bookcases filled with glittering folios of the Talmud and other volumes of holy lore, and came back with one containing the page he had named

"Find it and let David see what you can do," his father said

Rubie complied, reading the text and interpreting it in Yiddish precisely as I should have done when I was eleven years old. He even gesticulated and swayed backward and forward as I used to do. To complete the picture, his mother, watching him, beamed as my mother used to do when she watched me reading at the Preacher's Synagogue or at home in our wretched basement. I was deeply affected

"He's all right!" I said

"He's a loafer, just the same," his father said, gaily. "If he had as much appetite for his Talmud as he has for his school-books he would really be all right." "What do you want of him?" Malkah interceded. "Doesn't he work hard enough as it is? He hardly has an hour's rest."

"There you have it! I didn't speak respectfully enough of her 'only son.' I beg your pardon, Malkah," Mr. Kaplan said, facetiously

The wedding had been set for one of the half-holidays included in the Feast of Tabernacles, about six months later. Mrs. Kaplan said something about her plans concerning the event. Fanny objected. Her mother insisted, and it looked like an altercation, when the head of the family called them to order

"And where are you going for your honeymoon, Fanny?" asked Mary

"That's none of your business," her sister retorted

"She's stuck up because she's going to be married," Mary jeered

"Shut your mouth," her father growled

"Do you know my idea of a honeymoon?" said I. "That is, if it were possible—if Russia didn't have that accursed government of hers. We should take a trip to Antomir." "Wouldn't that be lovely!" said Fanny. "We would stop in Paris, wouldn't we?"

Fanny and her mother resumed their discussion of the preparations for the wedding. I scarcely listened, yet I was thrilled. I gazed at Fanny, trying to picture her as the mother of my first child. "If it's a girl she'll be named for mother, of course," I mused. I reflected with mortification that my mother's name could not be left in its original form, but would have to be Americanized, and for the moment this seemed to be a matter of the gravest concern to me

My attitude toward Fanny and our prospective marriage was primitive enough, and yet our engagement had an ennobling effect on me. I was in a lofty mood.

My heart sang of motives higher than the mere feathering of my own nest. The vision of working for my wife and children somehow induced a yearning for altruism in a broader sense. While free from any vestige of religion, in the ordinary meaning of the word, I was tingling with a religious ecstasy that was based on a sense of public duty. The Synagogue of the Sons of Antomir seemed to represent not a creed, but unselfishness. I donated generously to it. Also, I subscribed a liberal sum to an East Side hospital of which Kaplan was a member, and to other institutions. The sum I gave to the hospital was so large that it made a stir, and a conservative Yiddish daily printed my photograph and a short sketch of my life. I thought of the promise I had given Naphtali, before leaving Antomir, to send him a "ship ticket." I had thought of it many times before, but I had never even sought to discover his whereabouts. This time, however, I throbbed with a firm resolution to get his address, and, in case he was poor, to bring him over and liberally provide for his future

My wedding loomed as the beginning of a new era in my life. It appealed to my imagination as a new birth, like my coming to America. I looked forward to it with mixed awe and bliss

Three or four months later, however, something happened that played havoc with that feeling

*I got married*

# BOOK XII

# MISS TEVKIN

# CHAPTER I

᾽ ON a Saturday morning in August I took a train for Tannersville, Catskill Mountains, where the Kaplan family had a cottage. I was to stay with them over Sunday. I had been expected to be there the day before, but had been detained, August being part of our busiest season. While in the smoking-car it came over me that from Kaplan's point of view my journey was a flagrant violation of the Sabbath and that it was sure to make things awkward.

Whether my riding on Saturday would actually offend his religious sensibilities or not (for in America one gets used to seeing such sins committed even by the faithful), it was certain to offend his sense of the respect I owed him. And so, to avoid a sullen reception I decided to stop overnight in another Catskill town and not to make my appearance at Tannersville until the following day

The insignificant change was pregnant with momentous results

It was lunch-time when I alighted from the train, amid a hubbub of gay voices. Women and children were greeting their husbands and fathers who had come from the city to join them for the week-end. I had never been to the mountains before, nor practically ever taken a day's vacation. It was so full of ozone, so full of health-giving balm, it was almost overpowering. I was inhaling it in deep, intoxicating gulps. It gave me a pleasure so keen it seemed to verge on pain. It was so unlike the air I had left in the sweltering city that the place seemed to belong to another planet

I stopped at the Rigi Kulm House. There were several other hotels or boarding-houses in the village, and all of them except one were occupied by our people, the Rigi Kulm being the largest and most expensive hostelry in the neighborhood. lt was crowded, and I had to content myself with sleeping-accommodations in one of the near-by cottages, in which the hotel-keeper hired rooms for his overflow business, taking my meals in the hotel

The Rigi Kulm stood at the end of the village and my cottage was across the main country road from it. Both were on high ground. Viewed from the veranda of the hotel, the village lay to the right and the open country—a fascinating landscape of meadowland, timbered hills, and a brook that lost itself in a grove—to the left. The mountains rose in two ranges, one in front of the hotel and one in the rear

The bulk of the boarders at the Rigi Kulm was made up of families of cloak-manufacturers, shirt-manufacturers, ladies'-waist-manufacturers, cigar-manufacturers, clothiers, furriers, jewelers, leather-goods men, real-estate men, physicians, dentists, lawyers—in most cases people who had blossomed out into nabobs in the course of the last few years. The crowd was ablaze with diamonds, painted cheeks, and bright-colored silks. It was a babel of blatant self-consciousness, a miniature of the parvenu smugness that had spread like wild-fire over the country after a period of need and low spirits.

In addition to families who were there for the whole season—that is, from the Fourth of July to the first Monday in October—the hotel contained a considerable number of single young people, of both sexes—salesmen, stenographers, bookkeepers, librarians—who came for a fortnight's vacation.

These were known as "two-weekers." They occupied tiny rooms, usually two girls or two men in a room. Each of these girls had a large supply of dresses and shirt-waists of the latest style, and altogether the two weeks' vacation ate up, in many cases, the savings of months

To be sure, the "two-weekers" of the gentle sex were not the only marriageable young women in the place. They had a number of heiresses to compete with

I was too conspicuous a figure in the needle industries for my name to be unknown to the guests of a hotel like the Rigi Kulm House. Moreover, several of the people I found there were my personal acquaintances. One of these was Nodelman's cousin, Mrs. Kalch, or Auntie Yetta, the gaunt, childless woman of the solemn countenance and the gay disposition, of the huge gold teeth, and

*why is he noticing marriageable women?*

the fingers heavily laden with diamonds. I had not seen her for months.

As the lessee of the hotel marched me into his great dining-room she rushed out to me, her teeth aglitter with hospitality, and made me take a seat at a table which she shared with her husband, the moving-van man, and two middle-aged women. I could see that she had not heard of my engagement, and to avoid awkward interrogations concerning the whereabouts of my fiancée I omitted to announce it

"I know what you have come here for," she said, archly. "You can't fool Auntie Yetta. But you have come to the right place. I can tell you that a larger assortment of beautiful young ladies you never saw, Mr. Levinsky. And they're educated, too. If you don't find your predestined one here you'll never find her. What do you say, Mr. Rivesman?" she addressed the proprietor of the hotel, who stood by and whom I had known for many years

"I agree with you thoroughly, Mrs. Kalch," he answered, smilingly. "But Mr.

Levinsky tells me he can stay only one day with us."

"Plenty of time for a smart man to pick a girl in a place like this.

Besides, you just tell him that you have a lot of fine, educated young ladies, Mr. Rivesman. He is an educated gentleman, Mr. Levinsky is, and if he knows the kind of boarders you have he'll stay longer." "I know Mr. Levinsky is an educated man," Rivesman answered. "As for our boarders, they're all fine—superfine."

"So you've got to find your predestined one here," she resumed, turning to me again. "Otherwise you can't leave this place. See?"

"But suppose I have found her already—elsewhere?"

"You had no business to. Anyhow, if she doesn't know enough to hold you tight and you are here to spend a week-end with other girls, she does not deserve to have you."

"But I am not spending it with other girls."

"What else did you come here for?" And she screwed up one-half of her face into a wink so grotesque that I could not help bursting into laughter

About an hour after lunch I sat in a rocking-chair on the front porch, gazing at the landscape. The sky was a blue so subtle and so noble that it seemed as though I had never seen such a sky before. "This is just the kind of place for God to live in," I mused. Whereupon I decided that this was what was meant by the word heaven, whereas the blue overhanging the city was a "mere sky." The village was full of blinding, scorching sunshine, yet the air was entrancingly ref reshing. The veranda was almost deserted, most of the women being in their rooms, gossiping or dressing for the arrival of their husbands, fathers, sweethearts, or possible sweethearts. Birds were embroidering the silence of the hour with a silvery whisper that spoke of rest and good-will. The slender brook to the left of me was droning like a bee. Everything was charged with peace and soothing mystery. A feeling of lassitude descended upon me. I was too lazy even to think, but the landscape was continually forcing images on my mind. A hollow in the slope of one of the mountains in front of me looked for all the world like a huge spoon.

Half of it was dark, while the other half was full of golden light. It seemed as though it was the sun's favorite spot. "The enchanted spot," I named it. I tried to imagine that oval-shaped hollow at night. I visioned a company of ghosts tiptoeing their way to it and stealing a night's lodging in the "spoon," and later, at the approach of dawn, behold! the ghosts were fleeing to the woods near by

Rising behind that mountain was the timbered peak of another one. It looked like the fur cap of a monster, and I wondered what that monster was thinking of

When I gazed at the mountain directly opposite the hotel I had a feeling of disappointment. I knew that it was very high, that it took hours to climb it, but I failed to realize it

It was seemingly quite low and commonplace. Darkling at the foot of it was what looked like a moat choked with underbrush and weeds. The spot was about a mile and a half from the hotel, yet it seemed to be only a minute's walk from me. But then a bird that was flying over that moat at the moment, winging its way straight across it, was apparently making no progress. Was this region exempt from the laws of space and distance? The bewitching azure of the sky and the divine taste of the air seemed to bear out a feeling that it was exempt from any law of nature with which I was familiar. The mountain-peak directly opposite the hotel looked weird now.

Was it peopled with Liliputians? Another bird made itself heard somewhere in the underbrush flanking the brook. It was saying something in querulous accents. I knew nothing of birds, and the song or call of this one sounded so queer to me that I was almost frightened. All of which tended to enhance the uncanny majesty of the whole landscape

Presently I heard Mrs. Kalch calling to me. She was coming along the veranda, resplendent in a purple dress, a huge diamond breastpin, and huge diamond earrings

"All alone? All alone?" she exclaimed, as she paused, interlocking her bediamonded fingers in a posture of mock amazement. "All alone? Aren't you ashamed of yourself to sit moping out here, when there are so many pretty young ladies around? Come along; I'll find you one or two as sweet as sugar," kissing the tips of her fingers

"Thank you, Mrs. Kalch, but I like it here."

"Mrs. Kalch! Auntie Yetta, you mean." And the lumps of gold in her mouth glinted good-naturedly

"Very well. Auntie Yetta."

"That's better. Wait! Wait'll I come back."

She vanished. Presently she returned and, grabbing me by an arm, stood me up and convoyed me half-way around the hotel to a secluded spot on the rear porch where four girls were chatting quietly

"Perhaps you'll find your predestined one among these," she said

"But I have found her already," I protested, with ill-concealed annoyance

She took no heed of my words. After introducing me to two of the girls and causing them to introduce me to the other two, she said: "And now go for him, young ladies! You know who Mr. Levinsky is, don't you? It isn't some kike. It's David Levinsky, the cloak-manufacturer. Don't miss your chance. Try to catch him."

"I'm ready," said Miss Lazar, a pretty brunette in white

"She's all right," declared Auntie Yetta. "Her tongue cuts like a knife that has just been sharpened, but she's as good as gold."

"Am I? I ain't so sure about it. You had better look out, Mr. Levinsky," the brunette in white warned me

"Why, that just makes it interesting," I returned. "Danger is tempting, you know. How are you going to catch me—with a net or a trap?"

Auntie Yetta interrupted us. "I'm off," she said, rising to go. "I can safely leave you in their hands, Mr. Levinsky. They'll take care of you," she said, with a wink, as she departed

"You haven't answered my question," I said to Miss Lazar

"What was it?"

"She has a poor memory, don't you know," laughed a girl in a yellow shirt-waist. She was not pretty, but she had winning blue eyes and her yellow waist became her. "Mr. Levinsky wants to know if you're going to catch him with a net or with a trap."

"And how about yourself?" I demanded. "What sort of tools have you?"

"Oh, I don't think I have a chance with a big fish like yourself," she replied

Her companions laughed

"Well, that's only her way of fishing," said Miss Lazar. "She tells every fellow she has no chance with him. That's her way of getting started. You'd better look out, Mr. Levinsky."

"And her way is to put on airs and look as if she could have anybody she wanted," retorted the one of the blue eyes

"Stop, girls," said a third, who was also interesting. "If we are going to give away one another's secrets there'll be no chance for any of us."

I could see that their thrusts contained more fact than fiction and more venom than gaiety, but it was all laughed off and everybody seemed to be on the best of terms with everybody else. I looked at this bevy of girls, each attractive in her way, and I became aware of the fact that I was not in the least tempted to flirt with them. "I am a well-behaved, sedate man now, and all because I am engaged," I congratulated myself. "There is only one woman in the world for me, and that is Fanny, my Fanny, the girl that is going to be my wife in a few weeks from to-day

Directly in front of us and only a few yards off was a tennis-court. It was unoccupied at first, but presently there appeared two girls with rackets and balls and they started to play. One of these arrested my attention violently, as it were. I thought her strikingly interesting and pretty. I could not help gazing at her in spite of the eyes that were watching me, and she was growing on me rapidly. It seemed as though absolutely everything about her made a strong appeal to me. She was tall and stately, with a fine pink complexion and an effective mass of chestnut hair. I found that her face attested intellectual dignity and a kindly disposition. I liked her white, strong teeth. I liked the way she closed her lips and I liked the way she opened them into a smile; the way she ran to meet the ball and the way she betrayed disappointment when she missed it. I still seemed to be congratulating myself upon my indifference to women other than the one who was soon to bear my name, when I became conscious of a mighty interest in this girl. I said to myself that she looked refined from head to foot and that her movements had a peculiar rhythm that was irresistible

Physically her cast of features was scarcely prettier than Fanny's, for my betrothed was really a good-looking girl, but spiritually there was a world of difference between their faces, the difference between a Greek statue and one of those lay figures that one used to see in front of cigar-stores

The other tennis-player was a short girl with a long face. I reflected that if she were a little taller or her face were not so long she might not be uninteresting, and that by contrast with her companion she looked homelier than she actually was

Miss Lazar watched me closely

"Playing tennis is one way of fishing for fellows," she remarked

"So the racket is really a fishing-tackle in disguise, is it?" I returned.

"But where are the fellows?"

"Aren't you one?" "No."

"Oh, these two girls go in for highbrow fellows," said a young woman who had hitherto contented herself with smiling and laughing. "They're highbrow themselves."

"Do they use big words?" I asked.

"Well, they're well read. I'll say that for them," observed Miss Lazar, with a fine display of fairness

"College girls?"

"Only one of them."

"Which?"

"Guess."

"The tall one."

"I thought she'd be the one you'd pick. You'll have to guess again."

"What made you think I'd pick her for a college girl?" "You'll have to guess that, too. Well, she is an educated girl, all the same."

She volunteered the further information that the tall girl's father was a writer, and, as though anxious lest I should take him too seriously, she hastened to add: "He doesn't write English, though. It's Jewish, or Hebrew, or something."

"What's his name?" I asked

"Tevkin," she answered, under her breath

The name sounded remotely familiar to me. Had I seen it in some Yiddish paper? Had I heard it somewhere? The intellectual East Side was practically a foreign country to me, and I was proud of the fact. I knew something of its orthodox Talmudists, but scarcely anything of its modern men of letters, poets, thinkers, humorists, whether they wrote in Yiddish, in Hebrew, in Russian, or in English. If I took an occasional look at the socialist Yiddish daily it was chiefly to see what was going on in the Cloak-makers' Union. Otherwise I regarded everything that was written for the East Side with contempt, and "East Side writer" was synonymous with "greenhorn" and "tramp." Worse than that, it was identified in my mind with socialism, anarchism, and trade-unionism. It was something sinister, absurd, and uncouth

But Miss Tevkin was a beautiful girl, nevertheless. So I pitied her for being the daughter of an East Side writer

The tennis game did not last long. Miss Tevkin and her companion soon went indoors. I went out for a stroll by myself. I was thinking of my journey to Tannersville the next morning. The enforced loss of time chafed me. Of the strong impression which the tall girl had produced on me not a trace seemed to have been left. She bothered me no more than any other pretty girl I might have recently come across. Young women with strikingly interesting faces and figures were not rare in New York

I had not been walking five minutes when I impatiently returned to the hotel to consult the time-tables

# CHAPTER II

I WAS chatting with Rivesman, the lessee of the hotel, across the counter that separated part of his office from the lobby. As I have said, I had known him for many years. He had formerly been in the insurance business, and he had at one time acted as my insurance broker. He was a Talmudist, and well versed in modern Hebrew literature, to boot. He advised me concerning trains to Tannersville, and then we passed to the hotel business and mutual acquaintances

Presently Miss Tevkin, apparently on her way from her room, paused at the counter, by my side, to leave her key. She was dressed for dinner, although it was not yet half past 4 o'clock and the great Saturday-evening repast, for which train after train was bringing husbands and other "weekenders" to the mountains, was usually a very late affair

The dress she now wore was a modest gown of navy blue trimmed with lace. The change of attire seemed to have produced a partial change in her identity.

She was interesting in a new way, I thought

"Going to enjoy the fresh air?" Rivesman asked her, gallantly

"Ye-es," she answered, pleasantly. "It's glorious outside." And she vanished

"Pretty girl," I remarked

"And a well-bred one, too—in the real sense of the word."

"One of your two-week guests, I suppose," I said, with studied indifference.

"Yes. She is a stenographer." Whereupon he named a well-known lawyer, a man prominent in the affairs of the Jewish community, as her employer. "It was an admirer of her father who got the job for her."

From what followed I learned that Miss Tevkin's father had once been a celebrated Hebrew poet and that he was no other than the hero of the romance of which Naphtali had told me a few months before I left my native place to go to America, and that her mother was the heroine of that romance. In other words, her mother was the once celebrated beauty, the daughter of the famous Hebrew writer (long since deceased), Doctor Rachaeless of Odessa

"It was her father, then, who wrote those love-letters!" I exclaimed, excitedly. "And it was about her mother that he wrote them! Somebody told me on the veranda that her name was Miss Tevkin. I did think the name sounded familiar, but I could not locate it." The discovery stirred me inordinately. I was palpitating with reminiscent interest and with a novel interest in the beautiful girl who had just stood by my side

At my request Rivesman, followed by myself, sought her out on the front porch and introduced me to her as "a great admirer of your father's poetry."

Seated beside her was a bald-headed man with a lone wisp of hair directly over his forehead whom the hotel-keeper introduced as "Mr. Shapiro, a counselor," and who by his manner of greeting me showed that he was fully aware of my financial standing

The old romance of the Hebrew poet and his present wife, and more especially the fact that I had been thrilled by it in Antomir, threw a halo of ineffable fascination around their beautiful daughter

"So you are a daughter of the great Hebrew poet," I said in English

"It's awfully kind of you to speak like that," she returned

"Mr. Levinsky is known for his literary tastes, you know," Shapiro put in

"I wish I deserved the compliment," I rejoined. "Unfortunately, I don't. I am glad I find time to read the newspapers

"The newspapers are life," observed Miss Tevkin, "and life is the source of literature, or should be."

"'Or should be!'" Shapiro mocked her, fondly. "Is that a dig at the popular novels?" And in an aside to me, "Miss Tevkin has no use for them, you know."

She smiled

"Still worshiping at the shrine of Ibsen?" he asked her

"More than ever," she replied, gaily.

"I admire your loyalty, though I regret to say that I am still unable to share your taste."

"It isn't a matter of taste," she returned. "It depends on what one is looking for in a play or a novel."

She smiled with the air of one abstaining from a fruitless discussion

"She's a blue-stocking," I said to myself. "Women of this kind are usually doomed to be old maids." And yet she drew me with a magnetic force that seemed to be beyond my power of resistance

It was evident that she enjoyed the discussion and the fact that it was merely a pretext for the lawyer to feast his eyes on her

I wondered why a bald-headed man with a lone tuft of hair did not repel her

A younger brother of Shapiro's, a real-estate broker, joined us. He also was bald-headed, but his baldness formed a smaller patch than the lawyer's

The two brothers did most of the talking, and, among other things, they informed Miss Tevkin and myself that they were graduates of the City College. With a great display of reading and repeatedly interrupting each other they took up the cudgels for the "good old school." I soon discovered, however, that their range was limited to a small number of authors, whose names they uttered with great gusto and to whom they returned again and again. These were Victor Hugo, Dumas, Dickens, Thackeray, George Eliot, Coleridge, Edgar Poe, and one or two others. If the lawyer added a new name, like Walter Pater, to his list, the real-estate man would hasten to trot out De Quincey, for example. For the rest they would parade a whole array of writers rather than refer to any one of them in particular. The more they fulminated and fumed and bullied Miss Tevkin the firmer grew my conviction that they had scarcely read the books for which they seemed to be ready to lay down their lives

Miss Tevkin, however, took them seriously. She followed them with the air of a "good girl "listening to a lecture by her mother or teacher

"I don't agree with you at all," she would say, weakly, from time to time, and resume listening with charming resignation

The noise made by the two brothers attracted several other boarders. One of these was a slovenly-looking man of forty-five who spoke remarkably good English with a very bad accent (far worse than mine). That he was a Talmudic scholar was written all over his face. By profession he was a photographer.

His name was Mendelson. He took a hand in our discussion, and it at once became apparent that he had read more and knew more than the bald-headed brothers. He was overflowing with withering sarcasm and easily sneered them into silence

Miss Tevkin was happy. B.ut the slovenly boarder proved to be one of those people who know what they do not want rather than what they do. And so he proceeded, in a spirit of chivalrous banter, to make game of her literary gods as well.

"You don't really mean to tell us that you enjoy an Ibsen play?" he demanded. "Why, you are too full of life for that."

"But that's just what the Ibsen plays are—full of life," she answered. "If you're bored by them it's because you're probably looking for stories, for 'action.' But art is something more significant than that. There is moral force and beauty in Ibsen which one misses in the old masters."

"That's exactly what the ministers of the gospel or the up-to-date rabbis are always talking about—moral force, moral beauty, and moral clam-chowder," Mendelson retorted

The real-estate man uttered a chuckle

"Would you turn the theater into a church or a reform synagogue?" the photographer continued. "People go to see a play because they want to enjoy themselves, not because they feel that their morals need darning."

"But in good literature the moral is not preached as a sermon," Miss Tevkin replied. "It naturally follows from the life it presents. Anyhow, the other kind of literature is mere froth. You read page after page and there doesn't seem to be any substance to it." She said it plaintively, as though apologizing for holding views of this kind

"Is that the way you feel about Thackeray and Dickens, too?" I ventured

"I do," she answered, in the same doleful tone

She went on to develop her argument. We did not interrupt her, the two brothers, the photographer, and myself listening to her with admiring glances that had more to do with her beautiful face and the music of her soft, girlish voice than with what she was saying. There was a congealed sneer on the photographer's face as he followed her plea, but it was full of the magic of her presence

"You're a silly child," his countenance seemed to say. "But I could eat you, all the same."

She dwelt on the virtues of Ibsen, Strindberg, Knut Hamsen, Hauptmann, and a number of others, mostly names I did not recollect ever having heard before, and she often used the word "decadent," which she pronounced in the French way and which I did not then understand. Now and then she would quote some critic, or some remark heard from a friend or from her father, and once she dwelt on an argument of her oldest brother, who seemed to be well versed in Russian literature and to have clear-cut opinions on literature in general.

She spoke with an even-voiced fluency, with a charming gift of language.

Words came readily, pleasantly from her pretty lips. It was evident, too, that she was thoroughly familiar with the many authors whose praises she was sounding. Yet I could not help feeling that she had not much to say. The opinions she voiced were manifestly not her own, as though she was reciting a well-mastered lesson. And I was glad of it. "She's merely a girl, after all," I thought, fondly. "She's the sweetest thing I ever knew, and her father is the man who wrote those love-letters, and her mother is the celebrated beauty with whom he was in love."

Whether the views she set forth were her own or somebody else's, I could see that she relished uttering them. Also, that she relished the euphony and felicity of her phrasing, which was certainly her own. Whether she spoke from conviction or not, one thing seemed indisputable: the atmosphere surrounding the books and authors she named had a genuine fascination for her. There was a naive sincerity in her rhetoric, and her delivery and gestures had a rhythm that seemed to be akin to the rhythm of her movements in the tennis-court

Miss Lazar passed by us, giving me a smiling look, which seemed to say, "I knew you would sooner or later be in her company." I felt myself blushing.

"To-morrow I'll be in Tannersville and all this nonsense will be over," I said to myself

The long-faced, short girl with whom Miss Tevkin had played tennis emerged from the lobby door and was introduced to me as Miss Siegel. As I soon gathered from a bit of pleasantry by the lawyer, she was a school-teacher

At Miss Tevkin's suggestion we all went to see the crowd waiting for the last "husband train."

As we rose to go I made a point of asking Miss Tevkin for the name of the best Ibsen play, my object being to be by her side on our walk down to the village. The photographer hastened to answer my question, thus occupying the place on the other side of her

We were crossing the sloping lawn, Miss Tevkin on a narrow flagged walk, while we were trotting along through the grass on either side of her, with the other three of our group bringing up the rear. Presently, as we reached the main sidewalk, we were held up by Auntie Yetta, who was apparently returning from one of the cottages across the road

"Is this the one you are after?" she demanded of me, with a wink in the direction of Miss Tevkin. And, looking her over, "You do know a good thing when you see it." Then to her: "Hold on to him, young lady. Hold on tight.

Mr. Levinsky is said to be worth a million, you know."

"She's always joking," I said, awkwardly, as we resumed our walk

Miss Tevkin made no answer, but I felt that Auntie Yetta's joke had made a disagreeable impression on her. I sought to efface it by a humorous sketch of Auntie Yetta, and seemed to be successful

The village was astir. The great "husband train," the last and longest of the day, was due in about ten minutes. Groups of women and children in gala dress were emerging from the various boarding-houses, feeding the main human stream. Some boarders were out to meet the train, others were on their way to the post-office for letters. A sunset of pale gold hung broodingly over the mountains. Miss Tevkin's voice seemed to have something to do with it

Presently we reached the crowd at the station. The train was late. The children were getting restless. At last it arrived, the first of two sections, with a few minutes' headway between them.

There was a jam and a babel of voices. Interminable strings of passengers, travel-worn, begrimed, their eyes searching the throng, came dribbling out of the cars with tantalizing slowness. Men in livery caps were chanting the names of their respective boarding-houses. Passengers were shouting the pet names of their wives or children; women and children were calling to their newly arrived husbands and fathers, some gaily, others shrieking, as though the train were on fire. There were a large number of handsome, well-groomed women in expensive dresses and diamonds, and some of these were being kissed by puny, but successful-looking, men. "They married them for their money," I said to myself. An absurd-looking shirt-waist-manufacturer of my acquaintance, a man with the face of a squirrel, swooped down upon a large young matron of dazzling animal beauty who had come in an automobile. He introduced me to her, with a beaming air of triumph. "I can afford a machine and a beautiful wife," his radiant squirrel-face seemed to say. He was parading the fact that this tempting female had married him in spite of his ugliness. He was mutely boasting as much of his own homeliness as of her coarse beauty

Prosperity was picking the cream of the "bride market" for her favorite sons. I thought of Lenox Avenue, a great, broad thoroughfare up-town that had almost suddenly begun to swarm with good-looking and flashily gowned brides of Ghetto upstarts, like a meadow bursting into bloom in spring

"And how about your own case?" a voice retorted within me. "Could you get a girl like Fanny if it were not for your money? Ah, but I'm a good-looking chap myself and not as ignorant as most of the other fellows who have succeeded," I answered, inwardly. "Yes, and I am entitled to a better girl than Fanny, too." And I became conscious of Miss Tevkin's presence by my side

Conversation with the poet's daughter was practically monopolized by the misanthropic photographer. I was seized with a desire to dislodge him. I was determined to break into the conversation and to try to eclipse him. With a fast-beating heart I began: "What an array of beautiful women! Present company"—with a bow to Miss Tevkin and her long-faced chum—"not excepted, of course. Far from it."

The two girls smiled

"Why! Why! Whence this sudden fit of gallantry?" asked the photographer, his sneer and the rasping Yiddish enunciation with which he spoke English filling me with hate

"Come, Mr. Mendelson," I answered, "it's about time you cast off your grouch. Look! The sky is so beautiful, the mountains so majestic. Cheer up, old man."

The real-estate man burst into a laugh. The two girls smiled, looking me over curiously. I hastened to follow up my advantage

"One does get into a peculiar mood on an evening like this," I pursued. "The air is so divine and the people are so happy." "That's what we all come to the mountains for," the photographer retorted

Ignoring his remark, I resumed: "It may seem a contradiction of terms, but these family reunions, these shouts of welcome, are so thrilling it makes one feel as if there was something pathetic in them."

"Pathetic?" the bald-headed real-estate man asked in surprise

"Mr. Levinsky is in a pathetic mood, don't you know," the photographer cut in.

"Yes, pathetic," I defied him. "But pathos has nothing to do with grouch, has it?" I asked, addressing myself to the girls

"Why, no," Miss Siegel replied, with a perfunctory smile. "Still, I should rather see people meet than part. It's heartbreaking to watch a train move out of a station, with those white handkerchiefs waving, and getting smaller, smaller. Oh, those handkerchiefs!"

It was practically the first remark I had heard from her. It produced a stronger impression on my mind than all Miss Tevkin had said. Nevertheless, I felt that I should much rather listen to Miss Tevkin

"Of course, of course," I said. "Leave-taking is a very touching scene to witness. But still, when people meet again after a considerable separation, it's also touching. Don't you think it is?"

"Yes, I know what you mean," Miss Siegel assented, somewhat aloofly

"People cry for joy," Miss Tevkin put in, non-committally

"Yes, but they cry, all the same. There are tears," I urged

"I had no idea you were such a cry-baby, Mr. Levinsky," the photographer said. "Perhaps you'll feel better when you've had dinner. But I thought you said this weather made you happy."

"It simply means that at the bottom of our hearts we Jews are a sad people," Miss Tevkin interceded. "There is a broad streak of tragedy in our psychology. It's the result of many centuries of persecution and homelessness. Gentiles take life more easily than we do. My father has a beautiful poem on the theme. But then the Russians are even more melancholy than we are. Russian literature is full of it. My oldest brother, who is a great stickler for everything Russian, is always speaking about it."

"Always referring to her papa and her brother," I thought. "What a sweet child."

Presently she and her long-faced chum were hailed by a group of young men and women, and, excusing themselves to us, they ran over to join them. I felt like a man sipping at a glass of wine when the glass is suddenly seized from his hand

Some time later I sat on a cane chair amid flower-beds in front of the Rigi Kulm, inhaling the scented evening air and gazing down the sloping side of the lawn. Women and girls were returning from the post-office, many of them with letters in their hands. Some of these were so impatient to know their contents that they were straining their eyes to read them in the sickly light that fell from a sparse row of electric lamps. I watched their faces.

In one case it was quite evident that the letter was a love-message, and that the girl who was reading it was tremendously happy. In another I wondered whether the missive had come from a son. It was for Miss Tevkin's return that I was watching. But the dinner-gong sounded before she made her appearance

*, Miss Tevkin likes plays, very educated*

*D is drawn to her sense of knowledge*

# CHAPTER III

DINNER at the Rigi Kulm on a Saturday evening was not merely a meal. It was, in addition, or chiefly, a great social function and a gown contest

The band was playing. As each matron or girl made her appearance in the vast dining-room the female boarders already seated would look her over with feverish interest, comparing her gown and diamonds with their own. It was as though it were especially for this parade of dresses and finery that the band was playing. As the women came trooping in, arrayed for the exhibition, some timid, others brazenly self-confident, they seemed to be marching in time to the music, like so many chorus-girls tripping before a theater audience, or like a procession of model-girls at a style-display in a big department store. Many of the women strutted affectedly, with "refined" mien. Indeed, I knew that most of them had a feeling as though wearing a hundred-and-fifty-dollar dress was in itself culture and education

Mrs. Kalch kept talking to me, now aloud, now in whispers. She was passing judgment on the gowns and incidentally initiating me into some of the innermost details of the gown race. It appeared that the women kept tab on one another's dresses, shirt-waists, shoes, ribbons, pins, earrings. She pointed out two matrons who had never been seen twice in the same dress, waist, or skirt, although they had lived in the hotel for more than five weeks. Of one woman she informed me that she could afford to wear a new gown every hour in the year, but that she was "too big a slob to dress up and too lazy to undress even when she went to bed"; of another, that she would owe her grocer and butcher rather than go to the country with less than ten big trunks full of duds; of a third, that she was repeatedly threatening to leave the hotel because its bills of fare were typewritten, whereas "for the money she paid she could go to a place with printed menu-cards."

"Must have been brought up on printed menu-cards," one of the other women at our table commented, with a laugh

"That's right," Mrs. Kalch assented, appreciatively. "I could not say whether her father was a horse-driver or a stoker in a bathhouse, but I do know that her husband kept a coal-and-ice cellar a few years ago."

"That'll do," her bewhiskered husband snarled. ""It's about time you gave your tongue a rest."

Auntie Yetta's golden teeth glittered good-humoredly. The next instant she called my attention to a woman who, driven to despair by the superiority of her "bosom friend's" gowns, had gone to the city for a fortnight, ostensibly to look for a new flat, but in reality to replenish her wardrobe. She had just returned, on the big "husband train," and now "her bosom friend won't be able to eat or sleep, trying to guess what kind of dresses she brought back."

Nor was this the only kind of gossip upon which Mrs. Kalch regaled me. She told me, for example, of some sensational discoveries made by several boarders regarding a certain mother of five children, of her sister who was "not a bit better," and of a couple who were supposed to be man and wife, but who seemed to be "somebody else's man and somebody else's wife."

At last Miss Tevkin and Miss Siegel entered the dining-room. Something like a thrill passed through me. I felt like exclaiming, "At last!"

"That's the one I met you with, isn't it? Not bad-looking," said Mrs. Kalch

"Which do you mean?"

""Which do you mean'! The tall one, of course; the one you were so sweet on.

Not the dwarf with the horse-face."

"They're fine, educated girls, both of them," I rejoined. "Both of them! As if it was all the same to you!" At this she bent over and gave me a glare and a smile that brought the color to my face. "The tall one is certainly not bad-looking, but we don't call that pretty in this place."

"Are there many prettier ones?" I asked, gaily

"I haven't counted them, but I can show you some girls who shine like the sun. There is one!" she said, pointing at a girl on the other side of the aisle. "A regular princess. Don't you think so?"

"She's a pretty girl, all right," I replied, "but in comparison with that tall one she's like a nice piece of cotton goods alongside of a piece of imported silk."

"Look at him! He's stuck on her. Does she know it? If she does not, I'll tell her and collect a marriage-broker's commission."

I loathed myself for having talked too much.

"I was joking, of course," I tried to mend matters. "All girls are pretty." Luckily Mrs. Kalch's attention was at this point diverted by the arrival of the waiter with a huge platter laden with roast chicken, which he placed in the middle of the table. There ensued a silent race for the best portions.

One of the other two women at the table was the first to obtain possession of the platter. Taking her time about it, she first made a careful examination of its contents and then attacked what she evidently considered a choice piece. By way of calling my attention to the proceeding, Auntie Yetta stepped on my foot under the table and gave me a knowing glance

The noise in the dining-room was unendurable. It seemed as though everybody was talking at the top of his voice. The musicians—a pianist and two violinists—found it difficult to make themselves heard. They were pounding and sawing frantically in a vain effort to beat the bedlam of conversation and laughter. It was quite touching. The better to take in the effect of the turmoil, I shut my eyes for a moment, whereupon the noise reminded me of the Stock Exchange

The conductor, who played the first violin, was a fiery little fellow with a high crown of black hair. He was working every muscle and nerve in his body.

He played selections from "Aïda," the favorite opera of the Ghetto; he played the popular American songs of the day; he played celebrated "hits" of the Yiddish stage. All to no purpose. Finally, he had recourse to what was apparently his last resort. He struck up the "Star-spangled Banner The effect was overwhelming. The few hundred diners rose like one man, applauding. The children and many of the adults caught up the tune joyously, passionately. It was an interesting scene. Men and women were offering thanksgiving to the flag under which they were eating this good dinner, wearing these expensive clothes. There was the jingle of newly-acquired dollars in our applause. But there was something else in it as well. Many of those who were now paying tribute to the Stars and Stripes were listening to the tune with grave, solemn mien. It was as if they were saying: "We are not persecuted under this flag. At last we have found a home." Love for America blazed up in my soul. I shouted to the musicians, "My Country," and the cry spread like wildfire. The musicians obeyed and we all sang the anthem from the bottom of our souls

'Miss T verly cultured

# CHAPTER IV

I WAS in the lobby, chatting with the clerk across his counter and casting glances at the dining-room door. Miss Tevkin had not yet finished her meal and I was watching for her to appear. Presently she did, toying with Miss Siegel's hand

"Feeling better now?" I asked, stepping up to meet them. "I hope you enjoyed your dinner."

"Oh, we were so hungry, I don't think we knew what we were eating," Miss Tevkin returned, politely

"Going to take the air on the veranda?"

"Why—no. We are going out for a walk," she answered in a tone that said as clearly as words that my company was not wanted. And, nodding with exaggerated amiability, they passed out

The blood rushed to my face as though she had slapped it. I stood petrified.

"It's all because of Mrs. Kalch's tongue, confound her!" I thought.

"To-morrow I shall be in Tannersville and this trifling incident will be forgotten." But at this I became aware that I did not care to go to Tannersville and that the prospect of seeing Fanny had lost its attraction for me. I went back to the counter and attempted to resume my conversation with the clerk, but he was a handsome fellow, which was one of his chief qualifications for the place, and so I soon found myself in the midst of a bevy of girls and married women. However, they all seemed to know that I was a desirable match and they gradually transferred their attentions to me, the girls in their own interests and the older matrons in those of their marriageable daughters. Their crude amenities sickened me. One middle-aged woman tried to monopolize me by a confidential talk concerning the social inferiority of the Catskills

"The food is good here," she said, in English. "There's no kick comin' on that score. But my daughter says with her dresses she could go to any hotel in Atlantic City, and she's right, too. I don't care what you say."

I fled as soon as I could. I went to look for a seat on the spacious veranda. I said to myself that Miss Tevkin and Miss Siegel must have had an appointment with some one else and that I had no cause for feeling slighted by them

I felt reassured, but I was lonely. I was yearning for some congenial company, and blamed fate for having allowed Miss Tevkin to make another engagement—if she had

The veranda was crowded and almost as noisy as the dining-room had been.

There was a hubbub of broken English, the gibberish being mostly spoken with self-confidence and ease. Indeed, many of these people had some difficulty in speaking their native tongue. Bad English replete with literal translations from untranslatable Yiddish idioms had become their natural speech. The younger parents, however, more susceptible of the influence of their children, spoke purer English.

It was a dark night, but the sky was full of stars, full of golden mystery.

The mountains rose black, vast, disquieting. A tumultuous choir of invisible katydids was reciting an interminable poem on an unpoetic subject that had something to do with Miss Tevkin. The air was even richer in aroma than it had been in the morning, but its breath seemed to be part of the uncanny stridulation of the katydids. The windows of the dancing-pavilion beyond the level part of the lawn gleamed like so many sheets of yellow fire. Presently its door flew open, sending a slanting shaft of light over the grass

I found a chair on the veranda, but I was restless, and the chatter of two women in front of me grated on my nerves. I wondered where Miss Tevkin and her companion were at this minute. I was saying to myself that I would never come near them again, that I was going to see Fanny; but I did not cease wondering where they were. The two women in front of me were discussing the relative virtues and faults of little boys and little girls. They agreed that a boy was a "big loafer" and a great source of trouble, and that a little girl was more obedient and clinging. It appeared that one of these two mothers had a boy and two girls and that, contrary to her own wish, he was her great pet, although he was not the "baby."

"I am just crazy for him," she said, plaintively

She boasted of his baseball record, whereupon she used the slang of the game with so much authority that it became entertaining, but by a curious association of ideas she turned the conversation to the subject of a family who owed the hotel-keeper their last summer's board and who had been accepted this time in the hope that they would pay their old debt as well as their new bills

Two men to the right of me were complaining of the unions and the walking delegates, of traveling salesmen, of buyers. Then they took up the subject of charity, whereupon one of them enlarged on "scientific philanthropy," apparently for the sheer lust of hearing himself use the term

I recalled that one of the things I was booked to do in Tannersville was to attend a charity meeting of East Side business men, of which Kaplan was one of the organizers. Two subscriptions were to be started—one for a home for aged immigrants and one for the victims of the anti-Jewish riots in Russia—and I was expected to contribute sums large enough to do credit to my prospective father-in-law

The multitudinous jabber was suddenly interrupted by the sound of scampering feet accompanied by merry shrieks. A young girl burst from the vestibule door, closely followed by three young men. She was about eighteen years old, well fed, of a ravishing strawberries-and-cream complexion, her low-cut evening gown leaving her plump arms and a good deal of her bust exposed. One of the rocking-chairs on the porch impeding her way, she was seized by her pursuers, apparently a willing victim, and held prisoner. Two of her captors gripped her bare arms, while the third clutched her by the neck. Thus they stood, the men stroking and kneading her luscious flesh, and she beaming and giggling rapturously. Then one of the men gathered her to him with one arm, pressing his cheek against hers

"She's my wife," he jested. "We are married. Let go, boys."

"I'll sue you for alimony then," piped the girl

Finally, they released her, and the next minute I saw them walking across the lawn in the direction of the dancing-pavilion

The man who had talked scientific philanthropy spat in disgust

"Shame!" he said. "Decent young people wouldn't behave like that in Russia, would they?"

"Indeed they wouldn't," his interlocutor assented, vehemently. "People over there haven't yet forgotten what decency is."

"Oh, well, it was only a joke, said a woman

"A nice joke, that!" retorted the man who had dwelt on scientific charity

"What would you have? Would you want American-born young people to be a lot of greenhorns? This is not Russia. They are Americans and they are young, so they want to have some fun. They are just as respectable as the boys and the girls in the old country. Only there is some life to them. That's all."

Young people were moving along the flagged walk or crossing the lawn from various directions, all converging toward the pavilion. They walked singly, in twos, in threes, and in larger groups, some trudging along leisurely, others proceeding at a hurried pace. Some came from our hotel, others from other places, the strangers mostly in flocks. I watched them as they sauntered or scurried along, as they receded through the thickening gloom, as they emerged from it into the slanting shaft of light that fell from the pavilion, and as they vanished in its blazing doorway. I gazed at the spectacle until it fascinated me as something weird. The pavilion with its brightly illuminated windows was an immense magic lamp, and the young people flocking to it so many huge moths of a supernatural species. As I saw them disappear in the glare of the doorway I pictured them as being burned up. I was tempted to join the unearthly procession and to be "burned" like the others. Then, discarding the image, I visioned men and women of ordinary flesh and blood dancing, and I was seized with a desire to see the sexes in mutual embrace. But I exhorted myself that I was soon to be a married man and that it was as well to keep out of temptation's way

Presently I saw Miss Tevkin crossing the lawn, headed for the pavilion. She was one of a bevy of girls and men. I watched her get nearer and nearer to that shaft of light. When she was finally swallowed up by the pavilion the lawn disappeared from my consciousness. My thoughts were in the dance-hall, and a few minutes later I was there in the flesh

It was a vast room and it was crowded. It was some time before I located Miss Tevkin. The chaotic throng of dancers was a welter of color and outline so superb, I thought, that it seemed as though every face and figure in it were the consummation of youthful beauty. However, as I contemplated the individual couples, in quest of the girl who filled my thoughts, I met with disillusion after disillusion. Then, after recovering from a sense of watching a parade of uncomeliness, I began to discover figures or faces, or both, that were decidedly charming, while here and there I came upon a young woman of singular beauty. The number of good-looking women or women with expressive faces was remarkably large, in fact. As I scanned the crowd for the third time it seemed to me that the homely women looked cleverer than the pretty ones. Many of the girls or matrons were dressed far more daringly than they would have been a year or two before. Almost all of them were powdered and painted. Prosperity was rapidly breaking the chains of American Puritanism, rapidly "Frenchifying" the country, and the East Side was quick to fall into line

The band was again playing with might and main. The vehement little conductor was again exerting every nerve and muscle. His bow, which was also his baton, was pouring vim and sex mystery into the dancers. As I looked at him it seemed to me as though the music, the thunderous clatter of feet, and the hum of voices all came from the fiery rhythm of his arm

Finally, I discovered Miss Tevkin. She was dancing with a sallow-faced, homely, scholarly-looking fellow. The rhythmic motion of her tall, stately frame, as it floated and swayed through the dazzling light, brought a sob to my throat

When the waltz was over and her cavalier was taking her to a seat I caught her eye. I nodded and smiled to her. She returned the greeting, but immediately averted her face. Again I felt as if she had slapped my cheek.

Was I repugnant to her? I thought of my victory over the acrimonious photographer at the railroad station. Had I not won her favor there? And it came over me that even on that occasion she had shown me but scant cordiality. Was it all because of Auntie Yetta's idiotic jest? She beckoned to Miss Siegel, who was on the other side of the hall, and presently she was joined by her and by some other young people.

She danced indefatigably, now with this man, now with that, but always of the same "set." I watched her. Sometimes, as she waltzed, she talked and laughed brokenly, exchanging jokes with her partner or with some other dancing couple. Sometimes she looked solemnly absorbed, as though dancing were a sacred function. I wondered whether she was interested in any one of these fellows in particular. I could see that it gave her special pleasure to waltz with that sallow-faced man, but he was the best dancer in her group, and so homely that I discarded the theory of her caring for him otherwise than as a waltzing partner as absurd. Nor did she seem to be particularly interested in anybody else on the floor. As I scrutinized the men of her "set" I said to myself: "They seem to be school-teachers or writers, or beginning physicians, perhaps. They probably make less than one-third of what I pay Bender. Yet they freely talk and joke with her, while I cannot even get near her."

Miss Lazar, half naked, had been dancing with various partners, most of all with a freckled lad of sixteen or seventeen who looked as though he were panting to kiss her. She and I had exchanged smiles and pleasantry, but in her semi-nudity she was far less prepossessing than she had been in the afternoon, and I had an uncontrollable desire to announce it to her, or to hurt her in some other way. Finally, seeing a vacant seat by my side, she abruptly broke away from the freckled youth and took it

"You'll have to excuse me, Ben," she said. "I'm tired."

Ben looked the picture of despair

"Don't cry, Ben. Go out and take a walk, or dance with some other girl."

"Is this your catch after many days of fishing?" I asked

"Nope. I'm angling for bigger fish. He's just Ben, a college boy. He has fallen in love with me this evening. When I dance with somebody else he gets awful jealous." She laughed.

"He's a manly-looking boy, for all his freckles."

"He is. But how would you like a little girl to fall in love with you?" I made no answer

"Why don't you dance?" she asked

"Not in my line." "Why?"

"Oh, I never cared to learn it," I answered, impatiently

"Come. I'll show you how. It's very simple."

"Too old for that kind of thing." "Too old? How old are you?"

"That's an indiscreet question. Would you tell me your age?"

"Indeed I would. Why not?" she said, with sportive defiance. "Only you wouldn't believe me."

"Why wouldn't I? Do you look much older?"

"Oh, you cruel thing! I'm just twenty-three years and four months to-day.

There!" she said, with embarrassed gaiety.

"A sort of birthday, isn't it? I congratulate you."

"Thank you."

"You're welcome."

A pause

"So you won't tell me how old you are, will you?" she resumed

"What do you want to know it for? Are you in the life-insurance business?"

Another pause

"Look at that girl over there," she said, trying to make conversation.

"She's showing off her slender figure. She thinks she looks awful American."

"You do have a sharp tongue."

"But you remember what Mrs. Kalch said: 'A sharp tongue, but a kind heart.'"

The band struck up a two-step

Ben was coming over to her, his freckled face the image of supplication. She shut her eyes and shook her head and the boy stopped short, his jaw dropping as he did so

"Don't be hard on the poor boy," I pleaded

"That's none of your business. I want you to dance with me. Come on. I'll teach you

I shut my eyes and shook my head precisely as she had done to Ben

She burst into a laugh. "Ain't you tired of being a wall-flower?"

"I love it."

"Do you really? Or maybe you want to watch somebody?"

"I want to watch everybody," I replied, coloring the least bit. "When you were dancing I watched you, and I thought—well, I won't tell you what I thought."

A splash of color overspread her face

"Go ahead. Speak out!" she said, with a sick smile

I took pity on her. "I'm joking, of course. But I do like to watch people when they dance," I said, earnestly. "They do it in so many different ways, don't you know." I proceeded to point out couple after couple, commenting upon their peculiar manner and the special expression of their faces. One man was seemingly about to hurl his partner at somebody. Another man was eying other women over the shoulder of the one with whom he danced, apparently his wife. One woman was clinging to her partner with all her might, while her half-shut eyes and half-opened mouth seemed to say, "My, isn't it sweet!"

Miss Lazar greeted my observations with bursts of merry approval. Encouraged by this and full of mischief and malice, I made her watch a man with tapering white side-whiskers and watery eyes who was staring at the bare bust of a fat woman

"You had better look out, for his watery eyes will soon be on you."

Miss Lazar lowered her head and burst into a confused giggle

"You're a holy terror," she declared.

I was tempted to take her out into the night and hug and kiss her and tell her that she was a nuisance, but the fear of a breach-of-promise suit held me in leash

I rose to go. As I picked my way through the crowd I watched Miss Tevkin, who sat between Miss Siegel and one of their cavaliers. Our eyes met, but she hastened to look away

"She has certainly made up her mind to shun me," I thought, wretchedly. "She knows I am worth about a million, and yet she does not want to have anything to do with me. Must be a Socialist. The idea of a typewriter girl cutting me! Pooh! I could get a prettier girl than she, and one well-educated, too, if I only cared for that kind of thing in a wife. Let her stick to her beggarly crowd!"

It all seemed so ridiculous. I was baffled, perplexed, full of contempt and misery at once. "Perhaps she is engaged, after all," I comforted myself, feeling that there was anything but comfort in the reflection

I was burning to have an explanation with her, to remove any bad impression I might have made upon her

An asphalt walk in front of the pavilion and the adjoining section of the lawn were astir with boarders. A tall woman of thirty, of excellent figure, and all but naked, passed along like a flame, the men frankly gloating over her flesh.

"Wait a moment! What's your hurry?" a young stallion shouted, running after her hungrily

In another spot, on the lawn, I saw a young man in evening dress chaffing a bare-shouldered girl who looked no more than fifteen

"What! Sweet sixteen and not yet kissed?" he said to her, aloud. "Go on! I don't believe it. Anyhow, I'd like to be the fellow who's going to get you."

"Would you? I'll tell your wife about it," the little girl replied, with the good humor of a woman of forty

"Never mind my wife. But how about the fellow who is going to marry you?"

"I'd like to see him myself. I hope he ain't going to be some boob."

The air was redolent of grass, flowers, ozone, and sex. All this was flavored with Miss Tevkin's antipathy for me

# CHAPTER V

THE next morning I awoke utterly out of sorts. That I was going to take the first train for Tannersville seemed to be a matter of course, and yet I knew that I was not going to take that train, nor any other that day. I dressed myself and went out for a walk up the road, some distance beyond the grove.

The sun was out, but it had rained all night and the sandy road was damp, solid, and smooth, like baked clay. It was half an hour before breakfast-time when I returned to my cottage across the road from the hotel.

As I was about to take a chair on the tiny porch I perceived the sunlit figure of Miss Tevkin in the distance. She wore a large sailor hat and I thought it greatly enhanced the effect of her tall figure. She was making her way over a shaky little bridge. Then, reaching the road, she turned into it. I remained standing like one transfixed. The distance gave her new fascination. Every little while she would pause to look up through something that glittered in the sunshine, apparently an opera-glass. I had never heard that opera-glasses were used for observing birds, but this was evidently what she was doing at this moment, and the proceeding quickened my sense not only of her intellectual refinement, but also of her social distinction.

Presently she turned into a byway, passed the grove, and was lost to view

I seated myself, my eye on the spot where I had seen her disappear. Somebody greeted me from the hotel lawn. I returned the salutation mechanically and went on gazing at that spot. I knew that I was making a fool of myself, but I could not help it. My will-power was gone as it might from the effect of some drug

When she reappeared at last and I saw her coming back I crossed over to the hotel veranda so as to be near her when she should arrive. I found several of the boarders there, including the lawyer, the photographer, and a jewelry merchant of my acquaintance. We all watched her coming. At one moment, as she leveled her opera-glass at a bird, the lawyer said: "Studying birds. She's a great girl for studying. She is."

"Studying nothing!" the photographer jeered. "It's simply becoming to her.

It's effective, don't you know."

The lawyer smiled sagely, as if what Mendelson said was precisely what he himself had meant to intimate

I was inclined to think that Mendelson was right, but this did not detract from the force that drew me to Miss Tevkin

When she reached the veranda the lawyer gallantly offered her a chair, but she declined it, pleasantly, and went indoors. Her high heels had left deep, dear-cut imprints in a small patch of damp, sandy ground near the veranda.

This physical trace of her person fascinated me. It was a trace of stern hostility, yet I could not keep my eye away from it. I gazed and gazed at those foot-prints of hers till I seemed to be growing stupid and dizzy. "Am I losing my head?" I said to myself. "Am I obsessed? Why, I saw her yesterday for the first time and I have scarcely spoken to her. What the devil is the matter with me?"

After breakfast we returned to the veranda. The jewelry-dealer and the lawyer bored me unmercifully. Finally I was saved from them by the arrival of the Sunday papers, but my reading was soon disturbed by the intrusions of a mother and her marriageable daughter. There was no escape. I had to lay down my paper and let them torture me. There was a striking family resemblance between the two, yet the daughter was as homely as the mother was pretty. "She isn't as prepossessing as her ma, of course," the older woman seemed to be saying to me, "but she's charming, all the same, isn't she?"

Miss Lazar was watching me at a respectful distance. Mrs. Kalch was deep in a game of pinochle in a small ground-floor room that gave out on the veranda. The window was open and I could hear Mrs. Kalch's voice. She seemed to have been losing. The little room, by the way, was used both as a synagogue and a gambling-room. In the mornings, before breakfast, it was filled with old men in praying-shawls and phylacteries, while the rest of the day, until late at night, it was in the possession of card-players

I wanted to wire Bender to send a message to Fanny, in my name, stating that I had been unavoidably detained in the city, but I lacked the energy to do so. I had not even the energy to extricate myself from the attentions of the pretty mother of the homely girl

That charity meeting bothered me more than anything else. One was apt to impute my absence to meanness. I pictured Kaplan's disappointment, and I felt like going to Tannersville for his sake, if for no other reason. The next best thing would have been to have Bender wire my contribution to each of the two funds. But I did not stir

The hotel-keeper came out to remind me of my train

"Thank you," I said, with a smile. "But the weather is too confoundedly good. I'm too lazy to leave your place, Rivesman. You must have ordered this weather on purpose to detain me."

I was hoping, of course, that my presence in this hotel would be unknown to the Kaplans, for some time at least. Soon, however, something happened which made it inevitable that they should hear of it that very evening

On Sundays the Jewish summer hotels are usually visited by committees of various philanthropic institutions who go from place to place making speeches and collecting donations. One such committee appeared in the dining-room of the Rigi Kulm at the dinner-hour, which on Sundays was between 1 and 3. It represented a day nursery, an establishment where the children of the East Side poor are taken care of while their mothers are at work, and it consisted of two men, one of whom was an eloquent young rabbi.

As the ecclesiastic took his stand near the piano and began his appeal my heart sank within me. I had once met him at Kaplan's house, where he was a frequent visitor, and had given him a check. It goes without saying that I had to give him a contribution now and to talk to him. At this I learned, to my consternation, that he was going to Tannersville that very afternoon

"Shall I convey your regards?" he asked

"Very kind of you," I answered, and I added in an undertone, out of Mrs.

Kalch's hearing, "Please tell Mr. Kaplan I'm here on an important matter and that I have been detained longer than I expected."

When he had gone over to the next table I said to myself: "I don't care.

Come what may."

In the evening, as the crowd swarmed out of the dining-room, it was greeted by a gorgeous sunset. Everybody appreciated its beauty, but Miss Tevkin and Miss Siegel went into ecstasies over it, with something of the specialist in their exclamations. As for me, it was the first rich sunset I had seen since I crossed the ocean, and then I had scarcely known what it was. The play of color and light in the sky was a revelation to me. The edge of the sun, a vivid red, was peeping out of a gray patch of cloud that looked like a sack, the sack hanging with its mouth downward and the red disk slowly emerging from it. Spread directly underneath was a pool of molten gold into which the sun was seemingly about to drop. As the disk continued to glide out of the bag it gradually grew into a huge fiery ball of magnificent crimson, suffusing the valley with divine light. At the moment when it was just going to plunge into the golden pool the pool vanished. The crimson ball kept sinking until it was buried in a region of darkness. When the last fiery speck of it disappeared the sky broke into an evensong of color so solemn, so pensive that my wretched mood interpreted it as a visible dirge for the dead sun. Rose lapsed into purple, purple merged into blue, the blue bordering on a field of hammered gold that was changing shape and hue; all of which was eloquent of sadness. It seemed as though the heavens were in an ecstasy of grief and everybody about me were about to break into tears

some of the old women gasped. "How nice!" "Isn't it lovely?" said several girls

"Isn't that glorious?" said Miss Tevkin. "It's one of the most exquisite sunsets I have seen in a long time." And she referred to certain "effects," apparently in the work of a well-known landscape painter, which I did not understand

I discovered a note of consciousness in her rapture, something like a patronizing approval of the sky by one who looked at it with a professional eye. Nevertheless, I felt that my poor soul was cringing before her

An epigram occurred to me, something about the discrepancy between the spiritual quality of the sunset and the after-supper satisfaction of the onlookers. I essayed to express it, but was so embarrassed that I made a muddle of my English. Miss Tevkin took no notice of the remark

The sunset was transformed into a thousand lumps of pearl, here and there edged with flame. In some places the pearl thinned away, dissolving into the color of the sky, while the outline of the lump remained—a map of glowing tracery on a ground of the subtlest blue. Drifts of gold were gleaming, blazing, going out. A vast heap of silver caught fire. The outlined map disappeared, its place being taken by a raised one, with continents, islands, mountains, and seas of ravishing azure

What was the power behind this sublime spectacle? Where did it come from? What did it all mean? I visioned a chorus of angels. My heart was full of God, full of that stately girl, full of misery

"If I only got a chance to have a decent talk with her!" I said to myself again and again

# CHAPTER VI

IT was Monday afternoon. The week-end boarders and many others had left, and I was still idling my precious time away on the big veranda, listening to the gossip of women who bored me and trying to keep track of a girl who shunned me. My establishment in New York was feverishly busy and my presence was urgently needed there. It was more than probable that Bender had wired to Tannersville to call me home. The situation was extremely awkward.

Moreover, I was beginning to feel uneasy about certain payments that required my personal attendance.

It was a quiet, pleasant afternoon. The boarders were scattered over the various parts of the hotel and its surroundings. Twenty-four of them, forming two coach parties, had gone to see some celebrated Catskill views, one to the Old Mountain House and the other to East Windham. Some were in the village. Miss Tevkin, wearing her immense straw hat, and with her opera-glass in her hand, was looking at birds in the vicinity of the hotel.

Thus rambling about leisurely, she sauntered over to the main road near the grove. A few minutes later she turned into the same path where I had watched her disappear on the morning of the day before. And once more I saw her vanish there

I went out for a walk in the opposite direction. Soon, however, I turned back, strolling with studied aimlessness, toward that spot

What was my purpose? At first I did not know, but by little and little, as I moved along, an idea took shape in my brain: If I met her alone I might force her to listen to me and let her see the stuff I was made of. I lacked courage, however. While I was priming myself for the coup I wished that it would be postponed. I dawdled. There were swarms of strange insects on the road, creatures I had never seen before. At first I thought they were grasshoppers, but they were gray and had wings. Every now and then I would pause to watch them leap (or were they flying?) and drop to the ground again, becoming part of the dusty road. I followed them with genuine interest, yet all the time I kept working on the speech that I was going to deliver to Miss Tevkin

I was lingering at a spot a few yards from the grove on the opposite side of the main road when suddenly twilight fell over half of the valley. I raised my eyes. Behold! an inky cloud was crawling over the mountains, growing in size as it advanced. A flash of lightning snapped across the heavens. It was as though the sky screened a world of dazzling glory into which a glimpse had now been offered by a momentary crack in the screen. The flash was followed by a devout peal of thunder, as if a giant whose abode was in those dark clouds broke into a murmur of glorification at sight of the splendors above the sky. The trees shuddered, awe-stricken. I went under cover. A farmer was chasing a cow. As my eyes turned toward the grove they fell on Miss Tevkin, who was standing at the farther end of it, under its leafy roof, facing the main road. My heart beat fast. I dared not stir

A shower broke loose, a great, torrential downpour. It came in sheets, with an impetuous, though genial, clatter. It seemed as though the valley was swiftly filling with water and in less than an hour's time it would reach the tops of the trees. I thought of Noah's flood. I could almost see his dove winging her way over the waters. The storm had been in progress but seven or eight minutes when it came to an end. The sky broke into a smile again, as if it had all been a joke.

Miss Tevkin left the shelter of the trees and set out in the direction of the hotel. I do not know whether she was aware of my proximity

It was clearing beautifully, when a new cloud gathered. This time a great, stern force, violent, vengeful, came into play. A lash of fire smote the firmament with frantic suddenness, shattering it into a myriad of blinding sparks, yet leaving it uninjured. There was a pause and then came a ferocious crash. The universe was falling to pieces. Then somebody seemed to be tearing an inner heaven of metal as one tears a sheet of linen. This released a torrent that descended with the roar of Niagara, as though the metal vault that had just been rent asunder had been its prison. Miss Tevkin ran back to cover. The torrent slackened, settling down to a steady rain, spirited, zealous, amicable again

In a turmoil of agitation I crossed over to her. Instead, however, of beginning at the beginning of my well-prepared little speech, I blurted out something else

"You can't run away from me now," I said, with timid flippancy

"Please, leave me alone," she besought, turning away

I was literally stunned. Instead of trying to say what I had in my mind and to force her to listen, I slunk away, in the rain, like a beaten dog

The shock seemed to have a sobering effect on me. I suddenly realized the imbecility of the part I had been playing, even the humor of it. The first thing I did upon reaching the hotel was to ask the clerk about the next train—not to Tannersville, but direct to New York. Going to see Fanny was out of the question now

There was a late train connecting with a Hudson River boat and I took it

# CHAPTER VII

WHEN I got home and my business reasserted its multitudinous demands on my attention, the Catskill incident seemed to be fading into the character of a passing summer-resort episode, but I was mistaken; the pang it left in my heart persisted

A fortnight after my return to the city I forced myself to take a trip to Tannersville. Fanny came to meet me at the train. As we kissed it was borne in upon me that I was irretrievably estranged from her. I tried to play my part, with poor success

"Are you worried, Dave? What's the matter with you?" Fanny demanded again and again.

Her "What's the matter with you?" jarred on me

I offered her sundry excuses, but I did not even take pains to make them ring true

Finally she had a cry and I kissed her tears away. While doing so I worked myself into a mild fit of love, but my lips had scarcely released hers when it was again clear to me that she was not going to be my wife

Our engagement was broken shortly after the family came back to the city.

That burden lifted, it seemed as though the memory of my unfortunate acquaintance with Miss Tevkin had suddenly grown in clarity and painful acuteness

Our rush season had passed, but we were busy preparing for our removal to new quarters, on Fifth Avenue near Twenty-third Street. That locality had already become the center of the cloak-and-suit trade, being built up with new sky-scrapers, full of up-to-date cloak-factories, dress-factories, and ladies'-waist-factories. The sight of the celebrated Avenue swarming with Jewish mechanics out for their lunch hour or going home after a day's work was already a daily spectacle

The new aspect of that section of the proud thoroughfare marked the advent of the Russian Jew as the head of one of the largest industries in the United States. Also, it meant that as master of that industry he had made good, for in his hands it had increased a hundredfold, garments that had formerly reached only the few having been placed within the reach of the masses. Foreigners ourselves, and mostly unable to speak English, we had Americanized the system of providing clothes for the American woman of moderate or humble means. The ingenuity and unyielding tenacity of our managers, foremen, and operatives had introduced a thousand and one devices for making by machine garments that used to be considered possible only as the product of handwork. This—added to a vastly increased division of labor, the invention, at our instance, of all sorts of machinery for the manufacture of trimmings, and the enormous scale upon which production was carried on by us—had the effect of cheapening the better class of garments prodigiously. We had done away with prohibitive prices and greatly improved the popular taste. Indeed, the Russian Jew had made the average American girl a "tailor-made" girl.

When I learned the trade a cloak made of the cheapest satinette cost eighteen dollars. To-day nobody would wear it. One can now buy a whole suit made of all-wool material and silk-lined for fifteen dollars

What I have said of cloaks and suits applies also to skirts and dresses, the production of which is a branch of our trade. It was the Russian Jew who had introduced the factory-made gown, constantly perfecting it and reducing the cost of its production. The ready-made silk dress which the American woman of small means now buys for a few dollars is of the very latest style and as tasteful in its lines, color scheme, and trimming as a high-class designer can make it. A ten-dollar gown is copied from a hundred-dollar model.

Whereupon our gifted dress-designers are indefatigably at work on the problem of providing a good fit for almost any figure, with as little alteration as possible, and the results achieved in this direction are truly phenomenal. Nor is it mere apish copying. We make it our business to know how the American woman wants to look, what sort of lines she would like her figure to have. Many a time when I saw a well-dressed American woman in the street I followed her for blocks, scanning the make-up of her cloak, jacket, or suit. I never wearied of studying the trend of the American woman's taste. The subject had become a veritable idée fixé with me

The average American woman is the best-dressed average woman in the world, and the Russian Jew has had a good deal to do with making her one.

My Fifth Avenue establishment occupied four vast floors, the rent being thirty-eight thousand dollars a year. The office floor, which was elaborately furnished, had an immense waiting-room with gold letters on doors of dull glass bearing the legends: "General Offices," "Show-rooms," "Private Offices," "Salesmen. Please show samples of merchandise between 9 and 12 A.M.," and "Information." The "Private Office" door led to a secluded little kingdom with the inscription "David Levinsky" on one of its several doors, another door leading from my private office to the showrooms

I employed a large staff of trained bookkeepers, stenographers, clerks, and cloak models. These models were all American girls of Anglo-Saxon origin, since a young woman of other stock is not likely to be built on American lines—with the exception of Scandinavian and Irish girls, who have the American figure. But the figure alone was not enough, I thought. In selecting my model-girls, I preferred a good-looking face and good manners, and, if possible, good grammar. Experience had taught me that refinement in a model was helpful in making a sale, even in the case of the least refined of customers. Indeed, often it is even more effectual than a tempting complexion

My new place was the talk of the trade. Friends came to look it over. I received numerous letters of congratulation, from mill men, bankers, retail merchants, buyers, private friends. My range of acquaintance was very wide.

In hundreds of American cities and towns there were business people with whom my firm was in correspondence or whom I knew personally, who called me Dave and whom I called Jim, Jack, or Ned. So, many of these people, having received my circular describing my new place, sent their felicitations. Some of these letters were inspired by genuine admiration for my enterprise and energy. All of them had genuine admiration for my success. Success! Success!

Success! It was the almighty goddess of the hour. Thousands of new fortunes were advertising her gaudy splendors. Newspapers, magazines, and public speeches were full of her glory, and he who found favor in her eyes found favor in the eyes of man

Nodelman scarcely ever left my place during the first three days. He would show visitors over the four floors with a charming pride, like that of a mother. Among the things he exhibited was the stub-book of my first check account, a photograph of the rickety house where I had had my first shop, and letters of congratulation from some well-known financiers. Bender, with a big, shining bald disk on his head, slender and spruce as ever, was fussing around with the gruff air of an unappreciated genius, while Loeb, also bald-headed, but fat and beaming, was telling everybody about the scraps he and I used to have on the road when he was a star drummer and I a struggling beginner

One of the men who came to congratulate me at my magnificent new place on Fifth Avenue was the kindly American commission merchant who had been the first to grant me credit when I was badly in need of it. As I took him over my immense factory, splendid showrooms, and offices, we recalled the days when it took a man of special generosity to treat a beginning manufacturer of my type as he had treated me. That was the time when woolen-mills would even refuse to bother with a check of a Russian Jew; he had to bring cash.

In the rôle of manufacturer he was regarded as a joke. By hard work, perseverance, thrift, and ingenuity, however, we had completely changed all that. By the time I moved to the avenue our beginners could get any amount of credit. The American merchants dealing in raw material had gradually realized our energy, ability, and responsibility—realized that we were a good risk, while we, on our part, had assimilated the ways of the advanced American business man

Another man who came to see my new establishment was Eaton, the Philadelphia buyer who had given me my first lesson in table manners. He had a small, but well-established, business of his own now, and it was with my financial aid that he had founded it. Our friendship had never flagged. Sometimes I go to spend a day or two in his cozy little house in North Philadelphia, where I feel as much at home as I do in Bender's or Nodelman's house

I assigned one of my office men to the special duty of looking up and inviting Mr. Even, the kindly old man who had bought me my first American suit of clothes and paid for my first American bath. He came back with the report that Mr. Even had been dead for over four years. The news was a genuine shock to me. It was as though it had come from my birthplace and concerned the death of a half-forgotten relative. It stirred a swarm of memories; but, of course, impressions and moods of this kind do not last long. I received requests for donations from all sorts of East Side institutions and I responded liberally. Mindels, the handsome doctor, made me contribute twenty-five hundred dollars to a prospective hospital in which he expected to be one of the leading spirits

There was dining , and wining. I was being toasted, complimented, blessed

One of these dinners was given in my honor by my office employees, salesmen, designers, and foremen. Bender, who presided, told, in an elaborate and high-flown oration, of his experiences as my school-teacher, of our walks after school hours, and of our chance meeting a few years later

Loeb made a rough-and-ready speech, the gist of which was a joke on the bottle of milk which I had spilled while in the employ of Manheimer Brothers and which had led to my becoming a manufacturer. His concluding words were: "There's at least one saying that has come true. I mean the saying, 'There's no use crying over spilled milk.' Mr. Levinsky, you certainly have no reason to cry over the milk you spilled at Manheimer's, have you?"

I had heard the witticism from him more than once before. So had some of the other men present. Nevertheless, he now delivered it with gusto, and it was received with a hearty roar of merriment, in which his own laughter was the loudest

Among the people who came to rejoice in my success were some whose appearance was an amusing surprise to me. One of these was Octavius, the violinist, who had had nothing but contempt for me in the days when to go twenty-four hours without food was a usual experience with me. He had scarcely changed. He entered my office with bohemian self-importance

"Glad to see you, Levinsky. I was glad to hear of your rise in the world," he said, somewhat pompously. "I can't complain, either, though. However, our fields are so different."

The implication was that, while I had succeeded as a prosaic, pitiable cloak-manufacturer, he had conquered the world by the magic of his violin and compositions. He never referred to olden times. Instead, he boasted of his successes, present and future. The upshot of the interview was that I sent a check to the treasurer of the free conservatory of which Octavius was one of the founders

I was elated and happy, but there was a fly in the ointment of my happiness.

The question, "Who are you living for?" reverberated through the four vast floors of my factory, and the image of Miss Tevkin visited me again and again, marring my festive mood. My sense of triumph often clashed with a feeling of self-pity and yearning. The rebuff I had received at her hands in the afternoon of that storm lay like a mosquito in my soul

# BOOK XIII

# AT HER FATHER'S HOUSE

# CHAPTER I

I MADE it my business to visit a well-known Hebrew book-store on Canal Street. I asked for Tevkin's works. It appeared that before he emigrated to America he had published three small volumes of verse and prose, that they had once aroused much interest, but that they were now practically out of print. I tried two other stores, with the same result. I was referred to the Astor Library, whose Hebrew department was becoming one of the richest in the world. Sitting down in a public library to read a book seemed to be an undignified proceeding for a manufacturer to engage in, but my curiosity was beyond considerations of this sort. Whenever I thought of Miss Tevkin I beheld the image of those three books—the only things related to her with which I was able to come in contact

Finally, on a Saturday afternoon, I found myself at one of the green tables of Astor Library. I was reading poetry written in the holy tongue, a language I had not used for more than eighteen years

Two of Tevkin's three little volumes were made up of poetry, while the third consisted of brief essays, prose, poems, "meditations," and epigrams. I came across a "meditation" entitled "My Children," and took it up eagerly. It contained but three sentences: "My children love me, yet my heart is hungry. They are mine, yet they are strangers. I am homesick for them even when I clasp them to my bosom."

The next "meditation," on the same page, had the word "Poetry" for its head-line

"The children of Israel have been pent up in cities," it ran. "The stuffy synagogue has been field and forest to them. But then there is more beauty in a heaven visioned by a congregation of worshipers than in the bluest heaven sung by the minstrel of landscapes. They are not worshipers. They are poets. It is not God they are speaking to. It is a sublime image. It is not their Creator. It is their poetic creation."

Several of the poems were dedicated to Doctor Rachaeles, and of these one of two stanzas seemed to contain a timid allusion to Tevkin's love for his daughter. Here it is in prosaic English: "Saith Koheleth, the son of David: 'All the rivers run into the sea, yet the sea is not full.' Ah! the rivers are flowing and flowing, yet they are full as ever. And my lips are speaking and speaking, yet my heart is full as ever

"Behold! The brook is murmuring and murmuring, but I know not of what. My heart is yearning and yearning, and I know not of what. I cherish the murmur of the brook. I cherish the pang of my lonely heart."

The following lines, which were also dedicated to Doctor Rachaeles and which were entitled "Night," betray a similar mood, perhaps, without distinctly referring to the poet's yearnings

"Hush! the night is speaking. Each twinkle of a star is a word from the world beyond. It is the language of men who were once here, but are no more.

A thousand generations of departed souls are speaking to us in words of twinkling stars. I seem to be one of them. I hear my own ghost whispering to me: 'Alas!' it says, 'Alas!'"

The three volumes were full of Biblical quaintness, and my estrangement from the language only added to the bizarre effect of its terse grammatical construction. I read a number of the poems, and several of the things in the prose volume. His Hebrew is truly marvelous, and much of the strength and charm of his message is bound up in it. As I read his poetry or prose I seemed to be listening to Jeremiah or Isaiah. The rhythm of his lines is not the only thing that is lost in my translation. There is a prehistoric vigor and a mystic beauty to them which elude the English at my command. To be sure, every word I read in his three little volumes was tinged with the fact that the author was the father of the girl who had cast her spell over me.

But then the thought that she had grown up in the house of the man who had written these lines intensified the glow of her nimbus

As I returned the books to the official in charge of the Hebrew department I lingered to draw him into conversation. He was a well-known member of the East Side Bohème. I had heard of him as a man who spoke several languages and was amazingly well read—a walking library of knowledge, not only of books, but also of men and things. Accordingly, I hoped to extract from him some information about Tevkin. He was a portly man, with a round, youthful face and a baby smile. He smiled far more than he spoke. He answered my questions either by some laconic phrase or by leaving me for a minute and then returning with some book, pamphlet, or newspaper-clipping in which he pointed out a passage that was supposed to contain a reply to my query. I had quite a long talk with him. Now and then we were interrupted by some one asking for or returning a book, but each time he was released he readily gave me his attention again

Speaking of Tevkin, I inquired, "Why doesn't he write some more of those things?" For an answer he withdrew and soon came back with several issues of The Pen, a Hebrew weekly published in New York, in which he showed me an article by Tevkin

"Have you read it?" I asked

He nodded and smiled

"Is it good?"

"It isn't bad," he answered, with a smile

"Not as good as the things in those three volumes?"

He smiled

"This kind of thing doesn't pay, does it? How does he make a living?"

"I don't know. I understand he has several grown children."

"So they support the family?"

"I suppose so. I am not sure, though."

"Can't a Hebrew writer make a living in New York?"

He shook his head and smiled

The dailies of the Ghetto, the newspapers that can afford to pay, are published, not in the language of Isaiah and Job, but in Yiddish, the German dialect spoken by the Jewish masses of to-day. I asked the librarian whether Tevkin wrote for those papers, and he brought me several clippings containing some of Tevkin's Yiddish contributions. It appeared, however, that the articles he wrote in his living mother-tongue lacked the spirit and the charm that distinguished his style when he used the language of the prophets. Altogether, Tevkin seemed to be accounted one of the "has-beens" of the Ghetto

One of the bits of information I squeezed out of the librarian was that Tevkin was a passionate frequenter of Yampolsky's café, a well-known gathering-place of the East Side Bohème

I had heard a good deal about the resort. I knew that many or most of its patrons were Socialists or anarchists or some other kind of "ists." After my experience at the Cooper Institute meeting, Yampolsky's café seemed to be the last place in the world for me to visit. But I was drawn to it as a butterfly is to a flame, and finally the temptation got the better of me

.

# CHAPTER II

THE café was a spacious room of six corners and a lop-sided general appearance.

It was about 4 o'clock of an afternoon. I sat at the end of one of the tables, a glass of Russian tea before me. There were two other customers at that table, both poorly clad and, as it seemed to me, ill-fed. Two tables in a narrow and dingier part of the room were occupied by disheveled chess-players and three or four lookers-on. Altogether there were about fifteen people in the place. Some of the conversations were carried on aloud. A man with curly dark hair who was eating soup at the table directly in front of me was satirizing somebody between spoonfuls, relishing his acrimony as if it were spice to his soup. A feminine voice back of me was trying to prove to somebody that she did much more for her sister than her sister did for her. I was wretchedly ill at ease at first. I loathed myself for being here. I felt like one who had strayed into a disreputable den. In addition, I was in dread of being recognized. The man who sat by my side had the hair and the complexion of a gipsy. He looked exhausted and morose.

Presently he had a fried steak served him. It was heavily laden with onions.

As he fell to cutting and eating it hungrily the odor of the fried onions and the sound of his lips sickened me. The steak put him in good humor. He became sociable and turned out to be a gay, though a venomous, fellow. His small talk raised my spirits, too. Nor did anybody in the café seem to know who I was or to take any notice of me. I took a humorous view of the situation and had the gipsy-faced man tell me who was who

"Shall I begin with this great man?" he asked, facetiously, pointing his fork at himself. "I am the world-renowned translator and feuilleton writer whose writings have greatly increased the circulation of the Yiddish Tribune."

Under the guise of playful vanity he gave vent to a torrent of self-appreciation. He then named all the "other notables present"— a poet, a cartoonist, a budding playwright, a distinguished Russian revolutionist, an editor, and another newspaper man—maligning and deriding some of them and grudgingly praising the others. Much of what he said was lost upon me, for, although he knew that I was a rank outsider, he used a jargon of nicknames, catch-phrases, and allusions that was apparently peculiar to the East Side Bohème. He was part of that little world, and he was unable to put himself in the place of one who was not. I subsequently had occasion to read one of his articles and I found it full of the same jargon. The public did not understand him, but he either did not know it or did not care

As he did not point out Tevkin to me, I concluded that the Hebrew poet was not at the café

"Do you know Tevkin?" I inquired.

"There he is," he answered, directing my glance to a gray-haired, clean-shaven, commonplace-looking man of medium stature who stood in the chess corner, watching one of the games. "Do you know him?"

"No, but I have heard of him. You did not include him in your list of notables, did you?"

"Oh, well, he was a notable once upon a time. Our rule is, 'Let the dead past bury it's dead.'"

I felt sorry for poor Tevkin. Turning half-way around in my seat, I took to eying the Hebrew poet. I felt disappointed. That this prosaic-looking old man should have written the lines that I had read at the Astor Library seemed inconceivable. The fact, however, that he was the father of the tall, stately, beautiful girl whose image was ever before me ennobled his face

I stepped over to him and said: "You are Mr. Tevkin, aren't you? Allow me to introduce myself. Levinsky."

He bowed, grasping my hand, evidently loath to take his eyes off the chess-players

"I read some of your poems the other day," I added

"My poems?" he asked, coloring

"Yes; I had heard of them, and as I happened to be at the Astor Library I asked for your three volumes. I read several things in each of them. I liked them tremendously."

He blushed again. "It seems an age since they were written," he said, in confusion. "Those were different days."

We sat down at a secluded table. To propitiate the proprietor and the waiter I ordered hot cheese-cakes. I offered to order something for Tevkin, but he declined, and he ordered a glass of tea, with the tacit understanding that he was to pay for it himself

"Why don't you give us some more poems like those?"

He produced his business card, saying, "This is the kind of poetry that goes in America."

The card described him as a "general business agent and real-estate broker." This meant that he earned, or tried to earn, an income by acting as broker for people who wanted to sell or buy soda-and-cigarette stands, news-stands, laundries, grocery-stores, delicatessen-stores, butcher shops, cigar-stores, book-stores, and what not, from a peddier's push-cart to a "parcel" of real estate or an interest in a small factory. Scores of stores and stands change hands in the Ghetto every day, the purchaser being usually a workman who has saved up some money with an eye to business

"Does it pay?" I ventured to ask.

"I am not in it merely for the fun of it, am I?" he returned, somewhat resentfully. "Business is business and poetry is poetry. I hate to confound the two. One must make a living. Thank God, I know how to look things in the face. I am no dreamer. It is sweet to earn your livelihood."

"Of course it is. Still, dreaming is no crime, either."

"Ah, that's another kind of dreaming. Do you write?"

"Oh no," I said, with a laugh. "I am just a prosaic business man." And by way of showing that I was not, I veered the conversation back to his poetry.

I sought to impress him with a sense of my deep and critical appreciation of what I had read in his three volumes. I spoke enthusiastically of most of it, but took exception to the basic idea in a poem on Job and Solomon

"It's fine as poetry," I said. "Some lines in it are perfectly beautiful.

But the parallel is not convincing."

"Why not?" he said, bristling up.

We locked horns. He was pugnacious, bitter, but ineffectual. He quoted Hebrew, he spoke partly in Yiddish and partly in English; he repeatedly used the words "subjective" and "objective"; he dwelt on Job's "obvious tragedy" and Solomon's "inner sadness," but he was a poor talker and apparently displeased with his own argument

"Oh, I don't make myself clear," he said, in despair

"But you do," I reassured him. "I understand you perfectly."

"No, you don't. You're only saying it to please me. But then what matters it whether a business agent has a correct conception of Solomon's psychology or not?" he said, bitterly. "Seriously, Mr. Levinsky, I am often out of sorts with myself for hanging around this café. This is the gathering-place of talent, not of business agents."

"Why? Why?" I tried to console him. "I am sure you have more talent than all of them put together. Do you think anybody in this café could write verse or prose like yours?"

He looked down, his features hardening into a frown. "Anyhow, I cannot afford the time. While I loiter here I am liable to miss a customer. I must give myself entirely to my business, entirely, entirely—every bit of myself. I must forget I ever did any scribbling." "You are taking it too hard, Mr. Tevkin. One can attend to business and yet find time for writing."

All at once he brightened up bashfully and took to reciting a Hebrew poem.

Here is the essence of it: "Since the destruction of the Temple instrumental music has been forbidden in the synagogues. The Children of Israel are in mourning. They are in exile and in mourning. Silent is their harp. So is mine. I am in exile. I am in a strange land. My harp is silent." "Is it your poem?" I asked.

He nodded bashfully

"When did you compose it?"

"A few weeks ago."

"Has it been printed?" He shook his head

"Why?"

"I could have it printed in a Hebrew weekly we publish here, but—well, I did not care to."

"You mean The Pen?"

"Yes. Do you see it sometimes?"

"I did, once. I am going to subscribe for it. Anyhow, the poem belies itself. It shows that your harp has not fallen silent."

He smiled, flushed with satisfaction, like a shy schoolboy, and proceeded to recite another Hebrew poem: "Most song-birds do not sing in captivity. I was once a song-bird, but America is my cage. It is not my home. My song is gone."

"This poem, too, gives itself the lie!" I declared. "But the idea of America being likened to a prison!"

"It is of my soul I speak," he said, resentfully. "Russia did not imprison it, did it? Russia is a better country than America, anyhow, even if she is oppressed by a czar. It's a freer country, too—for the spirit, at least.

There is more poetry there, more music, more feeling, even if our people do suffer appalling persecution. The Russian people are really a warm-hearted people. Besides, one enjoys life in Russia better than here. Oh, a thousand times better. There is too much materialism here, too much hurry and too much prose, and—yes, too much machinery. It's all very well to make shoes or bread by machinery, but alas! the things of the spirit, too, seem to be machine-made in America. If my younger children were not so attached to this country and did not love it so, and if I could make a living in Russia now, I should be ready to go back at once."

"'Comfort ye, comfort ye, my people, saith your God,'" I quoted, gaily.

"It's all a matter of mood. Poets are men of moods." And again I quoted, "'Attend unto me, O my friend, and give ear unto me, O my comrade.'" I took up the cudgels for America

He listened gloomily, leaving my arguments unanswered. By way of broaching the subject of his daughter I steered my talk to a point that gave me a chance to refer to his little "meditation," "My Children." "How well you do remember my poor little volumes," he said, greatly flattered. "Yes, 'My children love me.' They are not children, but angels.

And yet—God save me from having to be supported by them. They bring in a considerable sum at the end of the week, and they hate to see me work or worry. But, oh, how sweet it is to earn one's own living! Thank God, I do earn my share and my wife's. My children are bitterly opposed to it. They beg me to stay home, but I say: 'No, children mine! As long as your father can earn his bread, his bread he will earn.' That's why my humdrum occupation is so sweet to me." At this he lowered his eyes and said, with the embarrassed simper which seemed to accompany every remark of his that implied self-appreciation, "I wrote something on this subject the other day, just a line or two: 'There are instances when the jewel of poetry glints out of the prose of trade.'"

The fact that his children contributed to the maintenance of the family nest was evidently a sore spot in his heart

His face, sensitive and mobile in the extreme, was like a cinematographic film. It recorded the subtlest change in his mood. The notion of its being a commonplace face seemed to me absurd now. It was a different image almost every minute, and my mental portrait of it was as unlike my first impression of it as a motion picture is unlike any of its component photographs

I parted from him without referring to his daughter, but I felt that I had won his heart, and it seemed to be a matter of days when he would invite me to his house

The next time I saw him, on an afternoon at Yampolsky's café again, there was an elusive deference in his demeanor. He seemed to me more reserved and ill at ease than he had been on the previous occasion. Finally he said, "I had no idea you were David Levinsky, the cloak-manufacturer."

My vanity was so flattered that I was unable to restrain my face from betraying it. I answered, with a beaming smile, "I told you I was in the cloak business, didn't I?"

"I don't think you did. Anyhow, I did not know what kind of a cloak-factory yours was," he said

"What kind do you mean?" I laughed.

"Well, I am glad to know you are so successful. There was somebody who recognized you last time you were here. Your secret leaked out."

"Secret! Well, what difference does it all make? To possess a talent like yours is a far greater success than to own a factory, even if mine were the largest in the world."

He waved his hand deprecatingly

Our conversation was disturbed by a quarrel between two men at a near-by table. I was at a loss to make out what it was all about. Tevkin attempted to enlighten me, but I listened to him only partly, being interested in the darts of the two belligerents. All I could gather was that they were story-writers of two opposing schools. I felt, however, that their hostility was based upon professional jealousy rather than upon a divergence of artistic ideals

Finally one of them paid his check and departed. Tevkin told me more about them. He spoke of the one who stayed in the café with admiration. "He's a real artist; some of his stories are perfect gems," he said. "He's a good fellow, too. Only he thinks too much of himself. But then perhaps this is an inevitable part of talent, the shadow that is inseparable from the light of genius."

"Perhaps it's the engine that sets it in motion, gives it incentive."

"Perhaps. I wish I had some of it." I reflected that he did seem to have some of "it." At all events, he did not seem to begrudge others their success. He spoke of the other people in the café with singular good-will, and even enthusiasm, in fact

Some of the people present I had seen on my previous visit. Of the others Tevkin pointed out a man to me who knew six languages well and had a working acquaintance with several more; another who had published an excellent Hebrew translation of some of the English poets, and a third whose son, a young violinist, "had taken Europe by storm."

An intellectual-looking Gentile made his entry. He shook hands with one of the men I had seen on the former occasion and seated himself by his side

"Either a journalist in search of material," Tevkin explained to me in answer to a question, "or simply a man of literary tastes who is drawn to the atmosphere of this place."

The café rose in my estimation

I learned from Tevkin that many of Yampolsky's patrons were poor working-men and that some of these were poets, writers of stories, or thinkers, but that the café was also frequented by some professional and business men. At this he directed my attention to a "Talmud-faced" man whom he described as a liquor-dealer who "would be a celebrated writer if he were not worth half a million." The last piece of information was a most agreeable surprise to me. It made me feel safe in the place. I regarded the liquor-dealer with some contempt, however. "Pshaw! half a million. He's probably worth a good deal less.

Anyhow, I could buy and sell him." At the same time I said to myself, "He's well-to-do and yet he chums around with people in whom intellectual Gentiles take an interest." I envied him. I felt cheap

I felt still cheaper when I heard that the literary liquor-dealer generously contributed to the maintenance of The Pen, the Hebrew weekly with which Tevkin was connected, and that he, the liquor-dealer, wrote for that publication

It appeared that Tevkin had an office which was a short distance from the bohemian café. I asked to see it, and he yielded reluctantly

"You can take it for granted that your office is a more imposing one than mine," he jested

"Ah, but there was a time when all my office amounted to was an old desk. So there will be a time when yours will occupy a splendid building on Wall Street."

"That's far more than I aspire to. All I want is to make a modest living, so that my daughters should not have to go to work. They don't work in a shop, of course. One is a stenographer in a fine office and the other a school-teacher. But what difference does it make?"

His office proved to be the hall bedroom of an apartment occupied by the family of a cantor named Wolpert. We first entered the dining-room, a door connecting it with Tevkin's "office" being wide open. It was late and the gas-light was burning. Seated at a large oval table, covered with a white oil-cloth, was Wolpert and two other men, all the three of them with full beards and with the stamp of intellectual life on their faces

"There are some queer people in the world who will still read my poetry," Tevkin said to them, by way of introducing me. "Here is one of them. Mr.

Levinsky, David Levinsky, the cloak-manufacturer."

The announcement made something of a stir.

Mrs. Wolpert brought us tea. From the ensuing conversation I gleaned that these people, including Tevkin, were ardent Zionists of a certain type, and that they were part of a group in which the poet was a ruling spirit. When I happened to drop a remark to the effect that Hebrew, the language of the Old Testament, was a dead language, Wolpert exclaimed: "Oh no! Not any longer, Mr. Levinsky. It has risen from the dead."

The other two chimed in, each in his way, the burden of their argument being that Hebrew was the living tongue of the Zionist colonists in Palestine

"The children of our colonists speak it as American children do English," said Tevkin, exultingly. "They speak it as the sons and daughters of Jerusalem spoke it at the time of the prophets. We are no dreamers. We can tell the difference between a dream and a hard fact, can't we?"—to the other two. "For centuries the tongue of our fathers spoke from the grave to us. Now, however, it has come to life again."

He took me into his "office," lighting the gas-jet in it. A few minutes later he shut the dining-room door, his face assuming an extremely grave mien

"By the way, an idea has occurred to me," he said. "But first I want you to know that I do not mean to profit by our spiritual friendship for purposes of a material nature. Do you believe me?"

"I certainly do. Go ahead, Mr. Tevkin."

"What I want to say is a pure matter of business. Do you understand? If you don't want to go into it, just say so, and we shall drop it."

"Of course," I answered

We were unable to look each other in the face.

"There is a parcel of real estate in Brooklyn," he resumed. "One could have it for a song."

"But I don't buy real estate," I replied, my cheeks on fire. He looked at the floor and, after a moment's silence, he said: "That's all. Excuse me. I don't want you to think I want to presume upon our acquaintance."

"But I don't. On the contrary, I wish it were in my line. I should be glad to—"

"That's all," he cut me short. "Let us say no more about it." And he made an awkward effort to talk Zionism again

# CHAPTER III

THE real-estate "boom" which had seized upon the five Ghettos of Greater New York a few years before was still intoxicating a certain element of their population. Small tradesmen of the slums, and even working-men, were investing their savings in houses and lots. Jewish carpenters, house-painters, bricklayers, or instalment peddlers became builders of tenements or frame dwellings, real-estate speculators. Deals were being closed, and poor men were making thousands of dollars in less time than it took them to drink the glass of tea or the plate of sorrel soup over which the transaction took place. Women, too, were ardently dabbling in real estate, and one of them was Mrs. Chaikin, the wife of my talented designer

Tevkin was not the first broker to offer me a "good thing" in real estate.

Attempts in that direction had been made before and I had warded them all off

Instinct told me not to let my attention be diverted from my regular business to what I considered a gamble. "Unreal estate," I would call it. My friend Nodelman was of the same opinion. "It's a poker game traveling under a false passport," was his way of putting it.

Once, as I sat in a Brooklyn street-car, I was accosted by a bewigged woman who occupied the next seat and whom I had never seen before

"You speak Yiddish, don't you?" she began, after scrutinizing me quite unceremoniously

"I do. Why?"

"I just wanted to know."

"Is that all?"

"Well, it is and it is not," she said, with a shrewd, good-natured smile.

"Since we are talking, I might as well ask you if you would not care to take a look at a couple of new houses in East New York."

I did not interrupt her and she proceeded to describe the houses and the bargain they represented

When she finally paused for my answer and I perpetrated a labored witticism about her "peddling real estate in street-cars" she flared up: "Why not? Is it anything to be ashamed of or to hide? Did I steal those houses? I can assure you I paid good money for them. So why should I be afraid to speak about them? And when I say it is a bargain, I mean it. That, too, I can say aloud and to everybody in the world, because it is the truth, the holy truth. May I not live to see my children again if it is not.

There!" After a pause she resumed: "Well?"

I made no reply

"Will you come along and see the houses? It is not far from here."

"I have no time."

She took up some details tending to show that by buying those two frame buildings of hers and selling them again I was sure to "clear" a profit of ten thousand dollars

I made no reply

"Well? Will you come along?"

"Leave me alone, please."

"Ah, you are angry, aren't you?" she said, sneeringly. "Is it because you haven't any money?"

The awkward scene that had attended Tevkin's attempt to get me interested in his parcel haunted me. I craved to see him again and to let him sell me something. To be sure, my chief motive was a desire to cultivate his friendship, to increase my chances of being invited to his house. The risk of buying some city lots in Brooklyn seemed to be a trifling price to pay for the prospect of coming into closer relations with him. Besides, the "parcel" seemed to be a sure investment. But I was also eager to do something for him for his own sake. And so I made an appointment with him by telephone and called at his wretched little office again

"Where is the parcel you mentioned the other day?" I began. "Where is it located?"

"Never mind that," he said, hotly. "There shall be no business between you and me. Nothing but pure spiritual friendship. I made a foolish mistake last time. I hate myself for it. If you were a smaller man financially I should not mind it, perhaps. As it is, it would simply mean that you help me out.

It would mean charity."

I laughed and argued and insisted, and he succumbed. We made an appointment to meet at Malbin's, a large restaurant on Grand Street that was known as the "Real Estate Exchange" of the Ghetto. There I was introduced to a plain-looking man who proved to be the then owner of the parcel, and closed a contract for a deed.

Encouraged by this transaction, Tevkin rapidly developed some far-reaching real-estate projects in which he apparently expected me to be the central figure. One afternoon as we sat over glasses of tea at Malbin's he said: "If you want to drink a glass of real Russian tea, come up some evening. We shall all be very glad to see you."

I felt the color mounting to my face as I said, "I don't think your daughter would like it."

"My daughter?" he asked, in amazement. "But I have three daughters."

"The one that spent some time at the Rigi Kulm in the Catskills last summer."

"Anna?" he asked, with still greater surprise, as it were

"I don't know her first name, but I suppose that's the one."

"If she was at the Rigi Kulm, it's Anna."

"Well, I had the pleasure of meeting her there, but I am afraid I was somewhat of a persona non grata with her," I said, in a partial attempt to make a joke of it

He dropped his glance, leveled it at me once more, and dropped it again

"Why, what was the matter?" he inquired, in great embarrassment

"Nothing was the matter. A case of dislike at first sight, I suppose."

"Still—"

"You'd better ask her, Mr. Tevkin." He made no reply, nor did he repeat his invitation. He was manifestly on pins and needles to get away, without having the courage to do so.

"So that's what you wanted to meet me for?" he muttered looking at the wall

"Well, I'll tell you frankly how it was, Mr. Tevkin," I said, and began with a partial lie calculated to bribe him: "I became interested in her because I heard that she was your daughter, and afterward, when I had returned to the city, I made it my business to go to the library and to read your works. My enthusiasm for your writings is genuine, however, I assure you, Mr. Tevkin.

And when I went to that café it was for the purpose of making your acquaintance, as much for your own sake as for hers. There, I have told you the whole story."

There was mixed satisfaction and perplexity in his look

The next morning my mail included a letter from him. It was penned in Hebrew. It read like a chapter of the Old Testament. He pointed out, with exquisite tact, that it was merely as a would-be courtier that I had failed to find favor in his daughter's eyes— something that is purely a matter of taste and chance. He then went on to intimate that if the unfortunate little situation rendered it at all inconvenient for me to visit his house he did not see why he and I could not continue our friendly relations

"If I have found as much grace in thine eyes as thou hast found in mine," he wrote, "it would pain me to forfeit thy friendship. Let the unpleasant incident be forgotten, then. I have a very important business proposition to make, but should it fail to arouse thine interest, why, then, let all business, too, be eliminated, and let our bond be one of unalloyed friendship. I have been hungry for a fellow-spirit for years and in thee I have found one at last. Shall I be estranged from thee for external causes?"

Whereupon he went into raptures over a prospective real-estate company of which he wanted me to be a leading shareholder. Companies or "combines" of this sort were then being formed on the East Side by the score and some of them were said to be reaping fabulous profits.

My Hebrew, which had never been perfect (for the Talmud is chiefly in Chaldaic and Aramaic), was by now quite out of gear. So my answer was framed partly in Yiddish, but mostly in English, the English being tacitly intended for his daughter, although he understood the language perfectly. I said, in substance, that I was going to be as frank as he was, that I did not propose to invest more money in real estate, and that I asked to be allowed to call on his daughter. The following passage was entirely in English: "I have made a misleading impression on Miss Tevkin. I have done myself a great injustice and I beg for a chance to repair the damage. In business I am said to know how to show my goods to their best advantage. Unfortunately, this instinct seems often to desert me in private life. There I am apt to put my least attractive wares in the show-window, to expose some unlovable trait of my character, while whatever good there may be in me eludes the eye of a superficial acquaintance.

"Please assure your daughter that it is not to force my attentions upon her that I am asking for an interview. All I want is to try to convince her that her image of me is, spiritually speaking, not a good likeness."

Two days passed. In the morning of the third I received a telephone-call from Tevkin, asking to meet me. Impelled by a desire to impress him with my importance, I invited him to my place of business. When he came I designedly kept him in my waiting-room for some minutes before I received him. When he was finally admitted to my private office he faced me with studied indifference. He said he had only a minute's time, yet he stayed nearly an hour. He asked me to come to his house. He spoke guardedly, giving vague answers to my questions. The best I could make of his explanation was that his daughter had been prejudiced against me by the fact that everybody at the Rigi Kulm had looked upon me as a great matrimonial "catch."

"My children have extremely modern ideas," he said. "Topsy-turvy ones." His face brightened, and he added: "The old rule is, 'Poverty is no disgrace.' Their rule is, 'Wealth is a disgrace.'" And he flushed and burst into a little laugh of approbation at his own epigram

"I suppose your daughter regarded me as a parvenu, an upstart, an ignoramus," I remarked

"No, not at all. She says she heard you say some clever things."

"Did she?"

"Still, your letter was a surprise to her. She had not thought you capable of writing such things."

What really had occurred between father and daughter concerning my desire to call I never learned

Tevkin's house was apparently full of Socialism. Indeed, so was the house of almost every intellectual family among our immigrants. I hated and dreaded that world as much as ever and I dreaded Miss Tevkin more than ever, but, moth-like, I was drawn to the flame with greater and greater force. I went to the Tevkins' with the feeling of one going to his doom

.

# CHAPTER IV

THE family occupied a large, old, private house in the Harlem section of Fifth Avenue, a locality swarming with our people. I called at 8 in the evening. It was in the latter part of March, nearly eight months after my unfortunate experience in the Catskills. I was received in the hall by Tevkin. He took me into a spacious parlor whose walls were lined with old book-cases and book-stands. There I found Anna and two of the other children of the numerous family. She wore a blouse of green velvet and a black four-in-hand tie. She welcomed me with a cordial handshake and a gay smile, as though all that had transpired between us had been a childish misunderstanding, but she was ill at ease. As for me, I was literally panic-stricken. It was at this moment, when I came face to face with her for the first time in the eight months following that Catskill incident, that I became aware of being definitely in love with her

The book-cases and book-stands were full to bursting. There was a piano in the room and two tables littered with books, prints, and photographs. The space between book-cases and over the piano was hung with etchings, crayons, pen-and-ink drawings, and photographs. The other two of Tevkin's children present were a chubby girl of twelve, named Gracie, and a young man of twenty-eight, two or three years older than Anna, named Sasha. Sasha had a half-interest in an evening preparatory school in which he taught mathematics, being now confined to the house by a slight indisposition

Mrs. Tevkin made her appearance—a handsome old woman of striking presence, tall, almost majestic, with a mass of white hair, with the beautiful features of the girl who was the cause of my being there. I thought of Naphtali. I had a desire to discover his address and to write him about my meeting with the hero and heroine of the romance of which he had told me a few months before I left Antomir. "I go to their house. She is still beautiful," I pictured myself saying to him. Her demeanor and the very intonation of her speech seemed to proclaim the fact that she was the daughter of that illustrious physician of Odessa. It did not take me long to discover, however, that under the surface of her good breeding and refinement was a woman of scant intellect

Seeing me look at the book-cases, she said: "These are not all the books we have. There are some in the other rooms, too. Plenty of them. It's quite a job for an American servant-girl to dust them."

Anna smiled good-humoredly

The next utterance of Mrs. Tevkin's was to the effect that one had to put up with crowded quarters in America—a hint at the better days which the family had seen in Russia

Anna's younger sister, Elsie, a school-teacher, came in. She had quicker movements and a sharper look than the stenographer and she bore strong resemblance to her father. Anna was the prettier of the two. We went down into the dining-room, where we found Russian tea, cake, and preserves.

Presently we were joined by George, an insurance-collector, who was between Anna and Sasha, and Emil, an artist employed on a Sunday paper, who was between Anna and Elsie. Emil was a handsome fellow with a picturesque face which betrayed his vocation. The crayons and the pen-and-ink drawings that I had seen in the library were his work. He had a pale, high forehead and a thick, upright grove of very soft, brown hair which I pictured as billowing in a breeze like a field of rye. "Just the kind of son for a poet to have," I thought

There was another son, Moissey. He was married and I did not see him that evening. His mother was continually referring to him

"I can see that you miss him," I said

"I should say so," Anna broke in. "He's her pet."

"Don't mind what she says, Mr. Levinsky," her mother exhorted me. "She just loves to tease me."

"Mother is right," Elsie interposed. "Moissey is not her pet. If somebody is, it's I, isn't it, ma?"

Anna smiled good-naturedly

"Gracie is my pet," Mrs. Tevkin rejoined

"Gracie and Moissey, both," Tevkin amended. "Moissey is her first-born, don't you know. But the great point is that he has been married only three months, and she has not yet got used to having him live somewhere else. She feels as if somebody had snatched him from her. When a day passes without her seeing him she is uneasy."

"Not at all," Mrs. Tevkin demurred. "I am thinking of him just now because—because—well, because we have all been introduced to Mr. Levinsky except him!"

"If two or three of the family were missing it wouldn't be so marked," Tevkin supported her, chivalrously. "But only one is missing, only one. That somehow makes you think of him. I feel the same way."

As he spoke it seemed to me that in his home atmosphere he bore himself with more self-confidence and repose than at the café or at his office. His hospitality had made him ill at ease at first, but that had worn off

"You can depend on father to find some defense for mother," remarked the picturesque Emil

At her husband's suggestion and after some urging the hostess led the way back to the parlor, or library, where she was to play us something. As we were passing out of the dining-room and up the stairs Tevkin seized the opportunity to say to me: "We live on the communistic principle, as you see. Each of us, except Mrs.

Tevkin and the little one contributes his earnings or part of them to the general treasury, my wife acting as treasurer and manager. Still, in the near future I hope to be able to turn the commune into a family of the good old type. My affairs are making headway, thank God. I sha'n't need my children's contributions much longer."

Mrs. Tevkin played some classical pieces. She had a pleasing tone and apparently felt at home at the keyboard, but it was to my eye rather than to my ear that her playing appealed. A white-haired Jewish woman at a piano was something which, in Antomir, had been associated in my mind with the life of the highest aristocracy exclusively. But then Mrs. Tevkin's father had been a physician, and Jewish physicians belonged, in the conception of my childhood and youth, to the highest social level. Another mark of her noble birth, according to my Antomir ideas, was the fact that she often addressed her husband and her older children, not in Yiddish or English, but in Russian. Compared to her, Matilda's mother was a plebeian

The only other person in the family who played the piano with facility and confidence was Emil.

I had never been in a house of this kind in my life. I was fascinated beyond expression

Anna's constraint soon wore off and she treated me with charming hospitality. So did Elsie. There was absolutely no difference in their manner toward me. Elsie gave me the attention which a girl usually accords to a close friend of her father's, and this was also the sort of attention I received from her older sister. It was as if the Catskill episode had never taken place and she were now seeing me for the first time

I met Moissey and his wife at my next visit. He was a man of thirty-two or more, tall, wiry, nervous, with large, protruding, dark eyes. He was "a dentist by profession and a Russian social democrat by religion," as his father introduced him to me

"Karl Marx is his god and Pleenanoff, the Russian socialist leader, is his Moses," the old man added

Moissey's wife looked strikingly Semitic. She seemed to have just stepped out of the Old Testament. She had been only about a year in the country, and the only language she could speak was Russian, which she enunciated without a trace of a Jewish accent or intonation. She scarcely understood Yiddish.

All this was uncannily at variance with her Biblical face. It seemed incredable that her speech and outward appearance should belong to the same person. To add to the discrepancy, she was smoking cigarette after cigarette, a performance certainly not in keeping with one's notion of a Jewish woman of the old type

The oldest two sons, Moissey and Sasha, spoke English with a Russian accent from which the English of all the other children was absolutely free. Mrs.

Tevkin's Russian sounded more Russian than her husband's. Emil, Elsie, and Gracie did not speak Russian at all

Barring Mrs. Tevkin, each adult in the family worshiped at the shrine of some "ism." Anna professed Israel Zangwill's modified Zionism or Territorialism. This, however, was merely a platonic interest with her. It took up little or none of her time. Her real passion was Minority, a struggling little magazine of "modernistic literature and thought." It was published by a group of radicals of which she was a member. Elsie, on the other hand, who was a socialist, was an ardent member of the Socialist party and of the Socialist Press Club. Politically the two sisters were supposed to be irreconcilable opponents, yet Anna often worked in the interests of Elsie's party. Indeed, the more I knew them the clearer it became to me that the older sister was under the influence of the younger

The two girls and their brothers had many visitors—socialist and anarchist writers, poets, critics, artists. These were of both sexes and some of them were Gentiles. Two of the most frequent callers were Miss Siegel and the sallow-faced, homely man who had danced with Anna at the Rigi Kulm pavilion.

He was an instructor in an art school From his talks with Emil and Anna I learned of a whole world whose existence I had never even suspected—the world of East Side art students, of the gifted boys among them, some of whom had gone to study in Paris, of their struggles, prospects, jealousies. I was introduced to several of these people, but I never came into sympathetic touch with them. I was ever conscious, never my real self in their midst.

Perhaps it was because they did not like me; perhaps it was because I failed to appreciate a certain something that was the key note to their mental attitude. However that may have been, I always felt wretched in their company, and my attempts at saying something out of the common usually missed fire

Was Anna interested in any of the young men who came to the house? I was inclined to think that she was not, but I was not sure

Among Elsie's closest friends or "comrades" was an American millionaire—a member of one of the best-known families in New York—and his wife, who was a Jewess, of whom I had read in the papers. I never saw them at the Tevkins', but I knew that they occasionally called on the school-teacher and that she saw a good deal of them at their house and at various meetings, a fact the discovery of which produced a disheartening impression on me. It was as though the sole advantage I enjoyed over Anna—the possession of money—suddenly had been wiped out

I sometimes wondered whether at the bottom of her heart Elsie did not feel elated by her close relations with that couple. That she herself was a stranger to all money interests there could be no doubt, however. And this was true of Anna and the other children. Elsie and Moissey were the strongest individualities in the family. Theirs were truly religious natures, and socialism was their religion in the purest sense of the term.

Elsie scarcely had any other great interest in life. Her socialism amused me, but her devotion to it inspired me with reverence. As for Moissey, good literature, as the term is understood in Russia, was nearly as much of a passion with him as Marxian socialism. His fervent talks of what he considered good fiction and his ferocious assaults upon what he termed "candy stories" were very impressive, though I did not always understand what he was talking about. Sometimes he would pick a quarrel with Anna over Minority and her literary hobbies generally. Once he brought her to tears by his attacks. I could not see why people should quarrel over mere stories. I thought Moissey crazy, but I must confess that his views on literature were not without influence upon my tastes. I did not do much reading in these days, so I may not have become aware of it at once. But at a later period, when I did do much reading, Moissey's opinions came back to me and I seemed to find myself in accord with them

To return to my visits at the Tevkins'. I told myself again and again that their world was not mine, that there was no hope for me, and that there was nothing for it but to discontinue my calls, but I had not the strength to do so. I never went away from this house otherwise than dejected and forlorn

Tevkin was charming in the fervent, yet tactful, hospitality with which he endeavored to assuage the bitterness of my visits. He seemed to say, "I see everything, my dear friend, and my heart goes out to you, but how can I help you?"

His wife tried to be diplomatic

"American young people imagine they own the earth," she once said to me, with a knowing glint in her beautiful eyes. "Some day they'll find out their mistake."

The hot months set in. The family nominally moved to Rockaway Beach for the season and my visits were suspended. Nominally, because Elsie and the boys and old Tevkin himself slept in the Harlem house more often than in their summer home. Elsie was wrapped up in the socialist campaign, which kept her busy every night from the middle of July to Election Day. She practically had no vacation. Anna made arrangements to spend her brief vacation with some of her literary friends who had a camp in Maine, but while she was in the city she came home to her mother and Gracie almost every evening. As for her father, whom I saw several times during that summer, he often sat up far into the night in Malbin's or some other restaurant, talking "parcels." He had become so absorbed in his real-estate speculations that he was rarely seen at Yampolsky's café these days. One evening, when he was dining with me at the private hotel in which I lived, and we were discussing his ventures, he said: "Do you know, my friend, I have made more than twelve thousand dollars?"

He tried to say it in a matter-of-fact, business-like way, but his face melted into an expression of joy before he finished the sentence.

"I tell it to you because I know that you are a real friend and that you will be sincerely glad to hear it," he went on

"I certainly am. I'm awfully glad," I rejoined, fervently

"I expect to make more. No more chipping in by the children! Anna shall give up her typewriting and Elsie her teaching. Yes, things are coming my way at last."

"Still, if I were you, I should go slow. The real-estate market is an uncertain thing, after all."

"Of course it is," he answered, mechanically

Since I bought that Brooklyn parcel and refused to go into further real-estate operations he had never approached me with business schemes again. There was not the slightest alloy of self-interest in his friendship, and he was careful not to have it appear that there was. He never initiated me into the details of his speculations, lest I should offer him a loan. He was quite squeamish about it

One day I offered him a hundred-dollar check for The Pen, the Hebrew weekly with which he was connected and upon which I knew him to spend more than he could afford

"I don't want it," he said, reddening and shaking his head

"Why?" I asked, also reddening

I was sorely hurt and he noticed it

"I know that you do it whole-heartedly," he hastened to explain, "but I don't want to feel that you do it for my sake."

"But I don't do it for your sake. I just want to help the paper. Can't I—" He interrupted me with assurances of his regard for me and for my motives, and accepted the check.

Was he dreaming of Anna ultimately agreeing to marry me— and my money? He certainly considered me a most desirable match. But I felt sure that he was fond of me on my personal account and that he would have liked to have me for his son-in-law even if my income had not exceeded three or four thousand dollars a year. He did not share the radical views of his children. He was much nearer to my point of view than they

# CHAPTER V

IT was December. There was an air of prosperity in Tevkin's house, but the girls would not give up their jobs. I was a frequent caller again. I was burning to take Anna, Elsie, and their parents to the theater, but was afraid the two girls would spurn the invitation

One day I was agreeably surprised by Elsie asking me to buy some tickets for a socialist ball. They were fifty cents apiece

"How many do you want me to take?" I asked

"As many as you can afford," she answered, roguishly

"Will you sell me twenty-five dollars' worth?"

"Oh, that would be lovely!" she said, in high glee

When I handed her the money I was on the brink of asking if it might not be rejected as "tainted," but suppressed the pleasantry

For me to attend a socialist ball would have meant to face a crowd of union men. It was out of the question. But the twenty-five dollars somehow brought me nearer to Elsie, and that meant to Anna also. I began to feel more at home in their company. Elsie was as dear as a sister to me. I went so far as to venture to invite them and their parents to the opera, and my invitation was accepted. I was still merely "a friend of father's," something like an uncle, but I saw a ray of hope now

"Suppose a commonplace business man like myself offered you a check for Minority," I once said to Anna.

"A check for Minority?" she echoed, with joyful surprise. "Well, it would be accepted with thanks, of course, but you would first have to withdraw the libel 'the commonplace business man.' Another condition is that you must promise to read the magazine." As I was making out the check I told her that I had read some issues of it and that I "solemnly swore" to read it regularly now. That I had found it an unqualified bore I omitted to announce.

Shortly after that opera night Tevkin provided a box at one of the Jewish theaters for a play by Jacob Gordin

I was quite chummy with the girls. They would jokingly call me "Mr.

Capitalist" and, despite their father's protests, "bleed" me for all sorts of contributions. One of these came near embroiling me with Moissey. It was for a revolutionary leader, a Jew, who had recently escaped from a Siberian prison in a barrel of cabbage and whose arrival in New York (by way of Japan and San Francisco) had been the great sensation of the year among the socialists of the East Side. The new-comer was the founder of a party of terrorists and had organized a plot which had resulted in the killing of an uncle of the Czar and of a prime minister. Now, Moissey, in his rabid, uncompromising way, sympathized with another party of Russian revolutionists, with one that was bitterly opposed to the theories and methods of the terrorists. So when he learned that Anna was collecting funds for the man who had been smuggled out of jail in a barrel, and that I had given her a check for him, he flared up and called her "busybody."

"You had better mind your own affairs, Moissey," she retorted, coloring

She essayed to defend her position, contending that the methods of the Russian Government rendered terrorism not only justifiable, but inevitable

"The question is not whether it is justifiable, but whether there is any sense to it," Moissey replied, sneeringly. "Revolutions are not made by plotting or bomb-throwing. They must take the form of an uprising by the masses."

"As if the Russian terrorists did not have the masses back of them! The peasantry and the educated classes are with them."

"How do you know they are?" Moissey asked, with a good-natured, but patronizing, smile

He spoke of the Russian working class as the great element that was destined to work out the political and economic salvation of the country, and at this he tactlessly dwelt on the Russian trade-unions, on what he termed their revolutionary strikes, and upon the aid Russian capitalists gave the Government in its crusade upon the struggle for liberty

I felt quite awkward. I wondered whether he was not saying these things designedly to punish me for the check I had given Anna for the terrorists.

He had always seemed to hold aloof from me, as if he were opposed to the visits of the "money-bag" that I was at his father's house. At this minute I felt as though his eyes said, "The idea of this fleecer of labor contributing to the struggle for liberty!"

I was burning to tell him that he lacked manners, and to assail trade-unionism, but I restrained myself, of course

Sometimes the girls and I would discuss the social question or literature, subjects upon which they assured me that I held "naïve" views. But all my efforts to get Anna into a more intimate conversation failed. For all our familiarity, it seemed as if we held our conversations through a thick window-pane. Nevertheless, in a very vague way, and for no particular reason that I was aware of, I thought that I sensed encouragement

Tevkin never again approached me with his real-estate ventures, but the very air of his house these days was full of such ventures. I met other real-estate men at his home. Their talk was tempting. my enormous income notwithstanding. Huge fortunes seemed to be growing like mushrooms all over the five Ghettos of New York and Brooklyn. I saw men who three years ago had not been worth a cent and who were now buying and selling blocks of property. How much they were actually worth was a question which in the excitement of the "boom" did not seem to matter. It is never a rare incident among our people for a man with a nebulous fortune of a few hundred dollars to plunge into a commercial undertaking involving many thousands; but during that period this was an every-day affair. At first I treated it like something that was going on in another country. But I had a good deal of uninvested money and my resistance was slackening.

At last I succumbed

One of the men I met at Tevkin's was Volodsky, the old-time street peddler, the man of the beautiful teeth whose push-cart had adjoined mine in those gloomy days when I tried to sell goods in the streets, and who had told me of the dower-money which his sister had lent him for his journey to America.

I had not seen him since then—an interval of over twenty years—and we recognized each other with some difficulty

The real-estate boom had found him eking out a wretched livelihood by selling goods on the instalment plan. Most of his business had been in the Italian quarter and he had learned to speak Italian far more fluently than he had English. A short time before I stumbled upon him at the Tevkins' he had built an enormous block of high, brick apartment-houses in Harlem. He had gone into the undertaking with only five thousand dollars of his own, and before the houses were half completed he had sold them all, pocketing an enormous profit. When we were peddlers together he had been considered a failure and a fool. He now struck me as a clever fellow, full of dash.

Nor did Volodsky represent the only metamorphosis of this kind that I came across. It was as though there were something in the atmosphere which turned paupers into capitalists and inane milksops into men of brains and pluck.

Volodsky succeeded in luring me into a network of speculations

Tevkin had an interest in some of these operations, and, as they were mostly concerned with property in Harlem or in the Bronx, his house became my real-estate headquarters. There were two classes of callers at his home now: the socialists and the literary men or artists who visited Tevkin's children and the "real-estate crowd" who came to see Tevkin himself. It came to be tacitly understood that the library was to be left to the former, while the dining-room, in the basement, was used as Tevkin's office. Being "a friend of the family," I had the freedom of both

"You're making a big mistake, Levinsky," Nodelman once said to me, with a gesture of deep concern. "What is biting you? Aren't you making money fast enough? Mark my word, if you try to swallow too fast you'll choke. Any doctor will tell you that."

I urged him to join me, but he would not hear of it. Instead, he exhorted me to sell out my holdings and give all my attention to my cloak business

"Take pity on your hard-earned pennies, Levinsky," he would say. "Else you'll wake up some day like the fellow who has dreamed he has found a treasure. He's holding on to the treasure tight, and when he opens his eyes he finds it's nothing but a handful of wind."

"I'll tell you what, Levinsky," he began on one occasion. "You ought to see some of those magician fellows."

"What for?" I asked

"Did you ever see them at their game? They'll put an egg into a hat; say, 'One, two, three,' and pull out a chicken. And then they say, 'One, two, three,' again and there's neither a chicken nor an egg. That's the way all this real-estate racket will end. Mark my word, Levinsky."

Bender nagged and pleaded with me without let-up. If I had had the remotest doubt of his devotion to me it would have been dispelled now. I was at my great mahogany desk every morning, as usual, but I seldom stayed more than two hours, and even during those two hours my mind was divided between cloaks and real estate or between cloaks and Anna. Bender was practically in full charge of the business. Instead, however, of welcoming the power it gave him, he made unrelenting efforts to restore things to their former state. He was constantly haranguing me on the risks I was incurring, beseeching me to drop my new ventures, and threatening to leave me unless I did so. Once, as he was thus expostulating with me, he broke down

"I appeal to you as your friend, as your old-time teacher," he said, and burst into tears

If it had not been for him I should have neglected my cloak business beyond repair. He handled me as a gambler's wife does her husband. He would seek me out in front of some unfinished building, at Tevkin's, or at some "boom" café, and make me sign some checks, consult me on something or other, or wheedle me into accompanying him to my factory for an hour or two. But the next day he would have to go hunting for me again

I had invested considerable money in my new affairs, and releasing it at short notice would not have been an easy matter. But the great point was that I was literally intoxicated by my new interests, and the fact that they were intimately associated with the atmosphere of Anna's home had much—perhaps everything—to do with it

I loved her to insanity. She was the supreme desire of my being. I knew that she was weaker in character and mind than Elsie, for example, but that seemed to be a point in her favor rather than against her. "She is a good girl," I would muse, "mild, kindly, girlish. As for her 'radical' notions, they really don't matter much. I could easily knock them out of her. I should be happy with her. Oh, how happy!" And, in spite of the fact that I thought her weak, the sight of her would fill me with awe.

One's first love is said to be the most passionate love of which one is capable. I do not think it is. I think my feeling for Anna was stronger, deeper, more tender, and more overpowering than either of my previous two infatuations. But then, of course, there is no way of measuring and comparing things of this kind. Anna was the first virgin I had ever loved.

Was that responsible for the particular depth of my feeling? "Oh, I must have her or I'll fall to pieces," I would say to myself, yearning and groaning and whining like a lunatic

My gambling mania was really the aberration of a love-maddened brain. How could Bender or Nodelman understand it? I found myself in the midst of other lunatics, of men who had simply been knocked out of balance by the suddenness of their gains. My money had come slowly and through work and worry. Theirs had dropped from the sky. So they could scarcely believe their senses that it was not all a dream. They were hysterical with gleeful amazement; they were in a delirium of ecstasy over themselves; and at the same time they looked as though they were tempted to feel their own faces and hands to make sure that they were real

One evening I saw a man whose family was still living on fifteen dollars a week lose more than six hundred dollars in poker and then take a group of congenial spirits out for a spree that cost him a few hundred dollars more.

One man in this party, who was said to be worth three-quarters of a million, had only recently worked as a common brick-layer. He is fixed in my memory by his struggles to live up to his new position, more especially by the efforts he would make to break himself of certain habits of speech. He always seemed to be on his guard lest some coarse word or phrase should escape him, and when a foul expression eluded his vigilance he would give a start, as if he had broken something. There was often a wistful look in his eye, as if he wondered whether his wealth and new mode of living were not merely a cruel practical joke. Or was he yearning for the simpler and more natural life which he had led until two years ago? We had many an expensive meal together, and often, as he ate, he would say: "Oh, it's all nonsense, Mr. Levinsky. All this fussy stuff does not come up to one spoon of my wife's cabbage soup."

Once he said: "Do you really like champagne? I don't. You may say I am a common, ignorant fellow, but to me it doesn't come up to the bread cider mother used to make. Honest." And he gave a chuckle

I knew a man who bought a thousand-dollar fur coat and a full-dress suit before he had learned to use a handkerchief. He always had one in his pocket, but he would handle it gingerly, as if he had not the heart to soil it, and then he would carefully fold it again. The effect money had on this man was of quite another nature than it was in the case of the bricklayer.

It had made him boisterously arrogant, blusteringly disdainful of his intellectual superiors, and brazenly foul-mouthed. It was as though he was shouting: "I don't have to fear or respect anybody now! I have got a lot of money. I can do as I damn please." More than one pure man became dissolute in the riot of easily gotten wealth. A real-estate speculator once hinted to me, in a fit of drunken confidence, that his wife, hitherto a good woman and a simple home body, had gone astray through the new vistas of life that had suddenly been flung open to her. One fellow who was naturally truthful was rapidly becoming a liar through the practice of exaggerating his profits and expenditures. There was an abundance of side-splitting comedy in the things I saw about me, but there was no dearth of pathos, either. One day, as I entered a certain high-class restaurant on Broadway, I saw at one of the tables a man who looked strikingly familiar to me, but whom I was at first unable to locate. Presently I recognized him. Three or four years before he had peddled apples among the employees of my cloak-shop. He had then been literally in tatters. That was why I was now slow to connect his former image with his present surroundings. I had heard of his windfall. He had had a job as watchman at houses in process of construction. While there he had noticed things, overheard conversations, put two and two together, and finally made fifty thousand dollars in a few months as a real-estate broker

We were furtively eying each other. Finally our eyes met. He greeted me with a respectful nod and then his face broke into a good-humored smile. He moved over to my table and told me his story in detail. He spoke in brief, pithy sentences, revealing a remarkable understanding of the world. In conclusion he said, with a sigh: "But what is the good of it all? The Upper One has blessed me with one hand, but He has punished me with the other."

It appeared that his wife had died, in Austria, just when she was about to come to join him and he was preparing to surprise her with what, to her, would have been a palatial apartment

"For six years I tried to bring her over, but could not manage it," he said, simply. "I barely made enough to feed one mouth. When good luck came at last, she died. She was a good woman, but I never gave her a day's happiness. For eighteen years she shared my poverty. And now, that there is something better to share, she is gone."

# CHAPTER VI

ONE of the many Jewish immigrants who were drawn into the whirl of real-estate speculation was Max Margolis, Dora's husband. I had heard his name in connection with some deals, and one afternoon in February we found ourselves side by side in a crowd of other "boomers." The scene was the corner of Fifth Avenue and One Hundred and Sixteenth Street, two blocks from Tevkin's residence, a spot that usually swarmed with Yiddish-speaking real-estate speculators in those days. It was a gesticulating, jabbering, whispering, excited throng, resembling the crowd of curb-brokers on Broad Street. Hence the nickname "The Curb" by which that corner was getting to be known

I was talking to Tevkin when somebody slapped me on the back

"Hello, Levinsky! Hello!"

"Margolis!"

His face had the florid hue of worn, nervous, middle age. "I heard you were buying. Is it true? Well, how goes it, great man?"

"How have you been?"

"Can't kick. Of course, compared to a big fellow like David Levinsky, I am a fly."

I excused myself to Tevkin and took Margolis to the quieter side of the Avenue

"Glad to see you, upon my word," he said. "Well, let bygones by bygones.

It's about time we forgot it all."

"There is nothing to forget."

"Honest?"

"Honest! Is that idiotic notion still sticking in your brain?"

"Why, no. Not at all. May I not live till to-morrow if it does. You are not angry at me, are you? Come, now, say that you are not."

I smiled and shrugged my shoulders

"Well, shake hands, then."

We did and he offered to sell me a "parcel." As I did not care for it, he went on to talk of the real-estate market in general. There was a restaurant on that side of the block—The Curb Café we used to call it—so we went in, ordered something, and he continued to talk. He was plainly striving to sound me, in the hope of "hanging on" to some of my deals. Of a sudden he said: "Say, you must think I'm still jealous? May I not live till to-morrow if I am." And to prove that he was not he added: "Come, Levinsky, come up to the house and let's be friends again, as we used to be. I have always wished you well." He gave me his address. "Will you come?"

"Some day."

"You aren't still angry at Dora, are you?"

"Why, no. But then she may be still angry at me," I said, indifferently

"Nonsense. Perhaps it is beneath your dignity to call on small people like us? Come, forget that you are a great capitalist and let us all spend an evening together as we used to." Was he ready to suppress his jealousy for the prospect of getting under my financial wing? The answer to this question came to me through a most unexpected channel

The next morning, when I came to my Fifth Avenue office (it was some eighty blocks—about four miles—downtown from "The Curb" section of Fifth Avenue), I found Dora waiting for me. I recognized her the moment I entered the waiting-room on my office floor. Her hair was almost white and she had grown rather fleshy, but her face had not changed. She wore a large, becoming hat and was quite neatly dressed generally

The blood surged to my face. Her presence was a bewildering surprise to me

There were three other people in the room and I had to be on my guard

"How are you?" I said, rushing over to her

She stood up and we shook hands. I took her into my private office through my private corridor.

"Dora! Well, well!" I murmured in a delirium of embarrassment

"I have come to tell you not to mind Margolis and not to call at the house," she said, gravely, looking me full in the face. "It would be awful if you did. He is out of his mind. He is—"

"Wait a minute, Dora," I interrupted her. "There'll be plenty of time to talk of that. First tell me something about yourself. How have you been? How are the children?" She was like an old song that had once held me under its sway, but which now appealed to me as a memory only. I was conscious of my consuming passion for Anna. Dora interested and annoyed me at once

I treated her as a dear old friend. She, however, persisted in wearing a mask of politeness, as if she had come strictly on business arid there had never been any other relations between us

"Everybody is all right, thank you," she answered

"Is Lucy married?"

"Oh, she has a beautiful little girl of two years. But I do want to tell you about Margolis. The man is simply crazy, and I want to warn you not to take him seriously. Above all, don't let him take you up to the house. Not for anything in the world. That's what brings me here this morning."

"Why? What's the trouble?"

"Oh, it would take too long to tell," she answered. "And it isn't important, either. The main thing is that you should not let him get into business relations with you, or into any other kind of relations, for that matter."

Her English was a striking improvement upon what it had been sixteen years before. As we continued to talk it became evident to me that she was a well-read, well-informed woman. I made some efforts to break her reserve, but they failed. Nor, indeed, was I over-anxious to have them succeed. She did speak of her husband's jealousy, however (though she dropped her glance and slurred over the word as she did so); and from what she said, as well as by reading between the lines of her statement, I gathered a fairly clear picture of the situation. Echoes of Max's old jealousy would still make themselves felt in his domestic life. A clash, an irritation, would sometimes bring my name to his lips. He still, sometimes, tortured her with questions concerning our relations

"I never answer these questions of his," she said, her eyes on my office rug. "Not a word. I just let him talk. But sometimes I feel like putting an end to my life," she concluded, with a smile

I listened with expressions of surprise and sympathy and with a feeling of compunction. A thought was sluggishly trailing through my mind: "Does she still care for me?"

Margolis had built up some sort of auction business, but his real-estate mania had ruined it and eaten up all he had except three thousand dollars, which Dora had contrived to save from the wreck. With this she had bought a cigar-and-stationery store on Washington Heights by means of which she now supported the family. He spent his days and evenings hanging around real-estate haunts as a penniless drunkard does around liquor-shops. He was always importuning Dora for "a couple of hundred dollars" for a "sure thing." This was often the cause of an altercation. Quarrels had, in fact, never been such a frequent occurrence in the house as they had been since he lost his money in real estate, and one of his favorite thrusts in the course of these brawls was to allude to me

"If Levinsky asked you for money you would not refuse him, would you?" he would taunt her

Now, that he had met me at "The Curb," he had taken it into his head that his jealousy had worn off long since and that he had the best of feelings for me. His heart was set upon regaining my friendship. He had spoken to her of our meeting as a "predestined thing" that was to result in my "letting him in" on some of my deals. Dora, however, felt sure that a renewal of our acquaintance would only rekindle the worst forms of his jealousy and make life impossible to her. She dreaded to imagine it

We spoke of Lucy again. It was so stirring to think of her as a mother. Dora told me that Lucy's husband was in the jewelry business and quite well-to-do

She rose to go. I escorted her, continuing to question her about Lucy, Dannie, her husband. It would have been natural for me to take her out by way of my private little corridor, but I preferred to pilot her through my luxurious show-rooms. We found two customers there to whom some of my office men and a designer were showing our "line." I greeted the customers, and, turning to Dora again, I asked her to finish an interrupted remark. We paused by one of the windows. What she was saying about Lucy was beginning to puzzle me. She did not seem to be pleased with her daughter's marriage

"She has three servants and a machine," she said, with a peculiar smile.

"She wanted it and she got what she wanted."

"Why?" I said, perplexed

"Everything is all right," she answered, with another smile

We spoke in an undertone, so that nobody could overhear us. The fact, however, that we were no longer alone had the effect of relieving our constraint. Dora unbent somewhat. A certain note of intimacy that had been lacking in our talk while we were by ourselves stole into it now that we were in the presence of other people

In the course of our love-affair she had often spoken to me of her determination not to let Lucy repeat her mistake, not to let her marry otherwise than a man she loved. We were both thinking of it at this minute, and it seemed to be tacitly understood between us that we were

At last I ventured to ask: "What's the trouble, Dora: Tell me all about it.

It interests me very much."

"I don't know whether there's anything to tell," she answered, coloring slightly. "She says she cares for her husband, and they really get along very well. He certainly worships her. Why shouldn't he? She is so beautiful—a regular flower—and he is old enough to be her father."

"You don't say!" I ejaculated, with genuine distress

"She is satisfied."

"Are you?"

"As if it mattered whether I was or not. I had other ideas about her happiness, but I am only a mother and was not even born in this country. So what does my opinion amount to? I begged her not to break my heart, but she would have her automobile."

"Perhaps she does love him."

She shook her head ruefully. "She was quite frank about it. She called it being practical. She thought my idea weren't American, that I was a dreamer.

She talked that way ever since she was eighteen, in fact. 'I don't care if I marry a man with white hair, provided he can make a nice living for me,' she used to say. I thought it would drive me mad. And the girls she went with had the same ideas. When they got together it would be, 'This girl married a fellow who's worth a hundred thousand,' and, 'That girl goes with a fellow who's worth half a million.' If that's what they learn at college, what's the use going to college?"

"It's prosperity ideas," I suggested. "It's a temporary craze."

"I don't care what it is. A girl should be a girl. She ought to think of love, of real happiness." (Her glance seemed to be the least bit unsteady.) "But I ain't 'practical,' don't you know. Exactly what my mother—peace upon her [this in Hebrew]—used to say. She, too, did not think it was necessary to be in love with the man you marry. But then she did not go to college, not even to school. Of what good is education, then?"

It was evident that she spoke from an overflowing heart, and that she could speak for hours on the subject. But she cut herself short and took another tack

"You must not think her husband is a kike, though," she said. "He is no fool and he writes a pretty good English letter. And he is a very nice man."

She started to go

"Tell me some more about Dannie," I said, on our way to the elevator

"He's going to college. Always first or second in his class. And one of the best men on the football team, too." She smiled, the first radiant smile I had seen on her that morning

"He's all right," she continued. And in Yiddish, "He is my only consolation." And again in English, "If it wasn't for him life wouldn't be worth living. Good-by," she said, as we paused in front of the elevator door. "Don't forget what I told you." She was ill at ease again

The elevator came down from the upper floors. We shook hands and she entered it. It sank out of sight. I stood still for a second and then returned to my private office with a sense of relief and sadness. My heart was full of love for Anna

# CHAPTER VII

IN a vague, timid way I had been planning to propose to Anna all along. My meeting with Dora gave these plans shape. Her unexpected visit revived in my mind the whole history of my acquaintance with her. I said to myself: "It was through tenacity and persistence that I won her. It was persistence, too, that gave me success in business. Anna is a meek, good-natured girl.

She has far less backbone than Dora. I can win her, and I will." It seemed so convincing. It was like a discovery. It aroused the fighting blood in my veins. I was throbbing with love and determination. I was priming myself for a formal proposal. I expected to take her by storm. I was only waiting for an opportunity. In case she said no, I was prepared for a long and vigorous campaign. "I won't give her up. She shall be mine, whether she wants it or not," I said to myself again and again. These soliloquies would go on in my mind at all hours and in all kinds of circumstances—while I was pushing my way through a crowded street-car, while I was listening to some of Bender's scoldings, while I was parleying with some real-estate man over a piece of property. They often made me so absent-minded that I would pace the floor of my hotel room, for instance, with one foot socked and the other bare, and then distressedly search for the other sock, which was in my hand. One morning as I sat at my mahogany desk in my office, with the telephone receiver to my ear, waiting to be connected with a banker, I said to myself: "Women like a man with a strong will. My very persistence will fascinate her." And this, too, seemed like a discovery to me. The banker answered my call. It was an important matter, yet all the while I spoke or listened to him I was conscious of having hit upon an invincible argument in support of my hope that Anna would be mine

At last I thought I saw my opportunity. It was an evening in April.

According to the Jewish calendar it was the first Passover night, when Israel's liberation from the bondage of Egypt is commemorated by a feast and family reunion which form the greatest event in the domestic life of our people

Two years before, when I was engaged to Fanny, I deeply regretted not being able to spend the great evening at her father's table. This time I was an invited guest at the Tevkins'. They were not a religious family by any means. Tevkin had been a free-thinker since his early manhood, and his wife, the daughter of the Jewish Ingersoll, had been born and bred in an atmosphere of aggressive atheism. And so religious faith never had been known in their house. Of late years, however—that is, since Tevkin had espoused the cause of Zionism or nationalism—he had insisted on the Passover feast every year. He contended that to him it was not a religious ceremony, but merely a "national custom," but about this his children were beginning to have their doubts. It seemed to them that the older their father grew the less sure he was of his free thought. They suspected that he was getting timid about it, fearful of the hereafter. As a rule, they saw only the humorous side of the change that was apparently coming over him, but sometimes they would awaken to the pathos of it

As we all sat in the library, waiting to be called to the great feast, he delivered himself of a witticism at the expense of the prospective ceremony

"You needn't take his atheism seriously, Mr. Levinsky," said Anna, the sound of my name on her lips sending a thrill of delight through me. "'Way down at the bottom of his heart father is getting to be really religious, I'm afraid." And, as though taking pity on him, she crossed over to where he sat and nestled up to him in a manner that put a choking sensation into my throat and filled me with an impulse to embrace them both

At last the signal was given and we filed down into the dining-room. A long table, flanked by two rows of chairs, with a sofa, instead of the usual arm-chair, at its head, was set with bottles of wine, bottles of mead, wine-glasses, and little piles of matzos (thin, flat cakes of unleavened bread). The sofa was cushioned with two huge Russian pillows, inclosed in fresh white cases, for the master of the house to lean on, in commemoration of the freedom and ease which came to the Children of Israel upon their deliverance from Egypt. Placed on three covered matzos, within easy reach of the master, were a shank bone, an egg, some horseradish, salt water, and a mush made of nuts and wine. These were symbols, the shank bone being a memorial of the pascal lamb, and the egg of the other sacrifices brought during the festival in ancient times, while the horseradish and the salt water represented the bitter work that the Sons of Israel had to do for Pharaoh, and the mush the lime and mortar from which they made brick for him. A small book lay in front of each seat. That was the Story of the Deliverance, in the ancient Hebrew text, accompanied by an English translation

Moissey, the uncompromising atheist and Internationalist, was demonstratively absent, much to the distress of his mother and resentment of his father. His Biblical-looking wife was at the table. So were Elsie and Emil. They were as uncompromising in their atheism as Moissey, but they had consented to attend the quaint supper to please their parents. As to Anna, Sasha, and George, each of them had his or her socialism "diluted" with some species of nationalism, so they were here as a matter of principle, their theory being that the Passover feast was one of the things that emphasized the unity of the Jews of all countries. But even they, and even Tevkin himself, treated it all partly as a joke. In the case of the poet, however, it was quite obvious that his levity was pretended. For all his jesting and frivolity, he looked nervous. I could almost see the memories of his childhood days which the scene evoked in his mind. I could feel the solemnity that swelled his heart. It appeared that this time he had decided to add to the ceremony certain features which he had foregone on the previous few Passover festivals he had observed. He was now bent upon having a Passover feast service precisely like the one he had seen his father conduct, not omitting even the white shroud which his father had worn on the occasion. As a consequence, several of these details were a novel sight to his children. A white shroud lay ready for him on his sofa, and as he slipped it on, with smiles and blushes, there was an outburst of mirth

"Oh, daddy!" Anna shouted

"Father looks like a Catholic priest," said Emil

"Don't say that, Emil," I rebuked him

Fun was made of the big white pillows upon which Tevkin leaned, "king-like," and of the piece of unleavened bread which he "hid" under them for Gracie to "steal."

As he raised the first of the Four Cups of wine he said, solemnly, with an effort of shaking off all pretense of flippancy: "Well, let us raise our glasses. Let us drink the First Cup."

We all did so, and he added, "This is the Fourth of July of our unhappy people." After the glasses were drained and refilled he said: "Scenes like this bind us to the Jews of the whole world, and not only to those living, but to the past generations as well. This is no time for speaking of the Christian religion, but as I look at this wine an idea strikes me which I cannot help submitting: The Christians drink wine, imagining that it is the blood of Jesus. Well, the wine we are drinking to-night reminds me of the martyr blood of our massacred brethren of all ages."

Anna gave me a merry wink. I felt myself one of the family. I was in the seventh heaven. She seemed to be particularly attentive to me this evening

"I shall speak to her to-night," I decided. "I sha'n't wait another day." And the fact that she was a nationalist and not an unqualified socialist, like Elsie, for instance, seemed to me a new source of encouragement. I was in a quiver of blissful excitement

The Four Questions are usually asked by the youngest son, but Emil, the Internationalist, could not be expected to take an active part in the ceremony, so Sasha, the Zionist, took his place. Sasha, however, did not read Hebrew, and old Tevkin had to be content with having the Four Questions read in English, the general answer to them being given by Tevkin and myself in Hebrew. It reminded me of an operatic performance in which the part of Faust, for instance, is sung in French, while that of Margarita is performed in some other language. We went on with the Story of the Deliverance. Tevkin made frequent pauses to explain and comment upon the text, often with a burst of oratory. Mrs. Tevkin and some of the children were obviously bored.

Gracie pleaded hunger

Finally the end of the first part of the story was reached and supper was served. It was a typical Passover supper, with matzo balls, and it was an excellent repast. Everybody was talkative and gay. I addressed some remarks to Anna, and she received them all cordially

By way of attesting her recognition of Passover as a "national holiday" she was in festive array, wearing her newest dress, a garment of blue taffeta embroidered in old rose, with a crêpe collar of gray. It mellowed the glow of her healthful pink complexion. She was the most beautiful creature at the table, excluding neither her picturesque younger brother nor her majestic old mother. She shone. She flooded my soul with ecstasy

Tevkin's religion was Judaism, Zionism. Mine was Anna. The second half of the story is usually read with less pomp and circumstance than the first, many a passage in it being often skipped altogether. So Tevkin dismissed us all, remaining alone at the table to chant the three final ballads, which he had characterized to his children as "charming bits of folk-lore."

When Mrs. Tevkin, the children, and myself were mounting the stairs leading up from the dining-room, I was by Anna's side, my nerves as taut as those of a soldier waiting for the command to charge. I charged sooner than I expected.

"Sasha asked the Four Questions," I found myself saying. "There is one question which I should like to ask of you, Miss Tevkin."

I said it so simply and at a moment so little suited to a proposal of marriage that the trend of my words was lost upon her

"Something about Jewish nationalism?" she asked

"About that and about something else."

We were passing through the hallway now. When we entered the library I took her into a corner, and before we were seated I said: "Well, my question has really nothing to do with nationalism. It's quite another thing I want to ask of you. Don't refuse me. Marry me. Make me happy."

She listened like one stunned

"I am terribly in love with you," I added

"Oh!" she then exclaimed. Her delicate pink skin became a fiery red. She looked down and shook her head with confused stiffness.

"I see you're taken aback. Take a seat; get your bearings," I said, lightly, pulling up a chair that stood near by, "and say, 'Yes.'"

"Why, that's impossible!" she said, with an awkward smile, without seating herself. "I need not tell you that I have long since changed my mind about you—"

"I am no more repellent, am I?" I jested

"No. Not at all," she returned, with another smile. "But what you say is quite another thing. I am very sorry, indeed." She made to move away from me, but I checked her

"That does not discourage me," I said. "I'll just go on loving you and waiting for a favorable answer. You are still unjust to me. You don't know me well enough. Anyhow, I can't give you up. I won't give you up. ("That's it," I thought. "I am speaking like a man of firm purpose.") "I am resolved to win you."

"Oh, that's entirely out of the question," she said, with a gesture of impatience and finality. And, bursting into tears of child-like indignation, she added: "Father assured me you would never hint at such a thing—never.

If you mean to persist, then—"

The sentence was left eloquently unfinished. She turned away, walked over to her mother and took a seat by her side, like a little girl mutely seeking her mamma's protection

The room seemed to be in a whirl. I felt the cold perspiration break out on my forehead. I was conscious of Mrs. Tevkin's and Elsie's glances. I was sick at heart. Anna's bitter resentment was a black surprise to me. I had a crushing sense of final defeat

# BOOK XIV

# EPISODES OF A LONELY LIFE

# CHAPTER I

IT was a severe blow. It caused me indescribable suffering. It would not have been unnatural to attribute my fiasco to my age. Had I been ten years younger, Anna's attitude toward me might have been different. But this point of view I loathed to accept. Instead, I put the blame on Anna's environment.

"I was in the 'enemy's country' there," I would muse. "The atmosphere around her was against me." I hated the socialists with a novel venom. Finally I pulled myself together. Then it was that I discovered the real condition of my affairs. I had gone into those speculations far deeper than I could afford. There were indications that made me seriously uneasy. Things were even worse than Bender imagined. Ruin stared me in the face. I was panic-stricken. One day I had the head of a large woolen concern lunch with me in a private dining-room of a well-known hotel. He was dignifiedly steel-gray and he had the appearance of a college professor or successful physician rather than of a business man. He liked me. I had long been one of his most important customers and I had always sought to build up a good record with him. For example: other cloak-manufacturers would exact allowances for merchandise that proved to have some imperfection. I never do so. It is the rule of my house never to put in a claim for such things. In the majority of cases the goods can be cut so as to avoid any loss of material, and if it cannot, I will sustain the small loss rather than incur the mill's disfavor. In the long run it pays. And so this cloth merchant was well disposed toward me. He had done me some favors before. He addressed me as Dave. (There was a note of condescension as well as of admiration in this "Dave" of his. It implied that I was a shrewd fellow and an excellent customer, singularly successful and reliable, but that I was his inferior, all the same—a Jew, a social pariah. At the bottom of my heart I considered myself his superior, finding an amusing discrepancy between his professorial face and the crudity of his intellectual interests; but he was a Gentile, and an American, and a much wealthier man than I, so I looked up to him.) To make my appeal as effective as possible I initiated him into the human side of my troubles. I told him of my unfortunate courtship as well as of the real-estate ventures into which it had led me

He was interested and moved, and, as he had confidence in me, he granted my request at once.

"It's all right, Dave," he said, slapping my back, a queer look in his eye.

"You can always count on me. Only throw that girl out of your mind."

I grasped his hand silently. I wanted to say something, but the words stuck in my throat. He helped me out of my difficulties and I devoted myself to the cloak business with fresh energy. The agonies of my love for Anna were more persistent than those I had suffered after I moved out of Dora's house.

But, somehow, instead of interfering with my business activities, these agonies stimulated them. I was like the victim of a toothache who seeks relief in hard work. I toiled day and night, entering into the minutest detail of the business and performing duties that were ordinarily left to some inferior employee.

Business was good. Things went humming. Bender, who now had an interest in my factory, was happy

Some time later the same woolen man who had come to my assistance did me another good turn, one that brought me a rich harvest of profits. A certain weave was in great vogue that season, the demand far exceeding the output, and it so happened that the mill of the man with the professorial face was one of the very few that produced that fabric. So he let me have a much larger supply of it than any other cloak-manufacturer in the country was able to obtain. My business then took a great leap, while my overhead expenses remained the same. My net profits exceeded two hundred thousand dollars that year

One afternoon in the summer of the same year, as I walked along Broadway in the vicinity of Canal Street, my attention was attracted by a shabby, white-haired, feeble-looking old peddler, with a wide, sneering mouth, who seemed disquietingly familiar and in whom I gradually recognized one of my Antomir teachers—one of those who used to punish me for the sins of their other pupils. The past suddenly sprang into life with detailed, colorful vividness. The black pit of poverty in which I had been raised; my misery at school, where I had been treated as an outcast and a scapegoat because my mother could not afford even the few pennies that were charged for my tuition; the joy of my childish existence in spite of that gloom and martyrdom—all this rose from the dead before me

The poor old peddler I now saw trying to cross Broadway was Shmerl the Pincher, the man with whom my mother had a pinching and hair-pulling duel after she found the marks of his cruelty on my young body. He had been one of the most heartless of my tormentors, yet it was so thrillingly sweet to see him in New York! In my schooldays I would dream of becoming a rich and influential man and wreaking vengeance upon my brutal teachers, more especially upon Shmerl the Pincher and "the Cossack," the man whose little daughter, Sarah-Leah, had been the heroine of my first romance. I now rushed after Shmerl, greatly excited, one of the feelings in my heart being a keen desire to help him

A tangle of wagons and trolley-cars caused me some delay. I stood gazing at him restively as he picked his weary way. I had known him as a young man, although to my childish eye he had looked old—a strong fellow, probably of twenty-eight, with jet-black side-whiskers and beard, with bright, black eyes and alert movements. At the time I saw him on Broadway he must have been about sixty, but he looked much older

As I was thus waiting impatiently for the cars to start so that I could cross the street and greet him, a cold, practical voice whispered to me: "Why court trouble? Leave him alone."

My exaltation was gone. The spell was broken.

The block was presently relieved, but I did not stir. Instead of crossing the street and accosting the old man, I stood still, following him with my eyes until he vanished from view. Then I resumed my walk up Broadway. As I trudged along, a feeling of compunction took hold of me. By way of defending myself before my conscience, I tried to think of the unmerited beatings he used to give me. But it was of no avail. The idea of avenging myself on this decrepit, tattered old peddler for what he had done more than thirty years before made me feel small. "Poor devil! I must help him," I said to myself.

I was conscious of a desire to go back and to try to overtake him; but I did not. The desire was a meandering, sluggish sort of feeling. The spell was broken irretrievably

# CHAPTER II

THE following winter chance brought me together with Matilda. On this occasion our meeting was of a pleasanter nature than the one which had taken place at Cooper Institute. It was in a Jewish theater. She and another woman, accompanied by four men, one of whom was Matilda's husband, were occupying a box adjoining one in which were the Chaikins and myself and from which it was separated by a low partition. The performance was given for the benefit of a society in which Mrs. Chaikin was an active member, and it was she who had made me pay for the box and solemnly promise to attend the performance. Not that I maintained a snobbish attitude toward the Jewish stage. I went to see Yiddish plays quite often, in fact, but these were all of the better class (our stage has made considerable headway), whereas the one that had been selected by Mrs. Chaikin's society was of the "historical-opera" variety, a hodge-podge of "tear-wringing" vaudeville and "laughter-compelling" high tragedy. I should have bought ten boxes of Mrs.

Chaikin if she had only let me stay away from the performance, but her heart was set upon showing me off to the other members of the organization, and I had to come

It was on a Monday evening. As I entered the box my eyes met Matilda's and, contrary to my will, I bowed to her. To my surprise, she acknowledged my salutation heartily

The curtain rose. Men in velvet tunics and plumed hats were saying something, but I was more conscious of Matilda's proximity and of her cordial recognition of my nod than of what was going on on the stage.

Presently a young man and a girl entered our box and occupied two of our vacant chairs. Mrs. Chaikin thought they had been invited by me, and when she discovered that they had not there was a suppressed row, she calling upon them to leave the box and they nonchalantly refusing to stir from their seats, pleading that they meant to stay only as long as there was no one else to occupy them. Our box was beginning to attract attention. There were angry outcries of "'S-sh!" "Shut up!" Matilda looked at me sympathetically and we exchanged smiles. Finally an usher came into our box and the two intruders were ejected

When the curtain had dropped on the first act Matilda invited me into her box. When I entered it she introduced me to her husband and her other companions as "a fellow-townsman" of hers

Seen at close range, her husband looked much younger than she, but it did not take me long to discover that he was wrapped up in her. His beard was smaller and more neatly trimmed than it had looked at the Cooper Institute meeting, but it still ill became him. He had an unsophisticated smile, which I thought suggestive of a man playing on a flute and which emphasized the discrepancy between his weak face and his reputation for pluck

An intermission in a Jewish theater is almost as long as an act. During the first few minutes of our chat Matilda never alluded to Antomir nor to what had happened between us at Cooper Institute. She made merry over the advertisements on the curtain and over the story of the play explaining that the box had been forced on one of her companions and that they had all come to see what "historic opera" was like. She commented upon the musicians, who were playing a Jewish melody, and on some of the scenes that were being enacted in the big auditorium. The crowd was buzzing and smiling good-humoredly, with a general air of family-like sociability, some eating apple or candy. The faces of some of the men were much in need of a shave.

Most of the women were in shirt-waists. Altogether the audience reminded one of a crowd at a picnic. A boy tottering under the weight of a basket laden with candy and fruit was singing his wares. A pretty young woman stood in the center aisle near the second row of seats, her head thrown back, her eyes fixed on the first balcony, her plump body swaying and swaggering to the music. One man, seated in a box across the theater from us, was trying to sneak to somebody in the box above ours. We could not hear what he said, but his mimicry was eloquent enough. Holding out a box of candy, he was facetiously offering to shoot some of its contents into the mouth of the person he was addressing. One woman, in an orchestra seat near our box, was discussing the play with a woman in front of her. She could be heard all over the theater. She was in ecstasies over the prima donna

"I tell you she can kill a person with her singing," she said, admiringly.

"She tugs me by the heart and makes it melt. I never felt so heartbroken in my life. May she live long."

This was the first opportunity I had had to take a good look at Matilda since she had come to New York; for our first meeting had been so brief and so embarrassing to me that I had come away from it without a clear impression of her appearance

At first I found it difficult to look her in the face. The passionate kisses I had given her twenty-three years before seemed to be staring me out of countenance. She, however, was perfectly unconstrained and smiled and laughed with contagious exuberance. As we chatted I now and again grew absent-minded, indulging in a mental comparison between the woman who was talking to me and the one who had made me embrace her and so cruelly trifled with my passion shortly before she raised the money for my journey to America. The change that the years had wrought in her appearance was striking, and yet it was the same Matilda. Her brown eyes were still sparkingly full of life and her mouth retained the sensuous expression of her youth. This and her abrupt gestures gave her provocative charm

Nevertheless, she left me calm. It was an indescribable pleasure to be with her, but my love for her was as dead as were the days when I lodged in a synagogue. She never alluded to those days. To listen to her, one would have thought that we had been seeing a great deal of each other all along, and that small talk was the most natural kind of conversation for us to carry on

All at once, and quite irrelevantly, she said: "I am awfully glad to see you again. I did not treat you properly that time—at the meeting, I mean.

Afterward I was very sorry."

"Were you?" I asked, flippantly.

"I wanted to write you, to ask you to come to see me, but—well, you know how it is. Tell me something about yourself. At this minute the twenty-three years seem like twenty-three weeks. But this is no time to talk about it.

One wants hours, not a minute or two. I know, of course, that you are a rich man. Are you a happy man? But, no, don't answer now. The curtain will soon rise. Go back to your box, and come in again after the next act. Will you?"

She ordered me about as she had done during my stay at her mother's house, which offended and pleased me at once. During the whole of the second act I looked at the stage without seeing or hearing anything. The time when I fell in love with Matilda sprang into life again. It really seemed as though the twenty-three years were twenty-three weeks. My mother's death, her funeral; Abner's Court; the uniformed old furrier with the side-whiskers, his wife with her crutches; Naphtali with his curly hair and near-sighted eyes; Reb Sender, his wife, the bully of the old synagogue; Matilda's mother, and her old servant—all the hinnan figures and things that filled the eventful last two years of my life at home loomed up with striking vividness before me

Matilda's affable greeting and her intimate brief talk were a surprise to me. Did I appeal to her as the fellow who had once kissed her? Had she always remembered me with a gleam of romantic interest? Did I stir her merely as she stirred me—as a living fragment of her past? Or was she trying to cultivate me in the professional interests of her husband, who was practising medicine in Harlem? When the curtain had fallen again Matilda made her husband change seats with me. I was to stay by her side through the rest of the performance. The partition between the two boxes being only waist-high, the two parties were practically joined into one and everybody was satisfied—everybody except Mrs. Chaikin

"I suppose our company isn't good enough for Mr. Levinsky," she said, aloud

When the performance was over we all went to Lorber's— the most pretentious restaurant on the East Side. Matilda and I were mostly left to ourselves. We talked of our native town and of her pious mother, who had died a few years before, but we carefully avoided the few weeks which I had spent in her mother's house, when Matilda had encouraged my embraces. In answer to my questions she told me something of her own and her husband's revolutionary exploits. She spoke boastfully and yet reluctantly of these things, as if it were a sacrilege to discuss them with a man who was, after all, a "money-bag."

My impression was that they lived very modestly and that they were more interested in their socialist affairs than in their income. My theory that she wanted her husband to profit by her acquaintance with me seemed to be exploded. She reminded me of Elsie and her whole-hearted devotion to socialism. We mostly spoke in Yiddish, and our Antomir enunciation was like a bond of kinship between us, and yet I felt that she spoke to me in the patronizing, didactical way which one adopts with a foreigner, as though the world to which she belonged was one whose interests were beyond my comprehension

She inquired about my early struggles and subsequent successes. I told her of the studies I had pursued before I went into business, of the English classics I had read, and of my acquaintance with Spencer

"Do you remember what you told me about becoming an educated man?" I said, eagerly. "Your words were always ringing in my ears. It was owing to them that I studied for admission to college. I was crazy to be a college man, but fate ordained otherwise. To this day I regret it."

In dwelling on my successes I felt that I was too effusive and emphatic; but I went on bragging in spite of myself. I tried to correct the impression I was making on her by boasting of the sums I had given to charity, but this made me feel smaller than ever. However, my talk did not seem to arouse any criticism in her mind. She listened to me as she might to the tale of a child

Referring to my uumarried state, she said, with unfeigned sympathy: "This is really no life. You ought to get married." And she added, gaily, "If you ever marry, you mustn't neglect to invite me to the wedding."

"I certainly won't; you may be sure of that," I said

"You must come to see me. I'll call you up on the telephone some day and we'll arrange it."

"I shall be very glad, indeed."

I departed in a queer state of mind. Her present identity failed to touch a romantic chord in my heart. She was simply a memory, like Dora. But as a memory she had rekindled some of the old yearning in me. I was still in love with Anna, but at this moment

I was in love both with her and with the Matilda of twenty-three years before. But this intense feeling for Matilda as a monument of my past self did not last two days

The invitation she had promised to telephone never came

I came across a man whom I used to see at the Tevkins', and one of the things he told me was that Anna had recently married a high-school teacher

.

# CHAPTER III

THE real estate boom collapsed. The cause of the catastrophe lay in the nature, or rather in the unnaturalness, of the "get-rich-quick" epidemic.

Its immediate cause, however, was a series of rent strikes inspired and engineered by the Jewish socialists through their Yiddish daily. One of the many artificialities of the situation had been a progressive inflation of rent values. Houses had been continually changing hands, being bought, not as a permanent investment, but for speculation, whereupon each successive purchaser would raise rents as a means of increasing the market price of his temporary property. And so the socialists had organized a crusade that filled the municipal courts with dispossess cases and turned the boom into a panic

Hundreds of people who had become rich overnight now became worse than penniless overnight. The Ghetto was full of dethroned "kings for a day only." It seemed as if it all really had been a dream

One of the men whose quickly made little fortune burst like a bubble was poor Tevkin. I wondered how his children took the socialist rent strikes

Nor did I escape uninjured when the crisis broke loose. I still had a considerable sum in real estate, all my efforts to extricate it having proved futile. My holdings were rapidly depreciating. In hundreds of cases similar to mine equities were wiped out through the speculators' inability to pay interest on mortgages or even taxes. To be sure, things did not come to such a pass in my case, but then some of the city lots or improved property in which I was interested had been hit so hard as to be no longer worth the mortgages on them

Volodsky lost almost everything except his courage and speculative spirit

"Oh, it will come back," he once said to me, speaking of the boom

When I urged that it had been an unnatural growth he retorted that it was the collapse of the boom which was unnatural. He was scheming some sort of syndicate again

"It requires no money to make a lot of money," he said. "All it does require is brains and some good luck."

Nevertheless, he coveted some of my money for his new scheme. He did not succeed with me, but he found other "angels." He was now quite in his element in the American atmosphere of breathless enterprise and breakneck speed. When the violence of the crisis had quieted down building operations were resumed on a more natural basis. Men like Volodsky, with hosts of carpenters, bricklayers, plumbers—all Russian or Galician Jews—continued to build up the Bronx, Washington Heights, and several sections of Brooklyn.

Vast areas of meadowland and rock were turned by them, as by a magic wand, into densely populated avenues and streets of brick and mortar. Under the spell of their activity cities larger than Odessa sprang up within the confines of Greater New York in the course of three or four years

Mrs. Chaikin came out of her speculations more than safe. She and her husband, who is still in my employ, own half a dozen tenement-houses. One day, on the first of the month, I met her in the street with a large hand-bag and a dignified mien. She was out collecting rent

# CHAPTER IV

IT was the spring of 1910. The twenty-fifth anniversary of my coming to America was drawing near. The day of an immigrant's arrival in his new home is like a birthday to him. Indeed, it is more apt to claim his attention and to warm his heart than his real birthday. Some of our immigrants do not even know their birthday. But they all know the day when they came to America. It is Landing Day with red capital letters. This, at any rate, is the case with me. The day upon which I was born often passes without my being aware of it.

The day when I landed in Hoboken, on the other hand, never arrives without my being fully conscious of the place it occupies in the calendar of my life. Is it because I do not remember myself coming into the world, while I do remember my arrival in America? However that may be, the advent of that day invariably puts me in a sentimental mood which I never experience on the day of my birth

It was 1910, then, and the twenty-fifth anniversary of my coming was near at hand. Thoughts of the past filled me with mixed joy and sadness. I was overcome with a desire to celebrate the day. But with whom? Usually this is done by "ship brothers," as East-Siders call fellow-immigrants who arrive here on the same boat. It came back to me that I had such a ship brother, and that it was Gitelson. Poor Gitelson! He was still working at his trade.

I had not seen him for years, but I had heard of him from time to time, and I knew that he was employed by a ladies' tailor at custom work somewhere in Brooklyn. (The custom-tailoring shop he had once started for himself had proved a failure.) Also, I knew how to reach a brother-in-law of his. The upshot was that I made an appointment with Gitelson for him to be at my office on the great day at 12 o'clock. I did so without specifying the object of the meeting, but I expected that he would know

Finally the day arrived. It was a few minutes to 12. I was alone in my private office, all in a fidget, as if the meeting I was expecting were a love-tryst. Reminiscences and reflections were flitting incoherently through my mind. Some of the events of the day which I was about to celebrate loomed up like a ship seen in the distance. My eye swept the expensive furniture of my office. I thought of the way my career had begun. I thought of the Friday evening when I met Gitelson on Grand Street, he an American dandy and I in tatters. The fact that it was upon his advice and with his ten dollars that I had become a cloak-maker stood out as large as life before me. A great feeling of gratitude welled up in me, of gratitude and of pity for my tattered self of those days. Dear, kind Gitelson! Poor fellow! He was still working with his needle. I was seized with a desire to do something for him.

I had never paid him those ten dollars. So I was going to do so with "substantial interest" now. "I shall spend a few hundred dollars on him—nay, a few thousand!" I said to myself. "I shall buy him a small business. Let him end his days in comfort. Let him know that his ship brother is like a real brother to him."

It was twenty minutes after 12 and I was still waiting for the telephone to announce him. My suspense became insupportable. "Is he going to disappoint me, the idiot?" I wondered. Presently the telephone trilled. I seized the receiver

"Mr. Gitelson wishes to see Mr. Levinsky," came the familiar pipe of my switchboard girl. "He says he has an appointment—"

"Let him come in at once," I flashed.

Two minutes later he was in my room. His forelock was still the only bunch of gray hair on his head, but his face was pitifully wizened. He was quite neatly dressed, as trained tailors will be, even when they are poor, and at some distance I might have failed to perceive any change in him. At close range, however, his appearance broke my heart

"Do you know what sort of a day this is?" I asked, after shaking his hand warmly.

"I should think I did," he answered, sheepishly. "Twenty-five years ago at this time—"

He was at a loss for words

"Yes, it's twenty-five years, Gitelson," I rejoined. I was going to indulge in reminiscences, to compare memories with him, but changed my mind. I would rather not speak of our Landing Day until we were seated at a dining-table and after we had drunk its toast in champagne

"Come, let us have lunch together," I said, simply

I took him to the Waldorf-Astoria, where a table had been reserved for us in a snug corner.

Gitelson was extremely bashful and his embarrassment infected me. He was apparently at a loss to know what to do with the various glasses, knives, forks. It was evident that he had never sat at such a table before. The French waiter, who was silently officious, seemed to be inwardly laughing at both of us. At the bottom of my heart I cow before waiters to this day.

Their white shirt-fronts, reticence, and pompous bows make me feel as if they saw through me and ridiculed my ways. They make me feel as if my expensive clothes and ways ill became me

"Here is good health, Gitelson," I said in plain old Yiddish, as we touched glasses. "Let us drink to the day when we arrived in Castle Garden."

There was something forced, studied, in the way I uttered these words. I was disgusted with my own voice. Gitelson only simpered. He drained his glass, and the champagne, to which he was not accustomed, made him tipsy at once. I tried to talk of our ship, of the cap he had lost, of his timidity when we had found ourselves in Castle Garden, of the policeman whom I asked to direct us. But Gitelson only nodded and grinned and tittered. I realized that I had made a mistake—that I should have taken him to a more modest restaurant. But then the chasm between him and me seemed to be too wide for us to celebrate as ship brothers in any place

"By the way, Gitelson, I owe you something," I said, producing a ten-dollar bill. "It was with your ten dollars that I learned to be a cloak-operator and entered the cloak trade. Do you remember?" I was going to add something about my desire to help him in some substantial way, but he interrupted me

"Sure, I do," he said, with inebriate shamefacedness, as he received the money and shoved it into the inside pocket of his vest. "It has brought you good luck, hasn't it? And how about the interest? He, he, he! You've kept it over twenty-three years. The interest must be quite a little. He, he, he!"

"Of course I'll pay you the interest, and more, too. You shall get a check."

"Oh, I was only joking."

"But I am not joking. You're going to get a check, all right."

He revolted me

I made out a check for two hundred dollars; tore it and made out one for five hundred

He flushed, scanned the figure, giggled, hesitated, and finally folded the check and pushed it into his inner vest pocket, thanking me with drunken ardor

Some time later I was returning to my office, my heart heavy with self-disgust and sadness. In the evening I went home, to the loneliness of my beautiful hotel lodgings. My heart was still heavy with distaste and sadness

# CHAPTER V

GUSSIE, the finisher-girl to whom I had once made love with a view to marrying her for her money, worked in the vicinity of my factory and I met her from time to time on the Avenue. We kept up our familiar tone of former days. We would pause, exchange some banter, and go our several ways. She was over fifty now. She looked haggard and dried up and her hair was copiously shot with gray

One afternoon she told me she had changed her shop, naming her new employer

"Is it a good place to work in?" I inquired

"Oh, it's as good or as bad as any other place," she replied, with a gay smile

"Mine is good," I jested

"That's what they all say

"Come to work for me and see for yourself."

"Will I get good wages?"

"Yes."

"How much?"

"Any price you name."

"Look at him," she said, as though addressing a third person. "Look at the new millionaire."

"It might have been all yours. But you did not think I was good enough for you." "You can keep it all to yourself and welcome."

"Well, will you come to work?"

"You can't do without me, can you? He can't get finisher-girls, the poor fellow. Well, how much will you pay me?"

We agreed upon the price, but on taking leave she said, "I was joking."

"What do you mean? Don't you want to work for me, Gussie?"

She shook her head

"Why?"

"I don't want you to think I begrudge you your millions. We'll be better friends at a distance. Good-by."

"You're a funny girl, Gussie. Good-by."

A short time after this conversation I had trouble with the Cloak-makers' Union, of which Gussie was one of the oldest and most loyal members

The cause of the conflict was an operator named Blitt, a native of Antomir, who had been working in my shop for some months. He was a spare little fellow with a nose so compressed at the nostrils that it looked as though it was inhaling some sharp, pleasant odor. It gave his face a droll appearance, but his eyes, dark and large, were very attractive. I had known him as a small boy in my birthplace, where he belonged to a much better family than I

When Blitt was invited to join the Levinsky Antomir Society of my employees he refused. It turned out that he was one of the active spirits of the union and also an ardent member of the Socialist party. His foreman had not the courage to discharge him, because of my well-known predilection for natives of Antomir, so he reported him to me as a dangerous fellow

"He isn't going to blow up the building, is he?" I said, lightly

"But he may do other mischief. He's one of the leaders of the union."

"Let him lead."

The next time I looked at Blitt I felt uncomfortable. His refusal to join my Antomir organization hurt me, and his activities in the union and at socialist gatherings kindled my rancor. His compressed nose revolted me now.

I wanted to get rid of him

Not that I had remained inflexible in my views regarding the distribution of wealth in the world. Some of the best-known people in the country were openly taking the ground that the poor man was not getting a "square deal." To sympathize with organized labor was no longer "bad form," some society women even doing picket duty for Jewish factory-girls out on strike.

Socialism, which used to be declared utterly un-American, had come to be almost a vogue. American colleges were leavened with it, while American magazines were building up stupendous circulations by exposing the corruption of the mighty. Public opinion had, during the past two decades, undergone a striking change in this respect. I had watched that change and I could not but be influenced by it. For all my theorizing about the "survival of the fittest" and the "dying off of the weaklings," I could not help feeling that, in an abstract way, the socialists were not altogether wrong.

The case was different, however, when I considered it in connection with the concrete struggle of trade-unionism (which among the Jewish immigrants was practically but another name for socialism) against low wages or high rent.

I must confess, too, that the defeat with which I had met at Tevkin's house had greatly intensified my hostility to socialists. As I have remarked in a previous chapter, I ascribed my fiasco to the socialist atmosphere that surrounded Anna. I was embittered

The socialists were constantly harping on "class struggle," "class antagonism," "class psychology." I would dismiss it all as absurd, but I did hate the trade-unions, particularly those of the East Side. Altogether there was too much socialism among the masses of the Ghetto, I thought

Blitt now seemed to be the embodiment of this "class antagonism."

"Ah, he won't join my Antomir Society!" I would storm and fume and writhe inwardly. "That's a tacit protest against the whole society as an organization of 'slaves.' It means that the society makes meek, obedient servants of my employees and helps me fleece them. As if they did not earn in my shop more than they would anywhere else! As if they could all get steady work outside my place! And what about the loans and all sorts of other favors they get from me? If they worked for their own fathers they could not be treated better than they are treated here." I felt outraged

I rebuked myself for making much ado about nothing. Indeed, this was a growing weakness with me. Some trifle unworthy of consideration would get on my nerves and bother me like a grain of sand in the eye. Was I getting old? But, no, I felt in the prime of life, full of vigor, and more active and more alive to the passions than a youth

Whenever I chanced to be on the floor where Blitt worked I would avoid looking in his direction. His presence irritated me. "How ridiculous," I often thought. "One would imagine he's my conscience and that's why I want to get rid of him." As a consequence, I dared not send him away, and, as a consequence of this, he irritated me more than ever

Finally, one afternoon, acting on the spur of the moment, I called his foreman to me and told him to discharge him

A committee of the union called on me. I refused to deal with them. The upshot was a strike—not merely for the return of Blitt to my employment, but also for higher wages and the recognition of the union. The organization was not strong, and only a small number of my men were members of it, but when these went out all the others followed their contagious example, the members of my Antomir Society not excepted

The police gave me ample protection, and there were thousands of cloak-makers who remained outside the union, so that I soon had all the "hands" I wanted; but the conflict caused me all sorts of other mortifications. For one thing, it gave me no end of hostile publicity. The socialist Yiddish daily, which had an overwhelmingly wide circulation now, printed reports of meetings at which I had been hissed and hooted. I was accused of bribing corrupt politicians who were supposed to help me suppress the strike by means of police clubs. I was charged with bringing disgrace upon the Jewish people

The thought of Tevkin reading these reports and of Anna hearing of them hurt me cruelly. I could see Moissey reveling in the hisses with which my name was greeted. And Elsie? Did she take part in some of the demonstrations against me? Were she and Anna collecting funds for my striking employees? The reports in the American papers also were inclined to favor the strikers.

Public opinion was against me. What galled me worse than all, perhaps, was the sympathy shown for the strikers by some German-Jewish financiers and philanthropists, men whose acquaintance it was the height of my ambition to cultivate. All of which only served to pour oil into the flames of my hatred for the union

Bender implored me to settle the strike

"The union doesn't amount to a row of pins," he urged. "A week or two after we settle, things will get back to their old state."

"Where's your backbone, Bender?" I exploded. "If you had your way, those fellows would run the whole business. You have no sense of dignity. And yet you were born in America."

I was always accompanied by a detective

One of the strikers was in my pay. Every morning at a fixed hour he would call at a certain hotel, where he reported the doings of the organization to Bender and myself. One of the things I thus learned was that the union was hard up and constantly exacting loans from Gussie and several other members who had savings-bank accounts. One day, however, when the secretary appealed to her for a further loan with which to pay fines for arrested pickets and assist some of the neediest strikers, she flew into a passion. "What do you want of me, murderers that you are?" she cried, bursting into tears.

"Haven't I done enough? Have you no hearts?"

A minute or two later she yielded

"Bleed me, bleed me, cruel people that you are!" she said, pointing at her heart, as she started toward her savings bank

I was moved. When my spy had departed I paced the floor for some minutes.

Then, pausing, I smilingly declared to Bender my determination to ask the union for a committee. He was overjoyed and shook my hand solemnly

One of my bookkeepers was to communicate with the strike committee in the afternoon. Two hours before the time set for their meeting I saw in one of the afternoon papers an interview with the president of the union. His statements were so unjust to me, I thought, and so bitter, that the fighting blood was again up in my veins

But the image of Gussie giving her hard-earned money to help the strikers haunted me. The next morning I went to Atlantic City for a few days, letting Bender "do as he pleased." The strike was compromised, the men obtaining a partial concession of their demands and Blitt waiving his claim to his former job

# CHAPTER VI

MY business continued to grow. My consumption of raw material reached gigantic dimensions, so much so that at times, when I liked a pattern, I would buy up the entire output and sell some of it to smaller manufacturers at a profit

Gradually I abandoned the higher grades of goods, developing my whole business along the lines of popular prices. There are two cloak-and-suit houses that make a specialty of costly garments. These enjoy high reputations for taste and are the real arbiters of fashion in this country, one of the two being known in the trade as Little Pans; but the combined volume of business of both these firms is much smaller than mine

My deals with one mill alone—the largest in the country and the one whose head had come to my rescue when my affairs were on the brink of a precipice—now exceeded a million dollars at a single purchase to be delivered in seven months. The mills often sell me at a figure considerably lower than the general market price. They do so, first, because of the enormous quantities I buy, and, second, because of the "boost" a fabric receives from the very fact of being handled by my nouse. One day, for instance, I said to the president of a certain mill: "I like this cloth of yours. I feel like making a big thing of it, provided you can let me have an inside figure." We came to terms, and I gave him an advance order for nine thousand pieces. When smaller manufacturers and department-store buyers heard that I had bought an immense quantity of that pattern its success was practically established. As a consequence, the mill was in a position to raise the price of the cloth to others, so that it amply made up for the low figure at which it had sold the goods to me

Judged by the market price of the raw material, my profit on a garment did not exceed fifty cents. But I paid for the raw material seventy-five cents less than the market price, so that my total profit was one dollar and twenty-five cents. Still, there have been instances when I lost seventy-five thousand dollars in one month because goods fell in price or because a certain style failed to move and I had to sell it below cost to get it out of the way. To be sure, cheaper goods are less likely to be affected by the caprices of style than higher grades, which is one of several reasons why I prefer to produce garments of popular prices

I do not employ my entire capital in my cloak business, half of it, or more, being invested in "quick assets." Should I need more ready cash than I have, I could procure it at a lower rate than what those assets bring me. I can get half a million dollars, from two banks, without rising from my desk—by merely calling those banks up on the telephone. For this I pay, say, three and a half or four per cent., for I am a desirable customer at the banks; and, as my quick assets bring me an average of five per cent., I make at least one per cent. on the money

Another way of making my money breed money is by early payments to the mills. Not only can I do without their credit, but I can afford to pay them six months in advance. This gives me an "anticipation" allowance at the rate of six per cent. per annum, while money costs me at the banks three or four per cent. per annum.

All this is good sport

I own considerable stock in the very mills with which I do business, which has a certain moral effect on their relations with my house. For a similar purpose I am a shareholder in the large mail-order houses that buy cloaks and suits of me. I hold shares of some department stores also, but of late I have grown somewhat shy of this kind of investment, the future of a department store being as uncertain as the future of the neighborhood in which it is located. Mail-order houses, on the other hand, have the whole country before them, and their overwhelming growth during past years was one of the conspicuous phenomena in the business life of the nation. I love to watch their operations spread over the map, and I love to watch the growth of American cities, the shifting of their shopping centers, the consequent vicissitudes, the decline of some houses, the rise of others. American Jews of German origin are playing a foremost part in the retail business of the country, large or small, and our people, Russian and Galician Jews, also are making themselves felt in it, being, in many cases, in partnership with Gentiles or with their own coreligionists of German descent. The king of the great mail-order business, a man with an annual income of many millions, is the son of a Polish Jew. He is one of the two richest Jews in America, having built up his vast fortune in ten or fifteen years. As I have said before, I know hundreds, if not thousands, of merchants, Jews and Gentiles, throughout this country and Canada, so I like to keep track of their careers

This, too, is good sport

Of course, it is essential to study the business map in the interests of my own establishment, but I find intellectual excitement in it as well, and, after all, I am essentially an intellectual man, I think

There are retailers in various sections of the country whom I have helped financially—former buyers, for example, who went into business on their own hook with my assistance. This is good business, for while these merchants must be left free to buy in the open market, they naturally give my house precedence. But here again I must say in fairness to myself that business interest is not the only motive that induces me to do them these favors.

Indeed, in some cases I do it without even expecting to get my money back.

It gives me moral satisfaction, for which money is no measure of value

# CHAPTER VII

AM I happy? There are moments when I am overwhelmed by a sense of my success and ease. I become aware that thousands of things which had formerly been forbidden fruit to me are at my command now. I distinctly recall that crushing sense of being debarred from everything, and then I feel as though the whole world were mine. One day I paused in front of an old East Side restaurant that I had often passed in my days of need and despair. The feeling of desolation and envy with which I used to peek in its windows came back to me. It gave me pangs of self-pity for my past and a thrilling sense of my present power. The prices that had once been prohibitive seemed so wretchedly low now. On another occasion I came across a Canal Street merchant of whom I used to buy goods for my push-cart. I said to myself: "There was a time when I used to implore this man for ten dollars' worth of goods, when I regarded him as all-powerful and feared him. Now he would be happy to shake hands with me."

I recalled other people whom I used to fear and before whom I used to humiliate myself because of my poverty. I thought of the time when I had already entered the cloak business, but was struggling and squirming and constantly racking my brains for some way of raising a hundred dollars; when I would cringe with a certain East Side banker and vainly beg him to extend a small note of mine, and come away in a sickening state of despair

At this moment, as these memories were filing by me, I felt as though now there were nobody in the world who could inspire me with awe or render me a service

And yet in all such instances I feel a peculiar yearning for the very days when the doors of that restaurant were closed to me and when the Canal Street merchant was a magnate of commerce in my estimation. Somehow, encounters of this kind leave me dejected.

The gloomiest past is dearer than the brightest present. In my case there seems to be a special reason for feeling this way. My sense of triumph is coupled with a brooding sense of emptiness and insignificance, of my lack of anything like a great, deep interest

I am lonely. Amid the pandemonium of my six hundred sewing-machines and the jingle of gold which they pour into my lap I feel the deadly silence of solitude

I spend at least one evening a week at the Benders. I am fond of their children and I feel pleasantly at home at their house. I am a frequent caller at the Nodelmans', and enjoy their hospitality even more than that of the Benders. I go to the opera, to the theaters, and to concerts, and never alone. There are merry suppers, and some orgies in which I take part, but when I go home I suffer a gnawing aftermath of loneliness and desolation

I have a fine summer home, with servants, automobiles, and horses. I share it with the Bender family and we often have visitors from the city, but, no matter how large and gay the crowd may be, the country makes me sad

I know bachelors who are thoroughly reconciled to their solitude and even enjoy it. I am not.

No, I am not happy

In the city I occupy a luxurious suite of rooms in a high-class hotel and keep an excellent chauffeur and valet. I give myself every comfort that money can buy. But there is one thing which I crave and which money cannot buy—happiness.

Many a pretty girl is setting her cap at me, but I know that it is only my dollars they want to marry. Nor do I care for any of them, while the woman to whom my heart is calling—Anna—is married to another man

I dream of marrying some day. I dread to think of dying a lonely man

Sometimes I have a spell of morbid amativeness and seem to be falling in love with woman after woman. There are periods when I can scarcely pass a woman in the street without scanning her face and figure. When I see the crowds returning from work in the cloak-and-waist district I often pause to watch the groups of girls as they walk apart from the men. Their keeping together, as if they formed a separate world full of its own interests and secrets, makes a peculiar appeal to me

Once, in Florida, I thought I was falling in love with a rich Jewish girl whose face had a bashful expression of a peculiar type. There are different sorts of bashfulness. This girl had the bashfulness of sin, as I put it to myself. She looked as if her mind harbored illicit thoughts which she was trying to conceal. Her blushes seemed to be full of sex and her eyes full of secrets. She was not a pretty girl at all, but her "guilty look" disturbed me as long as we were stopping in the same place

But through all these ephemeral infatuations and interests I am in love with Anna

From time to time I decide to make a "sensible" marriage, and study this woman or that as a possible candidate, but so far nothing has come of it

There was one woman whom I might have married if she had not been a Gentile—one of the very few who lived in the family hotel in which I had my apartments. At first I set her down for an adventuress seeking the acquaintance of rich Jews for some sinister purpose. But I was mistaken. She was a woman of high character. Moreover, she and her aged mother, with whom she lived, had settled in that hotel long before it came to be patronized by our people. She was a widow of over forty, with a good, intellectual face, well read in the better sense of the term, and no fool. Many of our people in the hotel danced attendance upon her because she was a Gentile woman, but all of them were really fond of her. The great point was that she seemed to have a sincere liking for our people. This and the peculiar way her shoulders would shake when she laughed was, in fact, what first drew me to her. We grew chummy and I spent many an hour in her company

In my soliloquies I often speculated and theorized on the question of proposing to her. I saw clearly that it would be a mistake. It was not the faith of my fathers that was in the way. It was that medieval prejudice against our people which makes so many marriages between Jew and Gentile a failure. It frightened me

One evening we sat chatting in the bright lobby of the hotel, discussing human nature, and she telling me something of the good novels she had read.

After a brief pause I said: "I enjoy these talks immensely. I don't think there is another person with whom I so love to talk of human beings."

She bowed with a smile that shone of something more than mere appreciation of the compliment. And then I uttered in the simplest possible accents: "It's really a pity that there is the chasm of race between us. Otherwise I don't see why we couldn't be happy together."

I was in an adventurous mood and ready, even eager, to marry her. But her answer was a laugh, as if she took it for a joke; and, though I seemed to sense intimacy and encouragement in that laugh, it gave me pause. I felt on the brink of a fatal blunder, and I escaped before it was too late.

"But then," I hastened to add, "real happiness in a case like this is perhaps not the rule, but the exception. That chasm continues to yawn throughout the couple's married life, I suppose."

"That's an interesting point of view," she said, a non-committal smile on her lips

She tactfully forbore to take up the discussion, and I soon dropped the subject. We remained friends

It was this woman who got me interested in good, modern fiction. The books she selected for me interested me greatly. Then it was that the remarks I had heard from Moissey Tevkin came to my mind. They were illuminating

Most of the people at my hotel are German-American Jews. I know other Jews of this class. I contribute to their charity institutions. Though an atheist, I belong to one of their synagogues. Nor can I plead the special feeling which had partly accounted for my visits at the synagogue of the Sons of Antomir while I was engaged to Kaplan's daughter. I am a member of that synagogue chiefly because it is a fashionable synagogue. I often convict myself of currying favor with the German Jews. But then German-American Jews curry favor with Portuguese-American Jews, just as we all curry favor with Gentiles and as American Gentiles curry favor with the aristocracy of Europe

I often long for a heart-to-heart talk with some of the people of my birthplace. I have tried to revive my old friendships with some of them, but they are mostly poor and my prosperity stands between us in many ways

Sometimes when I am alone in my beautiful apartments, brooding over these things and nursing my loneliness, I say to myself: "There are cases when success is a tragedy."

There are moments when I regret my whole career, when my very success seems to be a mistake

I think that I was born for a life of intellectual interest. I was certainly brought up for one. The day when that accident turned my mind from college to business seems to be the most unfortunate day in my life. I think that I should be much happier as a scientist or writer, perhaps. I should then be in my natural element, and if I were doomed to loneliness I should have comforts to which I am now a stranger. That's the way I feel every time I pass the abandoned old building of the City College

The business world contains plenty of successful men who have no brains.

Why, then, should I ascribe my triumph to special ability? I should probably have made a much better college professor than a cloak-manufacturer, and should probably be a happier man, too. I know people who have made much more money than I and whom I consider my inferiors in every respect

Many of our immigrants have distinguished themselves in science, music, or art, and these I envy far more than I do a billionaire. As an example of the successes achieved by Russian Jews in America in the last quarter of a century it is often pointed out that the man who has built the greatest sky-scrapers in the country, including the Woolworth Building, is a Russian Jew who came here a penniless boy. I cannot boast such distinction, but then I have helped build up one of the great industries of the United States, and this also is something to be proud of. But I should readily change places with the Russian Jew, a former Talmud student like myself, who is the greatest physiologist in the New World, or with the Russian Jew who holds the foremost place among American song-writers and whose soulful compositions are sung in almost every English-speaking house in the world. I love music to madness. I yearn for the world of great singers, violinists, pianists. Several of the greatest of them are of my race and country, and I have met them, but all my acquaintance with them has brought me is a sense of being looked down upon as a money-bag striving to play the Mæcenas. I had a similar experience with a sculptor, also one of our immigrants, an

East Side boy who had met with sensational success in Paris and London. I had him make my bust. His demeanor toward me was all that could have been desired. We even cracked Yiddish jokes together and he hummed bits of synagogue music over his work, but I never left his studio without feeling cheap and wretched

When I think of these things, when I am in this sort of mood, I pity myself for a victim of circumstances

At the height of my business success I feel that if I had my life to live over again I should never think of a business career

I don't seem to be able to get accustomed to my luxurious life. I am always more or less conscious of my good clothes, of the high quality of my office furniture, of the power I wield over the men in my pay. As I have said in another connection, I still have a lurking fear of restaurant waiters

I can never forget the days of my misery. I cannot escape from my old self.

My past and my present do not comport well. David, the poor lad swinging over a Talmud volume at the Preacher's Synagogue, seems to have more in common with my inner identity than David Levinsky, the well-known cloak-manufacturer

*duality of identity*

*└ payback*

*└ no satisfaction in life*

Made in the USA